THE POEMS AND TRANSLATIONS OF

Sir Richard Fanshawe

THE POEMS AND TRANSLATIONS OF Sir Richard Fanshawe

Volume I

EDITED BY

PETER DAVIDSON

Lecturer in English and Comparative Literature, University of Warwick

CLARENDON PRESS · OXFORD

1997

Oxford University Press, Great Clarendon Street, Oxford OX2 6DP
Oxford New York
Athens Auckland Bangkok Bogota Bombay Buenos Aires
Calcutta Cape Town Dar es Salaam Delhi Florence Hong Kong
Istanbul Karachi Kuala Lumpur Madras Madrid Melbourne
Mexico City Nairobi Paris Singapore Taipei Tokyo Toronto Warsaw
and associated companies in
Berlin Ibadan

Oxford is a trade mark of Oxford University Press

Published in the United States by
Oxford University Press Inc., New York

British Library Cataloguing in Publication Data
Data available

Library of Congress Cataloging-in-Publication Data
Fanshawe, Richard, Sir, 1608–1666. [Selections, 1997]
The poems and translations of Sir Richard Fanshawe/edited by Peter Davidson.
— (Oxford English texts)
Includes bibliographical references and indexes.
1. Latin poetry—Translations into English. 2. Romance poetry—Translations into English. 3. Boethius, d. 524—Translations into English. 4. Martial—Translations into English. 5. Horace—Translations into English. I. Davidson, Peter. II. Title.
PR3433.F7A6 1997
821′.4—dc20 96-31088

ISBN 0-19-811737-X

1 3 5 7 9 10 8 6 4 2

Typeset by Pure Tech India Ltd, Pondicherry
Printed in Great Britain
on acid-free paper by
Biddles Ltd,
Guildford and King's Lynn

PATRIS MEMORIAE SACER

Deus miserere clementer animae patris mei, ejusque peccata dimitte; meque eum in aeternae claritatis gaudio fac videre, per Christum Dominum nostrum.

PREFACE

A list of short titles and sigla for manuscripts follows the Textual Introduction. There are, however, a few points of referencing and annotation which require notice.

In the cases of texts with unconventional pagination, several apparent inconsistencies need to be explained. Unpaginated preliminary pages are referred to by printer's signatures wherever possible. Books which lack any pagination are referred to by signatures. The Spanish text of *Querer por solo Querer* (Madrid, 1623) is foliated by the printer on the rectos, rather than paginated in any conventional sense, and references are accordingly given by folios.

References to manuscripts are by folios of the manuscripts as they now exist, except in cases where there is consistent contemporary pagination and no modern foliation. References to uncatalogued manuscripts provide obvious difficulties, especially the extreme case of MS V, and the principle has been to give the clearest indication possible of the location of the text cited.

Texts of seventeenth-century works are cited in a modern and scholarly edition where such an edition exists. Otherwise they are cited in what is generally accepted as their earliest reliable form. However, there are some departures from this policy: Waller is quoted from the third edition of 1678, as it is the first printing of his works to contain all the poems to which reference is made; and the same principle has governed the selection of the two printed sources for the works of George Buchanan. References to Beaumont and Fletcher are drawn, where possible, from the modern edition, or otherwise variously from the folio edition of 1647 and from that of 1679: the Folio of 1647 omits many of the songs in the plays. In the Folio of 1679 the songs are printed from original sources for the first time, whereas the body of the text is a second edition. A letter of Sir Kenelm Digby's is given both manuscript and printed references, as the modern text, although accurate, is not found in a scholarly work.

The problem of Aubrey is always with us: Clark's edition of the *Brief Lives* has obviously been used whenever possible. One passage which Clark omits has been taken from the edition of *Remaines of Gentilisme and Judaisme* by James Britten.

References to the texts of Donne or King are to the modern Clarendon Press editions; any reference to earlier twentieth-century editions is only to notes contained therein. Where possible, *lapidaria* and works of art are cited by a printed reference or transcription in a scholarly work.

Classical texts are quoted in the Oxford edition, except in the case of the *Metamorphoses* of Ovid, where the highly respected edition of B. J. van Proosdij has also been consulted. Although references are made throughout the commentary to recent classical texts, the seventeenth-century texts of works translated by Fanshawe have been read and compared.

In the explanatory notes to this edition, references to books which are reasonably freely available to a scholar are by page number in the chosen edition, but are not given in full. Only works in manuscript or otherwise hard of access are quoted entire.

I am indebted for financial assistance to the Scottish Education Department; the Administrators of the Judith E. Wilson Fund; the Administrators of the Allen Scholarship in the University of Cambridge; and the Research Expenses Fund of Clare College, Cambridge. The University of Warwick have supported this work with research leave; I am indebted to the British Academy, not only for supporting a term of leave, but also for a most generous grant towards research expenses. Generous support was also forthcoming from the Harold Hyams Wingate Foundation.

Thanks are due to the following libraries and their librarians: Beinecke Rare Book Library, Yale University; Bibliothèque Nationale, Paris; Bodleian Library, Oxford; Boston Public Library, Boston, Mass.; the British Library; Cambridge University Library; the Library of Christ Church, Oxford; Coimbra University Library; Library of Congress, Washington, DC; Edinburgh University Library; Folger Shakespeare Library, Washington, DC; the Library of the Foreign and Commonwealth Office, London; Fundação de Casa de Braganza, Lisbon, Portugal; Glasgow University Library; Henry E. Huntington Library, San Marino, California; Hertfordshire Records Office; the Historical Manuscripts Commission, London; the Houghton Library, Harvard University; the Library of Jesus College, Cambridge; the Leicestershire Records Office; the Lilly Library, Bloomington, Indiana; the J. Pierpont Morgan Library, New York; the Carl Pfortzheimer Library, New York; the National Library of Scotland; the Sterling Memorial Library, Yale University; the Library of Trinity College, Cambridge; the Library of the University of Toronto; Valence House (London Boroughs of Barking and Dagenham Libraries); and Vanderbilt University Library, Nashville, Tennessee.

Thanks are due also to the following individuals who contributed to the first state of this edition as a Cambridge doctoral thesis: Richard Andrewes; Miss K. Andreyev; Dr R. Bolgar; Professor C. Boxer; Jerome Boytim; Isabel Brown, the late Professor G. Bullough; Sr. Don Jose-Luis Camaño; F. C. Collieson; Mrs H. Corlett; Professor J. P. Cutts; Dr Brian Donaghey; Miss L. C. Dunn; Mr and Mrs Richard Fanshawe; Dr M. Foot; D. J. Hall; C. C. D. Haswell; Major J. Haswell; James Howson; Miss Patricia Huskinson; Dr T. Knighton; Robert Latham; Guy Lee; Sr. E. Lisboa of the Portuguese Embassy, London; Dr M. McKendrick; C. T. Nodder; Ms D. Osnowitz; Steven Parks; Dr G. Parry; Dr J. Rathmell; D. J. Roberts; Professor Andrew Sabol; the Hon. J. A. Stourton; Robert Taylor; Dr T. Webb; and Miss R. C. Wehlau.

Particular thanks for this first stage are due to my supervisors, friends, and advisers: the late P. J. Croft; E. E. Duncan-Jones; Margaret Ezell; Janet Fairweather; Dr J. P. W. Gaskell; Mark Gibson; Dr M. A. Halls; Geoffrey Hill; Anny Jones; Dr Richard Luckett; Alan and Susanna Powers; Professor M. A. Radzinowicz; Simon Rees, and, especially, the late Sir Geoffrey Keynes.

Thanks are due to those who have assisted the transformation of thesis into book: Kim Scott Walwyn and Frances Whistler of the Oxford University Press; Jane Reid, secretary of the Wingate Foundation; Mark Kilfoyle, Carol Morley, Sandra Raphael, and Jennifer Drake-Brockman who have been far more than research assistants. Thanks are also due to Sr. E. Lisboa of the Portuguese Embassy and Dr D. De Lario of the Spanish Embassy; and Professor Roger Walker, Dr Kate Bennett, and Dominic Montserrat have given most generous help.

Carol Morley has advised on all matters relating to the drama; the translation and emendation of Fanshawe's Latin works owes much to Dominic Montserrat and Jane Stevenson.

Acknowledgement of more general support is due to the University of Warwick, particularly to the Department of English and Comparative Literature and to the Vakgroep Engels in the University of Leiden. This work owes much to the generous friendship of Kate Chedgzoy; Alastair and Cecilia Hamilton; Georgina Paul; Sabina Sharkey; Nigel Smith; and Adriaan van der Weel. Jane Stevenson has done more than can readily be quantified, on this and on all other counts.

CONTENTS

CHRONOLOGY OF SIR RICHARD FANSHAWE

This chronology represents an attempt to collate *Memoirs* with the evidence of the letters on pp. 328–35 of this work and of the dated prose works on pp. 318–26. The result serves to throw some doubt on the accuracy of *Memoirs* as a source for Fanshawe's life: either Lady Fanshawe has conflated several journeys to France in the years 1646–50 and confused them, or else there is textual corruption of some kind at pp. 122–3 of *Memoirs*. Wherever possible, material has also been collated with, and documented from, *Manuscripts of J. M. Heathcote of Conington Castle* (HMC, HMSO, 1899).

1608	Sir Richard Fanshawe born in June at Ware Park, Hertfordshire (baptized 12 June), youngest son of Sir Henry Fanshawe, third King's Remembrancer, and of his wife Elizabeth (*née* Smythe).
1616	Death of Sir Henry Fanshawe.
c. 1620	Enters Thomas Farnaby's school in Cripplegate, London.
1623	Enters Jesus College, Cambridge.
1626	Enters the Inner Temple. First poetic compositions.
1631	Death of Fanshawe's mother.
1632–4	Travels in France and Spain.
1635	Appointed secretary to Lord Aston, Ambassador to Spain and travels to Madrid.
1636	Visits the Aston family at Tixall in Staffordshire, in the autumn. MS A compiled about this time.
1638	*Chargé d'affaires* in Madrid after the departure of Lord Aston. Returns to England.
1639–41	Appointed secretary to the Council of War in Ireland.
1641	Appointed fifth King's Remembrancer.
1643	After debating their differences with the Parliamentarian poet and translator Thomas May; joins the King and court at Oxford.
1644	Appointed Secretary for War to the Prince of Wales. Marries Ann Harrison at Wolvercote on 18 May. MS F compiled about this time; MS H would also appear to date from his time in Oxford. Fanshawe's portrait (now at Valence House, Barking) painted by William Dobson.
1645	A son, Harrison, born 23 February and dies 10 March. Fanshawe goes from Oxford to Bristol with the Prince of Wales in March. Lady Fanshawe follows in May. In July they go to Barnstaple in Devon.
1646	With the Prince at Tavistock in the first days of January, and travels on with him to Launceston, Truro, and Pendennis Castle. In Penzance in March, sailing from Land's End to the Scilly Isles on about 24 March and on to Jersey in April. Goes with Lady Fanshawe to Caen in early

August. Lady Fanshawe thereafter to London. Fanshawe's movements are less certain, but he appears to have travelled in France and to have delivered a letter to the Prince of Wales.

1647 It seems likely that Fanshawe is still on the Continent. He travels from Caen to England shortly after 5/15 August, and is in hiding in London by the end of August. *1647* (the translation of *Il Pastor Fido* without the 'additional poems') published. Fanshawe visits Charles I at Hampton Court in September or October and receives instructions to go as Extraordinary Ambassador to Spain. These instructions to him as Ambassador dated from Hampton Court on 9 October. Fanshawe and Lady Fanshawe go to France in October and visit Henrietta Maria at Paris in December. Fanshawe returns to England in the last few days of December.

1648 Compounds for £300 in January and lives privately in London. *1648* published. A son, Richard (the first of three of that name) born 8 June (d. 1659). Summoned in September to attend the Prince of Wales in the Downs, and goes on to Paris in October and then to Ireland, arriving in Cork by the end of November. Made Treasurer of the Navy.

1649 Probably still in Ireland. Lady Fanshawe and Fanshawe certainly together at Cork in May and in Limerick in November and December. Fanshawe again ordered to Spain by a letter of Charles II, 20/30 August, dated from St Germain's, instructing him to meet Lord Cottington and Sir Edward Hyde (the future Earl of Clarendon) at San Sebastian, if the Marquis of Ormonde will grant him leave to depart from Ireland.

1650 In February Fanshawe and Lady Fanshawe sail from Galway to Spain, reaching Malaga late in March. They arrive in Madrid on 16 May and are still there on 17/27 July. In September they travel to San Sebastian and thence to Calais in October, briefly to Paris, and again to Calais (9/19 November). Lady Fanshawe travels to England. Fanshawe travels via Holland to join Charles II in Scotland.

1651 Lady Fanshawe in London and Hertfordshire, Fanshawe with the King in Scotland. Captured after the Battle of Worcester (September) and brought prisoner to London, where he is imprisoned at Whitehall. Lady Fanshawe obtains his release on bail on the grounds of his ill health (November). He lodges in London with Lady Fanshawe, but forbidden to publish overtly political writings.

1652 Seriously ill for the first half of the year. The first issue of *1652*. He recovers in the summer and goes to Bath in August, travelling thereafter to Hertfordshire. Second, corrected issue of *1652*.

1653–4 Fanshawe and Lady Fanshawe take up residence in March at Tankersley Park in Yorkshire. He translates *The Lusiad, Querer por solo Querer*, and *Fiestas de Aranjuez* into English.

1654 Daughter, Ann, dies in late July. Fanshawe and Lady Fanshawe move soon after from Tankersley to Hamerton in Huntingdonshire.

1655 Lodges in Chancery Lane in London, apart from a visit in February to Frogpool in Kent. *1655* published. Fanshawe translates part of *The Lusiad* into Latin.

1656 Fanshawe and Lady Fanshawe both in bad health. They go in September to Hertfordshire.

1657 Ill health continues. They go to Bath in August and take up residence thereafter at Ware in Hertfordshire.

1658 After the death of Cromwell in September, Fanshawe goes to London and obtains a pass to travel abroad as tutor or companion to the eldest son of the Earl of Pembroke. He travels to Paris in November. *1658* published.

1659 In Paris; appointed Secretary of the Latin Tongue to Charles II in June. In the same month Lady Fanshawe joins her husband in Paris, having forged her name on a pass for herself and her children. On 9/19 July, a letter of Sir Edward Hyde's promises the patent for Fanshawe's appointment as Master of the Requests. In another letter of 16/26 July, he acknowledges receipt of both Latin and English poetry from Fanshawe and expresses a desire to see the translation of *Querer por solo Querer*. Son, Richard (the first of that name) dies in October. In December both travel to Calais and Lady Fanshawe briefly visits England to raise money.

1660 Travels directly to Brussels to meet Charles II. Lady Fanshawe follows via Nieuwpoort, Bruges, and Ghent. Fanshawe appointed Master of the Requests. They move with the court to Breda in Brabant where Fanshawe is knighted in April, and then to The Hague, where Fanshawe fails to secure one of the positions of Secretaries of State to the King. Fanshawe and Lady Fanshawe return with the King to England in May, and take lodgings in Portugal Row in London.

1661 Elected Member of Parliament for Cambridge University; drafts Spanish translations of letters from Charles II to the Portuguese royal family in July and August. By (presumably secret) instructions of Charles II, dated 23 August, Fanshawe instructed to travel to Portugal and to gather information there on international affairs relating to that country. His official instructions as Envoy Extraordinary to Portugal, also issued in August, concerned with the completion of arrangements for the marriage of Charles II and Catherine of Braganza. Appointed as temporary ordinary Ambassador by a letter of Charles II dated from Hampton Court on 30 August, Fanshawe departs for Lisbon in September. He returns to London in December. The greater part of the material from 1652 issued in *The Poems of Horace*, edited by Alexander Brome.

1662 Attends the marriage of Charles II and Catherine of Braganza on 21 May. Lady Fanshawe presented to the Queen. A letter of Charles II to the King of Portugal, dated from Hampton Court 7 August, mentions Fanshawe as

Ambassador to Portugal. Fanshawe leaves with his family for Lisbon in August, arriving on 14 September.

1663 Fanshawe and his family in Lisbon. Son, Richard (the second of that name) born prematurely on 26 June and dies the same day. Fanshawe composes a Latin epitaph on him. MS B probably completed about this time. Fanshawe recalled to England, leaving Lisbon on 23 August and arriving in early September. On 21 September he is appointed Privy Councillor and sworn on 2 October.

1664 Appointed Ambassador to Spain by a letter of credence from Charles II to Philip IV, dated 13 January. With his family he leaves for Madrid on 21 January, landing at Cadiz on 7 March and travelling overland. They arrive at Vallecas on 30 April and finally settle in Madrid on 16 August. In October they visit Aranjuez and the Escorial. *1648* reissued.

1665 Son, Richard (the third of that name) born in Madrid on 6 August. On 17 December Fanshawe and the Duke of Medina de las Torres negotiate a conditional treaty between Spain and England, 'and the articles for the ajustment between Spaine and Portugal'. This treaty is not ratified. Although Fanshawe's household later protest that a draft had been sent to London, allowing ample time for a reply, it is held in England that Fanshawe has exceeded his instructions and that this action was the chief reason for his subsequent recall, leading to the appointment of the Earl of Sandwich as Ambassador Extraordinary to Madrid.

1666 A letter to Lady Fanshawe dated 12/22 February refers to their children giving a private performance in the Embassy of parts of *Querer por solo Querer*. Returns from Lisbon 8 March. On 26 March Fanshawe learns that he has been recalled as Ambassador and that the Earl of Sandwich has been appointed in his place. Letters of revocation are delivered 29 May by the Earl of Sandwich. On 5/15 June he is taken ill, 'taken sike like an ague, but turned to a malignant, inward feavour'. He dies on 16/26 June. Lady Fanshawe brings his embalmed body back to England, and he is temporarily buried in All Hallows Church, Hertford.

1667 Fanshawe's chaplain, Henry Bagshawe, publishes *A Sermon . . . occasioned by the Death . . . of his late Excellency Sir Richard Fanshawe.*

1668 A long biographical notice of Fanshawe appears in David Lloyd's *Memories . . . of those that Suffered.*

1670 Fanshawe reburied in St Mary's, Ware and a monument erected. *Querer por solo Querer* and *Fiestas de Aranjuez* published, apparently privately. Lady Fanshawe presents a number of copies to their friends.

1671 *Querer por solo querer* and *Fiestas de Aranjuez* issued for public sale. *The Poems of Horace* reissued.

1676 Lady Fanshawe writes her *Memoirs*. *1648* reissued. Elkanah Settle's adaptation of *Il Pastor Fido* (1647) performed at the Duke's Theatre.

1677 An edition of *Il Pastor Fido* (1647) published, as adapted by Elkanah Settle.

1679 The sheets of *1670* reissued with a new title-page as *Zeli Daura, Queen of Tartaria.*

1680 Lady Fanshawe dies. *The Poems of Horace* reissued.

1687 Brief biography of Fanshawe in Winstanley's *The Lives of the Most Famous English Poets.* Fanshawe also mentioned as a poetic model in the preface to Philip Ayres's *Lyric Poems.*

1689 *1648* reissued twice.

1691 Long biography of Fanshawe in Gerald Langbaine's *An Account of the English Dramatick Poets.*

1692 Last reprinting of *1648.*

1694 Sir Richard Fanshawe the younger dies.

1702 Publication of *Original Letters of His Excellency Sir Richard Fanshawe*, a collection of diplomatic correspondence.

TEXTUAL INTRODUCTION

I. SOURCES FOR THIS EDITION

Throughout the manuscript descriptions which follow it may be assumed that manuscripts are written on paper, and that they are laid out in the usual form for seventeenth-century poetical manuscripts of a continuous single column. Any exception is noted.

Two hands need to be identified. Sir Richard Fanshawe's own hand, a confident italic with a characteristic Greek 'e', may be referred to Sir W. W. Greg's *English Literary Autographs* (Oxford, Oxford University Press, 1925–32), ii, lv. The hand of Lyonel Fanshawe, Fanshawe's cousin and secretary, may be identified from several ALS among the uncatalogued papers of V.

All dimensions are height × breadth in millimetres.

Manuscript Sources Listed by Location

British Library, London

Add. MS 15,228
Siglum: A
Dimensions: 184mm × 106mm
Composition: In its present state, the manuscript consists of two unbound octavo notebooks, bound together, making a total of 73 folios. The first of the two notebooks runs from f. 1r to f. 49v and has original pagination, pp. 1–79. This pagination runs out at f. 41r. The second of the two notebooks runs from f. 50r to f. 73v. Pagination begins at f. 50r and runs out on f. 67r, pp. 1–35.

The manuscript was rebound in 1969. The leaves have been sewn, in their original gatherings, onto guards. The modern binding is of blue cloth, its black leather spine blocked in gold with 'Poems' and its catalogue number. The modern binding measures 198mm × 128mm. The manuscript is generally in good condition, but ff. 1–2 have been torn, so that text has been lost from the centre of the page.
Hands: Two scribal hands; autograph alterations and additions. A cramped secretary hand with ornate capitals has written ff. 2–39 and ff. 50–67. A second secretary hand, rather timid but with a distinctive upper-case 'L', has written ff. 39v–46r and ff. 67v–73r. There are

autograph additions and alterations on ff. 2r and v, 3r, 6r, 15r, 16r, 25r and v, 26r and v, 27r and v, 29v, 33r and v, 34r and v, 38r and v, 39v, 40r and v, 41r and v, 67v, 68r and v, and 72r. Folios 47r to 48r are autograph throughout.
Date: Before 1637. Both notebooks which compose the modern Add. MS 15,228 may have been started at any time from Fanshawe's going down from Cambridge (the Latin poem on f. 2r and v suggests that the University was fresh in Fanshawe's mind, but that he had left it). In the first notebook, 'On the Escuriall . . .' may reasonably be supposed to date from after Fanshawe's first visit to Spain in 1632–4. In the second notebook we have a firm date for the last poem 'On a Lady that vowed . . .' of the autumn of 1636. The pattern of the hands in the manuscript suggests that the two notebooks were started separately, the first for translations from Boethius and Martial, the second for translations from Horace. The first scribal hand copies translations into the beginnings of both notebooks and some original poems into the first: ff. 2–39 and 50–67. The poems copied by the later scribal hand (ff. 39v–46r and 67v–73r) contain no internal evidence to suggest that they are earlier than Fanshawe's first visit to Spain. It is reasonable to suppose that the poems in the later scribal hand were copied into both notebooks in the early 1630s. Fanshawe's autograph additions and alterations may date from after the autumn of 1636.
Provenance: In Fanshawe's possession in the 1630s. The manuscript was bought for the British Museum as Lot 195 of the Bright sale in 1844.
Contents: f. 1r [originally the cover of the first notebook; scribbles, practising of words and pen-strokes, apparently not in Fanshawe's autograph]; f. 1v [blank]; f. 2r *Ad Almam . . . Cantab . . .* [Latin verses to the University of Cambridge, much mutilated]; f. 3r [Translations of the Metres from Boethius *De Consolatione Philosophiae*] I, 1; f. 3v, I, 2; f. 4r, I, 3; f. 4r, I, 4; f. 4v, I, 5 [a lacuna of one line at l. 16 may represent a 'planned blank' as at f. 13v]; f. 5v, I, 6; f. 6r, I, 5; f. 6v, II, 1; f. 6v, II, 2; f. 7r, II, 3; f. 7v, II, 4; f. 8r, II, 5; f. 9r, II, 6; f. 9v, II, 7; f. 10r, II, 8; f. 10v, III, 1; f. 11r, III, 2; f. 11v, III, 3; f. 12r, III, 4; f. 12r, III, 5; f. 12v, III, 6; f. 12v, III, 7; f. 13r, III, 8; f. 13v, III, 9 [this *metrum* has a lacuna of about fifteen lines in the middle. The copyist has left a deliberate blank at the bottom of f. 13v and the head of f. 14r. This is one of a number of planned blanks in the Boethius translations in this manuscript, at points where Fanshawe had obviously not completed his translation at the time when the manuscript was copied, although the blanks indicate that he intended to do so]; f. 14r, III, 10; f. 14v, III, 11; f. 15r, III, 12; f. 16r, IV, 1; f. 16v [planned blank for IV, 2]; f. 17r, IV, 3; f. 18r, IV, 4; f. 18v, IV, 5 [planned blanks for missing lines]; f.

19r [planned blank for IV, 6]; f. 20r, IV, 7; f. 20v, V, 1; f. 21r, V, 2; f. 21v [planned blank for V, 3]; f. 22r [planned blank for V, 4]; f. 23r, V, 5; f. 23v, Psalme 45; f. 25r [*Epigrams* of Martial] I, 63; f. 25r, V, 62; f. 25v, VIII, 2; f. 26r, VIII, 35; f. 26r, VIII, 56 [cancelled by Fanshawe]; f. 26v, VIII, 70; f. 26v, X, 2; f. 27r, X, 23; f. 27r, X, 50; f. 27v, X, 66; f. 27v, XII, 44; f. 28r, XII, 48; f. 28r [Epigram] 'Aufidius moriens . . .' [Latin and English]; f. 28v, X, 26; f. 28v, VIII, 30; f. 29r, An Oade, 'Splendidis longum valedico nugis'; f. 30r [Untitled], 'My quench't and discontinu'd Muse'; f. 30v, An Oade on the sight of a gentlewoman at Church; f. 32r, An Oade by occasion of his Majestys Proclamation for Gentlemen to goe into the Country; f. 35r, Upon the report of fowre Kings dead at once; f. 35v [Randolph's 'Upon the Newes of the King of Sweden's Death']; f. 36v, Martial, *Epigram* X, 19; f. 37r [Untitled first version of 'A Canto of the Progresse of Learning']; f. 39v, In Domum quam Phillipus Secundus Rex Hispaniarum aedificavit Escuriis, et Sancto Laurentio Dedicavit; f. 42v, On the Escuriall built by Philipp the second of Spayne and dedicated to St. Lawrence; f. 47r, Martial, *Epigram* VIII, 56 [Fanshawe's autograph]; f. 49r [Laundry list]; f. 49v [Blank]; f. 50r [Translations of the *Odes* of Horace] I, 1; f. 51r, I, 2; f. 52r, I, 3; f. 53r, I, 4; f. 53v, I, 5; f. 54r, I, 8; f. 54v, I, 13; f. 55r, I, 18; f. 55v, II, 3; f. 56r, II, 8; f. 56v, II, 10; f. 57r, II, 14; f. 58r, III, 7; f. 58v, III, 11; f. 59v, III, 20; f. 60r, III, 24; f. 61v, IV, 2; f. 63r, IV, 3; f. 63v, IV, 4; f. 65r, IV, 7; f. 65v, *Epode* 16; f. 67v, The Progress of Learning; f. 72v, On a great Ruby sett in a Ring with many Diamonds about it; f. 73r, On a Lady that vowed not to curle her hayre till her Brother returned from beyond Sea; f. 73v [Blank].

Add. MS 32,133

Siglum: M

Dimensions: 229mm × 166mm

Composition: ff. 78. The manuscript, rebound in dark blue morocco with blue leather corners and spine (cover: 237mm × 187mm), spine lettered in gold with title and catalogue number, consisted originally of a bound folio notebook. Folio 1 is a single sheet, the second sheet of a bifolium of which the cognate leaf (presumably bearing the title) is now wanting. Folio 79 is also a single sheet: the last bifolium appears to have been a pair of blank leaves of which the last leaf is lost. The manuscript entered the British Museum in 1883, at which time it was rebound and the leaves were sewn onto guards in their original gatherings. The manuscript is in good condition, apart from wanting one leaf from beginning and end.

Hands: The body of the text is in the hand of Lyonel Fanshawe. There are a few words, irrelevant to the text, written on f. 78v in the

hand of Ann, Lady Fanshawe. On ff. 3v–14r, f. 15v, and f. 16r and subsequently, there are scribbles, erasures, and 'improvements' in an eighteenth-century hand.
Date: presumably 1664–6, at which time Lyonel Fanshawe was his cousin's secretary. The text varies from the printed version of *1670*. The readings in this manuscript appear to represent an earlier state of the text.
Provenance: Presumably in Fanshawe's possession in Madrid, and in the possession of Lady Fanshawe after his death. It may be conjectured that it remained in the Fanshawe family at least until the later eighteenth century. It was bought from J. Lully for the British Museum in 1883.
Contents: ff. 1–3, Prologue; f. 4r [Blank]; f. 4v, 'The Persons in the first Acte'; ff. 5r–78v [The text of] *Querer por Solo Querer*; f. 78 [In Lady Fanshawe's hand, in pencil] 'Sunt mala plura pessima'.

MS Egerton 2982
(Volume V of *Miscellaneous Theological and Literary Works*, once the property of the Heath and Verney families.)
Siglum: Eg.
Composition: This 'manuscript' of 292 folios is the creation of the binder. A very miscellaneous set of loose papers of various sizes has been sewn onto guards and bound within red morocco covers 414mm × 253mm with red leather corners and spine. The upper board is stamped in gold with a crest bearing the motto 'SIC DONEC'.
Contents, Dimensions, Hands: ff. 153–4, bifolium 304mm × 194mm; contains 'On his Majesties Great Shipp Lying almost finished in Woolage dock. Anno 1637'. Scribal hand, with alterations in Fanshawe's autograph; ff. 155–6, bifolium, 283mm × 206mm, scribal hand with autograph alterations, 'On his Majestie's Great Ship', the English and Latin versions written in double column; f. 156v is blank; ff. 157–8, bifolium, 307mm × 203mm, in the hand of Francis Heath (cf. *British Museum, Catalogue of Additions to the Manuscripts, 1916–1920*, London, printed for the Trustees of the British Museum: 1933, p. 319, for the identification of this hand). It contains 'What 'tis he loves in his Mistresse' and is attributed with the initials 'R. ff.'; ff. 166–8, bifolium and single sheet, 193mm × 147mm, in illegible secretary hand, possibly Francis Heath writing in great haste, contains 'Dialogue of Utrechia and Thirsis' in Latin and English; ff. 175–242 consist of a disbound small folio notebook (228mm × 173mm) in the hand of Sir John Heath, containing translations of the *Epigrams* of Martial. On f. 192v the translation of V, 62 is ascribed in a marginal note to 'R.F.'

Date: The collection covers a wide span of time from *c.*1600 to 1680. The pieces by Fanshawe may be dated to the 1630s.
Provenance: Heath and Verney families until at least 1680. Entered the British Museum in March 1919, when the manuscript reached its present form and was bound.

Evelyn Papers [in process of cataloguing].
Siglum: Eve.
Three single sheets, containing 'Dominae Navigaturae' and 'Methodus Amandi'.

MS Harley 6917
Siglum: Har.
Dimensions: 199mm × 150mm
Composition: Commonplace Book, foliated 1–105.
f. 51v (p. 94) On a faire Ruby set in a Ring with many diamonds about it.
Date: *c.*1637–40.

Bodleian Library, Oxford

MS Firth c. 1
Siglum: F
Dimensions: 298mm × 197mm
Composition: The manuscript is in folio and is in its original binding of brown calf stamped with the crest of Edward, second Viscount Conway (a moor's head filleted about the temples and surmounted with a coronet). In the late nineteenth century the spine has been repaired and blocked in gold 'SIR RICHARD FANSHAWE'S POEMS'. It is in good condition, apart from the loss of some leaves from the end. There is no modern foliation; the original pagination begins at f. 3r and carries through to the last surviving leaf, f. 62, pp. 118.
Hand: The manuscript is very much a fair copy, made in a single, extremely neat hand with a number of secretary forms. The scribe uses a fine italic for headings and emphasized words. There are inscriptions by subsequent owners on f. 1v, f. 2r, and f. 63. The manuscript gives the impression that it has been compiled with considerable care, and with Fanshawe's approval.
Date: It is hard to date the manuscript precisely. Its owner, Edward, second Viscount Conway, died in 1655. More precisely, it is obviously later than 1637, later than the final form of A; but it must also antedate Fanshawe's publication of *1648* in that it displays variant readings of poems published in *1648* which accord with A. This is to say that another

revision must have taken place between the compilation of this manuscript and the making of the final versions printed in 1648, which narrows the possible years to 1637–47. If this carefully arranged and copied manuscript was made for Fanshawe himself, presumably for presentation or for scribal publication, it must therefore further antedate the decision to publish a thematically linked group of poems in *1648* and to separate them from translations of Horace. It may be noted that this manuscript does not contain any translations of Boethius or Martial (the apprentice works of A), and that although it contains a number of translations from the Spanish it does not contain all the poems published in *1648*. Taking these factors into account, it might be suggested that the years 1641–5, years in which Fanshawe was in England and comparatively settled, are the most probable years for compilation.

Provenance: ?Fanshawe himself; Edward, second Viscount Conway; unknown; Joseph Warton 1788; the last leaves were torn away before it came into the possession of Professor Firth and thence to the Bodleian.

Contents: f. 1r [Blank]; f. 1v [inscription in the hand of Professor Firth]: 'This volume contains the miscellaneous poems of Sir Richard Fanshawe . . . it gives many various readings, and (I think) in most cases superior readings'; f. 2r [Title-page] *Diuers Poems / the Table where of is at the end / of this Booke. / Cicero in Oratione pro Archia, / Poeta / Haec Studia delectant domi; non impediunt / foris; pernoctant nobiscum, peregrinantur, / rusticantur.* [also inscription, in 18th-century hand] Joseph Warton 1788; f. 2v, *The Loues of Dido and Aeneas. The Argument*; f. 3r (p. 1.), *The Fourth Books of the Aeneads*; p. 31 [Translations of *Odes* of Horace], I, 1; p. 33, I, 2; p. 35, I, 3; p. 37, I, 4; p. 38, I, 5; p. 38, I, 8; p. 39, I, 9; p. 40, I, 13; p. 41, I, 18; p. 42, II, 2; p. 43, II, 3; p. 44, II, 4; p. 45, II, 8; p. 46, II, 10; p. 48, II, 14; p. 49, II, 15; p. 50, III, 7; p. 51, III, 11; p. 53, III, 24; p. 56, III, 27; p. 59, IV, 2; p. 62, IV, 4; p. 65, IV, 7; p. 67, *Epode* 1; p. 68, 14; p. 69, 16; p. 72, *Sonnets translated out of Spanish*, 'Soare high, my Love, check not thy gallant flight'; p. 72, 'That louelie mouth, which doth to taste invite'; p. 73, *To a River.* 'O thou cleare honour of the Christall Mayne'; p. 74, 'That virgin-Rose, which while she grew (though crown'd)'; p. 74, 'With such varietie and daintie skill'; p. 75, *To a Rose.* 'Blowne but i'th'morning, thou shalt fayde ere Noone'; p. 75, 'Behold how *Marius*, from *Minturnus* lake'; p. 76, '*Phillis* i'th'Sunne proyning her locks did sit'; p. 76, *A great Favorit beheaded.* 'The bloudie trunke of him, who did posesse'; p. 77, *To one very rich and very foolish.* 'Thee, senseles Stock, because th'art richly guilt'; p. 77, 'Thou, Love, by whome the naked Soule is view'd'; p. 78, 'To hope is good, but with so wild applause'; p. 79, 'O endlesse Smart, and endlesse wisht to be'; p. 79,

'Whether thou curle, or trence thy native gold'; p. 80, *A Cupid of Diamonds sent to a Ladie after parting from her in her disdaine.* 'Banisht from life, to seeke out death I goe'; p. 80, 'Strange Tyrranie! with smiles to kill your Lovers'; p. 81, 'Though bound to Rocks of Faith with golden chaine'; p. 82, *The Praise of the Winde.* 'If words are winde, which (guilt with eloquence)'; p. 82, Originalls. *An Ode upon occasion of His Majesties Proclamation in the yeare 1630. Commanding the Gentrie to repaire to their Estates in the Countrie*; p. 87, *On a faire Rubie set in a Ring with manie Diamonds about it*; p. 88, *In Aedes Magnificas, quas Philippus Secundus, Rex Hispaniae, Escuriis aedificavit, et S. Laurentio dedicavit*; p. 93, *On the Escurial, built by King Phillip the Second of Spaine; and dedicated to St. Laurence*; p. 100, *On His Majesties Great Ship lying almost finisht at Woolage Anno* 1637; p. 104, *Ad maximam totius orbis Navem sub auspiciis Caroli Magnae-Britanniae Regis constructam, Anno Domini* 1637; p. 108, *The Progresse of Learning* [This poem ceases on p. 116. The rest of the manuscript is wanting. There is a note to this effect on the endpaper in the hand of Professor Firth].

MS Malone 13
Siglum: Malone
Dimensions: 196mm × 143mm
Composition: Commonplace Book, iv + 318 pages, bound in brown morocco.
Date: 1630s.
p. 95 (f. 49r) 'Yet shee was fayre; yet dyd her grace'; the poem is untitled and is not attributed.

MS Wood F 34
Siglum: Wood
Date: 1637–48.
ff. 142–3. Bifolium, 326mm × 215mm, containing 'On his Majesties Great Ship', in the same hand, and with the same layout of English and Latin in double column, as ff. 155–6 of Eg.

MS Jones 56
Siglum: Jones
Dimensions: 367mm × 234mm
Date: 1637–48.
f. 13. 'On his Majesties Great Shippe lyinge allmost finished in Wollage Docke. Anno Domini 1637.' ff. 14–15r 'The same in Latin.'

Henry E. Huntington Library, San Marino, California

HM 904

Siglum: C
Dimensions: 191mm × 143mm
Composition: The Commonplace Book of Constantia Aston (Fowler) is a quarto notebook of 200 leaves bound in the original brown calf, with gold tooling.
Hand: Chiefly that of Constantia Aston.
Date: The manuscript was obviously copied carefully over a considerable period. The Huntington catalogue suggests 1630–50. The poems by Fanshawe, on the evidence of the state of the texts, would seem to have been copied *c.* 1636–9.
Contents: ff. 185v–186r, A Dreame; ff. 187–8, 'Celia hath for a brothers absence sworne' [attributed to] 'Mr R.F.'; f. 188v The Nightingall [attributed to] 'Mr R.F.'

HM 116

Siglum: H
Dimensions: 140mm × 90mm
Composition: The Commonplace Book of a member of the University of Oxford. In its original form, this manuscript was a small pocket notebook with 90 leaves, continuously paginated 1–180. It was rebound in light-brown calf, with gold tooling, about 1830, at which time the original notebook was disbound and was interleaved with blank pages 148mm × 160mm.
Hand: A minute italic, which contrives to write an average of thirty-five lines on a very small page. The hand, which is the same throughout, is presumably that of the compiler of the manuscript, but there is no indication of original ownership.
Date: The collection includes so many fugitive verses on Oxford topics that it would be reasonable to suppose that the copies from Fanshawe were made between 1643 and 1645, when he was in Oxford. If we conjecture, on the evidence of Fanshawe's letter to John Heath dated from Dublin 26 December 1640 (pp. 329–30), that he had been emotionally attached to Constantia Aston in the late 1630s it is perhaps unlikely that he would have circulated his poems to the Aston daughters (poems which had been dropped by the time that F was compiled) after his marriage in May 1644. Thus the date of this manuscript could be fixed at 1643–4. It is hard to believe that the compiler of this manuscript did not have access to unusually good texts of Fanshawe's

work, which would support the assumption that it was copied while Fanshawe was in Oxford. This manuscript is valuable in that it provides the only indication surviving of the revised texts of certain poems which Fanshawe did not choose to include in either F or *1648*.
Provenance: Original owner unknown; sold as lot 577 of the sale of Lord Kingsborough's library, Dublin, 1842; but it appears to have been interleaved and rebound for Joseph Haselwood before this (Haselwood has written on some of the blank interleaves); later owners appear to have included Alex. Chalmers and the Huth Library, from whence it passed to the Huntington.
Contents: A group of poems by Fanshawe are found on pp. 154–66; p. 154, On his Majesties great Shipp, Lying almost finish'd at Woolage, Anno 1637; p. 158, In Nave celeberrima sub auspiciis serenissimi Regis Angliae constructam super ripam Thamesis. Anno Domini 1637; p. 161, On a faire Rubie sett in a ring with many Diamonds about it; p. 162 On two most beautifull Sisters: rowed on the Trent; under the allegorie of swans; p. 163, On one of the same Sisters, haveing made a Vow not to curle her hayre (which was extreame fayre) untill a brother of hers returned from Travayle; p. 164, On the Wedding-day of his deare friend; p. 165, A Cupid of Diamonds sent to a Lady after parting from her in her disfavour; p. 165, To a friend fearing his relapse into an old Love; p. 166, To a Rose.

London Boroughs of Barking and Dagenham Libraries

Uncatalogued Fanshawe Papers, at Valence House
Siglum: V
Composition: This collection of papers, covering a span of time from the late sixteenth to the early eighteenth century, is vast in extent and bewildering in its disorganization. Much of the disorder appears to have been caused by the antiquary H. C. Fanshawe in the late nineteenth century. A catalogue is being undertaken by Professor Roger Walker of Birkbeck College in the University of London.

Since the 1970s a start has been made on sorting the seventeenth-century papers. They have been collected into large loose-leaf binders, the individual leaves being enclosed in transparent envelopes. Three single leaves require notice. The first is a leaf approximately 275mm × 193mm bearing 'Effigiei inscriptum' in the hand of Lyonel Fanshawe. The second is a damaged leaf measuring approximately 298mm × 197mm, also in the hand of Lyonel Fanshawe, containing part of the dedication to the *Specimen Rerum a Lusitanis* as in MS B (cf. *Textual Introduction*, vol. ii) ('Vidisti Lector... tantum non perfectus'), with two additions in Fanshawe's autograph on the recto and one on the verso. The third is another leaf of the same dimensions and hand, containing the 'Elogia poetae' and the Latin sonnet '*Vasco*, triumphanti qui signa per aurea *Soli*', both of which are found in the interpolation in B which divides the two Books translated from Camões. These three leaves, it must be assumed, come from a lost collection of Latin poems made in Madrid between 1664 and 1666. It is quite clear that the two leaves from the *Specimen Rerum a Lusitanis* were designed to be sent to the scribe of B, as one of Fanshawe's additions is a direction for the drawing of a shield to be found at f. 5r of B.

University Library, Cambridge
(Ex the collection of the late Sir Geoffrey Keynes.)

Commonplace Book of Henry Rainsford (not yet catalogued)
See Sir Geoffrey Keynes, *Bibliotheca Bibliographici* (London, Trianon Press: 1964), p. 4.
Siglum: Rainsford
Dimensions: 173mm × 90mm
Composition: Octavo notebook, containing academic notes and a collection of contemporary verses, copied in Oxford *c.* 1643–5.
Contents: f. 22, A Cupid of Diamonds sent to a Lady after parting in her disfavour.

Printed Sources Listed in Chronological Order

Thomas May's *Supplementum Lucani*, 1640
SUPPLEMENTUM / LUCANI / LIBRI VII. / *Authore* / THOMA MAIO / ANGLO. // *Venturi me tegue legent.* LUC. / [Device of eagle with scroll inscribed 'NIL PENNA SEDVSVS'] / LUGDUNI BATAVORUM. // Typis WILHELMI CHRISTIANI / M) I) CXL [MDCXL]
Short Title: *May*
12°.
Fanshawe's '*Ad. Cl. Virum* / THOMAM MAIUM / Anglo-Lucanum' is on sig. *6r–*7v. Copy in the Cambridge University Library.

A Proclamation . . . 1645

A PROCLAMATION, / For all Persons within Our Quarters in the County of DEVON . . . Imprinted at *Exeter* by ROBERT BARKER, and JOHN BILL, Printers / to the Kings most Excellent Majesty, 1645.
Single unfolded sheet. Copy in the British Library.

A Message from His Highnesse . . . 1648

A MESSAGE: / FROM HIS HIGHNESSE: / The Prince of Wales, / DELIVERED / *To the right Honorable the Lord Baron of Inchiquin / Lord President of Mounster, in a Councell of War / at Corcke the 28. of November, 1648. / By Richard Fanshawe Esquire, imployed by / his Highnesse into Ireland.* / [Block of the Royal Arms] / Printed at Corck, in the yeare 1648. and are / to be sold at Roches building.
4° Signed. A–B.
The text given below is a conflation of two damaged copies in the Cambridge University Library.

The second and augmented edition of *Il Pastor Fido* (1648)

IL / PASTOR FIDO / The faithfull Shepheard / WITH / An ADDITION of divers other / POEMS / Concluding with a short Discourse / OF THE LONG / CIVILL WARRES / OF / ROME. / To His Highnesse / THE PRINCE OF / WALES. // By *Richard Fanshawe*, Esq. // HORAT. / *Patiarque vel inconsultus haberi.* // LONDON: / Printed for *Humphrey Moseley*, and are to be sold at his Shop at the / Princes Armes in S. *Pauls* Church-yard. 1648.
4° A^4 A^4 a^2 B – $2R^4$, xviii + 312 pp.
Wing G2175; Greg 629 (all)
Short Title: *1648*

(This book is a reissue of the complete text of the 1647 edition of *Il Pastor Fido*, Wing G2174. These original sheets, including the *Pastor Fido* and two poems to the Prince of Wales, are numbered from Sig. B1 onwards pp. 1–223, and are signed A–Ff.)
p. 217, Presented to His Highnesse the Prince of Wales, At his going into the West, *Ann. M.DC.XLV.* Together with *Cesar's Commentaries*; p. 219, Presented to His Highnesse, *In the West*, Ann. Dom. 1646. Moseley's 1648 issue includes all these sheets with the addition of an extra Sig. A at the beginning and Sigs. Gg to Rr at the end, numbered pp. 225–312.
Contents: Sig. A2r Epistle: To the Hope and Lustre Of Three Kingdomes, Charles Prince of VVales, Duke of Cornwall, &c; A3v, The Printer to the Reader; A4r, An index of the severall things contained in

this Booke. [The sheets of Wing G2174 as noted above follow]; p. 225, An Ode upon occasion of his Majesties Proclamation; p. 230, In Aedes magnificas quas *Phillipus* Secundus *Hispaniarum* Rex Escuriis aedificavit, et Santo *Laurentio* dedicavit; p. 231, The Escuriall; p. 240, Ad eximiae magnitudinis Navem sub auspiciis Caroli Magnae Britanniae Regis constructam. *Anno Dom.* 1637. Cui postea nomen Regina Marium; p. 241, On His Majesties Great Shippe lying almost finisht in *Woolwich* Docke. Anno Dom 1637. and afterwards called The Soveraigne of the Seas; p. 250, *Written by Mr.* T. C. *of his* Majesties Bed-Chamber; p. 251, Ex Lingua Anglicana. Methodus Amandi; p. 254, *By* Mr. T. C. *likewise*; p. 255, *Dominae Navigaturae* ex Lingua Anglicana; p. 256, A Canto of the Progresse of Learning; p. 263, The Ruby; p. 264, A friends Wedding; [*Sonnets Translated out of Spanish*]: p. 265, *A Rich Foole*; p. 266, *Hope*; p. 266, *Constancie*; p. 267, *A Rose*; p. 268, *A Picture*; p. 268, *A River*; p. 269, *A Nightingale*; p. 269, *A Cupid of Diamonds Presented*; p. 270, *The Spring*; p. 271, The Fourth Booke of *Virgills Aeneis* on the *Loves of Dido* and *Aeneas. The Argument of the three preceding Bookes, By way of Introduction*; p. 273, The Fourth Books of *Virgills Aeneis* on the *Loves* of *Dido* and *Aeneas*; p. 297, A Happy Life out of *Martiall*; p. 298, On the Earle of *Straffords* Triall; p. 299, Two Odes out of *Horace*, relating unto the Civill Warres of *Rome* [Ode III, 24; Epode 16]; p. 303, A Summary Discourse of the Civill Warres of Rome . . . [Prose Discourse].

The Collection was reprinted in 1664, 1676, 1692: none of these 8° reprints has any textual significance. A reprint of Elkanah Settle's altered version of the play *Il Pastor Fido*, first printed in 1677, appeared as late as 1736.

The text is taken from the copy in the possession of the present editor, University of Warwick, England, collated with the copies in Trinity College, Cambridge and the University Library, Cambridge.

The second and corrected issue of *Selected Parts of Horace*, 1652

Wing H2786, with the corrections noted below. Not recorded by Wing as a second state.

Selected PARTS / OF / HORACE, / Prince of LYRICKS; / AND / Of all the Latin Poets the fullest fraught / with Excellent MORALITY. / Concluding With a Piece out of AUSONIUS, / and another out of VIRGIL. / Now newly put into English. / Dux VITae Ratio. / [Engraved plate with monogram of R. FANSHAWE surrounded by a wreath] / *London*, printed for *M.M. Gabriel Bedell, and T. Collins*, / and are to be sold at their shop at the *middle-Temple-Gate*, 1652.

8° [A]^{1} B – N^{8}.

Short Title: *1652*

The pages of the book are numbered in pairs, Latin facing English; in all copies of the uncorrected state the pages signed F are wrongly numbered, viz. 32; 35, 35; 34, 34; 33, 33; 36, 36; 39, 39; 38, 38; 37. In the two surviving corrected copies (Beinecke Library, Yale; Jesus College, Cambridge) the line 'Dux VITae Ratio' on the title-page is above, not below the plate. In both these copies the errors of Sig. F have been corrected. 8°, signed B–N, paginated continuously 1, 1–95, 95. Both of the known copies of this state have a Fanshawe family provenance: the Jesus College, Cambridge copy was presented by H. C. Fanshawe in the 1900s; the Beinecke copy bears the book-plate of Althea Fanshawe, the eighteenth-century poet, and her inscription on the title-page 'Corrected by the Translator himself Sir Richard Fanshawe Bt' might show that the annotations on that copy represent family tradition, although the ascription of the annotations requires some caution. There are one or two convincing textual corrections, but the dull marginalia appear to be in a later seventeenth-century hand. There are occasional 'improvements' apparently in an eighteenth-century hand.

This copy (Beinecke pressmark Gnbh a 652r. Copy 2) was probably prepared for Fanshawe: it is on fine paper, the presswork is of high quality, and the titles and margins are hand-ruled in brown ink.

Contents: p. 1, *Ode* I, 1; p. 2, I, 2; p. 4, I, 4; p. 5, I, 5, I, 8; p. 6, I, 9; p. 7, I, 13; p. 8, I, 3; p. 9, I, 18; p. 10, I, 27; p. 11, I, 31; p. 12, I, 24; p. 13, I, 34; p. 14, II, 1; p. 15, II, 2; p. 16, II, 3; p. 17, II, 4; p. 18, II, 8; p. 19, II, 10; p. 20, II, 13; p. 22, II, 14; p. 23, II, 15, II, 16; p. 25, II, 27; p. 27, III, 1; p. 29, III, 3; p. 31, III, 4; p. 34, III, 5; p. 36, III, 7; p. 37, III, 9; p. 38, III, 11; p. 40, III, 16; p. 41, III, 24; p. 43, III, 27; p. 46, III, 29; p. 48, III, 30; p. 49, IV, 2; p. 51, IV, 3; p. 52, IV, 4; p. 55, IV, 5; p. 56, IV, 7; p. 57, IV, 8; p. 59, IV, 9; p. 61, *Epode* 1; p. 62, 2; p. 64, 7; p. 65, 14; p. 66, 16; p. 68, *Ode* I, 37; p. 71, *Discourses* I, 6; p. 76, II, 1; p. 79, II, 6; p. 83, III, 1; p. 86, III, 5; p. 88, III, 10; p. 90, III, 2; p. 92, AUSONIUS *His Roses*; p. 94, VIRGIL'S BULL. *Out of his Third Book* of Georgicks.

La Fida Pastora, 1658

Wing F1343.

LA FIDA PASTORA. / Comoedia Pastoralis. / Autore / FF. ANGLO-BRITANNO / *Adduntur nonulla varii argumenti* / *Carmina ab eodem.* / [Engraved plate: monogram of 'R. Fanshawe' in a wreath] / DUX VITAE RATIO. / LONDINI, / Typis *R. Danielis*, Impensis *G. Bedell* & T. *Collins*, / apud quos veneunt proxime januam Templi Mediani / in vico dicto *Fleet-Streete*. 1658.

8° * [4]A – F[8] G[4], vi – 103pp.
Short Title: *1658*
Contents: sig. A2v, Personae Dramatis; sig. A3r, Author ad Opusculum; pp. 1–86, *La Fida Pastora* [Latin version of Fletcher's *The Faithfull Shepheardesse*]; p. 87 [second title-page] OPUSCULA / [engraved plate with monogram as for first title-page] / DUX VITAE: RATIO / LONDINI, / Impensis *G. Bedell* & T. *Collins*, / apud quos veneunt proxime januam Templi Mediani / in vico dicto *Fleet-streete*. 1658; p. 89, In Aedes magnificas quas PHILIPPUS SECUNDUS Hispaniarum Rex Escuriis aedificavit; p. 93, Ad eximiae magnitudinis Navem sub auspiciis *Caroli* Magnae Britanniae Regis prope constructam; p. 96, Maius Lucanizans; p. 98, Methodus Amandi; p. 100, Dominae Navigaturae; p. 101, Serenissimae Reginae Sueciae. [Epistle dedicating *Querer por solo Querer* to the Queen of Sweden]; p. 103, Lectori; The copy in the Cambridge University Library, pressmark o*. 5.18 has been used.

Arthur Clifford, *Tixall Poetry, with notes and illustrations by Arthur Clifford*
Edinburgh, J. Ballantyne and Co., 1813.
Short Title: *Tixall*
2°.
Contents: p. 213, A Dreame by Mr. Fanshawe; p. 214, Celia by Mr. Fanshawe.
Copy in the possession of the present editor, University of Warwick, England.

II. SCOPE AND LIMITATIONS OF THIS EDITION

This edition attempts to present a complete text of Fanshawe's surviving literary works, with the exception of *Il Pastor Fido* (1647) which exists in an excellent modern edition, *A Critical Edition of Sir Richard Fanshawe's 1647 Translation of Giovanni Battista Guarini's Il Pastor Fido*, ed. Walter F. Staton and William E. Simione (Oxford, Clarendon Press, 1964). *The Lusiads* (1655) are given here despite the existence of Geoffrey Bullough's edition, *The Lusiads in Sir Richard Fanshawe's Translation* (London and Fontwell, Centaur Press, 1963) because fresh textual evidence has become available. See Textual Introduction, Volume II.

Three prose works and a number of letters have been included: 'A Summary Discourse of the Civil Warres of *Rome*' is particularly important because it is an integral part of the careful thematic arrangement of *1648*. The two pieces of political prose give context to Fanshawe's political poems of the 1640s, as do the hitherto-unpublished letters given at the end of this volume.

For the two groups containing Fanshawe's original English poems, the unpublished poems of the 1630s and 1640s called here 'Early Poems from Manuscript' and those of *1648*, an attempt has been made to give all substantive variants, including all legible manuscript cancellations.

For *1652* the demands of the text are different: the copy-text is the poet's corrected copy of the printed text, and the variants from MSS F and A are considerably earlier than the final version. It is not possible to reconstruct a complete history of the evolution of the final text. In this case, rather than overburden a translation with apparatus, only substantive variants of literary importance have been given.

The sparse variants which it is possible to give for the Latin poems are reproduced in full.

A full commentary has been supplied for Fanshawe's original poems, but for the Latin works and translations an attempt has been made at economy of commentary.

III. ABOUT THE SOURCES FOR THIS EDITION

In view of the hazards and uncertainties of Fanshawe's life and of the times in which he lived, the rate of survival of the sources for this edition is remarkably good. As the itemization of sources shows, only one group of poems (those published with *Il Pastor Fido* in *1648*) cannot be given from either a printed text marked up by Fanshawe or his immediate family, or from a manuscript originating close to the poet himself. Every available copy of *1648* has been examined in vain for autograph corrections like those which Fanshawe made in one copy of *1652* and three copies of *1655*. (Lady Fanshawe hand-corrected a number of presentation copies of *1670*.) The copy of *1648* from the library of Charles II, now in the Houghton Library of Harvard University, lacks any annotation or correction.

In every case but *1648*, the sources which have been used for this edition represent Fanshawe's works in a form which is at least close to the poet's final intentions; allowing, that is, for the imperfections which must be expected of any text which has been through the hands of copyist or compositor, and which are not always removed by authorial correction.

Paradoxically, time and chance have been kinder to the texts of Fanshawe's works than family piety has been: the family copy of *1652* and the manuscript of *Querer por solo Querer* (MS M) are both disfigured by later 'improvements', and the Edwardian antiquary H. C. Fanshawe scattered and disarranged what must once have been a remarkably comprehensive collection of family papers. The remains are now secure at Valence House and are being ordered and catalogued.

IV. GENERAL STATEMENT OF EDITORIAL POLICY

Arrangement

The most logical order for the arrangement of Fanshawe's poems is dictated by the strong unity of the collections in which he himself published them: the poems in *1648* form a unified group with a strong thematic pattern; *1652* is united by the common source of the poems translated. This edition begins with a group of 'Early Poems from Manuscript' which are arranged chronologically, and thereafter follows the ordering of the poems as they were published in the texts printed in Fanshawe's lifetime. There are two exceptions to this rule: (i) Poems by Boethius, Horace, and Martial have been ordered and numbered according to standards accepted by modern classical scholarship. The standardized numbering at the head of translations from Latin poets is editorial; and (ii) Latin poems which were published first in *1648* remain in their place in the sequence of that volume, rather than with the group formed by their republication in *1658*. Variants found in the text of *1658* are recorded as part of the apparatus to the *1648* text. Two translations from Horace appear in the two contexts in which Fanshawe published them: *1648* and *1652*.

Modifications of Copy-Text

a. Spelling

The letters u, v, i, and j have been replaced by their modern equivalents. Capital F has replaced ff. Contractions and numerals have been expanded. Apart from this, the principle with regard to spelling has been to adhere to the diversity of the original. Standard contractions have been expanded.

b. Punctuation

A range of sources which covers a period of 40 years presents diverse problems of punctuation, requiring varying degrees of attention in the different sections of the work. Individual cases are examined in more detail below, but the following principles apply to the edition as a whole:

No attempt has been made to impose punctuation according to modern conventions. Original punctuation is retained throughout, except in the very few cases where there appear to be compositors' errors, in which cases the minimum alteration has been made;

1652 is pointed to direct the speaking voice, although it has suffered at the hands of the compositor; *1648* works on the same principle. The punctuation of the early manuscripts is sparse, rhetorical, unobtrusive;

In practice, this means that original punctuation is preserved, except for the removal of a small number of otiose commas from mid-line which serve neither to separate phrases nor to mark any possible rhetorical pause; the alteration of a few full stops in *1648*, apparently compositors' errors, which usurp the place of a comma in mid-phrase. The apostrophe is used with notable consistency in the sources, both in the marking of elision and possession. This edition seeks to preserve the original usage;

Running inverted commas to indicate *sententiae* are preserved in this edition.

c. Italicization

Italics are used consistently in the sources for emphasis, inconsistently for proper names. They have been taken exactly from the copy-texts, except in a few cases of patent compositor's error. These have been supplied with caution and only where they are demanded to indicate reported speech, or where a balancing emphasis is clearly required within a phrase.

d. Capitalization

The use of capitals is reasonably consistent in the sources and has been reproduced faithfully with the following minor exception: in Eg. and A a few lines beginning with an inexplicable lower-case letter have been replaced with upper-case.

Variant and Alternative Readings

Variant readings are given at the bottom of the text page. In the case of manuscript sources, a cancellation of literary interest is treated as a variant, but is marked thus: '[*canc.*]'. An uncancelled alternative reading is cued in the text and given at the foot of the relevant page. In those poems in *1648* and *1652* where the copy-text prints Fanshawe's own notes in the margin this original arrangement has been retained. There is no case where an authorial note could be mistaken for an alternative reading.

The only exception to the rule for the representation of variants is the early untitled version of 'A Canto of the Progresse of Learning' in A, which bears little relation to the poem in its final form and is given after it in the body of the *1648* text. The first version of 'The Fourth Booke of Virgill's Aeneis. On the Loves of Dido and Aeneas' from MS F seems, on the other hand, to take its place most usefully as a conventional variant to the *1648* text. When a number of texts are recorded as showing a particular variant there may be accidental differences between them; in every case the form recorded is that of the first text cited.

Summary of Principles

The principle of this edition is simple: once a copy-text has been chosen it is followed in all details except in cases of compositor's error, in which cases emendation is kept to an absolute minimum. Unless there is a variant text to support an emendation, only unequivocal printer's errors in copy-text are emended.

V. POEMS OF DUBIOUS AUTHORSHIP

The canon of Fanshawe's work is well defined. There are only three cases which require notice in this context:

(i) The unascribed poem 'Upon the funerall of Mrs Pawley's daughter' from Beinecke Library, Yale University, MS Osborn B4 1634, ff. 50v–51r, which may show some trace of Fanshawe's collaboration. The evidence for this is wholly internal.

(ii) In the Huntington Library, San Marino, California, the manuscript HM16522 ascribes Sir John Denham's 'The Western Wonder' to Fanshawe on f. 43v. The volume's binding bears the same crest (a moor's head filleted) as F, indicating that it comes from the same library, that of Edward, second Viscount Conway (d. 1655). This provenance is the one tenuous claim which Fanshawe might have to its authorship. Not only is the poem clearly in Denham's distinctive style, but it is also included in the definitive edition of Denham's *Poems and Translations* (1668). Denham's own annotated copy of this edition (in the Beinecke Library, Yale University) gives no indication that the poem owes anything to collaboration.

(iii) MS Rawl. D. 261.1 in the Bodleian Library, Oxford ascribes translations (not in *1652*, F, or A) to 'Sir R.F.' They are of Horace, *Odes* I, 12 and I, 22. The manuscript dates from the 1670s. It is copied literally, if carelessly, from Alexander Brome's *The Poems of Horace*, in the printed texts of which both translations are attributed to 'Sir T.H.', that is, to Sir

Thomas Hawkins. In Hawkins's *Odes of Horace* neither translation appears, but, on the other hand, the copyist of MS Rawl. D. 261.1 may well have mistaken the initials at the heads of these two poems. Given the nature of the manuscript, which has no authority and bears marks of haste, there is no reason to accept this attribution. The early folios of the manuscript indicate that it was copied by an undergraduate, James Gibson, for another undergraduate who had admired a printed copy of Brome's *The Poems of Horace*.

VI. LOST WORKS

The only work by Fanshawe mentioned in any contemporary document which appears not to have survived is a piece of autobiographical writing pertaining to the year 1651. The reference is on p. 135 of the *Memoirs*:

> You [Sir Richard Fanshawe the Younger] may read your father's demeanour of his self in this affaire [the battle of Worcester], writ by his own hand in a book amongst your books, and it's a great masterpiece, as you will find.

It is possible, as a number of Fanshawe's Latin works exist in a fragmentary form (and all in the hand of Lyonel Fanshawe) amongst the *disiecta membra* of V, that these represent the remains of a collection of Latin poems made in Madrid in the years 1664–6, when Lyonel Fanshawe was his cousin's secretary. If this is so, then any uncollected material which this collection may have contained may be accounted lost.

vii. STEMMATA AND STATEMENTS OF EDITORIAL POLICY FOR THIS EDITION, SECTION BY SECTION

Stemma for Fanshawe's Work before 1648

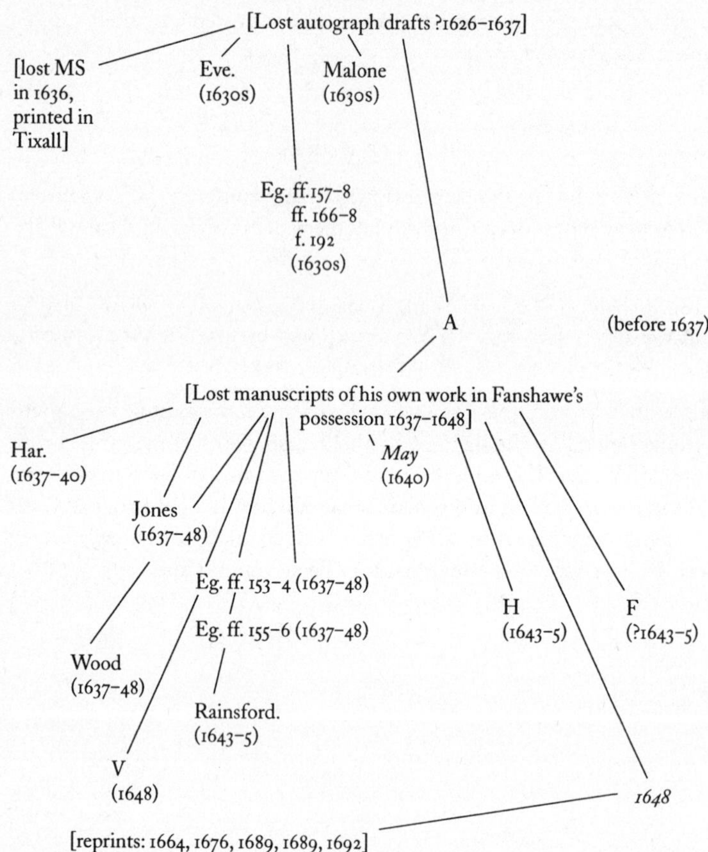

Sources for this Edition Dating from before 1648

The complicated interrelations of the sources for Fanshawe's earlier poetry demand an explanation to supplement the stemma.

It is reasonable to assume that Fanshawe had in his possession from *c.*1626 until 1648 a body of autograph and scribal copies of his own poems, copies which are now lost. This body of work obviously grew with the years until it contained the poems in *1648*, F, and H.

In the 1620s Fanshawe was writing and translating some of those poems which are now in A. The Boethius and Martial, the first attempts with Horace, belong to these years. It is not impossible that the poems copied in Eve. and Malone precede the compilation of A. Fanshawe's friends the Heaths seem to have made copies of his poems over a number of years and ff. 157–8 of Eg. may possibly date from the late 1620s in that they contain a poem which is not preserved in A.

A is Fanshawe's first attempt to collect his own works, a selection, it may be assumed, rather than a comprehensive collection. Eg. f. 192 was obviously copied after A, in that the *Epigram* of Martial's given there in Fanshawe's translation is in a version reworked from the one in A. It is possible that ff. 166–8 of Eg. were copied at the same time. So far all manuscript copies apart from Malone can be seen to proceed from the circle of Fanshawe's relations and friends.

The poem on the last folio of A provides at least a conjectural final date for that collection: we know that the two poems to the daughters of Lord Aston were composed in the autumn of 1636. The first manuscript, the poet's own, which is now lost, was copied by Constantia Aston at the time and sent in a letter to her brother (*Tixall*, pp. 383–4). At some time after this one of the two poems was copied into A, bringing that collection to a close.

After 1637, there were more commonplace copies from the growing corpus of Fanshawe's poems. Har. and Jones are the only ones of these which are not connected with Fanshawe's circle. The Heaths had the copy of 'On his Majesties Great Ship' which is found on ff. 153–4 of Eg. This was revised in Fanshawe's autograph and recopied in English and Latin on what is now ff. 155–6 of Eg. Wood derives from this copy, and is in the hand of the same scribe. About this time also, three of Fanshawe's poems were copied into C by his friend Constantia Aston. We may presume that the complimentary poem for Thomas May's *Supplementum Lucani* (Leiden, 1640) was printed from copy which Fanshawe supplied for his friend's book.

The corpus of Fanshawe's work continued to grow. By the time that he arrived in Oxford in 1643, it included many of the sonnets translated from Spanish. The copy in Rainsford would plausibly date from this time. H is something of a puzzle, since the name of its compiler remains unknown; there is no doubt, however, that it is an Oxford manuscript of the 1640s. It might be suggested that H is copied from Fanshawe's manuscripts, since it includes a good number of his poems in particularly careful and attractive texts. Fanshawe has obviously revised some of his earlier work, but the poems to the daughters of Lord Aston still remain. It might be argued that this could suggest that H was copied before Fanshawe's marriage in 1644.

F, like A, is a selection from a larger body of work. The careful division of F into translations and originals, and the scrupulous presentation of the whole, might suggest that it was the fair copy for a scribal publication. It need not be assumed that it constitutes fair copy for a projected printed edition. Its comparatively sombre selection, and the omission of the Aston poems, suggest a date towards the end of Fanshawe's time in Oxford.

No manuscript survives to illuminate the stages by which the F poems were divided to form the nuclei of *1648* and *1652*. It is obvious that *1648* is no pirate edition; indeed, Fanshawe returned to the same stationer, Humphrey Moseley, for the carefully produced *1655*. Equally the years 1647–8 were unusually troubled ones for Fanshawe as for the rest of England. The texts in *1648* may have been supplied by Fanshawe in another manuscript, now lost, of the same kind as F and A; they represent a more sophisticated form of those poems in F which are also in the printed text. Several new poems have been added for which no manuscript survives. They may have been composed after F was compiled or they may simply not have been selected for F out of that corpus of manuscript work which appears to have accompanied Fanshawe through the first years of his poetic career.

Editorial Policy for 'Early Poems from Manuscript'

In this edition 'Early Poems from Manuscript' is the editorial title for that group of poems consisting of surviving works dating from before 1648, which Fanshawe did not choose to publish in *1648*. Their arrangement is essentially chronological, with the exception that translations from classical authors are grouped according to the accepted numbering of their originals.

The earliest poems are 'Ad almam . . . Cantab . . .', the translations from Boethius, Psalm 45, and Martial. The text of all of these is taken from the unique copies in A, with the exception of Martial, Epigram V, 62, which exists in a later and more sophisticated version in Eg. The translation of Horace *Odes* III, 20 is from A. Fanshawe does not include this poem either in F or *1652*. Also from unique copies in A are the 'Oade. Splendidis longum valedico nugis' and its second part, which begins 'My quencht and discontinued Muse'. 'Upon the report of fowre Kings dead at once' is from the unique copy in A; and 'What 'tis he loves in his Mistresse' is from the unique copy in Eg. The poem is hard to date. It has subject-matter and tone in common with the poem which follows it in this edition. The version of the 'Oade on the sight of a Gentlewoman at Church' is taken from A, as a more authoritative text than Malone; while the two poems to the daughters of Lord Aston are from H, a text which has been thoroughly revised from the earlier versions in A and C.

'To a friend fearing his relapse into an old Love' comes from the unique copy in H. Its place in Fanshawe's canon is, in this editor's opinion, secure, although there is no attribution in the manuscript: it comes in the middle of a group of Fanshawe poems; it is a translation from Argensola; and it is very much in Fanshawe's style. The group of 'Sonnets translated out of Spanish' with which the 'Early Poems' end are those sonnets from F which Fanshawe did not print in *1648*; and 'Effigei inscriptum' is taken from the unique copy in V. Where variants exist in an earlier manuscript they are given in full.

Despite their diversity, these poems present few editorial problems which are not covered by the general principles of the edition. Contractions are numerous, punctuation is generally sparse, but in all these manuscripts there is no instance of obvious textual corruption. The texts are therefore given faithfully, with those minimal emendations of spelling and punctuation outlined in the earlier part of this Introduction. Standard contractions are silently expanded. Interlinear space marked by a diagonal pen-stroke in A is observed.

Editorial Policy for 1648

This is the most complicated section of the edition, in that Fanshawe did not see the text through the press and no copy of the printed text has been found with any contemporary annotation or correction.

The copy-text has to be *1648*, despite the carelessness of the printing. There are numerous copies of *1648* poems in earlier manuscripts, but to attempt a conflation would be to produce a text which would assuredly not convey Fanshawe's intentions.

While the printing of *1648* may fall far short of the ideal, there is no doubt that the texts from which the compositor worked were good. The latest wholly authoritative text of any of the *1648* poems is in F, but this records a distinct and earlier state of the text.

The note from 'The Printer to the Reader' on sig. A3v of *1648* admits to the literal errors which a reader may emend with 'skill and good judgement'. Accidentals in the edition, it is true, are very careless; spelling of proper names is erratic; the Latin poems contain patent errors. For all this, there is only one point where there seems to be real substantive error.

Accordingly, the policy in this edition has been the silent correction only of the very few unequivocal printer's errors in spelling and punctuation. Otherwise an attempt has been made to preserve the text in the form of *1648* lightly emended after reference chiefly to F, H, and A, rather than in a form which substitutes manuscript for printed readings wholesale.

All manuscript variants are given in the apparatus, but only on a few exceptional occasions have they been adopted into the text. The titles at the heads of the poems are from the text of *1648* rather than from the List of Contents on sig. A4 in that volume.

The arrangement of *1648*, including the prose discourse 'A Summary Discourse of the Civill Warres of *Rome*', is preserved, including the two Horatian translations which also appear in *1652*.

Stemma for 1652

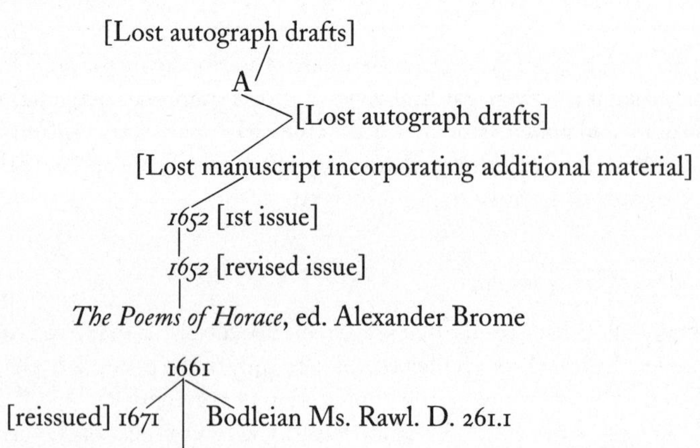

Editorial Policy for 1652

The Beinecke copy of the corrected issue of *1652* is used as copy-text. Corrections from the errata leaf are incorporated into the text given here. Later manuscript additions to the Beinecke copy of *1652* are ignored, with the exception of two convincing textual corrections to I, 1 and I, 4. (These brief corrections are in a hand resembling that of Lady Fanshawe. The otiose marginalia are in a distinctly later hand.)

Regarding the relation of copy-text to variant texts, there is no surviving authorial manuscript for the whole of *1652*. Earlier versions of some of the poems are found in A and F, but it is obvious that the text as it stands in F is a long way from the final version. Variance between *1652* in its corrected state and in its unrevised state consists only of printer's errors which the later issue corrects.

1652 in its corrected state is still far from ideal. There are occasional literal errors, uncorrected by Fanshawe, which have survived into the revised state of the text. Punctuation is in general consistent, but occasionally careless. It has been emended with great caution only at points where the sense of the poem is endangered. The few literal errors are corrected cautiously by reference to the Latin original.

The standardization, or numbering, of the poems is editorial, as is their rearrangement into the accepted order for the Horatian sequence. The Latin text, which is printed opposite the English text in *1652*, is not reproduced. Variance in headnotes between *1652* and F is not recorded.

Editorial Policy for 1658

La Fida Pastora is taken from *1658*, the only text in which this work exists. The text in *1658* is in general carefully printed, but names of characters prefixed to speeches have been corrected for this edition by reference to Fletcher's English original.

Editorial Policy for Prose Works and Letters

The *Proclamation* of 1645 is taken literally from the original broadside; and *A Message from his Highnesse*, 1648 is taken literally from the original pamphlet. There are two damaged copies in the Cambridge University Library. In one the first leaf is missing; in the other the later leaves are illegible. Otherwise they are identical, so the process of conflation is a very simple one.

Letters are printed from autograph, as recorded in their margins. Contractions have been expanded. Since Fanshawe is always admirably clear in his dating, the dates are given as in the originals with Fanshawe's indications of Old Style and New Style.

LIST OF SIGLA AND SHORT TITLES

MANUSCRIPTS

A	British Library, Add. MS 15,228
B	Fundação da Casa de Braganza, Lisbon, Portugal, MS (uncatalogued) of *Specimen Rerum a Lusitanis*
C	Huntington Library, San Marino, California, HM 904
Eg.	British Library, MS Egerton 2982, vol. v.
Eve.	British Library, Evelyn Papers
F	Bodleian Library, Oxford, MS Firth c. 1
H	Huntington Library, San Marino, California, HM 116
Har.	British Library, MS Harley 6917
Jones	Bodleian Library, Oxford, MS Jones 56
M	British Library, Add. MS 32,133
Malone	Bodleian Library, Oxford, MS Malone 13
Rainsford	University Library, Cambridge. Commonplace Book of Henry Rainsford (uncatalogued)
V	London Boroughs of Barking and Dagenham Libraries, Valence House, Fanshawe papers (uncatalogued)
Wood	Bodleian Library, Oxford, MS Wood F 34

PRINTED BOOKS

Bawcutt	Sir Richard Fanshawe, *Shorter Poems and Translations*, ed. N. W. Bawcutt (Liverpool, Liverpool University Press, English Reprints Series, 1964)
Heywood	Thomas Heywood, *A True Description of his Majesties Royall Ship, Built this year 1637 at* Wooll-*witch in* KENT (London, 1637)
May	Thomas May, *Supplementum Lucani* (Leiden, William Christian, 1640)
Memoirs	*The Memoirs of Ann, Lady Fanshawe*, ed. John Loftis (Oxford, Clarendon Press, 1979)
1648	Sir Richard Fanshawe, *Il Pastor Fido… with an addition of divers other poems* (London, 1648)
1652	Sir Richard Fanshawe, *Selected Parts of Horace* (London, 1652)
1655	Sir Richard Fanshawe, *The Lusiad* (London, 1655)
1658	Sir Richard Fanshawe, *La Fida Pastora; Opuscula* (London, 1658)
1670	Sir Richard Fanshawe, *Querer por solo Querer; Fiestas de Aranjuez* (London, 1670)
Tixall	Arthur Clifford (ed.), *Tixall Poetry* (Edinburgh, Ballantyne, 1813)

Early Poems from Manuscript

Ad Almam[Cantab[

[*A* f. 2r]

Accipe Templicolae te[
   Respuis, et dubit[
Ius colo, susp[
   Sed qu[ ]eram:
Quem tulit in pr[ ]e Parentis,
   Non ardor r[ ] fames.
Alma Parens, a[ ]estis abibam,
   Si liqui Gran[ ] aquas,
Nec dum etiam L[ ]tantibus undis
   Vester in in[ ] languet Amor.
Saepe ego sub noc[ ] deprendat Amantem;
   Ad Musas pr[ ]gineosque Choros.
Hic etenim nullae veniam meruere Camenae,
   Nec florilem Laurum Barbara Rura ferunt.
Suscipe Reliquias legum versusque colonos,
   Et quassos cupido chara reconde sinu.
Fas proferre oculis ante hac invisa prophanis:
   Fas sit vulgari dicere voce sacra.
Et mihi velle fuit, numeros vibrari Latinos
   Et dare quod possem dicere jure meum.
Languida non propriae noverunt otia linguae,
   Neglectusque Furor destituebat opus.
]ituri Transfuga voces,
   ] vix canit ore rudi.
]ostquam inde recessit,
   ]iuet aegra sonis.
] transferre Latinas,
   ]e Britanna rosis.

19–24] Iste Liber patriam non prodit transfuga linguam, / Balbutire mea sed peregrinus amat. / Mens erat, ac notis numeros tentare Latinos, / Et dare quod possum dicere jure meum. / Longa sed exiles fregissent olia vires, / Neglectusque furor destitu[eba]t opus. *A* [*canc.*]

[The *Metres* from Boethius' *De Consolatione Philosophiae*] [*A* ff. 3r–23r]

I, 1

I, who in flowry youth wrote flowry Rymes,
  Now sad, write sad ones, like the Tymes.
The Muses with torne hayre indite to mee,
  And true teares blurr my Elegie.
Them yett no adverse chance could make recoyle,
  And leave me freindless in exile.
My quondam crowne when I was young and jolly,
  Quits me not old and melancholy.
For come is Age with Antidate of Cares,
  Which to my Age have added theirs.
My head bloosms early Snow, and the loose Rine
  Lashes my decrepit Chine.
Happy, when death comes not, uncalld, to joyd:
  And comes, oft calld, to men destroyd.
Ah! what deafe eares hee turnes to wretches cryes?
  And (cruell) shuts not weepinge eyes!
When fortune on mee her fraile goods did rayne
  How neere was I to have bin slayne.
Now, for shee clowds with frowns her worning face,
  Abhorred Life goes a slow pace.
Why, frends, did you so oft mee happy call?
  Hee was not happy that could fall.

1–2] Lo I, that whilome lusty notes did rayse, / Now sadd am forct to sing sadd layes *A* [*canc.*] 4] blurr] blott *A* [*canc.*] 5–8] These yette no feare nor terror could prevent / From followinge to banishment: / The honour of my Springe and flowring prime / Comforts mee in my winter time *A* [*canc.*] 9 with Antidate of Cares] hastened with Cares sharp spurs *A* [*canc.*] 10 have . . . theirs] hath . . . hers *A* [*canc.*] 11 bloosms . . . the] beares . . . my *A* [*canc.*] 13–14] Blest death! that crowds not to the rich mans feast / And, bidd, will bee the poore mans guest *A* [*canc.*] 15 wretches cryes] miserys *A* [*canc.*] 16] And will not close the weepinge eyes *A* [*canc.*] 19–20] Now for shee hides her fickle face away, / Unwellcome life prolongs its stay *A* [*canc.*]

I, 2

In what low bottomes drownd his spright
Growes dull, and makes her selfe a Night
Darkning her Sunne, when waves of Care
With worldly Tempests raysed are?

Hee that was wont with a free eye
To reade the great booke of the Skye,
Veiwd the redd Chariott of the Sunne,
Survey'd the cold fyres of the Moone,
Nay the small print each starr that steeres
His wandring course through sundry Spheares
Knew, and their places. And moreover
Study'd the reasons to discover
Whence ratlinge winde the Sea disturbs,
What spirit turnes the constant Orbes,
Or why the Sunne rising i'th' East
Waters his horses in the West,
Who tempers the Springs *lusty howrs
With his calme breath, to deck with flowrs
The Earths warme bosome, and could tell yee
Who gave plumpe Autumne her great belly,
And the most inward secretts knew
Of nature, which shee tells to few:
Now lyes with his minds light lightless,
And heavy chaines his neck depress,
Which make him for to hange the head,
With eyes to th' Center rivetted.

I, 3

Then darkness left mee, the mist putt to flight,
   And I receiv'd my former sight.
As when swift Corus clouds the starry bands,
   And in heav'ns eyes the water stands;

* milder

Sol hides himselfe, and heav'n weepes out her eyes,
While night comes tumbling from the skyes.
Her if the Thracian Rover beat away,
And reskew false arrested day;
Phoebus comes forth, and with new burnisht rayes
The wondring lookers on doth daze.

I, 4

Hee that, in quiett sureness putt,
Hath trodd proud fate under his foot,
And, lookeing straight on either chance,
For neither changes countenance;
Him not the Ocean when it raves
And topsy-turvy turnes the waves,
Nor swift Vesevus that expires
Through broken chymnys smoaky fyres,
Nor the hott thunderbolt of Jove,
That strikes ambitious Tow'rs, cann move.
Why should wee Tyrants feare so much
That threaten without pow'r to touch?
Hope no good, nor feare no harme,
And their weake anger you disarme.
Butt hee that hopes or is afrayd,
Because hee has his fort betrayd,
Doth cast away his Sheild and fly,
And knitts a chaine to draw him by.

I, 5

O Maker of the spangled Spheare,
That, fixt in thy eternall Chayre,
Do'st turne about the starry wheele,
And mak'est those fyres a Law fulfill;
That now the Moone, proud of stolne light,
With her bigg lookes the starrs doth fright,
Now when the ownour comes in place,
Lookes black with pale and guilty face.
And Hesperus that comes cold out

I' th' Eveninge, turnes his horse about
And ushers day with paler Starr,
Whom now they clepen Lucifer.
Thou, when as leaveless Winter's come,
Contractst the day in lesser roome;
Thou, when hott summer turnes againe,
Appointst the Night as short a rayne.

Makeing West-Windes the leaves restore
Which Boreas from the branches tore.
And the hott Dogg in milky Roade
Bake the corne Arcturus sow'd.
Nothinge repugnant to old Lawes
From its appointed byas drawes.
All things with pow'rfull bands thou ty'st
Save Man. Him only thou deny'st
Within due limitts to restrayne.
Else why doth chance so madly raigne
In humane things? The punishments
Of guilt are layd on Innocents.
Butt wicked men sitt thron'd, and putt
On pious necks their impious foot.
Bright vertue lyes under a Clowde,
And to good men the meed's allowd
Of wicked.

Them nothinge hurts; not perjury,
Nor fraud ore varnisht with a ly.
Butt, when they list a head to make,
Ev'n mighty Monarchs they doe shake
That shoake whole Nations with their frowne
At length on wretched Earth looke downe
Thou that of things dost knitt the bands;
Man not the least worke of thy hands
Is tost about on Fortunes Seas.
Thou Neptune the rough waves appease,

I, 6

When the Crabb starr doth sweat
Through Phoebus soultry heat,

Hee that will then goe trust
His grayne to barren dust,
Deceived of his seed
May upon Akornes feed.

Hunt not the Purple woods
For Vi'letts, when the floods
Are bridled up with frost,
And the feilds tempest-tost.
Nor, if thou wine wouldst tast,
Press in impatient hast
The summer grapes: but gather
Those fruites in Autumne rather.
God proper times hath sett
For things; and will not lett
The seasons shuffled bee
Which hee hath cutt to thee.
So they that (hasty) ryde
At unfitt howres, besyde
This Roade Chalkt out by God,
As good at home have *bode.

I, 7

The starrs defac't
With a darke Night,
Beinge so cast,
Cann shedd no light.
If the rough South
Make Neptune roare,
And foame at mouth
Like to boyle o're;
The late smooth flood,
And pure as light,
Troubled with mudd,
Resists our sight.
And the swift Brook
That, runninge cleare,

* rode

12 Resists] Rejects *A* [*canc.*]

From Mountaines tooke
His swift Careere;
If a loose Rock
Chance in his way
To cast a block,
His course doth stay.
By a true Light
Wouldst thou too see?
From path of Right
Nor justled bee?
Sorrow dispell,
Terrours allay,
Pleasures repell,
Nor lett hope stay.
Clouds dim that Soule
And mudd doth stayne,
And rubs controwle
Where theise things raigne.

II, 1

Shee when by turnes shee fawnes and chides,
And ebbs and flows like boyleing tydes,
Shee kicks late feared Monarchs downe,
And lifts the Captive to a Crowne.
Shee is not mov'd with wretches moanes,
Butt, haveing caus'd enjoyes their groanes.
Thus Fortune playes, thus proves her might,
And showes it for a wondrous sight
Unto her servants, if one howre
Saw a mans begg'rey and his powre.

II, 2

If plenty, emptyinge all her horne,
  Powr'd on us many goods,
As Sands about the shore are borne

21–4] Thou too if sooth / Thou cleare wouldst see / From path of truth / Nor justled bee *A* [*canc.*] 29 dim] darke *A* [*canc.*]

When Eurus chafes the floods;
Or lights hung out in heav'ns great Hall
In a cleere starry Night;
Men would not therefore cease at all
To moane their wretched plight.
Though all their pray'rs were heard by God,
Of his great Wealth too free,
And honours gi'n them by the loud;
What's gott forgott would bee.
And, goblinge downe what was bestowne,
They'de gape more wide againe.
What bridle is of force alone
Their appetites to raigne?
When that which ought to quench the fyre
Doth kindle it the more?
They are not rich, that still desyre,
And still complayne th' are poore.

II, 3

When Phoebus from his Rosy Coach
Begins to scatter light,
The starrs grow pale at his approach
Dampt with a glorious Night.
When Zephyrus from teemeing mouth
Breaths Roses through the Wood,
Lett tempests ruffle from the South
You shall not see a budd.
Oft times no frowne at all deformes
The forehead of the Sea;
Oft Boreas with bitter stormes
Plows up the watry Lea.
If the worlds beauty bee so frayle,
And chang'd with ev'ry gust,
Go trust to men that quickly fayle,
To fickle fortune trust.
Theres nothinge certaine here below,
Butt that nought here is so.

II, 4

Hee that would wary found
  An everlastinge Seate
Not to bee throwne to ground
  With stormes that on it beat;
And would the Sea defy
  Threatning an overflow;
Lett him the high hill fly,
  And *thirsty sands below.
Those angry tempests thwack
  Assayld with a full blast;
Theise, being weake i' th' back,
  Their slideing burthen cast.
Shunning the dang'rous lock
  Of a sweet scituation,
Build mee upon a rock
  Thy stable habitation.
Then though the hoarse winds chafe,
  Cramming with wracks the waves,
Thou in thy Castle safe
  From all their idle braves,
Mayst lead a quiett age,
  And laugh at heaven's rage.

II, 5

Too happy times of yore
Content with Natures store!
That, free from idle ryott,
Supt late on Akorne dyett.
Nor mixt the God of wine
With hony Christalline:
Nor steept in Tyrian die
White wolls of Araby.
Their bedd was wholesome grass
Where sleepe no stranger was;

* sucking

The running brooke their Wine,
Their Canopy a Pine.
No Guest yett carv'd the deepe,
Not to one part did sweepe
The universall store.
Then Canons did not roare;
Nor blood, in fury spilt,
Sanguin'd the horrid hilt.

For who would bee so madd,
Where warr was to bee had
And no reward of Warr,
Once to begin a Jarr?
Would God our dayes at last
In the old Mould were cast!
Butt Ætna raignes in us
Cruelly covetous.
Oh who did first unfold
Mines of concealed gold?
And Gemms, the light abhord,
Deare dangers of their Lord?

II, 6

What havock Nero made 'tis plaine,
The Cyty fyr'd, and Fathers slayne:
Whose hands, in brothers death imbru'd,
Hee washt more foule in Mothers blood;
And running o're with greedy ey
Each limme o' th' cold Anatomy,
Could with dry balls, forgetting duty,
Sit C'roner on her murthered beauty.
Yett hee did all the Nations sway,
Whom rydeing Phoebus doth survey
From his farr riseing, till hee steepe
His tresses in the Westerne deepe.
Those that are prest beneath the Teame
Of frozen Pleiades; And them
On whom the skorching South doth beate
Boyleing the Sunne with dubbled heate.

Had power the powre at length to tame
This Nero, or his rage reclaime?
Oh, 'tis a lamentable case
Where a madd Man beares the Mace.

II, 7

Who thinks the choisest good is fame,
   And makes that all his ayme;
Lett him the narrow Earth compayre
   With the wide Realme of ayre,
And it will shame his glorys all,
   That cannot stuff a ball.

Why doe proud men in vaine attempt
   Themselves from fate t'exempt?
Though thy Fame reacht the farthest Seas,
   Learning all languadges,
And ev'ry pillar speakes thy story;
   Death makes a mock of glory.
Hee levells hills with dales, the base
   With men of royall race.
Where's true Fabritius now become?
   Where all the Starrs of Rome?
A little skrowle writt with their name
   Is borne i' th' beake of fame.

Wee know their names, butt them not know,
   That were dust long agoe.
Why then yee ly to th' world unshowne;
   Nor cann fame make you knowne.
Butt if yee reckon after death
   You live in others breath;
When time stoops to your Memory
   A second death you dy.

II, 8

That the fowre seasons raigne
By turnes, and Fayth mayn taine;

That a firme Peace cements
The fighting Elements;
That Phoebus the bright day
In his gilt Coach doth draw;
That Phoebe rules the night
Which Hesper forth did light;
That greedy Seas forbeare
Their neighbours marke to stirre,
Nor their blew armes expand
To owerlay the Land:
This Chaine of things hee knitts,
To whom the Earth submitts
And Sea and Heav'n above
The all commandinge Love.

If hee should slack his Bow,
They, that so frendly show,
Would straightway battayle wadge;
And this well ordered Stage,
Which joyntly they sustayne,
Strive to unbuild againe.

Hee diff'rent Nations too
With holy Leages doth glew.
Hee likewise with chast hand
Tyes fast the Marryadge band.
And hee conditions drawes
Twixt frends, and faithfull Lawes.
Blest men if, what doth sway
The heav'ns you would obay!

III, 1

Hee that ingenuous ground would sow,
First rids it of the shrubbs that grow,
The stones pickt out, and bushes shorne,
That Ceres may goe bigg with Corne.
More sweetly tasts the Attick Hive
After a sowre praeparative.
The starrs doe make a braver show

When the rough South hath ceast to blow.
When Lucifer hath chac't the Night
The day displayes her Rosy light.
Thou likewise the false goods discard,
Then seeke the true ones afterward.

III, 2

How strongly Nature swayes the raynes
Of things, with what wise lawes mayntaines
The great World, and in what a Chaine
(That may bee stretcht, ne're burst in twaine)
Shee doth all Creatures lead; I singe
With shrill voyce to the warbling stringe.
Though Affrick Lyons learne to weare
Gold chaines, and a curst Master feare,
And feed from hand: if they tast gore,
They wake, and with a hideous Roare
Come to themselves. They breake the yoake
With which their Infant necks were broake,
And their torne Master is the first
That hansels their revengeing thirst.

The chattring bird, that loves to gadd,
If in a Wyar Cage bee had;
Though sugar for her and large fare
Man's playing providence prepare
With busy pleasure; if by happ,
Skipping in her little trapp,
Shee spy deare woods through the grate;
Shee doth refuse her dayntyes straight,
Love-pineing for the Woods shee longs,
The Wood's the theame of all her songs.

A Cyence, that by some mischance
Grew crooked, hangs the countenance:
If it unbending hands lett goe,
The upright topps to heaven grow.
The Sunne arises in the East
And takes his progress to the West;

Butt by a path that no man knowes,
Comes to the place where he arose.
All things to their beginning tend,
And that being compast, have their end.
And all the Creatures generally
Doe in this principall agree,
To period where they did begin;
And this is called Natures ringe.

III, 3

Though a rich Miser in a golden Ryver
Still powr'd vaine riches on his unquencht Liver,
And *strang his neck with Erithrean Beades,
And fatted Oxen in a hundred Meades;
Nor biteing Cares would liveing leave his head,
Nor his wealth (fickle frend) pursue him dead.

III, 4

Though Nero sparkling Stones putt on,
And clad him sumptuously,
Hee livd abhor'd of every Man
For his dire Luxury.
Yett hee with meetless staves install'd
Unworthy Officers.
Cann honour then bee happy cald
Which such a wretch conferrs?

III, 5

Lett them that Powre affect
Their stubborne mindes subject,
Nor (lustfull) suffer it
To a base yoake submitt.
For though thou boast to rule
Both Inds, and farthest Thule,
Yett; if though canst not skare

* dekt

Out of thy breast black Care,
Nor wretched feare exile,
Th'art impotent the while.

III, 6

All men that tread this Ball
  Their births from one stock gather;
For there's one Sire of all
  And the same Foster Father.
Hee gave the Sunne his beames,
  Hee gave Diana hers;
Hee stockt the Earth with men,
  And peopled hea'vn with starrs.
Hee closd in paste of clay
  Soules of a higher place:
So every Mortall may
  Boast an Heroick race.
What crack yee of your blood?
  If yee looke back so farr
As the first fountaine God
  No men ignoble are.
Unless for villany
  His blood attaynted bee.

III, 7

All pleasures have this property,
They stinge whom they doe gratify:
And, like a Bee when in your chopps
Shee hath distilled her Nectar drops,
They fly away, and leave behinde
  A forked arrow in the minde.

III, 8

Ah! what a wretched ignorance
  Doth humane mindes intrance?

On trees yee seeke not golden Mines,
  Nor Jewells upon Vines.
Yee doe not dragg the cliffs for fish
  To furnish out your dish.
Nor, if you a Kidd would have,
  Fish yee the Tyrrhene wave.
Nay the very Nookes they know
  Hidd *in the waves below:
Where Purple fish doe haunt, and which
  In Orient Pearle is rich;
What Shoares the tend'rest fish afford,
  What with rough Urchins sto'rd.
Butt where the bliss they seeke should bee
  Blinded they cannott see:
And, what in Heav'n is to bee found,
  They digg for †under ground.
How shall I for theise fooles invent
  A worthy punishment?
Still lett them wealth and honours crave;
  And when at length they have
Gott the false goods with much adoe,
  Then lett them know the true.

III, 9

Oh thou that keepst thy worke with watchful eye
Still in repayre, Maker of Earth and Skye,
That from the worlds beginning bidd time runne,
And, fixt thy selfe, giv'st all things motion;
Whom no externall cause [
  ] but thine owne goodness which thou art,
Of envy voyd. Thou wroughtst all things wee see
By the fayre glass of the Dyvinity;
Beareing in thee the image of this frame,
And stamping thyne owne Image in the same:
And madst the perfect all of perfect parts.
Thy hand attones the Elements, and parts
Their fighting Natures, that moyst yoake with dry,

* under † in the

And hott with cold his Choll'rick heat layd by;
That neither her owne burthen sinks the Earth,
Nor subt'ler fyre aspires above his byrth.
[ ]
Dispell these clowds of earth eclipse my sight,
And shine in thy full pride, for thou art light,
Thou good mens rest; Thou art i'th' Race o' th' Soule
The start, the Coach, the Guide, the Way, the Goale.

III, 10

Come hither ev'ry captive mynde,
Whom your owne inbred passions binde
With traytrous chaines. Here take a Seate
After your dayes toylesome heate:
Here's a harbour safe and warme,
Sanctuary from the storme.
The wealth that Tagus banks infold,
And Hermus weltring in his gold,
And all the Jewells white and greene
That in the soultry Indys bin;
Will but dazle your weake sight
And plunge you deeper in your night.
The lusture, that them so commends,
Was hatcht in Earths obscurest denns.
The light, in which the Hea'vn excells,
The darkness of the Soule dispells.
If on that light your eye but fixe
You'l think the Sunne in an Eclipse.

III, 11

Who truly longs the truth to see
Nor would with errour blinded bee,
Inward lett him bend his sight,
And to himselfward turne the light,
And teach his minde to find, the things
Shee seekes without, in her owne springs.
So what was clowded late will soone

Bee cleere and open as the Noone.
The soule, in Earthy matter drencht,
Has not all her fyer quencht.
Some sparks of truth doe still remaine,
Which learning fanns into a flame.
For how could wee so readyly
Sometimes to questions reply
Wee ne're were taught, unless some Ray
Undrowned in the bottome lay?
And if that Plato bee divine
His Muse doth learning thus define
To bee a rubbing up of what
Wee knew before and had forgott.

III, 12

[ ]
The Thracian Bard of old,
Lamenting his Spouse cold,
After his dolefull song
Had drawne the woods along,
Stopt running Brookes careere,
And that the fearless Deere
With cruell Wolves did heard,
Nor Hares the Greyhounds feard
Which his harpes silver sound
Now to the peace had bound;
When still the flame increast
That torturd his greivd breast,
Nor songs their Author easd
Which all things else appeasd;
Calling high hea'vns his foes
Downe to the shades hee goes.

There temp'ringe sug'red words
To his harpes twanging Cords,
Whatever choicer spells
Hee drew from Thesp'ian wells

1 of old] while he *A* [*canc.*] 2 Spouse cold] dead feere *A* [*canc.*] 15 high] the *A* [*canc.*]

What madd griefe could indite,
What madder Love could write
Hee weepes stirring the Vaults:
And with sweet Pray'r doth press
Hell's Judge for her release.
The triple dogg stands mute
Charm'd by the pow'rfull Lute.
The Furyes, wont to skorch
Black Soules with restless torch,
Now cry. Ixions wheele
Stopt by his verse stands still.
Nor Tantalus now longs
For drinke, hee drinks the Songs.
The Vultur too forgoes
Her Quarr, and devowr's those.
At length, wee are o're come
Cry'd the mov'd King of Doome:
Let the man have away
His wife bought with his Lay.
Butt with this Law, that, till
Hee pass the bounds of Hell,
Hee looke not back. O Jove
Who cann give Lawes to Love?
Love is his owne great Law.
Alas! Ev'n at day-daw
Orpheus, whilst hee did see,
Lost his Eurydice.
This Tale may prove your story
Whoere you bee that, sorry,
From the Infernall Hole
Would draw up your poore Soule.
For if, o'recome, yee skew
To hell from whence yee flew;
Your Soules, which you had e'ne
Drawne up, fall back ageene.

IV, 1

For I have wings with which to fly
  Into the summitts of the sky.
On which when thy swift soule is borne
  Shee'l looke downe on the Earth with skorne;
Transcend the mighty space of Ayre,
  And leave the Clouds behind her farr;
Then vault upon the fy'ry Speare
  Strooke with the whirling of the Spheare;
Untill shee reach the starry Pole,
  And *ride with Phoebus cheek by jole:
Or with cold Saturne ly purdew
  A Sold'our of the starry Crew:
Or ride the Circuite with some starr
  That guilds the night with his bright Carr.
Where having had enough disport,
  Shee shall forsake the outward Court;
And ride the back of heav'n, with sight
  Made to endure the fearefull light.
There, keepes his state the King of Kings,
  Manageing the Raynes of things:
And, fixt, his whirling throne doth steer
  The Worlds cleeresighted Overseer.
This way, if thou perchance retyre,
  Which now forgott thou dost inquire;
Lo here my Country, thou wilt say,
  Hence I came, and here I'l stay.
Hence if thou please to cast thy sight
  Upon the low forsaken Night;
Thou't see these feared Tyrants, then,
  That banisht thee, are banisht men.

IV, 3

Ulisses weary Sayles,
That had trod many a mile

* walke

By Sea, stiff Easterne gales
Did cast upon the Isle
Where the fayre Queene, ygrew
From Phoebus blood divine,
Usd for her guests to brew
Magick-infected wine.
Whom when her pow'rfull Drugg
Had diversely transmew'd,
One gruntles like a Hogg:
Another, that indu'd
A Lybian Lyon, growes
In tooth and clutches; Hee
Like to a wolfe that showes,
Thinkeing to cry (Ay mee!)
Could nought but howles express.
This, like a Tyger, come
From Ind'an wilderness,
Walkes tame about the roome.
And though God Mercury,
Pytty'ng his many harmes,
The Admirall did free
From his badd Hoastess charmes;
Yett have his men her wine
Allready gulletted,
Already, tur'nd to swine,
For corne on Akorne feed.
And their fayre Nature's lame,
Bereft of shape, and mute;
Only mens Soules remayne,
Greiv'd to informe a brute.
Alas, poore feble charme,
And weakely poisned bowle,
That could translate the forme,
Butt not transforme the Soule!
Mans strengths are placed farr
Back in his secrett breast;
Those dramms more pow'rfull are
To make a man a beast,
That by a subtle stealth,
Leaveinge unhurt the skinne,

Pearce to the hidden wealth,
And melt the soule within.

IV, 4

Why do yee kindle such debate,
  And with your proper hands provoke your fate?
If it bee death you seeke, hee speeds
  Without your spurrs, nor checks his winged steeds.
Whose death Snakes, Beares, and Boares conspire,
  Eate one another by intestine *fyre.
Is't cause your manners different are
  You battayle joyne, and wadge injur'ous warr,
And blood of one another spill?
  That is not a suffic'ent cause to kill.
Would you that each his due should have?
  The good for Love, the badd for pytty, save.

IV, 5

[ ]
If the sick Moone impayre her light,
Infected by the Jaundyd night,
And by obscuringe her owne Rayes
Gives lesser tapers leave to blaze;
The publick Errour all admire,
And with thick stroakes their kettles tyre.
No man admires, when Bor'as raves,
Lashing the shoares with angry waves;
Nor that the Clowd-built snowy Pyles
Are ruind by Apollo's smiles.
[
]
Lett Clowdes of errour bee away
And they will bee as cleere as day.

* Ire

IV, 7

Atrydes, after tenn yeeres fight,
With Phrygian ruines did requite
His brothers wronged Nupt'alls. Hee,
To give the Graec'an fleet a free
Passage thorough the Azure flood,
And purchaceing a winde with blood;
Putt off a father, and the Preist
Launcht with sadd knife his daughters breast.
Ulisses his lost men did weepe
Whom Polyphemus, stretcht asleepe
Through his vast Cave, had byry'd late
In his deepe wombe. Butt his eye straight
Putt out by the Nerit'an speare
For teares of him payes bloody teare.
Alcides his hard labours fame:
The haughty Centaures hee did tame;
The spoyle from cruell Lyon reft;
The Harpyes with sure arrowes cleft;
Pulld the Hesper'an fruite, the Snake
That kept the Orchard broad awake;
And brought away the golden Vaine;
Drag'd Cerberus in triple Chaine:
Hee gave the tyrant just reward,
And fedd his horses with their Lord:
Hydra burnt out her poyson spent:
And Achelous, his horne rent
On his hurt brow ashamed shrunke
Into his waves the broken trunke:
On Africk sands Anteus flunge;
Cacus appeasd Evanders wronge.
And that stronge back, that Heav'n should prop,
The Boare did with his spumme bedropp.
His latest labour was, to beare
On unbent neck the heav'nly Spheare:
And, to requite his latest paynes,
Who heav'n sustain'd Him heav'n sustaynes.

19 Pulld] Tooke *A* [*canc.*]

Then on brave Soules where the great way
Of their example leads you: Nay,
Flinch not my hearts: Earth disregarded
With heav'n's rewarded.

V, 1

From Parth'yan Rocke, where flying fight arrests
   His darts in the pursuers breasts,
Together Tygris and Euphrates rise,
   And straightways part with watry eyes.
If e're they meete and aunc'ent leaugs renew,
   And what they carry doe meet too;
Ships, and uptorne trees with mutu'all greeting
   They wonder at their casu'all meetinge.
Yett them the falling order of the tyde
   And the declining Earth did guide.
So things, that seeme at randome to remayne,
   Are govern'd by a secrett rayne.

V, 2

The Hony Poet Homer height,
Calls Phoebus cleare with spotless light.
Yett cannot hee with his dull Eye
The Center of the Earth discry;
Nor peirce into the deepes below.
The great Worlds Architect not so.
Him, from his Tow'r surveying all,
Earth cannot stop with her thick ball;
Nor Night with her black mantle blinde:
Hee with one twinkle of his minde
Sees whatsoever is, or was,
Or shall hereafter come to pass.
Who since alone hee all doth see,
There is indeed no Sunne but hee.

V, 5

In what asort of shapes the creatures walke the round!
Some goe upon their gutts, sweeping the dusty ground,
And gath'ringe up themselves, upon the sand engrayle
With their degen'rous breasts a long continu'd trayle.
There are that fann the winde, on wingd ambassadge sent,
And with light pin'ons cleave the liquid firmament.
Another sort with feet to digg the Earth doth love,
Wandring o're verdant fields, or through a silent grove.
Butt though that each of theise a diverse forme endew,
Yett all have downward lookes, which pull their Souls downe too.
Only Mankind of all have lofty heads by byrth,
And an erected face, made to despise the Earth.
This upward shape (O Man) may lesson thee thus much
(Unless, being made of Clay, thy understanding's such)
To rayse thy minde likewise, and in this manner thinke;
My Earthly part aspires, why should my hea'vnly sinke?

Psalme 45

[*A* ff. 23v–24v]

Eructavit cor meum verbum bonum

My heart boyles o're with what I shall rehearse,
And my full bosome bubbles out new verse.
My tounge my minde, my hand would match my tounge
In expedition, whilst I sing a song
Touching the King. The King, to whom for face
May none compayre that comes of mortall race.
Whom sweetness decks, and grace it selfe doth flow
About his lipps, where Roses ever blow.
Goe on unconquerd Worthy, on thy thigh
Gird thy good sword, with pow'r and Majesty.
Lett truth and Justice guide thy Char'otts path,
And Mercy which reteynes thy headlong wrath:
Those shall advance thyne honour: thy right hand
Shall sow its myracles in ev'ry Land.
A grove of Arrows in thy Quiver grows,
Which vengeance whetts to conquer the Kings foes.

Nor shall the Earth, Nor Sea, Nor terme of dayes
Thy Empyre bound, which a just Scepter swayes.
Thou lovest right'ousness therefore above
Thy fellowes all doth thee thy Father love;
And 'noynted thee with gladsome oyle: which cloys
Thy peoples mindes with unexpressed joyes.
From Iv'ry Cheasts thy Roabes are taken out
Which cast their odour through the Ayre about:
Sweet breathing Aloes and costly Reume
Which Myrrha drops, and Casias soft perfume.
Amonge thy honourable women stand
The seed of Kings to runne at thy command.
Butt the deare partner of thy bedd, the Queene,
Before the rest at thy right hand is seene:
Her head with gold, with gold her bosome shines,
Which yellow Ophir sent from Eastern Mynes.
Hearken, O daughter, and incline thyne eare,
And in thy mindfull breast my speeches beare:
Henceforth forgett thy Country and thy Sire,
Nor the acquaintance of thy youth desire.
Only behold thy King, and only prize,
That doates upon thy lipps, and weares his eyes
Only to see thy beauty. Call him Lord,
And worship him to reape no small reward.
That Tyre, the Empress of the Ocean
Shall bring thee gold and Purple, and each man
Famous for wealth, or wealthy in renowne
Shall seeke thy Grace from ev'ry neighbouring Towne.
The gallant slip of Ægipts royall stemme
Is glorious all, all bright with gold and gemme.
And her face decks her cloths, and her sweet Mine
Excells her face; behold, O King, thy Queene.
In Roabe of nedleworke they bring her in,
Accompany'd with Virgins of her Kinn:
Whom crowded pompe, glad murmurs, favouring cryes
Guide to thy Pallace with melodious noyse.
Butt, least thou miss too much thy frends, in place
Of Parents lost shall come a glorious Race:
Which thou shalt see to governe in all lands,
And yoake proud Nat'ons under their commands.

Nor shall my Song be silent of thy Name
Illustri'ous Queene, but I'le bequeath thy fame
To late Posterity, where it shall runne
As farr, and as unweary'd, as the Sunne.

[*Epigrams* of Martial] [*A* f. 25r]

I, 62

De Laevina casta et ad Baias adultera

Laevina that was more then Sabine chast,
  And then her rigid husband straighter lac't;
While now in Lucrine Baths shee laves,
  Now in Avernian and Baian waves;
Takes fyre, and running with a page away,
  Who came Penelope, goes Helena.

V, 61 [*Eg.* f. 192v]

Of Marianus

Who's that spruce Gallant, that still like a Burr
Sticks to thy wife so close? That crisped Sir;
That still is whispring somewhat in her eare?
Who leanes so with his elbow on her chaire?
Who wanton rings on ev'ry finger weares?
On whose sleek'd limms not the least haire appeares?
Nott speake?
                    Who? Hee? My wife's Sollictor 'tis.
A very sowre and serious man I wiss.
You may a Proctour in his lookes discerne.
Chius Aufidius was not more sterne.
Oh! To bee beaten how well dost thou merit!
And for a Wittal, Shankes place to inherit!

5 Takes] Caught *A* [*canc.*]   6 goes] went *A* [*canc.*]

1] What's that crispt man, that ever like a burr *A*   2 so close?] What is *A*   3] That whispers something in her tender eare *A*   4 leanes so with his] leaneth his right *A*   5–6] That does a Ring upon his band-string ty, / Nor the least hair exasperates his thigh? *A*   11–12 Oh, thou deserv'st to have the Boyes runne after, / And Play'rs expose thee to the publick laughter *A*

Thy wives Sollictor, hee? That crisped fan?
Her Pope as soone. Hee's thy Attorney: Man.

VIII, 3

[*A* f. 25v]

De suo Epigrammatum scribendum studio

Five may suffice, or six, or seav'n bookes may,
 And cloy us too: Muse wilt thou ne're leave play?
For shame desist; now fame cann make the summe
 No more: My booke is worn with ev'ry Thumbe.
And when Messala's Monument shall rust,
 And Lycinus high stones *dissolve to dust;
Mee mouths shall reade, and many a Traveller
 My verses to his Native Cyty beare.
I ceast; when thus one of the Nine reply'd
 (Her hayre and slubbred Gowne with oyntment dy'd)
Unthankfull, theise sweet trifles canst thou leave?
 How canst thou better idle howres deceive?
Wouldst thou thy Sock to Tragick Buskin change,
 And Warrs feirce Clarions in like numbers clange?
That swelling Pedagogues thee with hoarce voyce
 May read, and great Girles hate thee, and good Boyes?
Lett grave and sterner witts such Poems write,
 Whom their Lampe sees in Labour at Midnight.
Butt season thou with Roman Salt thy booke;
 And in that Glass lett men see how they looke;
†For though thou seeme to tune a slender Reed,
 Thy Oaten Pipe some Trumpetts doth exceed.

VIII, 30

[*A* f. 28v]

What Wee see playd upon Domitian's Stage,
 Was held a gallant deed in Brutus age.

* crumble † And

13 Sollictor, hee] Sollicitour *A*

3 desist . . . make the summe] ha'done . . . adde no more *A* [*canc.*] 4] To mee. My booke by ev'ry Thumbe is woare *A* [*canc.*]

1 What Wee see] Wee see that *A* [*canc.*]

How hee doth graspe the flames, injoys his payne;
How in th'astonisht fyre his hand doth raigne!
Hee stands his owne spectatour, and envys
His right hands fate, burnt like a Sacrifize:
And, if they did not force him to retyre,
Would thrust his left into the weary fyre.
I will not aske his cryme after an Act
So noble, and will only know this fact.

VIII, 35

[*A* f. 26r]

In Pessimos coniuges

When as you are so like in life,
A wicked man, a wicked wife,
I wonder you should live at strife.

VIII, 55

[*A* f. 47r]

Ad Flaccum

Thou wondrest, since our *Age* past *Times* excells,
And great ROME greater, with her *Captain*, swells;
Where sacred MARO's wit is, and why None
Doth trumpet *Warrs* in such a thundring Tone.
Revive MAECENAS, MARO will revive:
And thou mayst VIRGILL in thy *Feilds* retrive.
Sterv'd TITIRUS had lost his Grounds b'undone
CREMONA, and lamented his sheep gone.
The *Tuscan* Knight did laugh, and from him chac't
Malignant Want; bid to retire in hast.
Take wealth (quoth hee) and Best of *Poets* make:

1–5] Since ours excells our Grandsires Age, and Rome / Is greater with her Emperour become; / Thou wondrest Maro's sacred witt's away, / Nor any chants Warr in so high a key. / Maecenas give, Maros will bee againe *A* [*canc.*] 7–8] Sadd Tityrus had lost his pasture nigh / to poore Cremona and begann to cry *A* [*canc.*]: Sterv'd Titirus his acres lost did weep / By poore Cremona, and his plundered sheep *A* [*canc.*] 9–10] The Tuscan smil'd, and chact malignant want / Bidd with a winged swiftness to avant *A* [*canc.*] 11 Best ... make] Prince ... prove *A* [*canc.*]

Ev'n our ALEXIS (doest thou eye him?) take.
At his Lord's Cupps *hee* stood, of Form divine,
With white Hand, powring, black *Falernian* Wine:
And gave it sugar'd with a Kisse, that might
Make tempted JOVE all other *Nectar* slight.
From the astonisht *poet* fell with this,
Dull GALATEE, and sun-burnt THESTILIS.
Forthwith conceiv'd *he* LATIUM in his Brain,
ARMS AND THE MAN; *who* at a GNAT did strain.
MARSI, and VARI, I omit: with more
Whom wittie GOLD inspired heertofore.
What then? If thou MAECENAS prove to mee,
Will I be VIRGIL? No: I'l MARSUS bee.

VIII, 70

[*A* f. 26v]

De Nerva

As is his *Nature such is Nerva's witt;
  Butt bashfullness makes him to cover it.
And when with thirsty lipps hee could have quaft
  All Helicon, hee takes a modest draught.
Contented with a little sprigg of Bayes
  To deck his browes, nor spreads his sayles to prayse,
Yett all men know, that have read Nero's rymes,
  Nerva is the Tybullus of our times.

X, 2

[*A* ff. 26v–27r]

Ad Lectorem

This booke, that slipt un'wares out of my hand,
  My better care a second time hath scand.

* calmeness

12] Thou shalt have o Alexis for thy Love *A* [*canc.*] To boot thine owne Alexis for thy Love *A* [*canc.*] 13–14] Hee, God-like, at his Master's board [arm] did stand / Filling black Alegant with marble [a white] hand *A* [*canc.*] 15] And gave the Cupp, with such a kiss to boot [as might] *A* [*canc.*] 16] As Jove himself might have him tempted to't *A* [*canc.*]: To tast the liquour Jove himself invite *A* [*canc.*] 17–22] Fat Galatee, dropt from the man amaz'd, / And Thestilis by Sol her beauty raz'd / Forthwith conceiv'd hee Italy in's pate / Armes, and the Man that erst strayn'd at a gnat. / 'Twould weary mee, ere I of Vari told, / And Marsi, and of Poets made of gold *A* [*canc.*]

You'l find some old, but smooth'd with a new fyle,
The most are new things; Reader, on both smile.
Reader, my wealth, whom when Rome gave, quoth shee,
I have no greater thing to give to thee.
By him thou shalt escape th'oblivious wave
Of *duller Lethe, and survive thy Grave.
Messala's Marble the wild figgtree teares,
And Crispus halfe-eat Tombe each Carter jeers
But Bookes nor theft can hurt, nor time consume;
Theise are a monument without a Tombe.

X, 20

[*A* ff. 36v–37r]

This booke, not learnd, nor grave enough,
Butt yett not voyd of common stuff,
Goe Muse to witty Pliny beare:
'Tis butt up Cheape, you'l soone bee there.
When you will Orpheus see (not farr)
Eve-dropping Pompey's Theater,
And round the wondring beasts, and Joves
King-bird, that from Idalian Groves
With ravisht Ganymed did fly
Into his Masters lapp. Hard by
Thy Pedoe's humble house thou't find
With a lesser Eagle sign'd.
Butt drunken Gyrle the learned doore
Beat not at ill howres, bee sure.
His dayes severe Minerva shares,
Whilst for the Judges hee prepares
What late Posterity may show
With Arpine papers. Safer goe
Att Candle-light, (to hide thy staynes)
This is thy howre: whilst Bacchus raigns
Under the Rose, when Oyntment shines,
Lett rigid Catos read my lines.

* stupid * lazy

4 things] ones *A* [*canc.*] 8 survive] outlive *A* [*canc.*]

X, 23 [*A* f. 27r]

De Marco Antonio

Quiett Antonius, haveing seen three scoare
  Of a well-Acted life, now nigh the Shoare,
Lookes back upon his deeds and moments past;
  Nor feares neere Lethe's bitter waves to tast.
No day, which he could wish he had not known:
  Which Hee could wish for night to cover, none.
A good man doubles his Time's stock: tis twise
  To live, past life with comfort to revise.

X, 26 [*A* f. 28v]

Varus, a Tribune late in Lagus land
  And fam'd Centurion of a Roman band:
Butt now in vaine expected on our coast,
  Thou ly'st in Pharian feilds a stranger ghost.
I could not wash thy cold face with my teares,
  Nor throw fatt Incence on the burning herse.
Verse I can give, thy lasting Memory
  T'embalme: false Aegypt canst thou theise deny?

X, 50 [*A* f. 27r and v]

De Scorpo

Break, Victory, thy Idumaean bands
  And, Favour, thump thy breast *instead of hands.
Lett Honour mourne, and widdow'd Glory teare,
  Her crowned locks, to strow the †early Beere.
Ah, Scorpus! Thou art ‡witherd in thy prime,

* and not thy palms   † untimely   ‡ blasted

3] deeds . . . moments] yeeres . . . story *A* [*canc.*]   5] No day wakes an unpleasant prospect, none *A* [*canc.*]: No day, which from his mind he would wish blown *A* [*canc.*] 6–7] He could wish bury'd in oblivion. / A good man his life's space doth amplifie *A* [*canc.*]   8] 'Tis twice to him the life past to enjoy *A* [*canc.*]: To live, and yet for past life to rejoice *A* [*canc.*]

2 thump] clapp *A* [*canc.*]

And swopst for black thy snowy steeds betime.
Thy race was ever quickly runne, but why
Was thy lifes race so too? Its Goale so nigh?

X, 66

[*A* f. 27v]

De Theopompo

Who was so proud, who could so cruell bee,
Fayre Theopompe, to make a Cooke of thee?
Could hee indure to see this face defy'ld
With soot? Theise locks with greasy fingers soyl'd?
Who rather shall present the Cupp? from whom
Will the touch't wine receive more rich perfume?
If such sweet boyes are for *this office tooke,
Why does not Jove make Ganymede his Cooke?

XII, 44

[*A* f. 27v]

Ad Marcum Unicum

Marcus, the partner of my blood and name,
Nor less a kinne in studyes, That your fame
Yeilds to your Brother's only, doth not prove
Your witt is less then his, but more your Love.
Your Eligies might looze Catullus charmes,
And winn Corinna from younge Ovids armes.
Nor want you winde to beare a bigger sayle,
Butt your Mayn-sheet you to your Brother vayle.

XII, 48

[*A* f. 28r]

In Lautum Invitatorem

If Brawne and Mushrumms bee your usuall fare
And not baytes layd for mee, Il' eate my share.

* the kitchin

6 for black thy snowy] thy white for sable *A* [*canc.*] 8 so too? Its Goale so nigh?] dispatcht so speedyly? *A* [*canc.*]

8 Why does not] Fayth then lett *A* [*canc.*]

2 eate] take *A* [*canc.*]

Butt if you looke Il' bless my selfe, and ranke yee
  My heire for five good bitts, Il' none I thanke yee.
Yett your meat's sweet, right sweet; yett 'twill not bee
  To morrow, not to day, not instantlie.
Witness your *Vomitt*, and your *Chamber* pott,
  And the damnd paper that wipes you know what.
Then, pray, th'effect of your high fare, what is't?
  A sallow cheek, a *clumsy foot or fist.
I would not buy, a Readers Feast so deare,
  A †Byshops dinner, nor my Lord Mayors cheere.
If Jove his nectar in my teeth should cast,
  It would to mee like sowreste Parges tast.
Seeke other guests, good ‡Feast-wright, such as dine
  Their belly's slaves, and will for it bee thyne.
Mee lett my Frend to suddayne chops invite,
  I like a supper that I cann requite.

[Epigram]

[*A* f. 28r]

Caufidius moriens dementibus omnia liquit:
  Turba dedit demens, inquit, et accepiet.

A dying lawyer Bedlam left his Heire:
  What Madmen gave, quoth hee, lett madmen share.

[Horace, *Ode* III, 20]

[*A* ff. 59v–60r]

To Pyrrhus

Knowst thou the danger (man) to wrong
A Lyoness of her deare younge?
Anon thou fearefull Ravisher
  Away will skerre:

When through the thickest shee shall roome
To fetch her bright Nearchus home,

* gouty   † Abbots   ‡ Feaster

5 right] most *A* [*canc.*]   8 damnd] poore *A* [*canc.*]

Twill bee old tugging which the prey
    Shall beare away.

Meane time while you your arrows draw,
And shee is whettinge her feirce claw:
The boy under his naked foot
    The palme will putt.

And with a gentle breath of Ayre
Refresh his odoriferous hayre:
Like Nireus or the ravisht pryde
    Of watry Ide.

An Oade

[*A* f. 29r and v]

Splendidis longum valedico nugis

Yee Vanitys of humane Race,
That lead fond youth the Wildgoose-chace,
    Mindless of after good;
    Bee-gone y'are understood.

Butt thou, my darling Vanity,
*Foe to my thriveing, Poetry,
    Whose love, begunne at first,
    My unwise Tutor nurst;

What witch, with her inchanting rodd,
Can loose mee from thy Charms, what God?
    Not Pegasus cann mee
    From thy Chymeras free.

Butt prethee leave mee, leave mee sweete,
And take thee to thy pritty feet.
    Oh heavens! Why did you sow
    The seed that may not grow?

* My learned folly

Goe, Wanton, where some witty heire,
That's tangled in thy worded snare,
  Invites thee with much coine,
  And Baths of choicest Wine.

There kindle thy Seraphick fyre
Where there is fuell, there aspire;
  To match the Eagles flight,
  Fedd for so proud a height.

Those that cann spare their idle howres
To cull from learned leaves the flowres,
  To make 'uhm curious posys;
  Those may pamper their noses.

In Rich mens gardens thou't bee held
A Flow'r, but in the poore mans feild,
  That him with Corne should feed,
  A flower is a weed.

Younger Brothers must not wedd
As they are by affection ledd;
  Alas! if that might bee,
  Id'e wive no Art but thee.

As 'tis both parts it doth behove
To leave betimes this foolish Love,
  And enter wiser bands:
  Then here lett us breake hands.

Thou catch some heire, (there's none will shunne
To meet thee) I to the Law will runne:
  Now then; unless th'adst lother
  Wee kept in hell together.

29 In . . . mens gardens] I'th . . . mans garden *A* [*canc.*] 36 wive no Art] know no wife *A* [*canc.*]

[*A* f. 30r and v]

My quench't and discontinu'd Muse
Her idle fyres againe renewes;
Which from my course do mee withdraw,
    The thriveing Law.

Oh! whether rapt in wakeing dreames,
Through Hills, through Dales, by tumbling streames,
(Places which sadd fancy loves)
    And silent Groves?

Yett I my reason place in sight,
And bidd mine eyes pursue that light;
Butt they (bewitch't) have fixt their gaze
    On t'other Rayes.

Whence, the free Councells of my frends,
Nor my owne choyce of better ends,
Nor this poore pleading without fee,
    Cann ransome mee.

I would not (fayne) spinn out my braynes
In Rhyme; This breast such work disdaynes,
And something, that to worth aspires,
    Faintly desires.

Which makes mee hate the Thespyan springs,
That trayne mee from more sollid things:
No fruits to shew of all my howres
    Only some flow'rs.

Butt Phoebus pulls mee by the arme,
And, foole, quoth hee, who does thee harme?
Trees have, that fruite in Autumne bring,
    Their flow'rs in spring.

Upon the report of fowre Kings dead at once [*A* f. 35r]

Grow fatt, pale death, and hide thy bones,
If currant rumour truly sings,
There's made into thy Stock at once,
    A Mournevell of Kings

And two of them, that may command
Our teares, are our Bohemiah, dead
In th'entry of his promisd Land,
    And that victor'ous Sweed

That with a slender Colony
The Eagle on her prey durst brave,
And, in the heart of Germany,
    Conquer'd himselfe a grave.

Kings are but mortall Gods I see,
And they must dy like men, and fall
Diff'ring from one of base degree
    Butt in their Funerall.

What it is he loves in his Mistresse [*Eg.* f. 157r and v]

'Though you are fairer then the day
Adorn'd with all the pride of May,
And in your lovely person beare
The various beauties of the yeare,
In you as native, as in Spring
The blossomes are, but not so perishing.

'Though Zephyrus, when he glides o're
The flowry feilds, and naturs store,
Sucking from thence the fragrancy
Which in the earths sweet lapp doth ly,
With all his [stelths], not borroweth
An aire so, well perfumd, as your owne breath.

15 base] meane *A* [*canc.*]

'Though all the wealth men covett so,
United in your selfe do growe,
And every gemme which Art refines,
In you with unforct lustre shines,
Where the sunn-beames which your eyes send
T'each other part, their proper splendour mend.

Though all, the world stiles rich, sweet faire,
In you as in a modell are,
And every parts just symmetrie
Make you a world of Harmony;
Tis not for these I serve, or sue,
Nor is it them I doate upon, but you.

You'r not from outward things defin'd,
But the inward vertues of youre minde.
The soule alone has power to give
To us a name. From thence wee live.
Nor are you faire, sweet, precious,
But as your soule, your better-selfe, is thus.

The redd and white, which doe compose
Your cheeke (like lawne spread ore the rose)
When I behold, I doe not see
Those barely, but chast modesty
And bashfull innocence, I find
In them the fairer beauties of your mind.

Your stately front (which arched lyes,
Smooth as the deepe; cleere as the skyes,
When neither winds furrow the maine,
Nor clouds the azur'd heavens staine)
Shows me what pure, and smooth, and free,
And peaceful thoughts within those lodges bee.

Mee thinks in your sweete sparkling eye
Inthroned sitt, mild majesty,
And awfull meekeness; having still
The pow'r but not the mind to kill;
Such as, whilst sweetely they invite,
Prescribe a fitting distance, to delight.

In every feature of your face,
And in each outward comely grace,
And fitt composure of the whole,
I veiew the graces of your soule;
Which so take up my heart, that you
I love for them, alone, and them for you.

An Oade on the sight of a gentlewoman at Church

[*A* ff. 30v–31v]

Yett shee was fayre, yett did her grace
Her meaner beautyes much advance;
And I preferd before her face
  Her Countenance.

And now my witt's already spent,
Nor that alone but Languadge lame,
For still was something excellent
  That wants a Name.

Il borrow of some other Creature,
And show you by a Metaphor:
Butt is there any thing in Nature
  That's like to her?

'Twas i' the Church, it was ev'n there
I saw her first; (forgive mee Skyes)
And yett I lookt on her, I sweare,
  With holy Eyes.

Nor sent them, standing at the Creed,
To spy where stood a hansome Mayde;
For then I had deserv'd indeede
  To have bin payd.

2 beautyes] beawty *Malone* [5–8 not in *Malone*] 10 show] shew't *Malone* 12 That's like] like *Malone* 13 i' the . . . it was] at the . . . t'was *Malone* 15] And yett I sweare I lookt on her *Malone*

By her sweet breath I did her find:
The Indy's were discover'd so
From Sea, by the perfumed winde
That thence did blow.

I askt who 'twas that Incence burn'd;
Is any here doth Saints adore?
Butt, when on her mine eyes I turn'd,
I scarce forboare.

Oh, if shee sent farr of so well,
More neere at hand what may shee bee?
Upon the bough how doth shee smell,
And spicy tree?

Some that hath tasted of those lipps,
(Redd with the blood of wounded hearts,
And where Lord Cupid ever dips
His poys'ned darts,)

Tell mee, for love of gentleness,
Doe not her kisses smell like balme;
Or Amber chaft in the sweet-Press
Of her owne palme?

Butt soft: It will not bee allow'd
(Bold Muse) that thou shouldst goe so farr:
Though fayre, thou may'st bee justly proud
To waite on her.

And undertake a Pilgrimage
A thousand mile on thy bare feet,
To that fayre wonder of the Age
Butt een'e to see't.

26 Is . . . doth] Are . . . doe *Malone* 29 sent] sents *Malone* 30 More] From *Malone* 31 doth] doe *Malone* 33 hath] have *Malone* 35 Lord] God *Malone* 42 shouldst] shalt *Malone* 46 A . . . mile] Of . . . myles *Malone*

Of two most beautifull Sisters rowed on the Trent; under the allegorie of swans [*H* p. 162]

Two stately swans sayle downe the Trent I saw
(Like spotlesse Ermynes charg'd on silver feild)
To which the Doves which Venus chariot drawe,
And Venus selfe, must Beautyes Scepter yeild.
Jove was not halfe so white when he was one,
And courted Laeda, in a snowy plume,
Nor ever such a takeing shape putt on
Of all which Love compell'd him to assume.
Faire kinne of Phaeton, who set on fyre
The World, Why doe yee so delight in floods
And bridling in a Thousande hearts desire
Quench his soft moovings with your mayden bloods.
Ah! since so many dwell in flames for you
Leave to be Swans: turne Salamanders too.

Of one of the same Sisters, having made a Vow not to curle her hayre (Which was extreame fayre) untill a brother of hers returned from Travayle. [*H* p. 163]

Phyllis hath for a Brothers absence sworne
(Rash oath!) that since her Tresses cannot mourne
In blacke (because unshorne Apollo's hayre
Darts not a greater splendour through the Ayre)
Sheele make them droope with her Neglect: forgett

Title] A Dreame *C*, *Tixall* 1–4] I saw two swans come proudly downe the streame / of Trent, as I his silver curles beheld. / To which the doves that drawe fayre Venus' Teame, / And Venus selfe must beautie's scepter yield *C*, *Tixall* 7 ever] never *Tixall* 8 which] that *C*, *Tixall* 9] Fayre Birds, allied to him that sett on fyre *C*, *Tixall* 11 bridling] kindling *C*, *Tixall* 12 with . . . mayden] in . . . gentle *C*, *Tixall* 13 dwell] live *C*, *Tixall* 14 turne] growe *C*, *Tixall*
Title] On a Lady that vowed not to curle her hayre till her Brother returned from beyond Sea *A*: Celia *Tixall*

1 Phyllis] Celia *C*, *Tixall*, *A* 5 with] in *C*, *Tixall*, *A*

Those Rings which her white hand in order sett,
And curiously did every Morning Curle
Into a Thousand Snares the bossed purle
Which makes the silver base, and doth behould
As a lesse Treasure the despised Gold.
But they are disobedient to Command,
And sweare they owe noe homage to her hand;
That Nature is their Mistresse; in her Name
The Priviledge which they were borne to clayme[;]
Scorning to have it said the hayre gave place
To the Perfections which each part doe grace.
So Wind themselves in Wreathes and curle now more
By Carelessnesse, than by her Care before,
Like a Crisp't Comet which the starres persue
In throngs and Mortalls with pale horrour View
Threatning some great one's fate, such light displayes
Her Brow: or like a Saint crowned with rayes.
Lady, What boots neglect of face or hayre?
You must use art if you will grow lesse fayre.

To a freind fearing his relapse into an old Love

[*H* pp. 165–6]

Art sure th'art free? how rare are well cur'd Lovers!
  Oft Wounds skynn'd fayrely are hide secret Ire.
For of the smallest sparke thy bosome covers
  Occasions breath will kindle the old fyre.
A pettish falcon rambles downe the Wind,
  And never meanes to see the falkner more,
Yet, having spi'de his tempting lure behind
  Comes faster in than e're shee did before.
Wranglings are Truce of Love. But all this storme
  Of Mutinous rage, which cryes out Liberty,
Thy Goddesse to a calme will soone transforme,
  If, Looking on thee with humanity

8 bossed] silver *C*, *Tixall*, *A*: wanton *A* [9–10 not in *C*, *Tixall*, *A*] 17 Wind... Wreathes] weave... Loopes *C*, *Tixall* 21 one's fate] one's death *C*, *Tixall*: man's death *A* 22 Brow] face *C*, *Tixall* crowned] that's crowned *C*, *Tixall* 24 will] would *C*, *Tixall*

Sweetly shee daigne to glaunce from Beauties skyes
One lightning, smile of her heart-charming Eyes.

Sonnets translated out of Spanish [*F* pp. 72–82]

I

Soare high, my Love, check not thy gallant flight
With thought of that ill-fated Youth, to whome
(Fallne like a Starre from his presumptuous heighth)
The greedie Sea was a Diaphane tombe.

Thy downie wings strech to the gentle winde,
Avoiding the dead sea of cold despaire,
And rays'd above the Clowdes, a passage finde,
To the inflamed Region of the Ayre.

With active circles crowne that golden Sphere,
'Gainst which the Royall Bird refines his sight,
Shewing what kinde he is by looking there,
And melt thy wings yet at the noblest Light.

Since to the Ocean, and her pearlie shore,
My glorious ruine addes one title more.

II

That lovelie mouth, which doth to taste invite
Balsamine moisture between pearles distill'd;
Not envying that immortall lickour fill'd,
To *Jove* by his from *Ida* stolne delight.

Touch it not, Lovers; on your lives abstaine;
For twixt her lipps, spreading his silken snares,
Like traytrous Snake mongst flowers to sting unwares,
Love, arm'd with all his poyson, doth remaine.

Let not those blossoms tempt you, which bedew'd
With pearles, and breathing virgin fragrancie;
The Morne presentes to the inchanted eye,
Like Roses from her purple bosome strewd.

Apples they are of *Tantalus*, indu'de
With mystick power, t'inflame, and to delude.

III

That virgin-Rose, which, while she grew (though crown'd
With prickles sweet) was glorie of the Vale
Dandled by wanton winds, fainting and pale
Yeelds up her purple honour to the ground.

The fragrancies she had, remaine in death;
Or may it not be sayd, she doth but rest
Against the Earth, like flowers, with rayne opprest.
How is she dead, that hath not lost her breath?

Her bloudlesse leaves, her native *Betis* mournes;
But not her sweetnes; groveling on his sands,
Exhausted *Tagus*, his hidd gold up-turnes.
She's now transplanted by the Maker's hands,

Amongst those flowers a better Morne adornes,
Whose fading deaw are the bright starrie Bands.

IV

Thou, Love, by whome the naked Soule is view'd,
Recounte to us, with what disdaines and hart
Of proofe could *Phillis* (with such forme endued)
Resist so long thy sharpest golden dart.

And those close doubts, and strugling reasons shew,
With which being vanquisht she her wound conceald.
If it were Pride, or Shame, which made her so,
Denye with language, what dumb shews reveal'd.

What we without could see, was that her face,
Like blushing Rose putt on a Crimson dye;
And her eyes hidd themselves with bashfull grace,
Like languishing *Apollo*, drawing nigh,

His races end; when his bright beames he shrowdes,
And, with Vermilion-flakes, adornes the Clowdes.

V

O endlesse Smart, and endlesse wisht to be,
Which as a ravisht pleasure I embrace,
My Capitall and bosome ennemie,
My Hell, in which my thoughts their Heaven place.

Since I'me enamourd of the Hellish payne,
And willingly thy scorching torments prove,
Why dost thou then unsought-for friendship faigne;
And doing acts of hate, art called Love?

I see the sweet rayes of her heav'nlie glance,
With which the hardest hart of Cristall thawes,
Her amorous and disdainefull Countenance,
And the effects are Ecchoes of the cause.

I feele a freezing flame, my bosome chill,
A scalding ice through everie veyne distill.

VI

Whether thou curle, or trence thy native gold,
And workst it pliant into everie forme,
Or leav'st it by thy Maydes to be unrolld
Falling about thy neck like *Danae's* storme:

Or whether richly 'tis enamelled
With chearful Emeralds, and blew Saphire veynes,
Or crown'd with tossing plumes, which hide thy head,
Hunting the Hart ore the enameld Playnes.

Venus mistakes thee for her rurall Lover,
  Whome late *Adonis* for his *Venus* tooke;
  Whilst change of dresses doth by turnes discover
  A lovelie Swaine, and Goddesse in thy looke.

But I, to whome they both united seeme,
In love with her, growe jealous strayte of him.

VII

Strange Tyrannie! with smiles to kill your Lovers?
  With shew of parley, is't not treacherie?
  T'inveigle Hope, which frustrated discovers
  How he that's favour'd most, shall surest dye.

Like the first Cherries (ripening in a Nett)
  Thy lipps are watcht; or as some minyon-flower
  In cover'd Potts on the Kings Tarras sett
  On which the raynie Heavens forbidd to lowre.

Few are lett in, the Gardner dares not touch it,
  Not the Sunne view it with too amorous rayes
  It shunnes the grosser ayres, least they should smutch it,
  With whose coye leaves the winde, even trembling, playes.

But *Cynthia*, 'tis a vice with faire-ones borne;
Yee bate with smiles, to catch whome yee may scorne.

VIII

Though bound to Rocks of Faith with golden chaine,
  Fair *Amarillis* stands before my sight
  Whilst sleeping in a peacefull calme the Mayne
  Presents to th'eye an object of delight.

And though soft Westerne gales (all doubt to cleare)
  The winde which swelles my Saile dispense my graines,
  And in the Heav'ns smooth forhead doth appeare
  A happie Period writt to crowne my paynes;

Yet on the fatall shore I can descrye
So manie uninterred bones of those,
Who thought Loves Ocean as secure as I,
That I mistrust it, yet for all these showes:

If sweet *Arion* doe not charme the Deepe,
If *Palinurus* at the Helme should sleepe.

IX
The Praise of the Winde

If words are winde, which (guilt with eloquence)
Like windes at sea, doe mens affections turne
Which way they list, and (lin'd with noble sense)
To highest place preferre the meanest borne

If that preferrement's winde, and all those Arts
To which these gallant Spiritts are inclin'd:
If life was winde, is winde, to winde converts,
And Beautie is the Musick of that winde:

If warre-begotten Honour be no more
Nor Vertue in her mortall Morall part,
Nor a good Name (although deserv'd before)
Nor all the Heart desires, or decks the Heart:

Let us esteeme the Winde then, since we finde,
That the worlds firmest Glorie, it is Winde.

Effigiei Inscriptum [*V* uncatalogued]

Altissimae sicut prosapiae ita et indolis Adolescentuli Jacobi Ducis Eboracensis, serenissimi Caroli primi (Magnae Britanniae Regis) Filii secundo-geniti, secundi Fratris nunc unici; Aetate ejus circiter 13, Ore (ut Moribus) virgineo; sorte Profugi; Mari tumultuante peribundo similis; ejecto Nauclero; conclamato navigio; Infixi scopulo; Innixi Anchorae, Thalassi-Archarum Tridenti, ad quod munus jam tunc designatus, primo quidem ab Inclytissimae Memoriae Patre, post autem a fratre Augustissimo:

Epigramma Propheticum
Anno Domini 1648

Uno Fratre, minor Jacobus in Orbe Britanno
  Altera stat vidui gloria spesque Soli.
Uno Fratre minor Tabula depingitur ista,
  Ferrea Fraternis Jura daturus Aquis.
En! Armata Venus, pelagoque (ut Cypria) pascens,
  Heu, tumido non hoc Marmore digne puer.
Sed subsidite Aquae, ne Vestras induat Iras,
  Cui tenera Virtus aspera fronte latet.

Poems from Il Pastor Fido, *1648*

IL PASTOR FIDO

The faithfull Shepheard

WITH
An ADDITION of divers other
POEMS

Concluding with a short Discourse
OF THE LONG
CIVILL WARRES
OF
ROME.

To His Highnesse
THE PRINCE OF
WALES.

By *Richard Fanshawe*, Esq.

HORAT.
Patiarque vel inconsultus haberi.

LONDON:

Printed for *Humphrey Moseley*, and are to be sold at his Shop at the Princes Armes in S. *Pauls* Church-yard. 1648.

TO THE

HOPE AND LUSTRE

Of Three Kingdomes,

CHARLES

Prince of *Wales*, Duke of *Cornwall*, &c.

SIR,

Your Gracious Reception of *Pastor-Fido* when hee was first presented to YOU by your Servant, shewing that Your *Highnesse* doth not despise the meanest SHEPHEARD, if *Faithfull*; is that which gives him boldnesse at this time, not onely to *come againe*, but also (being ambitious to advance his *Kindred* with *himselfe*) to bring his Brothers (the *Additionall Poems*) to partake the same honour.

They are by *him* as the elder and better Courtier, comming out of the Schoole of GUARINI, *pre-instructed* to approach Your ROYALL HIGHNESSE, if not without *Rusticitie* yet without *Irreverence*: And, to take up and minister such *Discourses* in your *Presence*, as (for the *Subject-matter* thereof, though in no other respect) may bee in some sort fit for a *Prince* of Your high *Birth* and *Hopes* to entertaine vacant Houres with; at least, that may not with any *Scurrility* offend at once both Your *Dignity* and your *Vertue*. *In* fine, SIR (such as they are) hee casts both *them*, and *himselfe*, with all humblenesse at Your Princely feet. As doth also

Your Highnesse

Most faithfull and ever dutifull and

obedient Servant,

RICHARD FANSHAWE.

AN ODE

Upon occasion of His MAJESTIES Proclamation in the yeare 1630. Commanding the Gentry to reside upon their Estates in the Country

Now warre is all the world about,
And everywhere *Erynnis* raignes,
Or else the Torch so late put out
The stench remaines.

Holland for many yeares hath beene
Of Christian tragedies the stage,
Yet seldome hath she play'd a Scene
Of bloudyer rage.

And *France* that was not long compos'd
With civill Drummes againe resounds,
And ere the old are fully clos'd
Receives new wounds.

The great *Gustavus* in the west
Plucks the Imperiall Eagles wing,
Than whom the earth did ne're invest
A fiercer King.

Revenging lost *Bohemia*,
And the proud wrongs which *Tilly* dud,
And tempereth the German clay
With Spanish bloud.

What should I tell of Polish Bands,
And the blouds boyling in the North?

Title. reside upon] *repaire to F* Title] An Oade by occasion of his Majestys Proclamation for Gentlemen to goe into the Country *A* 3 the...late] her...new *F*: her...late *A* 9 that] which *F* 11 are] were *A* 13 *Gustavus* in the] *Germanicus* i'th *F*, *A* west] west. *1648* 16 fiercer] braver *F*, *A* 19 tempereth] tempering *A*

Gainst whom the furied Russians
  Their Troops bring forth,

Both confident: This in his purse,
And needy valour set on worke;
He in his Axe; which oft did worse
  Th' invading Turke.

Who now sustaines a Persian storme:
There hell (that made it) suffers schisme
This warre (forsooth) was to reforme
  Mahumetisme.

Onely the Island which wee sowe,
(A world without the world) so farre
From present wounds, it cannot showe
  An ancient skarre.

White Peace (the beautiful'st of things)
Seemes here her everlasting rest
To fix, and spreads her downy wings
  Over the nest.

As when great *Jove* usurping Reigne
From the plagu'd world did her exile
And ty'd her with a golden chaine
  To one blest Isle:

Which in a sea of plenty swamme
And Turtles sang on ev'ry bowgh,
A safe retreat to all that came
  As ours is now.

Yet wee, as if some foe were here,
Leave the despised Fields to clownes,

23 furied] furred *F*, *A* 26 needy] forraign *A* on worke] a-worke *F* 27 Axe] Sword *F*: Arme *A* 29–32] Who 'gainst the *Persian* now unsheathes / His crooked Cemetar sharp-sett; / And *Mahomet* dire furie breathes / gainst Mahomet *F*: Who now with Persians hath a bout, / Their swords with mutu'all blood made wett; / And Mahomett is fallen out / With Mahomett *A* 33 sowe] owe *F*, *A* 41 usurping] in's brazen *A* 49 some] the *A*

And come to save our selves as twere
   In walled Townes.

Hither we bring Wives, Babes, rich clothes
And Gemms; Till now my Soveraigne
The growing evill doth oppose:
   Counting in vaine

His care preserves us from annoy
Of enemyes his Realmes to'invade,
Unlesse hee force us to enjoy
   The peace hee made.

To rowle themselves in envy'd leasure
He therefore sends the Landed Heyres,
Whilst hee proclaimes not his owne pleasure
   So much as theirs.

The sapp and bloud o'th land, which fled
Into the roote, and choackt the heart,
Are bid their quickning pow'r to spread
   Through ev'ry part.

O, 'twas an act, not for my muse
To celebrate, nor the dull Age
Untill the country aire infuse
   A purer rage!

And if the Fields as thankfull prove
For benefits receiv'd, as seed,
They will, to quite so great a love,
   A *Virgill* breed;

A *Tytirus*, that shall not cease
Th' *Augustus* of our world to praise

51 come] seeke *A*   53 Wives] wife *F*, *A*   58 his Realmes] our State *F*, *A*   61–4] Therefore the happy Lords of Land / Sends to their Vine and Figgtree home / (I would not stay the Kings command / If I were one) *A* [*canc.*]   65 which] that *A*   75 quite] quitt *A*   so great a] my Soveraign's *A*   77 *Tytirus*] *Tytirus F*, *A*: *Pytirus 1648*   that] who *F*   78 praise] raise *F*

In equall verse, author of peace
And *Halcyon* dayes.

Nor let the Gentry grudge to goe
Into those places whence they grew,
But thinke them blest they may doe so
Who would pursue

The smoaky glory of the Towne,
That may goe till his native earth,
And by the shining fire sit downe
Of his owne hearth,

Free from the griping Scriveners bands,
And the more byting Mercers books;
Free from the bayt of oyled hands
And painted looks?

The country too ev'n chopps for raine:
You that exhale it by your power
Let the fat dropps fall downe againe
In a full showre.

And you bright beautyes of the time,
That waste yourselves here in a blaze,
Fixe to your Orbe and proper clime
Your wandring rayes.

Let no darke corner of the land
Be unimbellisht with one Gemme,
And those which here too thick doe stand
Sprinkle on them.

Beleeve me Ladies you will finde
In that sweet life, more solid joyes

82 those . . . whence] the . . . where *A* 85 glory] glories *F*, *A* 86 may] might *F*, *A* 98 That waste] Which spend *F*: That spend *A* [After 100] Like those bright starrs that never peepe / Into the other Hemyspheare, / Nor water in the Westerne deepe / Their thirsty Beare *A* [*canc.*] 105 Beleeve] And trust *F*, *A*

More true contentment to the minde
  Than all Town-toyes.

Nor *Cupid* there lesse bloud doth spill,
But heads his shafts with chaster love,
Not feathered with a Sparrowes quill
  But of a Dove.

There shall you hear the Nightingale
(The harmelesse Syren of the wood)
How prettily she tells a tale
  Of rape and blood.

The lyrricke Larke, with all beside
Of natures feathered quire: and all
The Common-wealth of Flowres int's pride
  Behold you shall.

The Lillie (Queene) the (Royall) Rose,
The Gillyflowre (Prince of the bloud)
The (Courtyer) Tulip (gay in clothes)
  The (Regall) Budd

The Vilet (purple Senatour)
How they doe mock the pompe of State,
And all that at the surly doore
  Of great ones waite.

Plant Trees you may, and see them shoote
Up with your Children, to be serv'd
To your cleane boards, and the fair'st Fruite
  To be preserv'd:

And learne to use their severall gummes,
"T'is innocence in the sweet blood
"Of Cherryes, Apricocks and Plummes
  "To be imbru'd.

113 shall] may *F, A*   [117–128 not in *F, A*]   124 (Regall) Budd] (Regall Budd) *1648*   131 boards] Board *A*   134 innocence] no sinne *A* [*canc.*]   135 Cherryes,] cherries *F, A*: Cherrye *1648*

In Aedes magnificas quas *Philippus* Secundus *Hispaniarum* Rex Escuriis aedificavit, et Sancto *Laurentio* dedicavit

Sideriae turres, et proxima machina mundo,
Cui natura loci dat inexpugnabile saxum
Temporibus, desueta movent in carmina mentem.
Hanc molem fecere manus? quot jugera tecti!
Ordo quis! et simplex immani corpore forma!
Tu semper *Regina*, et nescia linquere fasces,
Tale nihil nova *Roma* vides, nec prisca videbas.
    Haec tibi (*Laurenti*) posuit ditissima Templa
Postquam quae fuerant *Quintinus* Marte *Philippus*
Dejecet, trepidis quoniam latuere sub aris
Inclusi muris hostes, et numine frustra
Cui Rex; Hic etiam liceat mihi sumere poenas,
Et gentem Hostilem sacris sepelire ruinis,
Sanguine fas temerare focos, majora daturo.
Protinus Escurias concepit: et undique jussit
Ferre viros, quorum melior natura dedisset
Artificemve manum, aut divinae mentis ideam.
Cuncti ergo, quos vel Regio longinqua, vel ipsum
Iunctas esse domos, odiis disjunxit iniquis,
Contribuunt operi magno, miscentque labores
Missus ab *Occiduo* properat niger incola mundo,
Captivique *Arabes*; Alter venit *Indus* ab *Ortu*;
Queis *Batavi* fecere latus; flavique *Sicambri*;
Danus adest *Graeco*, nativum *Gallus Iberum*
Adjuvat, Atque *Anglus* dotalis, et *Itala* pubes
Fortibus *Hispanis* verso jam subdita fato.
Omnis Terra coit. Nec vox diversa *Piorum*

Title. et Sancto] et easdem *Sancto 1658* [after] 3] Divitis Italiae resonet Palatia fama / Aere gravi, domibusque cavis respondeat Echo; / Hoc stupeat, summi residens in culmine montis, / Et digito numeret postes, atque atria monstret *A* [*canc.*] 4] Quae moles tam magna manus? Lustingera tecti? *A* 9 *Quintinus*] *Quintini 1658*: *Quintinis F, A* [12–14 *ital.* in *1658*] 14 focos, majora daturo] forum, et dabo plura relictis *A* 16 dedisset] dedisset *1658, F, A*: dediscet *1648* 17 Artificemve] Artificemque *F* 18 quos] quos *1658, F, A*: quot *1648* 23 flavique] rubrique *F, A* 24 adest] adest *1658, F, A*: ades *1648* 25] Adiuvat et iunctus dotalibus Italus Anglis *A*

Interrumpit opus. Nunc aequat machina nubes
Divisa in ternas partes. Hinc *Limina* dantur
Devoto vitae meliori, animaque supernas
Contemplanti arces resupina, ad cetera caeco.
  Inde nec angusto *Collegia* limite surgunt,
Fingere molle lutum, et formandis apta Pupillis
Artibus, et vita. Reliquum sibi *Regius Author*
Vendicat, et totum capit Angulus ille *Philippum.*
Exerat alta caput mediis *Ecclesia* tectis.
  Nec minor augusto prudentia munere Regis
Qua largas disponit opes, et partibus aptat
Quae decet ornamenta; Modo non fingit eodem
*Heroas, Sanctos*que, et acuta mente *Sophistas.*
  Qua Monachi vivunt, *Res Sacra!* Nihilque prophani
Religiosa domus irrumpit limina; vitas
Sanctorum narrat paries, et plurima servat
Arca sacerdotum vestes, auroque nitentes
Et gemmis (mundum *Sponsae*) tum sancta supellex,
Reliquae, quas *Rex divinos cogit in usus*
Omne sacrum rapiente manu. Quae tanta Tabellas
Dicere lingua potest, numero pretioque carentes,
Omnes Coelicolas, quos inter *Christus* ubique est!
  Hic verbum caro sit, praebent praesepia cunas.
Doctores docet hic magni sapientia Patris;
Ecce flagellat opes Templo! Miracula cerne?
Nunc *Sacram instituit mensam*; Nunc *orat in horto*:
Jam vinctus recipit penecilli *verbera* crudi,
Jam necti sibi vult, jam *rumpit vincula mortis.*

  Omnis ibi est. Et juncta illi (quod et ipse jubebat)
Pone lavans digitos moestissima *Magdalena*,
Quam bene docta manus, pectus perfecit eburnum?
Accensasque pudore genas? Aurumque capilli
Fusile! At, O! tantos poteras ars fingere fletus?
Haud equidem falsi apparent, et plurimus illos

28 aequat... nubes] surgit... coelo *1658*   49 Omnes Coelicolas] Cunctas Coelicolum *F*, *A*   54 penecilli *verbera* crudi] crudelis *verbera* lori *1658*   57 moestissima] moestissima *1658*, *F*, *A*: maestissima *1648*   59] Et flammans caelium vultus] Aurumque capilli *A*   60 fletus] fletus *1658*, *F*, *A*: flectus *1648*

Peccator cupit esse suos. Sed quid vetitum Arti,
Si laetas animas, si non imitabile fulgur
Gloriae, et humani voti depingere summam
Soleus dextra volet? Quae, quamvis excidit auso,
Nescio quid Caeleste tamen praestringit ocellos,
Incantat mentem, caelorum accendit amores.

Ista *Monasterium* decorat *Collegia* libris
Bibliotheca duplex. Impressos continent una,
Una Manuscriptos; quorum pars magna (character
Quos Arabum signat) *Turcis* erepta, Trophaei
Martis, oliviferae sunt instrumenta *Minervae*.
Ora virum circum pingunt, quos vindicat umbra
Ingenii lux clara sui, et virtutibus aequa
Posteritas.
Fessi tandem successimus *Aulae*.
Res alia est: Mauras stupeas longo ordine pugnas.
It nigrum campis agmen, comitante Megera,
Christata galea, et nudo plus ore, tremendos.
Heu! frustra, Heu! pugnas *Rodorice*, et Praeteris ipsum
Mavortem luctans fato. Cum virgine rapta
Vertebas in te arma *Ducis*, Populumque trahebas
Exemplo, vitiis nimium Regalibus, aptum;
Tum tua Sceptra dabas, quae *virtus* sera reposcit.
Olim (longa tamen veniet post tempora tempus,)
Cum solitas poterit renovare *Hispania* vires;
Cum redeat nitor antiquus, sectique *Leonum*
Excrescant ungues, et vellera fulva jubarum.
Hic, alias veluti cum noctem Pictor opacum
Vult usurpati decedere limite Mundi,
Arte fugam tenebrarum, et candida castra diei
Exprimit, ingenuos dextra miscente colores;
Sic procul expulsis cernes albescere Mauris
Picturam: Nox atra comis, ut montibus, haeret.

66 praestringit] praestringit *1658*, *F*, *A*: praestringet *1648* 71 Trophaei] *Trophea 1658* 78 It] It *1658*, *F*, *A*: Id *1648* 83] Luxuriae exemplo (vitiis Regalibus aptum *A* 85 Olim ... tempora] Olim ... Saecula *F*: Quondam ... saecula *A* 86 solitas] veteres *F*, *A* [87–8 Wanting in *F*, *A*] 88 jubarum] jubarum *1658*: juborum *1648* 89 alias] alibi *1658* 94 atra] sola *1658* 94] Picturam, solos tingit iam caros capillos *A* [*canc.*]

Parte alia *Austraicum* videas bellare *Johannem.*
Concurrere Rates; sonitu loca lata fremebant
Fulminis humani, plenumque cadavere multo
Jam mare sanguineo, veluti *Leo*, rugiit ore.
Aeolus invidit magnus de rupe ruinis.
Vos autem quae damno salo? Quis inane veretur
Murmur anhelantum? raro perit una carina
Obruta naufragio, quam jam damnaverat Orco
Vectorisve Scelus, sua vel quia venerat hora.
Obruit hic Classes oriens ex navibus ipsis
Tempestas, et major hyems. His intonat antro
Raucus, et ignavis homines, Pater, exprobrat *Euris.*
Semper tuta fides; *Christi* victoria velis
Tandem sistit, aqua madidis et sanguine pennis.
Haec animos illi *Juveni* dare tanta valebat
Ut sceptra, et Magnae thalamos speraret *Elizae.*
Jamque opus exactum est. Longis jam debita votis
Templa vocant sanctum, qui non quaesiverat isse;
Scilicet ingentes illa tellure callores
Craticulamque novam (tectorum ea forma) timebat
Vanos esse metus verum experientia monstrat,
Nam cum fumat humus, rabiatque Canicula flammis
Hispanos per agros; illic placidissimus horror
Frigida membra quatit. Facit hoc, qui creber anhelat
Ventus vicini dura ad fastigia montis,
Et *Marmor* calcatum, et *Fons*, et *lumen ademptum.*
Quid *Mors* interea? Quae te clementia caepit!
(Rumpere surgentes aliquid facientibus annos
Importuna soles, et magnis invida rebus,
Segnibus indulgens canos et inutile tempus)
Hic res magna agitur: Quid praepetis impedit alas?
Visceribus terrae tenuis quo semita ducit,

96 fremebant] tremebant *F*, *A* 96–7] Noctantur puppes, pugna mare servit Eoum: / Ferte citi flammas, dato tela extinguite flammas / Turra [ ] clamant pessit cadere aequore Christus *A* [*canc.*] 99] Eolus horrisonis invidit rupe ruinis *A* 102 *damnaverat*] devoverat *1658* 103] *Vectoris crimen, vel quod sua venerat hora F*, *A* 104 *Obruit*] *Destruit F*, *A* 108 sistit] inclinat *F*, *A* 113 illa] esse hac *F*, *A* tellure] tellure *1658*, *F*, *A*: tedure *1648* 114] Compertus (*Diana* velut quae Lampada fratris / Expavet) ad notos pallet *Laurentius ignes F*, *A* 116 rabiatque Canicula flammis] Canis et diffuderit ignes *1658* 118 hoc] hoc *1658*, *F*, *A*: haec *1648* 119 fastigia montis] vestigia clivi: fastigia clivi *A* 123 rebus] rebus *1658*, *F*, *A*: robus *1648*

Speluncam non fessa manus post omnia format.
Formatam gemmis ornant: et Jaspide compta
Frangit avernales obscura luce tenebras,
Ornatam sacrant dirae *(Palatia) Morti*
Hoc expectavit donum, quod maluit illa
Quam lachrymis populi, et saturari funere Regis.
O! (pretiosa licet, licet acrem flectere Parcam
Divitiis poteras, et te cinis ipse superbit)
Haud capias *Dominum*, Nec tantus sudet in urna,
Qui fecit totum scelus est in parte locari.
Sis Tumulus Regum: *Tumulus Domus ipsa Philippi est.*

The Escuriall

A Fabricke is the subject of my verse,
The best and greatest, but the universe:
Whose massy Towers to heaven seem to climbe
And scorne the idle battery of old time.
How thicke the Courts! How smooth the pavements lye!
Of what vast parts what perfect Symmetry!
That *Phoenix Rome*, which burnt by barbarous foes,
More glorious since out of hir ashes rose,
Yet did not, doth not, such a building see,
In her youths pryde, or ages Majestie.
Spaines King unto St. *Laurence* vow'd this place
When at St. *Quintins* siedge he did deface
The Temple of that Saint, because his foes,
After the Towne no longer could oppose,
Intrencht them there, whilest vainly they rely
On the walls strength, or *Philips* piety.
Who with the Saint besiedged thus did treate;
Let it not be prophaneing of thy seate,
If with bold Armes ev'n here I wreake my fury,
And enemies with holy ruines bury,

The occasion of building this house and dedication of it.

136 locari] iacere *F, A*

Title] *On the Escurial, built by King Philippe the Second of Spaine and dedicated to St. Laurence F, A* 7–8] Rome, the world's Queene, (too patient of the whipp / Of her perpetuall Dictatorship) *A* 10 or] nor *F, A* 16 or] and *F, A* 17 besiedged . . . did] resolved . . . . to *F, A*

Thy *Altars* quencht with blood, for which I sweare
Lowd fame shall to the farthest Nations beare
The News of an eighth wonder, when in *Spaine*
I raise thee fairer shrines, a prouder Fane.
Forthwith conceiv'd hee in his Princely thought
Th'Escuriall. From every part are sought
They to whom Heaven a rich Idea gave,
Or that by art more skill in working have.
All therefore whom the distance of the clime
Or neighbourhood it selfe (which is oft tyme
The greatest barre) at further distance set,
In the great labour with joynt forces met.
The sallow late found *Indian* comes to worke
From a new world from *Fesse* the captive Turke,
The other *Indians* from the East repaire,
All which with mingled *Germans* chequer'd are
And *Flemmings* white. The *Greeke* and *Dane* combine,
And *Frenchmen* with the native *Spaniards* joyne.
The fine *Italian* there doth emulate
Our *English* joyn'd with *Spaine* by Mariage late
All tongues are met, yet no confusion there,
Because this Pile to Pious end they reare.
'Tis up. And like the *Spanish* Gerion
Hath three proportion'd bodyes joyn'd in one.
First there's a *Covent* for the man whose whole
Devotion is above, whose Dove-like soule
Seel'd with an Angells quill, hath eyes to finde
The way to Heav'n, but to the world is blinde.
   A *Colledge* next its faire dimensions spreads,
To mould soft clay, and settle tender heads
With knowledge and with vertue. What remaines
The *Founder* for his Royall Court retaynes.
One corner holds the King, amidst the rest
A Church extends on high its Towred crest.
   Nor was the wise contrivance of the King
In ordering his Guift, lesse than the thing;
Who gave each part his due, and gravely weigh'd

22 Lowd] That *F, A*   38 *Spaniards*] *Spanyards F, A*: *Spaniard 1648*   40 joyn'd] linkt *F, A*   42 Pile] Worke *F, A*   43 up] rear'd *A*   49 its] her *F, A*   56 his] this *A*   57 each part] each *A*

That *Saints, Clearks, Worthies*, are not one way made.
  Within the *Covent* every thing is pure,
No Ornament prophane into that doore
May presse, nor History but of some Saint
Staine the religious wall with blushing paint.
There, holy *Vestments* many a Coffer fill,
Rich in the matter, Richer in the skill.
(To decke the *Spouse*) there, *Reliques* are (to set
Hir off with patches) which the King did get
From Graves and Ruines. Above all behold
The Pictures, there, too numerous to be told,
Too precious! And they all are of the blest,
And all *Christs* Acts are lively there exprest.
  Behold him borne a man, or God exil'd!
The Doctours taught their lesson by a Child
(His Fathers wisedome)! See the Temple purg'd
(The money changers from their tables scourg'd)!
Loe there his Miracles successively!
Loe here his Supper, there his Agony!
Ah! how the bloudy pencell here doth wound
His sacred body to the Pillar bound!
There Crucifi'd (alas!) he yeilds his breath,
And here he triumphs over hell and death.
  You have him all. And by him (as was meet)
The *Magdalene* that bath'd his blessed feet.
How well the Paynter to the life exprest
The soft and swelling Ivory of hir brest?
Hir flashing Cheekes? Hir long bright haire unroll'd,
And spilt upon the ground like molten Gold?
But oh, hir teares! and could he paynt them too?
(A sinner wisht them his they seem'd so true)
Yet what so hard, but art made proud assayes?
When Heav'n it selfe (whose outward beauties daze
Mans feeble eyes, but from whose inward light
The Angells with their wings must skreen their sight

The Monastery and Church.

The pictures there.

62 Staine] Dye *F, A* 65 the] *Christ's F* *Reliques* are (to set] thousand Reliques are *F, A* 66] Sought by the King, whose griping hand did spare *F, A* 67 From Graves and Ruines] Nought that was sacred *F, A* 74 tables] Boards being *F, A* 77 doth] did *F* 78 sacred] tender *F, A* 80 And] But *F, A* 85 flashing Cheekes] face of woe *A* 90 When] Since *F, A*

Titians Glory.

When in the dreadfull presence they doe stand)
Is there decyphered by bold *Titians* hand?
Where, though it fail'd, yet something Heav'nly takes
Our sence, our soule, and love of Heav'n awakes.
  Such is the *Convent.* On the other side

The Colledge with the Lybraries.

The *Colledge* is with *Libraries* supply'd,
One stor'd with printed bookes, another fraught
With *Manuscripts* from diverse Countreyes brought,
But most (which in *Arabick* letters writ
Conteyne the deepest mysteries of wit)
From the *Turks* hands the *Christians* did gayne.
So *Mars* his spoiles adorne *Minerva's* Fane.
And round their pictures are plac'd properly

Pictures there.

Whom their great learning from the darke doth free,
And that which robs from none his envy'd praise
Posteritie.

The Kings Palace, with the pictures therin

Here breath—unto the Palace then proceed
There other *Paintings*, other objects feed
The Honour-starved minde. The horrid wall

The invasion of Spain by the Moores.

Showes how the Conquering *Moores* made spoyle of all.
The blacke Troops hide the Field, fear'd when they wore
The plumed Caske, but fear'd without it more.
  In vayne thou fightst *Rodrigo* with thy fate,
Doeing such acts as *Mars* might imitate.
No; when thy *Generall* to new alarmes
Thou drav'st by's Daughters Rape, turning thy armes
Against thy self, and didst thy Land betray
By *Royall vice*, then, then, thou gav'st away
Thy Crowne, which too-late vertue would recall.
Yet time shall be (long hence) when *Spaine* shall fall
To her old Lords, hir Lyons nailes grow out,
And all her with'red glories freshly sprout.
  The paynter shifts his scene: as when hee'l make
A morne against the night possession take.
Ore the usurped world, the darkeness hyes

104 adorne *Minerva's* Fane] *Minerva* entertaine *F, A* 105 are plac'd properly] fittly placed bee *A* 109 Here breath] Breath here *A* 112 *Moores*] *Moores F, A*: *Moore 1648* 115 fightst] fightst *F, A*: fights *1648* 120 *Royall*... then, then] Leading... O then *F, A*

Before the light, *Dayes* purple Ensigne flyes:
So may you see, when as the *Moores* are gone,
The Picture dawne, and blacke is us'd alone
About the haire, as when (though now 'tis light)
Yet on the cloudy hills there hangs some night.

The expulsion of the Moores.

Another Chamber at full length display'd
The cruell fight before *Lepanto* made,
The Gallyes shockt; the Ocean roar'd that day
Like a full Lyon blouded with the prey.
And all the shoares, and all the billowes round,
With noyse of mortalls thunder did resound.
From either battaile rose confused cryes.
Whilst *Eolus* such monstrous wracks envyes.
And thus the lazie tempests doth upbraid,
What Tragedie act you? Or who's afraid
At your vaine noyse? you drowne (perhaps) a few
Craz'd Barques, condemn'd before to vengeance due,
Because some guilty passengers they beare,
Or whom ripe Fate oretakes at Sea; But here
Whole Navies perish without rockes or shelves,
By greater Tempests from the Ships themselves.
Thus storm'd hee; whilst uncertaine victory
Between both Fleets: did long time wav'ring fly
At length upon the Christians Fleet shee stood,
Hir wings being clogg'd with water and with blood.
This glorious day made the brave *Austria* seeme
Worthy a Crowne, and *Englands* Martiall *Queene*.

The battaile of Lepanto.

So now the worke is finished, and fit
To have the Saint invokt t' inhabite it.
Who, loth, approacht. He fear'd that Climates ire
And *Gridiron*-house. *The burnt Childe dreads the fire.*
But glad experience satisfies his doubt:
For when the furious *Dogg-starre* raves throughout
The *Spanish* soyle which smoakes like kindled flaxe,

130 dawne] cleares *F, A* 138 mortalls] humane *A* 142 *Tragedie act you*] mischief doe you worke *F, A* 144 *Craz'd*] *Poore A* [after] 148] *Is this our Jurisdiction ore the Sea, / To reade Man Lectures of Humanitie? F, A* 153 the brave] *John of A* 157 that] the *F, A* 158] And as the Moone growes pale at Phoebus' fire *F, A* [after] 158] With no lesse terrour can he thinke of *Spaine. / Saint Laurence* doubted to be broyl'd againe. *F, A* 160 raves] *rowes* 1648

And with the anguish of his byting cracks
Here pleasing horrour through each Limbe doth shoote,
Caus'd by the Marble freezing under foote,
And the cold springs, and by the wynd which still
Breaths freshnesse, panting up the neighbouring hill.
  Where then was *Death* wandring about the Earth?
(He strangles great foundations in the birth,
Anticipating in his best of yeares
The busied man, whilst droanes attaine gray haires,
And their superfluous life to length is spunne,)
Where wert thou envyous *Death* whilst this was done?
  Beneath the building is a darksome vault, The Parthia.
Which after all th' unwearyed workeman wrought,
Then deckt it sumpteous, and a glim'ring light
From the rich *Jasper* breakes the thicker night.
It is *Deaths Palace, their Kings burying place,*
Where over Crowned heads he waves his Mace.
The hungry Monster waited for this bit,
To feasting on a King preferring it,
And unto Gen'rall Blacks. But precious *Cave*
(Though dust it selfe grow proud of such a Grave
Which brib'd ev'n Fate) yet doe not thou presume
To crowd the *Founder* in a narrow Tombe.
Though thou alone mayst all their Kings content,
The house is (*all*) *but Philips Monument.*

163 horrour] horrour *F*, *A*: honour 1648 164 Marble freezing] freezing Marble *F*: frozen Marble *A* 173 is] lurkes *F*, *A* 175 deckt] deckt *F*, *A*: decke *1648* 178 waves] shakes *F*, *A* 186 *but*] *King F*, *A*

Ad eximiae magnitudinis Navem sub auspiciis Caroli Magnae Britanniae Regis constructam. Anno Dom. 1637. *Cui postea nomen* REGINA MARIUM

Escuriale Maris, quod jam post saecula multa
Ars pariebat Anus, plus et te diligit unam
Mater, quam cunctas quas fecerat ante Carinas:
Te *Thamesis* vix ipse capit tumefactus; Abyssi
Divitias, Monstrumque novum: tibi flumina *Betis*
Nil aequale vident, *Rodanusve* capacibus undis,
Aut septem-gemini navalia barbara *Nili*
Alite digna Ratis qui te, plaudente volatu,
Maeonioque canens tollat super Æthera versu.
Digna tuo Domino, cujus *Freta-clausa* coronae
Parent: injustis quae si quis liberet Armis,
Uni jam tantam tibi fas confidere litem.
Grandis in Oceano jam pandes carbasa parvo,
Carbasa quae prisci Saeclum meruere *Noachi*,
Cum mundus fuit Oceanus, cum cuncta creata
Sulcavere Fretum, Navi contenta minore.
  Quis te jactat Avus? Que sacrae Robora sylvae
In tantum crevere latus? spoliisve triumphas
Multorum nemorum? Genuit tam fortia mala

Title. *Regis constructam*] *Regis prope constructam 1658* In Navem celeberrimam sub auspiciis serrenissimi Regis Angliae constructam super ripam Thamesis. Anno Domini 1637 *H*: *Ad maximam totius orbis Navem sub auspiciis Caroli Magnae-Britanniae Regis constructam, Anno Domini* 1637 *F*: *In eximiae Magnitudinis Navem sub auspiciis CAROLI Magnae Britanniae Regis fabricatam Anno Domini* 163[ ] *Eg. II*, *Wood*: The same in Latine *Jones* 2 pariebat] produxit *Jones* 4 tumefactus] fluviosus 4 *F*, *Eg. II*, *Wood*, *Jones* 5 flumina] livida *1658*, *H*, *F*, *Jones* 6 capacibus] tumentibus *H*, *F*, *Eg. II*, *Wood*, *Jones* 6] Flumina nil aequale vident, nil Maximus *Ister 1658* 7 Aut] Nil *1658* 8 Alite digna Ratis qui] Digna ratis penna quae *Jones* 10–11] Digna tuo Domino, qui poscit et humida Regna / Iure Patrum, nolintque suo si cedere Gentes *Eg. II*, *Wood* 11 liberet] liberet *1658*, *H*, *F*, *Jones*: liberat *1648* 13 Carbasa parvo] turgida aperto *H* 17] Intemerata diu sacrae quae robora Sylvae *Eg. II*, *Wood* 19 Genuit tam] Dedit haec tam *Eg. II*, *Wood* fortia mala] ingentia ligna *1658*

Anglia? vel Dani montes? vel Suevia, duras
Erudiens tolerare nives puerilibus annis,
Et saevos Boreae flatus mollire gemendo,
Ut tandem aequoreas superent assueta Procellas?
  Quis Titulus te deinde manet? Quae nomina magnae
Æqua rei? Tu Navis eris, sive insula Deli
Errans per tumidum vulsis radicibus aequor?
Quis titulus formamque tuam, Palmasque futuras
Paucis litterulis (vates) comprendet in auro?
Princeps esse velis? sed quantum *Principe* major?
Serviet ille tibi, solitus non ferre priorem.
Regis nomen aves? Sed jam tibi *Carolus* illud
Praeripuit, *Magnus* poteris tu *Carolus* esse.

Nomina Navium primae magnitudinis Apud Anglos.

An tua vis *Prisco* deberi nomina Regi
Qui vinctum terrae pelagus, Sceptroque tridentem,
Noluit avelli, gladio tutatus utrumque?
Vix equidem dubito; celsa nam conspice Prora
Ut micat auratis fortissimus *Edgar* in armis!
Vendicat ense Fretum, et pedibus prostrata superbis
Agnoscunt Dominum septem Regalia colla.
Inter vicinas O Insula clara coronas
Quam Rex Classe sua circumdedit ipse quotannis!
Non tam tuta fores si Daemonis arte *Baconus*
Maenia caeruleae junxisset ahenea Fossae.
Quantus et ille fuit septem qui remige Regum
Impulit exiguam, conducens ipse, Carinam
Fluminibusque intravit ovans *Cestrensia Templa!*
Jura mari dedit inde simul, normamque regendi
Imperiis quae stare volunt; Quibus uncta gubernat
Majestas, lentant magnates Remige, Miles

Monachus Anglus qui fabulose dicitur pigisse olim cum diabolo uti Britanniam muro aheneo cingeret.

22] Erudiens scopulis Ventos placare gemendo *Eg. II, Wood* 23 Ut tandem aequoreas superent] Ut tandem Ponti ferrent *H*: Ut post aequoreas tolerent *Eg. II, Wood* 25 Deli] (ut olim) *Eg. II, Wood* 30 ferre] nosse *H, Jones* 32 Praeripuit] Arripuit *Jones* 34 vinctum] iunctum *H, F, Eg. II, Wood* 36 nam conspice Prora] tam Puppe videmus *H, Jones*: nam *F* 37 micat] nitet *H, F, Jones* *Edgar* in] *Edgarus H, F, Jones* 38 ense Fretum] ipse Mare *H, F, Jones* 42 si Daemonis arte *Baconus*] Magica si Monachus arte *H, Jones*: Magna si Monachus arte *F* 46 Fluminibusque . . . *Cestrensia*] Exoniisque . . . pulcherrima *H, F, Jones*: Atque undis . . . Cestrensia *Eg. II*, [not in *Wood*] 48] Imperiis quae stare velint; ubi sacra gubernat *H, F, Jones* 49 *lentant . . . Miles*] sudant . . . Vulges *Eg. II* 49–50] Maiestas, lentant Proceres, variisque Popellus / Fervet in officiis, Nullo sed munere vitae *H, F, Jones, Wood*

Bellica, *Sacra sacri*, *tractant Fabrilia Fabri*.
At nullo officio, nullo qui munere vitae
Instituit fungi, dormit super aequora vector
Ægrotans Patriaeque incumbit inutile pondus.
Sed Navis nos ipsa vocat: quam *Rector* aquarum
Deperit, infandam volvens sub pectore curam.
Fervet avens totisque petit Te fluctibus; Ipse
Rauca voce rogat properes, Zephyrusque susurro.
Bisque die indulget lachrymis, mandataque Amantis
Fertque refertque aestus, *Thamesis*que per ostia currit,
Scire jubat quae forma Ratis est, quae causa morandi,
Quando venire velit, quando velit agmina mitti
Undarum Domino *Sponsam* ductura potenti,
Fluctuat expectans, positaeque in montibus altis
Adventum speculantur aquae *Rectricis Aquarum*.
Ecce venit! cultu splendens ut Regia virgo!
Anchora pendet iners, *Crux Anglica* purpurat auras.
Albam pone stolam (Regum de more vetusto)
Excipit ancillans turgenti flamine ventus.
Tu magnis opibus, magnoque superba decore,
Incedis lento passu *Regina Profundi*.
Eximiumque decus Formae, motusque venustos,
In speculo componis aquae placitura *Marito*.
Amens sed *Thamesis* tanta laetatus Alumna
Nunquam tam tumido currebat flumine, nulla
Oceano Patri tantum dedit unda tributum.
Agmine jam nitido Proceres glomerantur Aquarum
Undique stipantes *Dominam*, canosque capillos
Exeruere senes late spumantibus undis.
Progrederis, placidisque volans illaberis undis.
Sic ratis at vitrium semper venias elementum.
Seu tu Bella geras, atque horrida fulmina mittas,
Roboreum complens armato milite ventrem,

51 At nullo officio] Tractans opus varium *Eg. II*: Fervit in officiis: nullo sed munere vitae *Wood* 52 Instituit fungi] Qui fungi voluit *H, F, Jones* 55 Deperit] Peperit *Jones* curam] Vulnus *Eg. II* 58 indulget] exundat *Jones* 60 Ratis] Rati *1658 H, F, Jones* 61 velit . . . velit] velis . . . velis *H, F, Eg. II, Wood, Jones* mitti] mittat *Eg. II, Wood* 65 Ecce venit! cultu] En, venis ornatu *H, F, Jones*: Tandem progrederis *Eg. II*: Iamque venis cultu *Wood* 75 unda] unde *Jones* 79] Venit io, clamant, placidisque illabitur undis *H, F, Eg. II, Jones*

Ut Trojanus equus trepidos ruiturus in hostes:
Mollibus aut spoliis Pacisque dicata Tryumphis,
Angliacas mittare *Rosas* aliena per arva
Spargendum, lachrimis quae crescant undique nostris:
Sive magis laetis velis ventoque secundo
Regali puero Parilem ductura Maritam.
At, Mare per multos postquam bene rexeris annos,
Cum vitae tibi Portus adest, Requiesque laborum
Ultima, non pereas infelix Naufraga Puppis,
Nec te jam fractam Pelago, seraque senecta,
Hostibus imbellis prodat jactantibus aetas;
Lenta nec ignavo consummat otia Portu,
Nec Thesea Ratis partes renovata per omnes,
Illudas Fato, Fato ludibria fias:
Sed tu sidereas *Nova Constellatio sedes*
Ascendas dono divum (felicia Nautis
Lumina fluctivagis) et Coelo naviga in Alto.

On His Majesties Great Shippe lying almost finisht in *Woolwich* Docke *Anno Dom.* 1637. and afterwards called *The Soveraigne of the Seas.*

Escuriall of the Sea: which art (now growne
After long practize, to perfection)
Made for hir ages comfort, and doates more
On thee alone, than all shee built before.

86 Spargendum] Spargere quae *H, Jones* undique] in littore *H, F, Jones* 89] Tunc cum longa dies plus Te superesse metavit *Eg. II* 92 seraque senecta] vincendoque victam *Eg. II*: tardaque Senectam *Wood* 96 Illudas] Illudens *1658* 97–9] Sed tu felici sero hinc ablata procella / Sidereas conscende domos, atque orbibus haere. / Inde potes cunctas Praetoria ducere navis / Noctivagisque procul sidus praeferre Carinis. / Nec tantum Fratresve Helenae, vel Plaustra Bootis / Vel Cytherea potens quantum tua Lumina quondam / Succurrent caeco perituris *Aequore* Nautis *Eg. II, Wood*

Title] On his Majesties great Shipp Lying almost finish'd at Woolage, Anno 1637 *H, F*: On his Majestie's great Ship The Soveraigne of the Seas *Eg. II, Wood*: On his Majesties Great Shippe lyinge allmost finished in Woolag Docke Anno Dom. 1637 *Jones, Eg. I* 1–4] Let my unskillful Muse presume to hayle / The tallest Shipp that ever Flew with Sayle / Thou pride and solace of old Art: than which / Neptune hath nought more wonderous nor more rich *Eg. I* [*canc.*]

Fairer than all which the rich Billowes keepe
From greedy eyes; New wonder of the deepe.
For which the *French Garoon*, *Nyles* sev'nfold streames,
The *Spanish Betis*, doe envy the *Thames*.
Worthy a better quill thy worth to raise,
Worthy that King whom so much Sea obeyes
On whose force only he might rest that plea,
For which the Ocean's but a narrow Sea:
Which hadst deserv'd (for larger scope and sway)
Thy pompous Sayles and streamers to display
In *Noahs* age, when the whole World was mayne,
And a lesse Shipp all creatures did conteyne.
  What Pedegree doth boast thee? From what wood,
Whose sacred Oakes so long untoucht had stood,
Sprung thy huge Masts? Or was't from more than one?
Did Brittish Forrests yeild these Ribbs alone?
Or *Denmarke* or cold *Norway* bring them forth,
Inur'd betimes to tempests of the North,
And then at length allow'd to be a Shipp
When they had serv'd a stormy Prentizshipp?
Then tell me, thou, that seemst a floating Isle,
What name dost thou aspire to, what great stile,
Which in a few gold letters may comprize
All beauty, and presage thee victories?
Since thou art so much greater than the *Prince*
Which to thee only sayes; I serve, and since
The meaner *Charles* takes the Kings name in vaine,
What canst thou be except *The Charlemaigne*?
Or will thy Royall Master Christen thee

7 *Nyles* sev'nfold streames] Envyes the Thames *H, F, Jones* 8 doe envy the *Thames*] and Niles seven-fold streams *H, F, Jones* 9 quill] pen *H, Jones, Eg. I* 11 On] In *Eg. I, Jones* 11] To which alone, He might confide, that Plea! *Eg. II, Wood* 12 For] To *Eg. I, Jones* Ocean's but] Ocean is *Eg. II, Wood.* 17–18] What superstitiously preserved Grove / (Sacred to Dian, or Olympick Jove) *Eg. II, Wood* 19 Sprung] Came *H, F, Eg. I, Jones* 19] These Gyant-Masts product? These Ribbs, did they *Eg. II, Wood* 20 Brittish] English *H* 20] Grow upon Albion Clifts? Or Scythia *Eg. II, Wood* 21 or] and *Eg. I, Jones* 21] Or the cold Hills of Norway bring them forth *Eg. II, Wood* 23–4] And then at length probation'd for the Flood / When they on Land ten thousand stormes had stood? *Eg. II, Wood* 24 a] theire *Eg. I, Jones* 25 that seemst] that art *H, Eg. I, Jones*: which art *F* 28 thee] thy *Eg. II, Wood, Jones* 31] The Charles already the Kings name hath tane *H, Eg. I, Jones*: The meaner *Charles* usurpes our Soveraigne's Name *Eg. II, Wood*

The Edgar, to revive his memorie
Who so long since ore Land and Ocean raign'd,
Scepter and Trident (joyn'd) with sword maintayn'd;
Upon thy gorgeous Beake when I behold
That warlick King compleatly arm'd in gold,
Whilst at his feet sev'n vassall Kings doe throw
Their crowned heads, methinks it must be so.
How bright 'mongst neighb'ring Crowns did *Brittayn* stand
When once a yeare hir King Saild round the Land,
Which with that wooden wall securer was
Than if it had been girdled in with Brasse?
And what a brave procession must that be,
When to proclaime his Empire ore the Sea,
Steering the Galley which those Kings did rowe,
To *Chester* Church in tryumph he did goe?
It did both seale his clayme, and represent
The image of a perfect Government,
Where, sitting at the helme the Monarch steeres,
The Oares are labour'd by the active Peeres,
And all the People distributed are
In other offices of Peace and Warre.
Whilst he that in the Common-wealth doth beare
No calling, is the Sea-sick passenger.

But to our Shipp, for which loud *Neptune* raves,
And seemes to long to daunce hir on his waves.
Boyling with love, he sends gale after gale
To sigh into hir shrowds his amorous tale.
Twice every day into *Thames* channell runne
His watry poasts to know when shee'l be done,
And when he may dispatch a full spring-tyde
To wedd (as Proxie) his betrothed bryde,
And bring hir where from hills of Frost on greene,

35–6] Who shooke so long ago his Crosse of Blood / And silver sword over the Azure Floode *Eg. I* [*canc.*] 37 Upon] For on *H, F, Eg. I, Jones* 41 Crowns] Realms *H, F, Eg. I, Jones* 44] Than if Frier Bacon had rays'd one of Brasse *H, Eg. I* [*canc.*] 44 girdled] circled *Eg. I, Jones* 48 *Chester*] *Exon H, F, Jones*: Exton *Eg. I* 49 clayme, and represent] Title and present *Eg. II, Wood* 50 image] modell *Eg. II, Wood* 52 *labour'd*] handled *H, F* 54 other] the lesse *H, Eg. I* 57 loud] great *Eg. II, Wood* 58 to... daunce] too... want *H, F, Eg. I, Jones* 60 into hir] in her soft *H, F, Eg. I, Jones* 62 know] see *Jones* 64] To marry in his name his promised Bride *Eg. I* 65 Frost] froth *Jones*

The Seas looke out to spye their comming *Queene*,
Behold she comes, deckt like a Royall Maide!
Hir Anchors are tuckt up, hir Flaggs display'd,
Which fann the Ayre, and offer in a scorne
Waves to the River, Purple to the Morne.
Hir chast white sayle is borne up by the winde,
Which, like a nimble Page, wayts close behinde.
She mixing hir much beauty with due state,
Moves soberly with a Majesticke gate,
And ore the christall streame, hir Lord to please,
A thousand gracefull gestures practizes.
But franticke *Thames* never so proudly ranne,
Did never river pay the *Ocean*
So great a tribute. The old Sea-Gods throng
In scaly flocks to wayt on hir along,
And froathing a high circuit round about,
Their gray curld heads above the waves thrust out.

O, welcome to the christall Element!
To Neptune alwayes welcome! whether bent
To Martiall proofes thou powre on hostile Lands
(As from *Troyes* wooden horse) bright armed Bands,
And thund'ring with thy hoarce Artillery
Against their Castles like a Castle lye;
Or giv'n to softer tryumphs of faire Peace,
Thou plant in forreigne soyles the sweet increase
Of Englands Royall Roses, when they goe
Deaw'd with the Subjects teares to make them grow;
Or that with gladder Sayles and fuller pride,

66 *Seas* looke...spye their] sea lookes...see her *Jones*: Seas looke...see her *Eg. I* 67 Behold] And now *Eg. II* [*canc.*], *Wood*: At length *Eg. II* 68] Her Anchor's upp, her English flaggs displaid *Eg. I* [*canc.*] 69–70] Which fanne the Ayre, and add with wanton play / Waves to the River, purple to the day. *H, F, Eg. I, Jones*: Where the pure white and Red do cume and goe / Like Tydes that every minute Ebbe and Flowe *Eg. I* [*canc.*] 72 a nimble] an humble *H, F*: a dutious *Eg. I, Jones* 73] Who, to make beauty prizd by keeping state *H, Eg. I, Jones* [75–6 absent from *H, Eg. I, Jones*] 77 But franticke] The frantic *Eg. I*: The pleased *Eg. I* [*canc.*] 80 scaly] stately *H* 81 high circuit] large Circle *Eg. II, Wood*: huge circuite *H, Eg. I, Jones* 87 hoarce] brasse *H, Eg. I, Jones* 88 Against] Before *Eg. I, Jones* 90 soyles the sweet] Countryes the *H*: Kingdomes the *Eg. I, Jones* 90] Transplant to friendly shoares the sweet Increase *Eg. II, Wood* 93] Or that with Sayles full blowne with Joy and Pride *Eg. II, Wood*: Or that with gladder Flaggs and fuller Pride *Eg. I, Jones*

Thou fetch for our young Prince a Princely Bride.
When running in the *Ocean* thy last stage,
Being then to end thy watry pilgrimage,
Let it not be by wracke; nor, feeble growne
With yeares, by any foe be overthrowne;
(Too proud a victory!) Nor pine away
Of slow consumption in inglorious Bay;
Nor like patcht *Theseus* Shipp (whereof the name
Of what it was only remayn'd the same)
Be mending still, and by that fallacy
Affect a perishing eternity;
But, lodg'd b' a happy storme upon some speare,
Be launcht *a sayling Constellation* there.
And thence (as *Am'rall of the World*) hang forth
A brighter Starre than that which from the North
Lights the benighted Seaman through the Mayne
So *Charles* his Shipp shall quite Ecclipse his *Wayne*.

Maius Lucanizans

Vivis (Io!) *Lucane* sacra revocantur ab urna
Purpurei manes, et *noto major Imago.*
Cesareo turgent exhaustae crimine venae,
Dum melior *Caesar* Capitolia, vindice versu,
Conspergit moriens, ipsumque cruore *Tonantem.*
Hoc tu *Maie* facis, divini pectoris haeres,
Linguarumque potens; Patrio seu carmine reddis
Quae peregrina suis cantavit Musa Quirinis;

Versio Lucani in linguam Anglicanam.

94 for our young] unto our *H*, *F*, *Eg. I*: unto a *Jones*: 95] When having raign'd i' th'ocean a long Age *H*, *F*, *Eg. I*, *Jones*: when having rul'd the Sea to a great Age *Eg. II*, *Wood* 96 then] now *H*, *Eg. I*, *Jones* 97 by] thy *H* 99] (Too proud a boast!) Nor bed-rid pine away *Eg. II*, *Wood* 100 inglorious] ignoble *H*, *Eg. I*, *Jones* 105] But snatcht by some high power to Heav'ns bright sphere *H*, *Eg. I*, *Jones*: But snatcht by some high power of Heav'ns bright sphere *F*: But by a Tempest cast upon some Spheare *Eg. II*, *Wood* 106 launcht *a sayling*] fixt another *H*, *Eg. I*, *Jones* [107–8 wanting in *H*, *F*, *Eg. I*, *Jones*] 109] Propitious to the Wand'rers on the Mayne *H*, *F*, *Eg. I*, *Jones* 110] Whilst Charles his ship is plac'd by Charles his Wayne, *H*, *F*, *Eg. I*, *Jones*: That *Charles* his Ship may quyte eclypse *His* Waine *Eg. II*, *Wood*

Title] Thomam Maium Anglo Lucanum *May* 8 Quae] Quod *May*

Seu, Duce jam rapto procedere longius audes,
Angliacaeque ferens victricia signa Camenae
Qua Romanae jacent, caeptis ingentibus addis:
Sive, tui Interpres, quae paucis auribus ante
Bella canebantur, Romae Romana remittis.
Nota vacillantem describit Lingua *Catonem*,
Qui moritur toto Mundi spectante Theatro.
Authorem, teque exuperas et utroque potitus
Culmine Parnassi, Doctis Plebique legeris
Quo recinente feros variata voce triumphos
Ad fluvium *Thamesis*, ripas tuba verberat ambas,
Hinc *Romana* sonans, respondens inde *Britanna*:
Angli Lucanum jactant, *Maium*que *Latini*.
O nobis, O plura refer! Quot *Praelia* restant
Exornanda tibi? Quos Musa sepultat *Amores*?
Heu! quantas pateris non semper vivere Mortes?
Plebem iracundam, et *Bruti* miserabile lethum,
*Uxoris*que fidem, *meritam non morte probari*;
Heu nimium sociata viro! nimium aemula Patris!
Atque ipsum dira proscriptum lege *Senatum*,
Et Ciceronem ipsum, Libertatisque (Tyrannis
Jam tribus oppressae) supremam audire querelam,
Te recitante juvat. Prima *Cleopatra* Camena
Dicta tibi, summo poscit jam carmine dici,
Nondum tota micat, media plus parte laborat
Luminis, et privata mori, *Regina* veretur,
Altisono properes nisi tu succurrere versu
Exaequesque animos dictis, anguesque ministres.
Formam pinge *Ducum* victricem; Haud tempore victam:
Pinge *Ducem* molli vinctum fera colla cathena:
Actiacasque acies; Tyroni ubi gloria cana
Cessit. Saepe *Virum* retrahebat conscia virtus

Supplementum eiusdem in Lingua Anglicana.

Supplementi versio in Linguam Latinam.

10–11] Caesaris et tollens Aquilas, quas straverat ipse / Lucanus moriens, Caeptis ingentibus addis *May* 13 canebantur] susurrabas *May* 14] Docta vacillantem canit et sua Lingua Catonem *May* 24 Heu] O *May* 25 *Plebem* iracundam] Iratam Plebem *May* 26 *morte*] igne *May* 32 poscit] possit *1658* 39 *Actiacasque*] *Actiacasque 1658*: *Actiacas* acies *1648*

Factorum veterum, *Martis*que innata Cupido,
Navali sed enim pugna plus posse probavit
Aequoream *Venerem*. Fugiens quem vincere posset,
Victricem sequitur fugientem: Et parte recedens
Imperii, laxas *Augusto* tradit habenas.
  Hic suspende Tubas. Hic cum *Nasone Maronem*,
Et Flaccum, dulcesque choros agnosse *Tuorum*.
Egregius *Victor* pacato carmine Mundo
Auscultat, totamque *Hederis* indulgent *Olivam*.
Emeritus vates agat otia grata sub illo.

Written by Mr. T.C. of his Majesties Bed-Chamber

I

Tell me, *Eutresia*, since my fate
And thy more powerfull Forme decrees
My heart an Immolation at thy Shrine,
Where it is ever to incline,
How I must love, and at what rate,
And by what steps, and what degrees
I shall my hopes enlarge, and my desires confine?

A

First when thy flames begin
See they burne all within,
And so, as lookers on may not descry
Smoake in a sigh, or sparkle in an eye,
I'de have thy love a good while there
Ere thine owne heart should be aware,
And I my selfe would choose to know it
First by thy care and cunning not to show it.

2

When my flame thine owne way is thus betrayd,
Must it be still afrayd?

43 Fugiens] fugit hunc *May*   49] Audivit, pinguique hederas ditavit oliva *May*

May it not be sharpsighted too as well,
And know thou knowst that which it dares not tell,
And by that knowledge finde it may
Tell it selfe ore a lowder way?

B

Let me alone a while,
For so thou maist beguile
My heart to a consent
Long ere it meant.
For whilst I dare not disaprove
Least that betray a knowledge of thy love,
I shall be so accustom'd to allow,
That I shall not know how
To be displeas'd when thou shalt it avow.

3

When by loves powerfull secret sympathy
Our Soules are got thus nigh,
And that by one another seene
There needs no breath to goe betweene,
Though in the maine agreement of our breasts
Our *Hearts* subscribe as *Interests*,
Will it not need
The Tongues signe too as *Witnesse* to the deed?

C

Speake then, but when you tell the tale
Of what you ayle,
Let it be so disorder'd that I may
Guesse onely thence what you would say,
Then to speake sence
Were an offence,
And twill thy passion tell the subtlest way
Not to know what to say.

Ex Lingua Anglicana.
Methodus amandi

I

Dic (quoniam Fatumque meum, tuaque optima Forma,
Fato omni major, cor hoc tibi destinat olim
Non extinguendis carpendum (ut victima) Flammis)
Quomodo amare decet, quantumque indulgeam amori?
Quid sperare jubes, vel desperare? quibusque
Fraena spei laxem gradibus, ponamve Furori?

A

Cum nata est nova Flamma tibi, tota ardeat intus:
Ut non indicium det spectatoribus ullum
Scintillante oculo, vel dum suspiria fumant.
Quin ipse insolitos ignores pectoris aestus,
Affectumque diu proprium; monstretque latentem
Prima meis oculis ars ipsa et cura tegendi.

2

More modoque tuo cum sic mea prodita flamma est,
Num trepidabit adhuc? oculos sibi sumere quondam
Non et amor poterit? nec te scire hoc sciet ille
Quod narrare pudor vetat? audacterque vel inde
Audebit fari, tacitus quod dixerat ante?

B

Paulum conticeas: sic illaqueata gradatim
Quam vellem citius concedam forsan amorem
Quippe tacere et ego nimio persuasa pudore,
Nec culpare tuam, videar ne noscere Flammam,

Title] *Methodus Amandi. 1658*: Dialogus inter Utrechiam et Thirsim *Eg.*: [Untitled in *Eve.*] 3] Vultet adoratis aeternum acendier aris *Eg.* 6 ponamve] ponamque *Eve.* 14 sibi] num *Eg.* 15 nec] Et *Eg.* 16 pudor] timor *Eg.*, *Eve.* 17 Audebit fari] Audeat effari *Eg.*, *Eve.* 18–19] Verba tacendo dabis melius [?] fraude uti victa / Quam vellem citius concedere cogar amori *Eg.*

Post ubi jam constet, jam consensisse videbor,
Spemque pudore datam non confirmare pudebit.

3

Cum prope se nostrae, Magnete potentis Amoris,
Contigerint Animae:
Voce nec indigeant, vanoque Interprete (vento)
Jam conspecta sibi per hiantia vulnera, corda
Quamvis alternis rata sint et inusta medullis
Foedera, non Linguas *Testes* (de more) vocemus?

C

Fare agedum: sed cum trepido depinxeris ore
Poenam animi, tam abruptus eat, sine et ordine sermo,
Ut vix eliceam dictis quid dicere velles.
Hic foret eloquium male sani crimen Amoris,
Et nil posse loqui Facundia major Amantis.

By Mr. T.C. *likewise*

Farewell faire Saint, let not the Seas and wind
Swell like the eyes and hearts you leave behind.
But smooth and gentle as the lookes you beare
Smile in your face, and whisper in your eare.
May no bold Billow venture to arise
That it may neerer gaze upon your eyes,
Lest Wind and Waves enamour'd of your forme
Should crowd and throng themselves into a storme.
But if it be your fate (vast Seas) to love,
Of my becalmed breast learne how to move.
Move then, but in a gentle lovers pace,

22 jam constet] constiterit *1658*: clara miret *Eg.* consensisse] consensisse *1658*, *Eg.*, *Eve.*: concessisse *1648* 24–5] Cum tacito magnete vocans amor / attrahat ambos *Eg.*: Cum sic fortis Amor caeco magnete coegit / Contiguas animas *Eve.* 27 conspecta] perspecta *Eg.* 28–9] Quamquam firma fatis [ ] conformia legi / [ ] niscentique dei fa [ ] ita ea f[oe]dera restant / Intendere manum non linguam more sigilli / Addere conveniet pacto, testemque vocare *Eg.* 30 agedum] igitur *Eg.* 31 abruptus eat] abrupta cadant *Eg.* 33 Hic . . . male sani] Tum . . . suspecti *Eg.*

No wrinckle nor no furrough in your face.
And you (Fierce winds) see that you tell your tale
In such a breath as may but fill her Sayle.
So whilst you court her each your severall way
You may her safely to her Port convey,
And loose her by the noblest way of wooing
Whilst both contribute to your own undoing.

Dominae Navigaturae
ex Lingua Anglicana

O Diva, O Formosa vale: non ventus et Æquor
Cordibus intumeant, oculisque similima nostris.
Sed vultus imitata tuos, pectusque serenum,
Mulceat Aura Aures, blandumque arrideat Æquor.
Nulla procax insurgat aquis audacibus unda,
Ut sic nempe tuos propius miretur Ocellos.
Ne forma vesana tua ventusque Fretumque
In rapidam sese impellant glomerentque procellam.
Sed si Fata volunt ut ametis vos (Freta Vasta)
Discite Fraenatos nostro de pectore motus.
Ergo movete (*sinam*) sed Amantum more movete,
Non sulcus sit Fronte minax non ruga senilis.
Et Tu (Vente ferox) nimio ne Flamine Flammam
Suspires moneo, sed tantum ut vela tumescant.
Sic dum fletis Aquae, dum Venti flatis *Amorem*,
Illa petet Portum Fluctu Flatuque secundis:
Dumque aliena salus propria sic empta ruina est
Nobiliore modo *Vos* amittetis *Amatam*.

Title] *Dominae Navigaturae. 1658, Eve.* 1 O Diva, O Formosa] Pulchra vale, Dea pulchra *Eve.* 4 blandumque] orique *Eve.*

A CANTO OF THE *Progresse of Learning*

Tell me O Muse, and tell me *Spencers* ghost,
What may have bred in knowledge such decay
Since ancient times, that wee can hardly boast
We understand those grounds they then did lay?
Much I impute to th' short'ning of the day,
(Our life, which was a stride, being shrunck t'a spanne)
Yet sure there are besides some rubbs i'th way.
Say then how *Learnings* Sunne to shine began?
And by what darke degrees it did goe backe in man?

Then thus when seeds of all things (from the wombe
Of pregnant *Chaos* sprung) were perfected;
Another *Chaos* (yet to be orecome)
Out of the Reliques of the former bred,
With ignorance this infant world orespred,
And having drown'd Reasons deviner Ray
In the dull lumpe of flesh, made men (the head)
Companions of their slaves: The Beasts and they
Promiscuously fed, Promiscuously lay.

As now they are, things were not sorted then;
Nor by division of the parts did breed
The publique harmony. For how should men
Manure the ground their minds being choakt with weed?
Or adde the last hand, which themselves did need?
Woods yet unto the Mountaines did not passe,
Nor Heards beneath in grassy Meadowes feed,

Title] *The Progresse of Learning F, A* 1 and tell me *Spencers* ghost] (for it concernes thee most *F, A* 1] When I consider in my serious thought *A* [*canc.*] 3 that wee can hardly boast] as that we scarce can boast *F*: that wee are hardly brought *A* 4 We] To *F, A* 6 Our] For *F* being shrunck] is shrunke *F*: shrunk *A* 7 there are besides] besides, there are *F, A* rubbs] letts *F, A* 10 Then thus] 'Tis this *F*: Tis thus *A* 10–11] They tell, when sprung from Chaos' fruitfull wombe / The seeds of all things now were perfected *A* [*canc.*] 12 Another] That a new *A* [*canc.*] 14 this] the *F, A* 15 drown'd] plung'd *A* 16 lumpe of flesh] fleshy lumpe *A* 22 being choakt] oregrowne *A* [*canc.*]

Nor Corne inrich the middle Grounds; but Grasse,
And woods, and stifled Corne, were shuffled in one Masse.

When thus sad Nature did her case deplore;
Why is the best of Creatures poore whilst I
Abound in wealth: or what availes my store
Heapt in a common field? O Jove deny
Thy fruitlesse gifts, or else cleare reasons eye:
And grant that they possesse those gifts alone
In whom that Reason most shall fructifie
For till for worth some difference be showne
Twixt man and man, twixt man and beast there will be none.

Jove heard: nor chose to blame her murm'ring Pray'r,
But remedy the cause, by sending *Wit*
(Which is the use of Reason.) To his Care
Th' unpollisht minde of man he did commit,
As with a Diamonds point to fashion it.
Bidding him gently glyde into his Heart
By such convenient meanes as he could get,
And that as Soveraigne Lord he should impart
Kingdomes and Provinces to them that tooke his part.

"A pregnant spirit short instructions serve
So buckling to his taske he did survey
All Creatures in this world, and might observe
To breake from *Womans* eye a brighter day
Than that which rising *Phoebus* did display.
On this fraile Basis the great worke begun:
The lesser World which yet in darkenesse lay,
With Weeds and Brambles wildly over run,
To purge that second *Chaos* found this second *Sunne.*

For whil'st Man gaz'd on the bewitching light,
An unknowne Passion entred at his Eye,

27 stifled] choaked *A* [*canc.*] 31 *Heapt*] *Lay'd A* 31] *Trod downe by common use? O Jove denie A* [*canc.*] 32 *cleare*] *ope A* [*canc.*] 33–4] *And grant the greatest portion of the one / To whom the other most cann fructifie. A* [*canc.*] 36 *man and beast*] *Beasts and him F*: *Beasts and man A* 37 chose to] would he *F*, *A* 38 the cause] her greife *A* [*canc.*] 42 glyde] slide *F*, *A* 45 them that] them, who *F*: those that *A* 48 in this] of the *A*

Which, strugling with his Reason, did exite
Her languisht spark through secret sympathy
Of flames that were ingendred mutually.
His narrow soule grew larger with her Guest,
And furnisht to enshrine a Deity:
Who now with Language his new love exprest,
And now with Thousand Tropes his smoother Language drest.

"*Love* is that fire which wise *Prometheus* caught
"From Heav'n it selfe to forge mans soule anew,
"(Which Feavours with it, and dead Palenesse brought
"Instead of Health, Repose, and Lively Hiew)
"When all these goods out of the Basket flew,
"*Hope* only to the bottome did remove.
"Yet had wee rather this sweet Hope pursue
"Than have our former State. And some approve
"With Losse of all those goods even a hopelesse Love.

Say you by whom this kindly flame's reprov'd,
Who layd the first stone of civilitie?
Whilst men sought sweet converse with them they lov'd,
And for advice in the New Malady,
With others too; which let in *Amitie*?
Who did the Organs first for Reason fit,
As by experience to this day wee see?
"For properly *Love* ripens the *Fooles* wit;
"But turnes some wise men Fooles by over rip'ning it.

Men thus conversing, soone the *Arts* were made,
And, that which all included, *Poetry*:
Under whose veyle were mystickly convey'd
The solid Grounds of all *Phylosophy*,
Ev'n to the homely Rules of *Husbandry*,
Which with such sugred Eloquence were drest,

57 strugling with] breathing on *F*, *A* 63 drest] drest *F*, *A*: rest *1648* 64 which wise] that wise *A*: indeed *A* [*canc.*] 67 Instead of] For ruin'd *A* 67] Instead of Health) Repose, and Lively Hiew *1648* 68 these] choise *A* 73 you] yee *F* kindly flame's reprov'd] powre is disapprov'd *A* 75 sought sweet] desyr'd *A* them] whome *F*, *A* 76 New] strange *F* 76] And to communicate their Malady *A* 84 mystickly] secretly *A* 86 Ev'n to the] And the more *F*, *A*

And Coucht in such Delightfull Harmony,
That they who could not crabbed Texts disgest,
To heare those flowing numbers, without number prest.

And now had *Wit* his noble taske perform'd;
For what could more for Mortalls be desir'd
Than to be decently susteyn'd, and form'd
With all the Ornaments their minds requir'd?
So to his Contemplations he retir'd,
Leaving the Countryes in propriety
To such as were by him for Rule inspir'd,
Who us'd them with a *Liberality*
That little differ'd from the old community.

But *Nature* was not so content whose thought
Is vast and ever Covetous of more:
For though to such a rare perfection brought
She held all nothing that was done before.
And therefore farther to improve her store,
Her wily head a counterfeit did frame,
Who in his lookes *Wits* perfect likenesse bore,
And by that stollen tytle dar'd to clayme
The Government of things, But *Craft* was his right name.

So well could he his subtile picklocks file
That in most minds his entrance he had made,
Partly deceiv'd with his pretended style,
And partly from their due Allegiance swayd
With *Guifts* of a strange force before them layd,
Which in the Oceans unknowne waves did lye,
(Now Sayl'd and div'd into) which *Earth* display'd
Forc't by a thousand tortures to discry,
Where her bright Gold was hid from *Phoebus's* envyous eye.

His precepts are; *From every thing to get*:
And each from other. But with legall show.

90 without number] plentyfully *A* 94 their minds] the minde *F* 103 held] counts *A* 106 lookes] face *A* 111 with] by *A* 112 due] true *F*, *A* 113 a strange] strange *A* 119 *each from other*] *from each other A*

(For that, he sayth, is liveing by his wit)
But the true *Wit* which all these things did owe,
From his just right he wrongfully did throw.
That only Title hath a solid Plea
Which he confirmes, if he did not bestow,
He is Lord Paramount of Land and Sea,
And all the world is held of *Craft* in *Capite*.

O Witt! *next* Jove *Creator of Mankind,*
Where dost thou now in secret corner sit,
Counting the Starrs with avaricious mind
Or brooding some immortall worke of wit
Whereby thou maist affected glory get,
Whilst thy poore Clients, outed of their right,
For nobler Sciences are made unfit,
"*Since Lamps that have no Oyle can give no light,*
"*And folly twere to shine when men have lost their sight?*

Thus some: who well affected did remaine,
To the old learned Age. Yet each of these
Had learn't a *Craft* his livelyhood to gaine;
And learnt withall the Liberall Sciences,
Forc't to give halfe obedience for his ease
To the new Government. But if his soule
(Not needing the dull world) her selfe might please,
She then would passe directly to her Gole,
And spurne the Golden Apples that before her rowle.

These Cryes fetcht *Wit* from the retyred shade
Of a delightfull Solitary Grove;
Who (wondring) saw what spoil his Foe had made
Of the most precious goods: He cry'd to *Jove*,
On *Nature* cry'd, that could such Change approve.
Then learnt he first to be Satyricall,
(Whose bitter'st Argument before was Love)
And let some words of hard Construction fall,
And ev'ry drop of inke was mingled with some Gall.

120] For then hee sayes it is the prize of Witt. *A* 124 bestow,] bestow *1648* 127 O Witt! *next*] *O Next to A* 136 who] that *A* 138 a *Craft*] some Trade *F:* a trade *A* livelyhood] maintenance *F* 144 spurne] scorne *A* 148 Of] In *A*

At last demands the Law. And he will try
By publique Justice before *Natures* Barre
To whom the World perteynes most rightfully.
Craft, (though possession were his surer farre)
His Plea of merit would not seeme to marre,
But nam'd a day his Title to abet;
On it the Creatures all assembled are,
Raunged by *Natures* Marshall as they met,
And all on the Successe their expectation set.

First *Wit* with copious Language did dilate
Those benefits which Man to him did owe,
Whom from a poore dishonourable state,
He made with blessings of all sorts to flow.
He said, whom he made Rulers first did know
To rule themselves. And if the World new Clad
With a few glitt'ring Trifles, (but for show)
Which *Craft* with dammage of true Goods did adde,
Seem'd now to have more wealth, it then more honor had.

Here ceas'd his speech. Then *Craft* reply'd to all
With Such a boldnesse as not blusht to slight
Th' immortall workes of *Wit*, which he did call
Chymera's of the Fancy, vaine and light
And urg'd the *Learned* had renounc't their right
In Earthly things, as he could represent
By diverse Instruments themselves did write,
Knowing they were unfit for Government,
As wholly unto idle Contemplations bent.

But that they did not truely Gold contemne
(Which all that have their Eyes must needs admire)
Only in boasting writings did Condemne
The thing which in their hearts they most desire.
Nor could the World his perfect State acquire,
Whilst not a Mettall was in Earth suppresst

154 will] would *A* 157 surer] stronger *A* 160 it] which *F*, *A* 168 themselves] *their Mindes F*, *A* 172 Then...reply'd to all] and...beganne withall *F*, *A* 184 most] did *A* 185 his] her *A* 186 in] by *A*

But a Fifth Element more bright than fire,
Which Poets ev'n denying had confest,
Styling the *Golden Age* what they would have *The best*.

That he found out; and *Gemms* of wond'rous price
Like which their Mistresse Eyes, Teeth, Lipps, they feign,
As things which have most vertue to entice.
And last, said he; *'Tis hamm'ring in this brayne*
To turne all things I touch to golden veyne.
This clos'd his speech; But left such stings behind
In Nature, biteing greedily at gaine,
That (seeming first to poyse it in her minde)
She judg'd the World to *Craft*, which *Wisedome* she defin'd.

The Philosophers Stone.

Her overpartiall Doome, she colour'd ore
With this pretext, that the world's Rule (now growne
More intricate through its increased store)
Requir'd a *Drudge* to tend that worke alone,
But *Wit* had many things to study on.
Then ended with a smooth fac'd Complement,
How *Him* she held in high opinion
Whom breaking up the Court, she from her sent
As infinitly prais'd, as not a jot content.

For his stout heart felt deepe disgraces wound,
And hardly could dissemble Injury,
Who, having long survey'd the Creatures round,
Leapt lightly on an *Eagle* perching by,
And Cry'd; *The Earth to me she may deny,*
But not the Heav'n. So, without making playne,
Directs his Flight to fair *Eternity.*
(*The Muses horse his nimble joynts doth strayne*
When he is spurr'd with Love, or nettled with disdaine.)

His active Circles Crowne *Sols* glorious Spheare:
Heav'n op'ning still new Beauties to his Eye

190 he found] found hee *A* 191 Teeth, Lipps] tooth, lipps *F*: lipps teeth *A* 193 said] quoth *A* *hamm'ring*] forging *F, A* 197 poyse] poyse *F*: Weigh *A*: spoyle *1648* 199 colour'd] cover'd *A* 201 its] her *F, A* 202 Requir'd a *Drudge*] Required one *A* 208 stout heart] high thought *F, A* 210 survey'd] beheld *F, A*

As he gets up, whilst Earth doth lesse appeare,
Where some presage his fall to *Poverty*,
The heighth will turne his braine, some others cry;
Some few in judging Eares his raptures poise,
(Who like a Larke doth singing mount the Skye)
They beare him up with their applausive noise,
At which in secret heart he not a little joyes.

But the faint *Bird* is not releeved so
Although her Rider cheer'd her what he might,
To whom the whole Terrestriall Globe below
Seem'd a meane Quarry to debase his flight
Yet forc't ere long for a small bait to light,
The hunger of his *Animall* to stay,
Though oft he cuffs it first, and oft doth slight.
But need Commands, and Flesh must needs obay,
So at the last he stoops and seazes the skorn'd prey.

As in a Torch wee see the bating flame
Unto its heav'nly country doth aspire,
But the wax softly shrinking from the same
Makes it for food from Heaven to retire,
And tend to Earthward with descending fire:
So *Wit* is forc't (some Maintenance to get)
To stoop to Earth against his owne desire;
But soone againe the fruitfull Earth doth quit,
To soare in Empty Ayre: (Heav'n send me better wit!)

Yet when this Eagle shall have cast her Bill,
And mew'd her mortall plumes, some thinke that he
Shall then attaine the topp of Heavens hill,
And Coeternall with his writings be,
Taking peculiar felicitie
In penning Hymnes of His Creators praise;
(That is the genuine use of *Poetry*)

221 braine] braines *F* 222 Some] A few *A* raptures] fancies *F*, *A* 223 Skye] skye *F*, *A*: Skyes *1648* 230 small] poore *A* 233 need Commands] hunger bidds *F*, *A* [244–252 and Motto wanting in *F*] 247 Coeternall with] more aeternall than *A* 249 penning Hymnes] frameing Psalmes *A* 250] (For there shall bee most use of Poetry) *A*

And for reward of those Coelestiall Layes
That hov'ring Cherubins shall Crowne him with fresh Bayes:

Non est mortale quod optas Cum sis mortalis.

[Untitled early version of 'A Canto of the Progresse of Learning']

[*A* ff. 37r–39r]

1

Before the Earth was held in severall
Twas one great feild where all the creatures fedd,
As in a Common (therefore termd the All)
Men mixt with beasts together in one shedd
Upon the ground did take a homely bedd:
Things were not sorted yett, for then there was
No Groves where shady trees were billetted,
Nor grass distinguisht from the corne, butt grass
And corne, and shady trees were shuffled in one Masse.

2

Till Mother Nature griev'd to undergoe
A second Chaos, made a suite to Jove
That upon her hee would a sonne bestow,
Whose care this wild confusion might remove,
And Husbandry her mangled state improve.
For why on Earth was so great plenty rain'd
Or why had men Soules gi'n 'um from above,
If reasonable men with beasts remayn'd
And in a world of wealth the world of want complayn'd?

3

Jupiter wearyed with her busy pray'r
(As nature ever is importunate)

251 And for reward] And that for meed *A* 252 *hov'ring*] flying *A* [*canc.*] [Motto not in *A*]

At length consented shee should have an heire.
His words had deeds, and shee conceived straight,
And after soone was eas'd of her sweet waight.
Without or pange or groane. Butt as the light
Breakes out, in wombe of cloudes imprison'd late,
So easyly came forth, and eke so bright,
This Child of Nature, sent from heav'n and Witt hee hight.

4

A Jolly boy, who, growne, soone understood
Why hee was sent: Hee saw and greiv'd to see
How man *too lavish of his †Royall blood,
Converst with Creatures of base pedigree:
Yet still saw left seeds of Divinity,
And lookes erect to heav'n whence hee was bredd,
Butt his soule clave to th' Center, as a tree
That to the Sunne lifts his aspireing head
While his degen'rous root to th' Earth is rivetted.

5

When, like to one that rak't in ashes spyes
A little fyer left since yesterday,
Gently hee nurses it, and first applyes
Dry leaves and slender clefts (for yett it may
Indure no stronger meate) then fagotts lay,
And with his tim'rous breath the Cyndar wake;
Till by degrees it doth at length display
A heatfull blaze: No less paynes did hee take
Till to a goodly flame mans sparke of reason brake.

6

First hee with Cupid them acquainted brings,
With whom this Witt kept dayly company;
And borrow'd of him oft his nimble wings
With which supported hee would sore on high,
And trace the golden people of the sky
And lent to him his fancy and conceipt

* forgetfull † noble

Feath'red with which his shafts would surer fly
This seem'd a likely meanes to worke the feate
Softning the breasts of men, and kind'ling *divine heat.

7

So when through Love they 'gan to like each other
Hee taught them speech their liking to declare,
Which least so generous a flame should smother,
Hee had invented to give passion ayre.
Inspir'd with Love, their thoughts more lofty are,
And skorne on Earthly things for to bee bent.
Or if they were, 'twas for the Love they bare
Their causes more then them from which th'invent
The Cyrcle of the Sciences. Thus farr witt went.

8

There ceas't. For his high minde did much disdayne
To file it selfe with seeking gold in myre,
Or finding out of trades, or hoarding grayne,
To feed, not men butt the unquencht desyre
Of Men, by adding fewell to their fyre.
For well hee saw there was for all enough
And thought that reason should bee busy'd high'r
Then with base carke to gather such vile stuff
Mens foggy flesh and their diviner soule to puff.

9

Butt greedy Nature was not of his minde
And murmur'd Jove had heard her butt in part.
Shee had a Sonne, and one that had refyn'd
The lesser world: Butt that was butt a partt
To what lay wast: And therefore in her heart
Shee beats and tosses how shee may attayne
To better that. Att length she teem'd with Art,
And in Adultery betweene them twayne
†Was Craft begott, and brought to th' world with mickle payne.

* a brave † Shee

10

This Youth was for her turne: for all that Witt
Thought base, and for ingenuous breasts too meane,
Hee undertooke to doe, and finish't it.
That soone the face of things was changed cleane,
Hee alter'd both the Actours and the scene.
For th' Earth that was a Common like the Sea,
Hee gave to sev'rall men as their demesne,
And lent to ev'ry secrett roome a key.
To hold (as their Chiefe Lord) of Craft in Capite.

11

And men that wont with knowledge beat their browes
Now study the new knowledge how to gaine:
Therefore the Earth they wound with cruell ploughs,
That them to feed doth spend her heart in vaine,
Which they with Art restore that they againe
May feede it downe. *Which seemes to bee exprest
†By Tytyus Bird, whom with her beake they fayne
To plough the hundred Acres of his breast,
Which still renewes, still to renew the Vulturs feast.

12

Nor so content, her very bowells wound,
And torture her with all the Art they may,
Till shee confess in what holes underground
Her wealth was hidd; farr from the envyous day
At length (orejoy'd) they find where her gold lay.
Nor yett does this their sacred thirst appease:
Butt through the waves seeke a forbidden way,
And trust their lives to stormy Pleyades,
If any wealth remayne, in or beyond the Seas.

* that maks it seeme no rest † Of

The Ruby

Hayle! whom the Diamonds proclayme their King;
Crowning as Peeres, as Guards envyroning;
Hayle! whom the rising Sunne where thou wert borne,
Invested in the purple of the Morne,
And his owne Beames, whilst thee my verse displayes
Thou swell'st at once, and blushest at thy praise.
  Like a red Sea thy trembling Mount of blood
Stands off i'th ayre and threats a Crimson flood
Over the Golden bancks, whilst our dimm'd sight
Mistakes for flowing waves thy floating light.
  Or as in Wine the subtile spirits move,
Making ev'n Temperance her selfe in love;
So rowles thy fiery and bewitching Eye,
Able to shake a vow of Poverty.
  But oh, how like my Cruell faire thou art!
Thy panting stone is her obdurate heart
Pegg'd in with Diamonds: or signifies
Her Lipp, severely guarded by her Eyes.

A friends Wedding

This day my friend is ty'de
  With pleasing Chaines to a sweet Bryde.
So well the Turtle Loves
  So well are coupled *Venus* Doves;
Which her blythe Sonne hath broake
  With rods of Mirtle to her yoake.
Out of thy Lazy bed,

Title] On a [*H, F, A, Har.*] faire [*H, F*] *great* [*A, Har.*] Rubie sett in a Ring with many Diamonds about it *H, F, A, Har.* 7 thy] a *A* 9 bancks, whilst our dimm'd] shoare; the while our *A*: bankes, while our dimm'd *Har.* 11 the subtile] those cheerfull *A* 12] With which ev'n Temperance is made in Love *A* 13 bewitching] enchanting *H, F, Har.* 14 shake] tempt *H, F, A, Har.* 16 panting] bloody *H, F, Har.* 17 Pegg'd in] Chayn'd downe *H, F, Har.*: Chayn'd in *A*

Title] On the Wedding-day of his deare friend *H* 2 sweet] chast *H* 5 blythe] Glad *H* 7 thy] your *H*

Get up my Muse, and lay thy head
With thy faire Friend the Morne,
This happy Marriage to adorne.
Why art thou yet so dull
When thou shouldst quaffe Castalia full
To th' health of the faire *BRIDE*;
In which her *LOVERS* is implyde,
Not yet? Then fetch the Sack;
Ile put thee to the gentle wrack.
Finde me a way to show
What happinesse I wish these two.
Of *PORTIAS* Love relate,
How constant she was to her Mate,
And hearing *Brutus* death,
By stopping it expir'd her breath:
And then of *ORPHEUS* tell,
And of a Husband that lov'd well;
Through Heav'n, hell, Earth and Sea
He cryd his lost *Euridice*,
That the Rocks groan'd againe,
Helping the Widdower to complaine,
And hell it selfe lamented,
And fates their cruelty repented.
Then wish this couple here
May prove as faithfull as they were,
But never their fate prove,
And only imitate their Love.
Not yet? Is this a day
For silence? Or doth silence say?
"Deepe streames runne without noise,
"And those that sound are hollow Joyes?

13] To the faire health o'th' Bride *H* 15 Not] Not *H*: Nor *1648* 17 a] some *H* 19 *PORTIAS*] Portias *H*: PORCIAS *1648* 28 Widdower] Widdowes *H* 29 lamented] relented *H*

Sonnets translated out of Spanish

A Rich Foole

Thee, senselesse Stock, because th'art richly guilt,
The blinded people without cause admire,
And Superstition impiously hath built
Altars to that which should have beene the fire.

Nere shall my tongue consent to worship thee,
Since all's not Gold that glisters and is faire;
Carving but makes an Image of a Tree:
But Gods of Images are made by Prayer.

Sabean Incense in a fragrant Cloud
Illustriously suspended ore thy Crowne
Like a Kings Canopy, makes thee allowd
For more than man. But let them take thee downe,

And thy true value be once understood,
Thy dull Idolaters will finde th'art wood.

Hope

To hope is good, but with such wild applause
Each promise *Fabius* thou dost entertain;
As if decreed thee by Fates certaine Lawes,
Or in possession *now* it did remaine.

Wisdome is arm'd 'gainst all that can succeed,
Tymes changes and his stratagems: For such
His nature is, that when his wings wee need
He will come creeping on his halting Crutch.

Title] *To one very rich, and very foolish F* 5 Nere] Nere *F*: Where *1648* 6 Since all's not] Nor thinke all *F*

Hope [untitled in *F*] 1 such] so *F* 5 that can] which may *F*

Doe not, if wise, then to thy selfe assure
  The future, nor on present goods rely,
  Or thinke there's any time from time secure:
  For then when Patience sees her Harvest nigh,

That mocking Tyrant in an instant reares
A wall between the Sicle and the Eares.

Constancie

Cloris i'th Sunne proyning her Locks did sit
  With Lilly hand and Combe of Ivorie,
  But scarce could you discerne the Combe in *it*,
  Nor see the Sunne, Ecclips'd when *those* were by.

Whilst the rich fleece about her Shoulders playes
  And the pure Brooke (whose Margent is her bed)
  Sucks from her two bright Sunnes delitious rayes
  Through Clouds of Gold with which they're shadowed;

Thus *Coridon* (chiding the flying howres,
  With such a voyce as made them faster fly)
  Invoakt the Pow'r which doth subdue all Powr's:
  In vayne (*O Love*) *is my Felicitie.*

If the sweet Flames, thy feathered shafts beganne
To Kindle, thy wings feathers doe not fanne!

The Fall

The bloudy trunck of him who did possesse
  Above the rest a haplesse happy state,
  This little Stone doth Seale, but not depresse,
  And scarce can stop the rowling of his fate.

Constancie [untitled in *F*]   1 *Cloris*] *Phillis F*   4 *those*] they *F*   10 fly] move *F*   12] In vaine my happines was given, O Love, *F*

The Fall Title] A great Favorit beheaded. *F*

Brasse Tombes which justice hath deny'd t' his fault,
The common pity to his vertues payes,
Adorning an Imaginary vault,
Which from our minds time strives in vaine to raze.

Ten yeares the world upon him falsly smild,
Sheathing in fawning lookes the deadly knife
Long aymed at his head: That so beguild
It more securely might bereave his Life;

Then threw him to a Scaffold from a Throne.
Much Doctrine lyes under this little Stone.

A Rose

Blowne in the Morning, thou shalt fade ere Noone:
What bootes a Life which in such hast forsakes thee?
Th'art wondrous frolick being to dye so soone:
And passing proud a little colour makes thee.

If thee thy brittle beauty so deceives,
Know then the thing that swells thee is thy bane;
For the same beauty doth in bloody leaves
The sentence of thy early death containe.

Some Clownes course Lungs will poyson thy sweet flow'r
If by the carelesse Plough thou shalt be torne:
And many *Herods* lye in waite each how'r
To murther thee as soone as thou art borne;

Nay, force thy Bud to blow; Their Tyrant breath
Anticipating Life, to hasten death.

5 fault,] fault. *1648* 7 an] an *F*: on *1648*
A Rose Title] *To a Rose F* 1 in the] but i'th' *F* 10 shalt] shouldst *F*

A Picture

Behold how *Marius* from Minturnian Lake
  Flying through *Africk* late by him orethrowne,
  A pittyfull Comparison doth make
  Betweene high *Carthage* ruines and his owne!

Thy Prides just fall which thou must one day mourne,
  In this dumbe Picture *Caelia* thou hast read
  For so doth Age, Loves Empire too oreturn,
  And pull downe Thrones in hearts established.

Thy glasse, where oft thou whetst each wounding grace,
  Will shew thee better farre the History
  Of *Marius*, and raz'd *Carthage*, in thy face:
  And *thou*, one Trophy of Times victory,

Shalt then confesse, to equall skornes expos'd,
Thy Beauty was a Tyrant soone depos'd.

A River

Thou clearer honour of the Christall Mayne,
  Sweet Rivulet, compos'd of liquid plate,
  Whose waters glide through this enamell'd plaine
  With sound harmonious, with stately gate;

Since *shee* is standing on thy happy brimme
  Who both enflameth and congeales my blood,
  Whilst Love with admirable skill doth limme
  Her portraict on thy smooth and quiet flood;

Move on thus Gently still, and doe not slacke
  The waving reynes unto the foaming bit

A Picture [untitled in *F*] 1 Minturnian] *Minturnus' F* 6 *Caelia*] *Phillis F* 12 *thou*] thou *F*: *then 1648*

A River Title] *To a River F* 1 Thou clearer] O thou cleare *F* 10 waving] waved *F*

With which thou now art pleased to pull backe
Thy headstrong Current: For it is not fit

Neptune with all the treasures he doth hold
Should so much beauty in his Armes infold.

A Nightingale

With such variety and dainty skill
Yon'd Nightingale devides her mournefull song,
As if tenne thousand of them through one bill
Did sing in parts the story of their wrong.

Nay shee accuses with such vehemence
Her Ravisher, I thinke she would incline
The conscious Grove thereof to have a sence
And print it on the Leaves of that tall Pine.

Yet happy *shee*, who may her paine declare
In moving Noates, and wand'ring through the woods
With uncut wings, by change divert her care!
But let *Him* melt away in silent floods,

Whom his *Medusa* turn'd into a stone,
That he might neither change, nor make his moane.

A Cupid of diamonds presented

Banisht from Life to seeke out death I goe
Which through the world so long I will pursue,

14 Armes] waves *F*

A Nightingale Title] The nightingall *C* [Untitled in *F*] 3 of them] others *C* 5 Nay . . . such vehemence] Yea . . . that life and flame *C* 7–12] The conscious groves to register his name / Upon the leaves, and barke of that tall pine: / But happy she that may her sorrow leave, / Since having wings to wander through the woods, / And bill to publish it she may deceave / Her payne. But let him powre forth silent floods *C*

A Cupid of diamonds presented Title] A Cupid of Diamonds sent to a Lady after parting from her in her [*H*, *F*, *Rainsford*] disfavour *H*: *disdaine F*, *Rainsford*

Till desp'rat Griefes at least have made men know
My Soule feares no divorcement but from you.

To thinke to mollifie you now were vaine,
For if my present services could not
Worke the least feeling in your cold disdaine,
What should I hope for absent and forgot?

Yet take this Gemme, which, as my melting Eye
My soft *affection* did at parting prove,
May Cipher to you now my *Constancie*.
Wear't in your bosome, tis the *God of Love*.

And once I'le try, if (as in Goldsmiths Art)
A Diamond Love can cut *a Diamond Heart*.

The Spring

Those whiter Lillies which the early Morne
Seemes to have newly woven of sleav'd Silke,
To which (on Banks of wealthy *Tagus* borne)
Gold was their Cradle liquid Pearle their Milke:

These blushing Roses, with whose virgin leaves
The wanton Wind to sport himselfe presumes,
Whilst from their rifled wardrobe he receives
For his wings Purple, for his breath Perfumes:

Both those, and these, my *Caelia's* pretty foote
Trod-up. But if she should her Face display,
And fragrant breast, they'd dry againe to th' Roote,
(As with the blasting of the Mid-dayes ray)

And this soft wind which both perfumes and Cooles
Passe like the unregarded breath of Fooles.

3 Griefes] Griefs *H*: grief *F*, *1648* least have] least ha' *H*: least have *F*: lest have *1648*

The Fourth Booke OF *VIRGILLS ÆNEIS* On the *Loves* of *DIDO* and *ÆNEAS*.

The Argument of the three preceding Bookes, By way of Introduction

ÆNEAS bound for *Italie*, is tost
By raging Seas to *Lybia's* guarded Coast,
Where *Dido* builds faire *Carthage* with that wealth
She with her selfe conveigh'd from *Tyre* by stealth;
For which *Pigmalion* her deare *Husband* slew,
And for *the same* sought *her* destruction too.
Pious Æneas, and his valiant Trayne,
The Royall Widdow there doth entertaine.
Who, though grasse growes where *Conquerd Troy* had stood,
Makes it her Pride to come of Trojan blood.
Yet thoughtfull *Venus*, who the *Punick Faith*
And *Rivall-Walls* in great suspition hath,
Fearing a change from *Interest of State*,
Or some *new Plot* from *Juno's ancient hate*
To those of *Troy*, which made *her* raise that storme:
Sends *Cupid*, maskt in young *Ascanius* forme,
To ceaze the *Fortresse Royall* (the *Queene's* Brest)
And make *Her* first a prisoner to her *Guest*.
Shee with a hundred questions streight began
Of *Troy*: Then askes the story of *the Man*
From first to last. *Hee* paynts his *Town's* sad *fall*
(Besieg'd ten yeares): *his owne flight* (*last* of all),

Title] *The Loves of Dido, and Aeneas. The Argument F* 1–34] *Aeneas* driven by a tempest upon the Coast of *Carthage*, was there royally entertained by Queene *Dido*; who entreates him to recounte the Storie of the Sack of *Troy*, and his Adventures afterwards; which is the subject of the First Booke of the *Aeneads*. In the Second, and Third Booke, till the end of it, *Aeneas* continues his Relation; whereupon followes most properly and elegantly the seeming-abrupt beginning of this Fourth Booke: *But Dido etc.* Because *Virgil* makes *Dido* enamoured chiefly with the sufferings, and heroicall valour of *Aeneas*, as she herself sayth: *How all his talke was Armes*! *F*

On his broad shoulders bearing through the *Fire*
His *vanquisht Gods*, and his *decrepid Sire*:
His poore *Wife* tripping after, and his *Boy*
With shorter steps (the growing *Hope* of *Troy*)
Shee mist: how *backe* amongst the *Swords* he flyes,
And in the *Flames* his *lost Creusa cryes*:
Not found; resum'd his venerable *Load*
With heavier Cheere, and *forward* (weeping) trod.
Then tells his sev'n-yeares *Travailes*; in which *Hee*
Was *tost* no lesse upon the *Land* than *Sea*:
Meeting his greedy Auditors. But how
It wrought with *Dido* this next Booke will show.

The Fourth Booke
OF
VIRGILLS ÆNEIS
On the *Loves* of
DIDO and *ÆNEAS*

But she who *Love* long since had swallowed downe,
Melts with hid fire; her wound doth inward weep:
The *Mans* much worth, his *Nations* much *Renowne*
Runs in her minde: His Lookes and words are deepe
Fixt in her breast: Care weanes her Eies from sleepe;
The *Morne* with *Phoebus* lampe the *Earth* survayd,
And drew *Heav'ns* veyle through which moist Starrs did creep;
When thus to her deare sister (sicke) she said
Anna what frightfull Dreames my wavering soule invade!

Who is this Man that visits our Aboads?
How wise! How valiant! What a Face he has!

Title] *The Fourth Booke of the Aeneads F* 1] But *Dido*, who Love's hooke long since had caught *F* 2 wound] wounds *1648* 2–50] Festers within, and waistes with choaked flame; / The Man's heroick worth runnes in her thought, / And his brave Nation's wide-extended fame; / Fixt in her breast, his lookes, and words remaine. / Care makes her watche, the long'd-for morne survayde / By *Phoebus* light, this low terrestriall frame, / And wip't from Heaven's face the humide shade, / When to her dearest Sister thus half-sick she sayde: // What dreames are mine! *Anne*, what a Guest have we! / How brave his meene! How all his talke was Armes! /

Well may hee be descended from the Gods.
Feare shewes ignoble minds: But hee (alas)
Tost with what Fates! through what warres did he passe!
Were I not well resolv'd never to wed
Since my first *Love* by death bereft me was:
Did I not loath the Nuptiall Torch and Bed,
To this one fault perchance, perchance I might be led.

For since my poore *Sicheus's* fatall howre
(Our household Gods besmear'd by brothers steele)
This only Man (I must confesse) had powre
To shake my constant Faith, and make it reele:
The footsteps of that ancient flame I feele.
But first *Earth* swallow me, or (Thunder slaine)
Jove naile me to the *shades*, pale *shades* of Hell,
And everlasting Night, before I staine
Thee (holy Chastitie) or thy faire Rites profane.

Hee tooke my love with *him* (and let him keep't
Cold in his Grave) to whom I first was tyde.
This said her bosome full of Teares she wept.
O dearer than my life! (*Anna* replyde)
Wilt thou forever live a dead mans Bride?
Nor prety Babes (Rewards of *Venus*) know?
Are *Ghosts* apeas'd, or Ashes satisfide
With this thinkst *thou*? What if before (thy woe
Yet greene and fresh) no husbands downe with thee would goe?

Not *Lybia's* King (Iarbas) skornd in *Tyre*
Before, with other *Chiefs* whom *Affrick* high

Wel may he boaste Celestiall pedegree. / *Feare shewes ignoble mindes*. But, ah, what harmes / Did he rush through! What deaths! what dire Alarmes! / Were I not wel resolv'd new Bands to shunne, / Since my first Love *Fates* ravisht from mine armes, / Did I not halfe repent I ere begunne, / To this one fault perchance my frailtie might be wonne. // For I confesse, since poore *Sicheus* death / By brother's hand, this onlie man doth move / My sense, and stagger'd fayth; I feele a breath / Stirre the old fire. But Earth my grave first prove, / Or strike me, a pale shadowe, Thund'ring *Jove* / To Hell, and night eternall, ere I stayne / Thee, *Chastitie*, or wrest thy Lawes. My love / Is gone with him, who did it first obtaine, / In whose cold Urne rakt up, ever let it remaine. // This speach a floud of gushing teares ensu'th. / O dearer then my life (then *Anna* sedd) / Wilt thou still mourne away thy widdow'd youth? / Nor reape the sweet fruits of a Marri'd bedd? / Doth Jealousie, thinkst thou, disturbe the dead? / Though, thee twice-scorn'd *Iarbas* could not move; / Though none of *Africk's* Kings, in Triumphs bredd, /

In Mettle, breeds? Wilt thou quench Loves sweet fire?
Nor yet consider whom thou'rt planted nigh?
Here (a fierce People) the *Getulians* lye,
Bitlesse *Numidian Horse*, and *Quicksands* dire
There mad *Barceans* block thee up, and drye
Deserts. What speake I of the bloodier ire
A Wolfe turn'd Brother breaths, and gathering Clouds from *Tyre*.

Auspicious Heav'ns, and *Juno's* care of *thee*,
The Trojan Navie hither (doubtlesse) led.
O (sister) what a Citie will this be!
How shalt thou see thy Scepter flourish! Wed
To *Troy*, how will the *Punick* Glory spread.

Aske but Heav'ns leave, thy Guest then (feasting) keepe,
Pretending 'tis unsafe to saile in winter,
When Ships are tost, and Pleiades doe weepe,
And ominous Skyes forbid, On Seas to venter.
These words, blew Love t' a flame; for doubts hope lent her,
And staunch her blushes. First in solemne wise
To *Phoebus*, *Bacchus*, *Ceres* (Lawes-Inventer)
Selected Lambs i'th' Fane they Sacrifize,
But *Juno* most atone who favours Nuptiall tyes.

The Queene her selfe (more beautious in those Rites)
Betweene the Crescent of a milke white Cow
The liquor powres: Or passing in their sights,
Unto the Gods with rev'rend grace doth bow,
Consults the panting lites, and payes her vow.
Alas, vayne Mysteries! Blind Priests aread
Which is the sacrifize is offer'd now?
Soft flames upon the Off'rers marrow feed,
And her concealed wound doth freshly inward bleed.

Thy yet fresh-bleeding sorrow could approve; / Hast thou the hart to quenche the kindelie heates of Love? // Nor dreadst *Numidias* expert horse, dry sands / of *Syrtis*, wilde *Getulias* warlike race, / *Barceans* nurst with spoile (ill-neighbour lands) / Besides *Tyre's* threates! Sure *Juno's* speciall grace, / And fav'ring Gods *Troy's* fleete did hither chace. / Thinke, Sister, what a strength to thy new Crowne, / this Match will adde. When *Troy* and *Tyre* inlace / Their boughes, and summe their Glories in one Towne, / How must it spreade in Empire, and in bright renowne! *F* 50 how will] how how will *1648* 56 staunch... wise] quencht... guise *F* 60 more] most *F*

Poore *Dido* burnes, and stung with restlesse Love
Runs raveing to and fro through every street
Runs like a Hinde, which in some covert grove
Where she securely graz'd in fruitfull *Creet*,
A woodman shooting at farre distance hit;
Drunke in her veynes the feather'd Iron lyes,
Nor he who made the wound doth know of it;
She through Dictean woods and pastures highs,
But carries in her side the Arrow which she flyes.

Shee takes *Æneas* with her up and downe,
And shews him the vast wealth she brought from *Tyre*,
The goodly streets and Bulwarkes of her Towne.
No lesse a thousand times did she desire
To shew unto him too her am'rous fire;
And oft began, but shame represt her tongue.
At night unto their banquets they retyre;
And *Troy's* sad fall againe she must have sung,
And at his charming Lips againe shee fondly hung.

When every one was parted to his rest,
And the dimme Moone trod on the heeles of day,
And setting Starres shew'd it high time to rest,
She in the empty house languisht away,
And on the Couch, which he had pressed, lay:
Absent she sees *him* whom her thoughts admire,
Him absent heares, or on her lappe doth stay
Ascanius the true picture of his sire,
As if she so could cheat her impotent desire.

All workes are at a stand; The youth for warre
Provide no Forts, nor trayning exercise;
Huge beames, and arches, which halfe finisht are,
Hang doubtfull in the Ayre, to fall, or rise,
And Towr's doe threat at once both Earth and Skyes.
Whom when as *Joves* deare wife perceiv'd so drown'd
In witchcrafts, and that *Fame*, with lowdest cryes,

88 dimme] dimm'd *F*

Could not awake her from the pleasing swound,
She thus accosted *Venus*, and her minde did sound.

Great glory sure, and goodly spoyles yee gaine
You and your Boy: A doughty enterprize
Yee have atchiev'd, and worthy to remaine
In lasting Marble, if two *Dietyes*
By subtlety one woman doe surprize.
Nor am I ignorant that, to defend
Your Race from feare of future Enemies,
Y' are jealous of my walls. But to what end
Should so neare friends as wee eternally contend?

Nay rather let us knit eternall Love,
And bind the Peace more strong with Hymens cord.
Yee have the thing for which so much ye strove,
Eliza with Loves fi'ry shaft is gor'd
Then rule we this joynt Towne with one accord,
And who shall ayd it most be now our strife.
Once let a Queen obey a Trojan Lord
And Tyrians (to preserve a Lovers life)
Call thee their Patronesse, as Dowry of his wife.

Venus (who saw her drift was to translate
To *Carthaginians* those Imperiall dues
Which were reserv'd for *Italy* by *Fate*)
Made this Reply. Who madly would refuse
So advantagious match, and rather choose
To war with you. If but the faire Event
According to your wise forecast ensues.
But Fates I feare me, nor *Jove* will consent
That *Tyrians* and *Trojans* in one Towne be pent.

And yet perchance you, lying in his breast
With a wives Rhet'rick may his Councells sway;
Then breake the Ice; I'll second the Request.
Leave that to me (said shee) and for a way
T' effect our wishes, marke my plot I pray.

133 wives] wife's *F*: wives *1648*

To morrow, when the Sun shall be discryde
To guild the Mountaines with his early'st ray,
Æneas and the Love-sick Queene provide
To have a solemne hunting in the Forrest wide.

Now I, when here they beat the Coppice, there
The Horsemen flutter, on their heads will powre
A pitchy cloud, and Heav'n with Thunder teare.
Their followers for shelter from the showre
By severall paths along the plaine shall skowre;
Maskt in darke night, unto one Cave they two
Shall come. There I will be; and (adde your pow'r,)
Tye such a knot as only Fates undoe;
I'l seale her his. Good Hymen shall be present too.

Venus seemes, nodding, to consent; and smiles
To see Dame *Juno's* craft. Meanewhile the Morne
Arose: And the choice youth, with subtle toyles,
Sharpe hunting-speares, fleet steeds in *Barbry* borne,
And sure-nos'd hounds tun'd to the Bugle-horne,
Are gone before. The Lords at doore expect
Whilst the Queene staies within her selfe t'adorne.
Her Palfrey stands with Gold and Skarlet deckt,
And champs the foaming Bit, as skorning to be checkt.

At length she comes, with a huge troope: Her Gowne
Of *Tyrian* dye, bordered with Flow'rs of Gold:
A Quiver by her comely side hung downe;
Gold Ribining her brighter haire enrolld,
Gold Buttons did her purple vesture hold.
The *Trojans* too, and blithe *Iulus* went
Above the rest, farre goodlyest to behold,
Æneas selfe his gladding presence lent,
And with his darkned trayne did *Dido's* trayne augment.

As when *Apollo* leaves his winter seates
Of *Lycia* and *Zanthus* floods, to see
His Country *Delos*, and his feast repeats;

159 comes] came *F*

About his Altars hum confusedly
Creets, Dryopes, and ruddy Nymphs: But hee
On *Cynthus* rides, and pleating doth enlace
His flowing haire with Gold, and his lov'd tree:
His shafts shogge at his backe. With no lesse grace
Æneas marcht. Such rayes displayd his Lovely face.

When in the Mountains now engag'd they were
And pathlesse woods. Loe Goats from summits cast
Runne tumbling through the bushes: Heardes of Deere
Another way come hurrying downe as fast,
And raise a cloud as through the dust they hast
Hot-spurre *Iulus* on his mettl'd horse
Out cracking all, now these, now those men past,
And wisht, 'mongst those faint Beasts, and without force,
Some Lyon, or tusk't Bore would crosse him in his course.

Meane while loud Thunder Heav'n's Pavilion teares,
Making a passage for th' ensuing raine:
The *Trojan* youth, and *Tyrian* followers,
And *Venus* Dardan-Granchild through the Plaine
Seeke sev'rall shelters: Rivers, like a Mayne,
Rush from the Mountaines round. One Cave that Lord
Of *Troy*, and she who did in *Carthage* raigne
Lighted upon. Earth gives the signall word,
And *Juno*, Queene of Marriage, doth their hands accord.

The guilty Heav'ns, as blushing to have been
An instrument this meeting to fulfill,
With flashing lightning shone: The Nymphs were seen
To weepe with all their streames, and from each hill
Were heard to murmur the presaged Ill.
That day did usher Death, and *Didos* shame:
For now shees arm'd, let men say what they will,
Nor seekes, as erst, to hide her am'rous flame:
She calls it Wedlock, gives her fault an honest name.

Fame straight through *Lybias* goodly towns doth post,
Fame a fleet evill, which none can outflye;

185 crosse] thwart *F*

Most strong she is when she hath travaild most,
First small through feare, but growne so, instantly,
That standing on the ground shee'l reach the Skye.
She was, the last birth Mother Earth did bring
When her proud anger did the Gods defie,
The Gyants sister, swift of foot and wing;
A huger never was, nor a more monstrous thing.

Most strange! There's not a Plume her body beares
But under it a watching Eye doth peepe,
As many tatling tongues, and listning Eares.
By night 'tween Earth and Heaven shee doth sweepe
Skreeching, nor shuts her Lids with balmy sleepe.
And all the day time upon Castle-gates
Or steeple-tops she doth strict watches keepe,
And frights great Cyties with her sudden Bates,
And with one confidence both truths and lyes relates.

She, glad of such a Prey whereon to plume,
Through peoples mindes truths mixt with falshood sent:
How one *Æneas* came from *Troy*, with whom
Fayre *Dido* deign'd to wed; And now they spent
In Revells the long winter, wholly bent
On brutish Love, drowning affaires of State:
These things she sow'd in mens rank mouths: then went
To King *Iarbas*, and did irritate
His minde with tales, and his old wrath exasperate.

A hundred Temples built to *Jove* had hee,
(Who unto Hammon forct *Gramantis* bore)
A hundred Altars burning constantly
(The Gods aeternal Centinells) each floore
Painted with bloud of beasts, with flow'rs each doore,
Who mad with Love, and with the bitter newes,
Before the Altars, and the Gods before,
Kneeling, with hands upheav'd to *Jove*, doth use
Great supplications and in this manner sues.

Jove, to whom Moores rich wine on Carpets drinke,
Seest this? Or when thy arme doth lightning shake

Giv'st thou false fire t'a cloud to make fooles winke?
And, when it thunders, dost thou only make
A rumbling ore our heads at which wee quake?
A stray, to whom our selfe (being hither fled)
Hir'd a small barren plot, for pity sake
With some restraints, refusd with us to wed,
And Don *Æneas* takes unto her Crowne and bed.

And now this *Paris*, with a quoife to stay
His Beard and powderd Locks, and's Beaver trayne
Of shee-men, gluts himselfe upon the prey;
Whilst we with guifts on guifts enrich thy Fane.
And make our person glorious in vaine.
Th'al pow'rfull heard these pray'rs; And cast his Eye,
On the new walls where th' am'rous paire remaine
Carelesse how desp'rate sicke their fame doth lye,
Then spake, and gave this charge to winged *Mercury.*

Goe Sonne, as swift as windes, in *Carthage* light.
Tell *Venus* sonne, whom loyt'ring there thou't see
Unworthy of that Fate which he doth slight,
That his faire Mother painted him to mee
Another man; And therefore twice did free
From *Graecian* swords; One, who with steddy rayn
Should manage proud and warlike *Italie*,
And prove himselfe of *Teucers* haughty strayne,
And the tryumphed World under his Lawes maintaine.

If not at all *this* him with glory fires,
Nor care of his owne greatnesse he doth show,
Why should he grudge his sonne the Roman spires?
What makes he here? What seekes he from a Foe?
Latium, and them who there expect to grow
From him, let him regard. Let him away.
This is th' effect, from me this let him know.
At once *Jove* ended, and the sonne of Maye
His greater sires commands prepar'd himselfe t' obey.

249 quoife] quoife *F*: quofe *1648*   250 Beaver] beaten *F*

First Golden Wings unto his feete he binds,
Which over Lands and over Seas that swell
Beare him aloft, as speedy as the Winds.
Then takes his rod. With this he calls from hell
Pale Ghosts, sends others in sad shades to dwell,
Gives sleepe and takes it from the drowzie brayne,
And seales up eyes with death. He doth repell
By pow'r of this the Heav'ns which part in twaine,
And through the watry Clouds he sayls as through a Main.

He soaring the lanke sides and Crowne disclos'd
Of craggy *Atlas*, whose necke props the Sky,
Atlas, whose Piney head to stormes expos'd
Is bound about with Clouds continually.
Thick on his aged backe the snow doth lye,
And down his dravell'd chine powre plenteous springs,
His beard in Icycles growes horridly.
Here lights the god poysd on his hov'ring wings.
Towards the Sea from hence his body headlong flings.

Like to a Bird, which round the Shores doth glide
And Fishy Rocks, skimming along the Bay;
So flyes 'tweene Earth and Heav'n, and doth divide
The Winde and Sandy Coast of *Lybia*,
Leaving his Mothers sire, the sonne of May.
Who Landing where the Sheep-coates lately were,
Sees how *Æneas* doth the workes survey,
Here building Tow'rs, and altring Turrets there,
He by his side a sword all Stard with Gemmes did weare.

Upon his shoulder to the Ayre displayd
A Robe of *Tyrian* Purple seem'd to flame,
Which *Dido* with her owne faire hands had made
And edgd the seams with gold. Here you doe frame,
(Said *Hermes*) hindring your owne Crowne and Fame,
High Towrs of *Carthage*, and, uxorious, rayse
Faire Walls whereof another beares the name:

277 that] which *F* 290 powre] powres *F* 301 Turrets] houses *F* 303 Upon] And on *F* 309 another beares] your Love must beare *F*

Marke now what *Jove* himselfe, whom Heav'n obaies,
And Earth, by his wing'd messenger unto you saies.

What make you here loytring in *Lybia*?
If glory of great actions fire not *you*,
Nor your owne Interest nor Fame you weigh;
Seeke your *Heires* good, *Iulus* hopes pursue,
To whom the *Latian* Crowne and *Rome* is due.
This having said *Cyllenius* vanisht quite
From mortall eyes, and back to Heaven flew.
Æneas at the vision shakes with fright,
His tongue cleaves to his jawes, his hair stands bolt-upright.

Hee is on fire to goe, and flye that Land
Of sweet inchantments, being skar'd away
By no lesse warning than the Gods command.
But (ah?) what shall he doe? How dare t'assay
With words the am'rous Queene? What should hee say
For introduction? His swift-beating thought
In doubtful ballance thousand things did lay,
And this way cast them, and then that way wrought,
At last this seemd the best when all wayes he had sought.

He cald *Sergestus*, *Mnesteus*, and the stout
Cloanthus, bids them fit immediatly
The Fleet, and draw their Companies about
The Port, their armes prepar'd, not telling why;
Meane while himselfe (when no least jealousie
To the good Queene should thought of breach betray
In so great Loves) an entrance would espye,
The season of soft speech, and dextrous way.
With readinesse and joy they doe him all obay.

But *Dido* found their plot. (whats hid from Lovers?)
Herselfe, who doubts ev'n safe things, first doth see't:
And the same tatling *Fame* to her discovers
That *Trojans* are departing with their Fleete.
Shees mad, stark mad, and runs through ev'ry street

330 cald] calls *F* 341 tatling] wicked *F* 343 runs] raves *F*

Like *Bacchus* She-Priests, when the god is in,
And they to doe him furious homage meete,
Citheron yelling with their mid-night dynne
Then thus t' *Æneas* speakes, nor stayes till he beginne.

Didst thou hope too by stealth to leave my land,
And that such treason could be unbetray'd?
Nor should my Love, nor thy late plighted hand,
Nor *Dido*, who would dye, thy flight have staid?
Must too this Voyage be in Winter made?
Through stormes? O, cruell to thy selfe, and mee
Didst thou not hunt strange Lands, and Scepters swayd
By others, if old *Troy* reviv'd should be;
Should *Troy* it selfe be sought through a tempest'ous Sea?

Mee fly'st thou? By these teares, and thy right hand,
(Since this is all's now left to wretched me)
By marriages *New* joyes, and sacred Band,
If ought I did could meritorious be,
If ever ought of mine were sweet to thee;
Pity our house, which must with my decay
Give early period to its soveraignty;
And put, I doe beseech thee, farre away
This cruell minde, If cruell mindes heare them that pray.

For *thee* the *Lybian* Nations me defie,
The Kings of *Scythia* hate me, and my *Tyre*:
For *thee* I lost my shame, and that, whereby
Alone I might unto the Starres aspire,
The chaster fame which I did once acquire.
To whom my Guest (for Husbands out of date)
Dost thou commit me ready to expire?
Why stay I? Till *Pigmaleon* waste my state?
Or on *Iarbas* wheeles, a captive Queene, to wayte?

Yet if before thou fled'st out of this place
Some childe at least I unto thee had borne,

347 t' *Æneas*] *Aeneas F* 355 should] could *F* 359 marriages *New*] marriage, new *F*: marriage's *New 1648* 363 its] her *F* 365 that] who *F* 369 aspire] aspire *F*: expire *1648*

If in my Court resembling but thy face,
Some young *Æneas* playd; I should not mourne
As one so quite deluded, or forelorne.
Here ceased *shee*. But *hee*, whom *Jove* had ty'd
With strict commands, his Eyes did no way turne,
But stoutly did his griefe suppresse, and hide
Under his secret heart. Then thus in short replyde,

For me, O Queene, I never will deny
But that I owe you more than you can say,
Nor shall I sticke to beare in memory
Eliza's name, [whilst memorie doth stay
In this frayle seate,] whilst breath these limbs doth sway.
But to the point. I never did intend
(Pray charge me not with that) to steale away:
And much lesse did I Wedlock-bands pretend,
Neither to such a treaty ever condescend.

Would Fates permit me mine owne way to take,
And please my selfe in choosing of a Land,
Ilium out of her ashes I would rake,
And gleane my Earths sweet Reliques, *Troy* should stand,
(The vanquisht Troops replanted, by my hand)
And *Priam's* Towrs againe to Heav'n aspire.
But now have I the Oracles command
To seeke great *Italy*; the same require
The Destinies. My Country's this; This my desire.

If you of *Tyre* with *Carthage* Towrs are tooke,
Why should our seeking *Latian* fields offend?
May not the *Trojans* too new mansions looke?
As oft as night moyst shadowes doth extend,
Over the Earth, and golden Stars ascend,
My Fathers chyding ghost affrights my sleepe:
My sonne, on whom that Realme is to descend,
And those deare Eyes doe freshly seeme to weepe;
Complaining that from him his destin'd Crowne I keepe.

381 strict . . . way] straight . . . wayes *F* 387–8] Eliza's name, whilst breath these limbs doth sway *1648* [Correction from *F*] 393 Would] Did *F* 396 my] mine *F* 410 his] this *F*

And now *Joves* Sonne (by both their heads I sweare)
Was sent to me, my selfe the God did see
In open day, and with these Eares did heare:
Then vexe not with complaints your selfe and mee,
I goe against my will to *Italy.*
Whilst thus he spake, shee lookt at him askew,
Rowling her lightning Eyes continually,
And him from head to foot did silent view,
When, being throughly heat, these thundring words ensue.

Nor Goddesse was thy Mother, nor the source
Of thy high blood, renowned *Dardanus*,
But some *Hyrcanian Tigresse* was thy Nource,
Out of the stony Loynes of *Caucasus*
Descended, cruell and perfidious.
For with what hopes should I thy faults yet cover,
Did my teares make thee sigh? Or bend, but thus,
Thine Eyes? Or sadnesse for my griefe discover?
Or if thou couldst not Love, to pity yet a Lover?

Whom first accuse I since these Loves began,
Jove is unjust, *Juno* her charge gives or'e,
Whom may a Woman trust? I tooke this man
Homelesse, a desp'rate wrack upon my shoare,
And fondly gave him halfe the Crowne I wore:
His Ships rebuilt, t' his men new lives I lent.
And now the Fates, the Oracles, what more?
(It makes me mad) *Joves* sonne on purpose sent
Brings him forsooth a menace through the Firmament.

As if the Gods their blissefull rest did breake
With thinking on thy Voyages. But I
Nor stop you, nor confute the words you speake.
Goe, chase, on Rowling billowes Realmes that fly,
With ficle waves uncertaine *Italy.*
Some courteous Rock (if Heav'n just curses heare)
Will be Revenger of my injury:

415] I tell you, I goe forc't to *Italie F* 441 that] which *F* 442 waves] windes *F*

When thou perceiving the sad Fate draw neere,
Shalt *Dido*, *Dido*, call; who surely will be there.

For when cold death shall part with dreary swoone
My Soule and Flesh; my ghost, where ere thou bee,
Shall haunt thee with dim Torch, and light thee downe
To thy darke conscience: I'l be Hell to thee,
And this glad newes will make Hell Heav'n to mee.

Here, falling as farre from him as she might,
She fainted ere her speech were finished:
Leaving him tossing in his tender spright
What he should say to her, or leave unsed,
Her Maides conveigh her to her Iv'ry Bed.
But *good Æneas*, though he faine would prove
To swage her griefe, and leave her comforted,
Peirc't to the soul with her so ardent Love,
Yet goes to view his Fleet, obedient unto *Jove*.

Aye, now the *Trojans* fall to worke for good,
And hale their Vessells downe from all the shoares;
The calkt Ships are on floate, and from the wood
They bring whole Oakes unwrought, and leavy Oares
For hast to fly away.
Through ev'ry gate they pack and trudge amayne:
As when the Emmets sally through Earths pores
To sack, for hoard, some barne full stuft with graine,
Remembring barren Winter must returne againe,

The black Troops March, and through the Meadows beare
The booty by a narrow path, some hale
The heavy Cornes; others bring up the Reere,
And prick them forwards that begin to fayle
The busie Labourers ev'ry path engrayle.
What sighs gav'st thou now *Dido*, looking out
From thy high Tow'r? How did thy sences quayle
Seeing the shoares so swarm'd, and round about
Hearing confused shoutings of the *Nautick Rout*?

461 Aye] By *F*: I *1648* 469 barren] that bare *F* 470 Troops] garde *F* 473 that begin] who beginne *F*: that begun *1648*

O Tyrant Love, how absolute thou art
In humane breasts! Againe shee's forc't to fly
To teares and pray'rs, and bow her prostrate heart
To the subduing passion, glad to trye
All cures before the last, which is to dye.
Sister, said shee, thou seest they all repaire
To th' Port: And only for a winde doe lye,
Inviting it with streamers wav'd ith' ayre:
Had I but fear'd this blow, I should not now despaire.

Yet try for me this once; For only thee
That perjur'd soule adores, to thee will shew
His secret thoughts: Thou, when his seasons bee,
And where the *Man's* accessible dost know.
Goe sister, meekly speake to the proud Foe.
I was not with the *Greeks* at *Aulis* sworne
To raze the *Trojan* name, nor did I goe,
'Gainst *Ilium* with my Fleet, neither have torne
Anchises ashes up from his profaned urne.

Why is he deafe to my intreaties? whether
So fast? It is a Lovers last desire
That he would but forsake me in faire weather,
And a safe time. I doe not now aspire
To his broake Wedlock-vow, neither require
He should faire *Latium*, and a Scepter leave:
Poore time I begge, my passions to retyre,
Truce to my woe; Nor pardon, but Reprieve,
Til griefs, familiar growne, have taught me how to grieve.

For sisterhood, for sence of my distresse,
Let me this last boone, ere I dye, obtayne.
This *Dido* spake. The sad Ambassadresse
Carries her teares, and brings them back againe.
(As brackish tydes post from and to the Maine)
But not an Ocean of bitter teares
Can alter, him, nor will he entertaine

482 subduing] all-mightie *F* 492 speake to] treate with *F* 502 Scepter] Kingdome *F* 505 how] but *F*

The flatt'ring force of words: He only heares
The Fates, and *Joves* command, which dams up his mild ears.

As an old Oake (but yet not weake with Eld)
Which showres and blasts to overthrow contend,
It cracks, and (the trunck shooke) leaves strow the field,
That sticks in Rocks; whose Roots tow'rds Hell descend
As farre as towards Heav'n the boughs ascend:
So stands the *Heros*, beat with winde and rayne,
His stout heart groanes, and his affections bend
Shooke with their sighs; But his resolves remaine
As unremov'd as Rocks, teares rowle their waves in vaine.

Then doth unhappy *Dido*, given ore
By her last hope, desire to dye. The light
Is irkesome to her eyes. To confirme more
Her purpose to imbrace eternall night,
Placing on th' Incence-burning Altars bright
Her guifts, the holy water she beheld
Converted to black Inke (Portentous sight!)
And the powr'd Wine to roaping blood congeal'd
This thing to none, not to her sister, she reveal'd.

A Marble Fane too in the house she had
Where lay her first Lords ashes, kept among
Her most adored Reliques, 'twas with sad
Darke Yew-tree, and the whitest fleeces hung.
Hence in the night she heard her husbands toung,
Call her, she thought. And oft the boading Owle
Alone on the house top harsh dirges sung,
And with long noates quavr'd a dolefull howle,
Besides old Prophesies, which terrifie her soule.

Cruell *Æneas* ev'n her sleepes torments:
And still shee dreames shees wandring all alone
Through a long way with steep and dark descents,
Calling her *Tyrians* in a Land, where none,
But some pain'd Ghost Eccho's her with a groane.
As when mad *Pentheus* troops of Furies fright,
Who sees a twofold *Thebes*, and double Sunne:

Or when *Orestes* flyes his Mothers sight,
Hunting His bloody track with Hel-hounds by torch-light.

Sunke then with griefe, possest with furyes, bent
On death, she plots the meanes, and in her Eye
A feign'd hope springing, hiding her intent
Accosts sad *Anne*. Partake thy sisters Joy,
I've found a way to make him burne as I,
Or turne me cold like him. Neere *Phoebus* set
At the lands end doth *Æthiopia* lye,
Where on great *Atlas* necke, the Heav'n thick set
With glorious Diamond-starres hangs like a Carkanet.

Of a great Sorceresse I have been told
There borne, who did th' *Hesperian* Temple keepe,
The Dragon fed, and sacred fruit of Gold
Watcht on the tree which she for dew did steepe
In Honey, and moyst Poppy causing sleepe.
Shee undertakes to cure the Love-sicke breast,
And whom shee list to plunge in Love as deepe,
The waters course in Rivers to arrest
And call down stars from Heav'n, and cal up ghosts from rest.

Under her tread thou shalt perceive Earth groane,
And Oakes skip from the hills, I sweare to thee
(Calling the Gods to Record, and thine owne
Sweet head) that forc't to these blacke Arts I flee.
Thou on some Tow'r a stack build secretly,
Lay on it the mans cloathes, and sword which lyes
Within, and, that which prov'd a grave to me,
My Wedding Bed. So doth the Witch advise,
Ev'n that I blot out all the traytors memories.

This said, grew pale. Yet thinkes not *Anne* that shee
With these new Rites her funerall doth shade,
Nor feares such Monsters, or worse extasie
Then at *Sycheus* death; Therefore obay'd
But *Dido*, a great Pile of wood being made

572 these] the *F*

The place with flow'rs and fatall Cypresse crown'd,
Thereon his cloaths and sword bequeathed layd,
His Picture on the Bed, the mistick ground
Knowne only to her selfe. Altars are placed round.

With haire dispread like a black falling storme,
Th' Inchantresse thunders out three hundred names,
Orchus, and *Chaos*, *Hecate*-triforme
Which Virgin *Dian's* triple-pow'r enseames,
She sprinkled too *Avernus* fabulous streames;
And hearbs were sought for, sprouting forth ripe Bane,
With brazen siccles, cropt in the Moones beames:
And puld from new borne Colt, that lumpe, which, ta'ne
From the Dammes mouth, no love t'her issue doth remain.

Her selfe in a loose vest, one foot unshod,
With meale in pious hands neer th'Altar drew,
Witnesse yee guilty starres and every God
(Saith she) I'm forc't to dye. Invokes them too
Who care of Lovers take (if any doe)
Unequally. 'Twas night, and conqu'ring sleepe,
With weari'd bodies the whole earth did strew;
When woods are quiet, and the cruell deep,
When stars are half way down, when fields stil silence keep.

And beasts and painted Birds, which liquid Springs
Inhabit, or which bushy Lands containe,
Nuzling their cares beneath sleepes downy wings,
Doe bury the past dayes forgotten paine;
All but the haplesse Queen, she doth refraine
From rest, nor takes it at her eyes or heart.
After long seeming dead, Love rose againe
And fought with wrath, as when two Tydes do thwart,
Whilst thus her big thoughts role and wallow to each part.

What shall I doe? shall I a suiter be
To my old suitors, scorned by the new,

585 Picture] pourtrait *F* 597 Altar] Altars *F* 613 wallow] tumble *F*

And wooe those Kings so oft despis'd by me?
What then? shall I the *Ilian* Fleet pursue,
And share all this mans fates? Yes, he doth shew
Such sense of my first aydes: Or say I wou'd,
Whom he hath mockt, will not his proud ships too
Reject? Ah foole, by whom the perjur'd brood
Of false *Laomedon* is not yet understood.

Grant they'd admit me, shall I flye alone
With Mariners? Or chace him with the power
Oth'emptyed Towne, and servants of mine owne,
And whom I scarce from *Tyre* by the roots up tore,
Compell to plough the horrid Seas once more?
No, dye as thou deservst, cure woes with woe.
Thou sister, first, when I my teares did showre
To quench these rising flames, thou didst them blow,
And out of cruell pity soldst me to the Foe.

Why might not I (alas) have mourn'd away
My widdow'd youth as well as Turtles doe?
Nor twice have made my selfe misfortunes prey,
Or to *Sicheus* ashes prov'd untrue?
These words with sighs out of her bosome flew.
Æneas slept aboord, all things prepard.
To whom againe *Joves* sonne with the same hiew
Divine, so silver-voyc'd, so golden hayr'd,
So straight and lovely shap't, thus rowsing him appear'd.

O Goddesse borne, now dost thou sleepe? nor know
How many dangers watch to compasse thee?
Nor heare this good wind whispering thee to goe?
Purpos'd to dye, great plots and dire broods she,
Who boyles with rage like a high going Sea.
Fly whilst thou mayst flye. If the morning finde
Thee napping here, the Sea will cover'd be
With Ships, the shoare with flames: Fly with the wind,
Trust that, but doe not trust a womans fickle mind.

621 Reject] Refuse *F*

This said, he mixt himselfe with night: But then
Æneas at these visions sore agast,
Starts out of sleepe, and cryes, up, up, O men,
Hoyse up your Sayles, flye to your Oares, row fast;
Behold a God from Heav'n again bids haste,
Cutting the wreath'd Cable. O, who ere
We follow thee, obey'd as late thou wast
Most gladly. Ayde what thou commandst, and steere
With prosp'rous stars bespoke as thou fly'st through their sphere.

This said, whipt out his Lightning Sword, and strooke
The fastning ropes. Like zeale his patterne bred
In all. They snatcht, they ran, the shoares forsook,
Their Sayles like wings over the waves were spread;
They comb'd with Oares gray *Neptunes* curled head.
And now *Aurora* scattered rosie light,
Upon the Earth from *Tythons* purple bed.
Whom *Dido*, having scouted all the night,
Discover'd from the Watch-Tow'r by her Ensignes white.

Seeing the Fleet sayle smoothly on, she knocks
Three or foure times her breast of Ivorie,
And tearing piteously her amber Locks;
O *Jove*, but shall he then be gone, said she,
And shall a stranger mock my Realme and me?
Shall not my pow'rs pursue him from the shoare,
And my tall Galleys man'd out instantly?
Arme, Arme, ye men of *Tyre*, bring fire-balls store,
Hoyse in a trice the sayles, tug stoutly at the Oare.

What talk I? or where am I? Doe I rave?
Poore *Dido*, now you see his heart; before
Could you not see it, when your Crowne you gave
To his dispose? Behold the faith he swore
Who sav'd his gods, and his old Father bore?
I'l strow him on the waves, his men first kill'd,
And spitted upon swords, and sawc't in gore,
Ascanius to him his last meale shall yeeld,
The Fathers yearning bowels with his bowels fill'd.

But this would be a doubtfull battaile. Bee't.
What should she feare whose wishes are to dye!
I will blow up the hatches burne the Fleet,
Sonne, Syre, and Nation in one Bon-fire frye,
And my selfe last to crowne the Tragedy.
O *Sol*, the Index of whose purging light,
Doth all the works of skilfull Nature try;
And *Juno* 'cause of this my wofull plight,
And *Proserpine*, cry'd through the Towns in dead of night.

And you revenging pow'rs, Gods which pertaine
To dying *Dido*; All of you incline
Your Deities to this my prayer; both deigne
Gently to heare, and lend me your divine
Assistance, due to such high wrongs as mine.
If one so clog'd with perjuries as he,
Must needs attaine the Port he doth designe,
And swim to shoare, because his Destiny
So wills, and such is *Joves* immutable Decree;

Yet vext b'a warlike people, forc't to flye,
Torne and divorc't from his deare sonnes imbrace,
Let him beg forraigne ayde, see his men dye
For crimes not theirs: And let him, when a peace
Shall be concluded by him with disgrace,
Enjoy nor Crown, nor life (then seeming good)
But be cut off in middle of his race,
And uninterr'd float on the restlesse Flood:
Thus pray I, these last words I powre out with my blood.

Then you, O *Tyrians*, breed your children in
Successive hate, so shall my wrong'd ghost rest;
Let Peace or Faith with these be held a sinne,
Some one of ours with fire and sword infest,
The proud *Æneiades* where ere they nest,
And through the world once more the straglers drive;
Now or hereafter, when your strength serves best;
Be shoares oppos'd to shoares, let our tydes strive
With theirs, and our late sons keep endless war alive.

699 to such high] unto such *F*

This said, she cast to flye dayes loathed beames,
And calls *Sichaeus* Nurse (her owne was dead.)
Good Nurse, goe bid my sister, dasht with streames,
Come straight, and bring the beasts I ordered
For Sacrifice: Doe thou too bind thy head
With holy Fillet, I will consummate
Rites well begun, to *Dis*, and fire the Bed
Where the mans Portraicts laid, t'annihilate
All care; so she did gallop at an old wives rate.

But *Dido*, fearing what she wisht, sad doome,
Rowling her blood-shot eyes, and in her face,
The palenesse of the death which was to come,
With trembling spots, rusht to that secret place,
And climbing the high Pile with furious pace,
The Dardan Sword, not therefore given, unsheath'd,
Spying the clothes and well-known bed, a space
She paws'd, till some few teares she had bequeath'd,
And leaning on that bed her latest speech she breath'd.

Sweet pledges, whilst the Fates and *Jove* so will'd,
Receive this soule, and free me from this woe,
I liv'd, and my good Fortunes circle filld;
And now my great Ghost to *Elizium* goe,
I built a famous City, saw it grow
To the perfection which it boasts this day;
Reveng'd my Husband on his brother-foe:
My too much happinesse had lackt allay,
If *Iliums* wandring Fleet had never past this way.

Then groveling on the bed, but shall I dye,
And not reveng'd? Yes, dye; what, so present
My selfe to *Dis*? Even so. Drink with thine eye
Fierce *Trojan* this flames Comet-like portent,
And let my death bode thee a dire event.
Here her Maids saw her with spread hands fall downe
Upon the reeking blade; A shrill cry went
To the high roofes, and through th' astonisht towne,
Swift as a Thunder-bolt the raging newes was blown.

748 had never] never had *F*

With sighs, laments, shriekes, and a female yell
Earth sounds, and Heavens high battlements resound,
As if, the foe let in, all *Carthage* fell,
Or mother walls of *Tyre* were brought to ground,
And Fanes and Houses one flame did confound.
Her frighted sister heares the balefull noyse;
She thumps her bosome, and with nayles doth wound
Her face, distracted through the prease she flyes,
And *Dido*, *Dido*, O my sister *Dido*, cryes.

Was *this* the businesse? wouldst thou cozen me?
Those fires, piles, Altars, hid they this beneath?
Skorndst thou in Fate thy sisters company?
I might have been invited to thy death,
One Sword, and one houre should have reft our breath.
Must I too build the Pile, and Heaven invoke
For this? Thy cruell hand extinguisheth
Thy selfe, and me, Senate and common folke,
And thy new-raised town, with one all-murth'ring stroke.

Teares bathe her wounds, suck her last breath my lips,
If any about hers yet hov'ring stayes.
This said, she passes the high stayres, and clips
Her halfe-dead sister, whom she fostring layes
To her warme breasts, and as the breath decayes,
Sighs new, the gore-blood with her garment dry'd.
Shee, striving her eyes heavy lids to raise,
Fainted againe, her wounds mouth gaping wide,
Vents by a neerer way her hearts groans through her side.

Thrice on her arme she did her body stay,
Thrice tumbled backward, and with rowling eyes
Groapt for, and sigh'd to finde, the glaring day.
Then *Juno* pitying her long Agonies,
And pangs of death, sent *Iris* from the skyes,
Her wrastling soule from twisting limbs t' untwine.
For since of age nor malady she dyes,
But by despaire nipt early, *Proserpine*
Had not yet cut her haire, and said, *This head is mine.*

So *Iris* her great Mistris will obeyes,
Descending to the Earth immediately
On curious wings, which the Suns oblique rayes
With water colours painted variously:
And standing right over her head (said she)
As I am bid, these vowed locks I beare
To Hells black Prince, and doe pronounce thee free
From bodies bonds. This said, cut off her hayre,
Heat left her, and th' uncaged Soule flew through the Ayre.

FINIS

A HAPPY LIFE
out of *Martiall*

The things that make a life to please
(Sweetest *Martiall*) they are these:
Estate *inherited*, not *got*:
A *thankfull* Field, *Hearth* alwayes hot:
City *seldome*, Law-suits *never*:
Equall Friends agreeing *ever*:
Health of *Body*, *Peace* of *Minde*:
Sleepes that till the Morning binde:
Wise Simplicitie, *Plaine* Fare:
Not *drunken* Nights, yet *loos'd* from *Care*:
A *Sober*, not a *sullen* Spouse:
Cleane strength, not such as *his* that Plowes:
Wish onely what thou *art*, to *bee*;
Death neither *wish*, nor *feare* to *see*.

On the Earle of *Straffords* Tryall

The Earle yet made a gallant stand, to be
Judg'd by *one* Kingdome, and *arraign'd* by *three*.
He might have fled at first, or made his skreene
A Royall Master, or a Gracious Queene;
But this had been the *Touch-stone* to decline,

T'ingage in Mortalls Quarrels, Powers Divine.
As artlesse Poets *Jove* or *Juno* use,
To play the Mid-wife to their labouring Muse.
No he affects a labour'd Scene, and not
To *cut*, but to *untye* the Gordian knot.
Then if 'twill prove no *Comedy*, at least
To make it of all *Tragedies* the best.
And that hee'l doe, I know not what past fact,
May speake him lesse, but for his lifes *last act*,
Times shall admiring read it, and *this age*,
Though now it *hisse*, *claps* when he leaves the Stage;
So *stand* or *fall*, none *stood* so, or so *fell*;
This farre-fam'd *Tryall* hath no paralell.
But if 'ith *Senate*, *Caesar* had been *try'd*,
As he was *stab'd*, whilst with their hands fast ty'd,
The Armies had lookt on, and left *the Cause*
Of *Rome* to *Tully* onely, and the *Lawes*,
Thus had great *Julius* spoke, and lookt; distill'd
Pharsalia, *Munda Thapsus* hard-fought Field
All into Speeches; and free *Cato* mov'd,
(Though he could never feare) yet then t'have *lov'd*,
And *pittyed* him: For mixt of *Peace* and *Warre*,
He was a *Souldier* and an *Oratour*.
A *Caesar*? or a *Strafford*? *Hee* resolv'd,
T'abide no *tryall*: *This*, to be *absolv'd*,
Or *dye*: Herein more like to *Otho* farre,
Who gave his blood to quench a *Civil Warre*.
Nor shall he dye, unlesse these broyles t'asswage
A yet *more Civill Warre* himselfe shall wage,
Turne (what hee usd so well for his defence)
Against *himselfe*, his conquering *Eloquence*.
Spend his whole stock of favour too, to bring
To the *Three Kingdomes a fourth* Power, *the King*:
A *Fourth Estate* adde to the *Parliament*:
And to the *Royall* give his *owne assent*.
So fell great *Rome* her selfe, opprest at length
By the united *Worlds*, and her *owne* strength.

The Earles pathetical Letter to the King, which is to be seene in print, wherein hee begges of his Majesty, to passe the Bill for his death, to quiet the Kingdomes.

Two Odes out of *Horace*, relating unto the Civill Warres of *Rome*

Against covetous rich men, Carm.lib.3. Ode 24

Though richer then unpoll'd
Arabian wealth, and Indian Gold,
Thou with thy workes shouldst drayne
The *Tyrrhene* and whole Ponticke Mayne;
Thou couldst not, when death layes
On *thee* his Adamantine Mace,
Thy *Minde* from *terrour* free,
Nor *Body* from *Mortality.*
Wiser the *Scythians*,
Whose Houses run on wheeles like Waynes;
And frozen Getes, whose field
Unbounded doth free *Ceres* yeeld:
Nor is't the custome there,
To sow a Land above a yeare;
And when that Crop is borne,
The rest releive it each by turne.
There Women mingle not,
For Sonne-in-Lawes a poyson'd pot;
Nor *Governe*: on their Dow'r
Presuming, or Adultrers pow'r.
Their Dow'rs *To be well bred*:
And *Chastity* flying the bed
Of others, their owne trust
Perswading, and the price of Lust.
Oh! he that would asswage
Our blood-shed and intestine rage:
If he would written have,
His Countries Father on his Grave;
Let him not feare t'oppose
Unbridled Licence to the Nose:
So shall he gaine great praise
In after times; since (wo the dayes!)
Wee envy living worth,
But misse it when 'tis laid in Earth;

For what doe our Lawes stand,
  If punishment weed not the Land?
What serves vaine Preaching for,
  Which cannot cure our lives? If nor
Those Lands which flames imbrace;
  Nor where the Neighb'ring *Boreas*,
Shuts up the Ports with cold,
  And snows fast nayl'd to the free-hold,
The Mariner repell?
  If crafty Merchants learne to quell
The horridst Seas? the feare
  Of that crime (*Want*) making them beare,
And doe all things, and balke
  Severer vertues narrow walke.
Would Heaven wee'd carry all
  Our wealth into the Capitall!
O in the next sea duck
  Our Jewels and pernicious muck,
Fewell of all that's naught!
  If we repent us as we ought,
Strike at the root of ills;
  And mould wee our too plyant wills
To rougher Arts: the Child
  Of Noble Linage cannot wield
A bounding Horse of Warre,
  Nay feares to him more skill'd by farre,
To stride off the Greeke bowle,
  Or the forbidden Dice to trowle,
The whilst his perjur'd Father
  Deceives his Partners trust, to gather
For one that hath no wit.
  So ill got wealth growes fast, and yet
Something still short doth come,
  To make it up *An even Summe*.

To the People of *Rome, Epod.* 16

Commiserating the Common-Wealth, in respect of the Civill Warres

Now Civill Warres a second Age consume,
  And Romes owne Sword destroyes poore *Rome.*
What neither neighbouring *Marsians* could devoure,
  Nor fear'd *Porsenas* Thuscan Pow'r;
Nor *Capua's* Rivall Valour, Mutinies
  Of *Bond-slaves*, Trechery of *Allyes*;
Nor *Germany* (blew-ey'd Bellona's Nurse)
  Nor *Hanniball* (the Mothers curse)
Wee (a blood-thirsty age) our selves deface,
  And Wolves shall repossesse this place.
The barb'rous Foe will trample on our dead,
  The steele-shod Horse our Courts will tread;
And *Romulus* dust (clos'd in religious Urne
  From Sunne and tempest) proudly spurne.
All, or the sounder part, perchance would know,
  How to avoid this *comming blow.*
'Twere best I thinke (like to the *Phoceans*,
  Who left their execrated Lands,
And Houses, and the Houses of their Gods,
  To Wolves and Beares for their abodes;)
T'abandon all, and goe where our *feet*
  Beare us by *Land*, by *Sea* our *Fleet.*
Can any man better advice affoord?
  If not, in name of Heav'n *Aboard*!
But you must sweare first to returne againe,
  When loosned Rockes float on the Maine,
And be content to see your Mother-Towne,
  When *Betis* washes the Alpes crowne;
Or *Appennine* into the Ocean flyes,
  Or new Lust weds Antipathies,
Making the Hynde stoop to the Tygers love,
  The ravenous Kite Cuckold the Dove;
And credulous Heards, t'affect the Lyons side,
  And Goats the salt Sea to abide.

This, and what else may stop our wisht returne,
  When all, or the good part have sworne,
Fly hence! Let *him* whose smooth and unfledg'd breast
  Misgives him, keep the rifled neast.
You that are men, unmanly griefe give o're,
  And sayle along the Thuscan shore,
To the wide Ocean. Let us seeke those Isles
  Which swim in plenty, the blest soyles:
Where the Earths Virgin-wombe plow'd is fruitfull,
  And the unproyned *Vine* still youthfull:
The *Olive Tree* makes no abortion there,
  And *Figges* hang dangling in the Aire;
Honey distills from Oakes, and *Water* hops
  With creaking feet from Mountaine tops.
The gen'rous Goats without the *Milk-maids* call,
  Of their full bags are prodigall;
No Evening Wolfe with hoarse Alarms wakes
  The Flocks; Nor breeds the up-land Snakes.
And farther (to invite us) the plump Graine,
  Is neither drunke with too much raine,
Nor yet for want of mod'rate watring dry:
  Such the blest *temper* of the Sky.
Never did *Jason* to those Ilands guide
  His Pirat-ship, and whorish Bride.
Sydonian *Cadmus* never toucht these shoares,
  Nor false *Ulysses* weary Oares.
No murraine rots the *Sheep*, no starre doth scorch
  The *Cattell* with his burning Torch.
When *Jove* with brasse the Golden-Age infected,
  These Iles he for the pure extracted.
Now Iron raignes, I like a statue stand,
  To point *Good Men* to a *Good Land*.

A Summary Discourse of the Civill Warres of *Rome*, extracted out of the best Latine writers in Prose and Verse.

To the Prince His Highnesse, upon occasion of the preceding Odes.

Most Excellent Prince,

When, by the subversion of *Carthage*, *Rome* had lost her two spurres, *Emulation* and *Feare*, she sunke presently in her vertue, I mean all her vertues, except her Fortitude; there was but too much of that left still to doe her selfe mischiefe withall: Yet, upon no unreasonable presumption that this also might languish with her much ease, and dissolving her self in pleasures, an *insurrection* there was in the neighboring Province of *Spain*; but this *abroad*, though manag'd with so contrary fortune to the *Romans*, that two of her Generals, one after another, were forced to condiscend to most dishonourable *Pacifications*, would have done her little hurt, had it not been the accidentall occasion of those Factions and Divisions *at home* that were not so easily extinguished, as either the *Fire-brand* that kindled them (*Ti Gracchus* the Tribune) by *Scipio Nasica*, or as the occasion it selfe (the potent City of *Numancia*) was by that other *Scipio*, who had done as much before to *Carthage*, of which unhappy *Divisions*, thus *Paterculus*. T. Gracchus.

Hoc initium in urbe Roma civilis sanguinis, gladiorumque impunitatis fuit, etc. Paterc. Franc. impres. p. 18.

This was the beginning of Civill Warre, and impunity of Swords in the City of Rome, *thenceforth Might overcame Right, and the most powerfull was held the best man*; *and the discords of the Citizens, used to be healed by* Accommodations, *were decided by the* Sword; *and Warres were entred into, not for the* Cause; *but according to* the Pay: *which is not to be wondred at, for examples doe not stop where they began, but though they* get in *at a* little cranny, *make themselves a* wide breach *to* come out *at. And when once* the Rule *is forsaken, we run amaine downe the hill, nor doth any man thinke that* dishonest *in* him, *which hath been* profitable *to* another.

In pursuance of this fury, about ten years after, *Caius Gracchus* stept into *action* (as the *Irish* call it) to play the second part of his *Brother*, *equall* in *vertues*, *equall* in *errour*, *equall* in *punishment*, in *wit* and *eloquence* far *superiour*; of both which brothers it is said, that if any moderate things could have contented them, they might have had those *Honours cast upon them* in a *quiet State*, which they *fisht for* in a *troubled*. The next that came upon the Stage *from contrary doores*, were *Cynna* and *Marius*, these were rough Gamesters (it was now growne past the power of the Pulpit (though from thence the first fire was flung abroad) to doe either good or harme in the matter) originally they had beene of *opposite Factions*, but being *expelled* the City for *severall causes*, they united their Forces to *enter* it (as they did immediately one after the other) upon a *joynt designe*, to feast there at once their *spleen* and *avarice*, the latter of which was by them then made *the vice of the times*.

C. Gracchus.

Cynna and *Marius*.

Omnia erant praecipitia in repub. nec tamen adhuc quisquam inveniebatur, etc. Pat. p. 32.

All things were in extreme in the Common-wealth, neither yet was any man found, that either durst give, *or had the face to* aske *the goods of a Roman Citizen*; *afterwards that also was added, that* Covetousnesse *should minister fuell to* Cruelty, *and that the proportion of mens* offences *should rise to proportion of their* money, *so that whosoever was* rich, *should consequently be guilty, and every one become the price of his owne danger, nor any thing seeme dishonest that was gainfull.*

By this meanes *the Game* play'd it selfe alone into the hands of *Sylla*, who having begun *a Set* with *Marius* some yeares before, and left it off when he had much the better of it, to prosecute a forreigne warre in *Asia*, and having been never to be withdrawne from that, to play out his first Game, and mingle in the *Civill broyles*, until hee had happily finished the *Forreigne Warre*, found the hearts of men thereby, (whether as an argument of the *goodnesse* or of the *greatnesse* of his mind) wonderfully prepared to receive him, whom they now looke upon:

Sylla.

Non ut Belli vindicem, sed Pacis Autorem: Not as a *part of the Warre*, but as an *Author of Peace*. Pat. p. 34.

Which opinion of him, his quiet March, with a singular care of the Fruits, Corne, Men and Cities, and his endeavour to *compose* things by *just Lawes* and *equall conditions*, looking with *one eye* upon *the Nobility*, and with *the other eye* upon the Commonalty, did exceedingly confirme:

Being himselfe a *Nobleman*, and the favorite of the *Common-people*. *Ibid.*

Crescebat interim indies Sullae excercitus,

Confluentibus ad eum optimo quoque et sanissimo.

By which meanes the Army of Sylla increased daily, through the confluence of the best and soundest-hearted men unto him.

But *He*, who was never *unhappy* till he assumed the sirname of *Happy*, that is, till he had overcome:

Ex successu animum sumens, Pat. p. 28.

(*Changing his mind upon successe.*)

Began to exercise those execrable *cruelties* and *oppressions* which are not to be paralell'd in any story either before or since that time for the greatnes and generality of them; his new invented horrour of *proscriptions*, not distinguishing betwixt *turbulent* and *quiet* spirits, nor scarcely betwixt *friend* and *enemy*; which if he could have forborne, and *managed* his unlimited power with the same Arts of *Moderation* by which he *got* it, he might have both *kept* it to himselfe, and also have *cut off* a long taile of mischiefs that were to come on his Country.

Videbantur finita Belli civilis mala, cum Sullae crudelitate aucta sunt. Pat. p. 35.

The mischiefes of Civill Warre seem'd ended, when by the cruelty of Sylla *they were* increased.

If your Highnesse demand the issue; this was *too hot to hold*: his power *burnt his fingers*, and hee was glad of himselfe to let it goe, finding it more safe to live a *private man*, and disarm'd amongst those very men whom he had so highly provoked (obliging them now with that voluntary Resignation of his exorbitant power) than with it to goe on still hated and feared in the midst of his Legions.

For brevity sake, I skip over that which they called *Bellum Italicum*, as an externall *Association*; that of the Bond-slaves, as *a Mutiny*; and that of *Cataline*, as a *Conspiracie*; rather than properly *Civill warres*: and come to what is of a piece with the former.

Amongst the *proscribed* of *Sylla* was *Julius Caesar*, then very young, who escaped that *Inquisition* to act afterwards the longest and greatest part in the *Tragedy* of these *civill Wars* against *Pompey* and his *sonnes*. The *Father* and *hee* were *at daggers drawing* long before they came to *blowes*; for not withstanding that there was *ambition* enough *in the best of them* to have ingaged them sooner: *the one not enduring an equall, nor the other a superiour*; yet *the worst of them* had *love* and *piety* enough *to his countrey*, and *good nature* enough to his *Ally*, at least whilst the Bond lasted (they were *Father* and *Son-in-law*) to come unwillingly to that work: To which may be added, that though *both* were enough *conscious*, and *confident* too enough, of their owne *valour* and *conduct*, yet *neither* of them found any thing to despise in his *Adversary*: But, Caesar and Pompey.

Cum justissimus quisquis et a Caesare et a Pompeio vellet dimitti exercitus: Pat. p. 52

When every good man would have had both Caesar and Pompey to have disbanded their Armies.

C. Curio tribunus pl. subiecit facem, vir, etc. Ibid. *Curio.*

C. Curio a Tribune of the people gave fire, a man, etc. Describing a third *Gracchus*. *Ad ultimum saluberrimas et coalescentis conditiones pacis, quas et Caesar iustissimo animo postulabat, et Pompeius aequo recipiebat, discussit, ac rupit unice cavente Cicerone concordiae publicae*. Ibid.

In fine, those most wholesome and healing Conditions of Peace, which both Caesar justly demanded, *and* Pompey *as* fairely entertained, *this* Curio *shooke in pieces, and broke off, not a man, but* Cicero *labouring for* Peace.

The conclusion of this War is sufficiently known, having crown'd *Ceasar* with that absolute Victory, which *hee* using with a clemencie and moderation, that *Sylla* could not light on, made *Rome* for a time very happy, and the name of *Ceasar* to this day an *Imperiall Title*; although it is true that he miscarried in *his owne person*, by the conspiracie of a few men, some out of a *good* intention, and some out of a *bad*, when the *people* in generall were now at the last infinitely satisfied with his Government, which opened the sluces to a new *civill Warre*. This was the Conjuncture in which *Horace* (living in that Age) thought it high time for him and all that Hor. Carm. lib. 1. Ode 14. To the Common-wealth renewing the Civill-Warre.

lov'd their Countrey, to cry, *Fire, fire*, and bring every one his Bucket to quench it.

(1) *What againe to Sea*, (quoth he in his allegoricall allusion, to a Shippe newly escaped from wrack?) (2) *what a Gods name dost thou mean?* (art thou mad?) (3) *Hug thy port*, (make much of the peace thou enjoyest) (4) *Dost not thou see how thy Oarmen are washt from the Decks* (the number of thy Souldiers impaired?) (5) *thy Main-mast spent* (Great *Pompey* slaine?) (6) *Thy Top-saile shot down*, (*Ceasar* himselfe stab'd) (7) *and that without ropes* (without Money, the nerves of Warre) *Thou canst not possibly live in so high a sea?* with more to the same purpose: And wilt thou that art a *Merchant-man*, drawing unto *thee* alone the Trade and wealth of the whole world, turn *Man of Warre* againe, to rob upon thy *owne coast?* (8) *Be not, be not over-confident of the thicknesse of thy sides* (thy walls or frontiers) *to beare out all stormes*. (9) *If thou hast not a longing to be made a Tennis-ball to the winds* (if thou hast not a mind neighboring Nations should laught at thee, if the Devill do not owe thee a shame) *take heed*, (10) *take heed how thou embayest*: But all this will not serve the turne, *Embayed* they are, and *embarqu'd* in a *New civill Warre*: *Brutus* and *Cassius* against *Octavius* and *Anthony*; which makes the Poet now *despaire of the fortune of the Common-wealth* to that degree, as to think of nothing but going to a *Plantation* in the second of the fore-going Odes; for why?

Rusticus expectat dum defluat amnis, at ille,
Labitur et Labetur in omne volubilis aevum.

It was his own description of *a fool that stood gaping by a River side to see when the water would bee all run out*. And *he* having seen and read how many Ages these miserable warres had lasted (with some holy dayes betweene) and how many faire *opportunities* and *Overtures* which promised an end to their calamities, (especially this last) had proved ineffectuall, resolved he would not prove such another foole himselfe. Yet though this war went on, and being determined by the Battell at *Philippi*, another as dismall sprang out of the ashes of it, between the Victors themselves; this same despairing *Horace* did live to see, and particularly to enjoy, other very different *times*, when the Common-wealth, after the defeat of *Mark Anthony* at the Battell of *Actium, being now quite*

(1) *O navis referent in mare te novi fluctus.*
(2) *O quid agis*
(3) *Fortiter occupa Portum*
(4) *Nonne vides ut nudum remigiolatus?*
(5) *Et Malus celeri sauctus Africo.*
(6) *Antennaeq; gemant?*
(7) *Ac sine funibus vix durare Carinae possint imperiosius Æquor, etc.*
(8) *Quamvis Pontica pinus, etc.*
(9) *Tu nisi ventis debes Ludibrium, cave, etc.*
(10) *Interfusa nitentes vites aequora Cycladas.*
Brutus and *Cassius.*
Horat.
Anthony.

tired out with civill Warres, submitted her selfe to the just and peacefull Scepter of the most Noble Augustus.

Tacit. p. 1. Qui cuncta discordiis civilibus fessa nomine principis sub imperium accepit.

Hic vir, hic est, tibi quem promitti saepius audis,
Augustus Caesar, divum genus, aurea condet
Saecula, qui rursus Latio, regnata per arva
Saturno quondam, super et Garamantas et Indos
Proferet imperium; jacet extra sidera Tellus,
Extra anni, solisque vias, ubi Coelifer Atlas
Axem humero torquet stellis ardentibus aptum.
Hujus in adventum jam nunc et Caspia Regna
Responsis horrent divum, et Maeotica tellus,
Et septem-Gemini turbant trepida ostia Nili.
Nec vero Alcides tantum telluris obivit,
Fixerit Eripidem cervam licet, aut Erymanthi
Placarit nemora, et Lernam tremeseceret arcu:
Nec qui Pampineis Victor juga flectit habenis,
Liber agens celso Nysae de vertice Tigres.

Augustus Virg. Æneid. lib. 6. in the person of *Anchises* Ghost, shewing *Æneas* his future progeny.

This is that man of men Augustus, hee
Whom (sprung from Heaven) Heaven oft hath promis'd thee,
That man that shall to Italy *restore*
The Golden Age *which* Saturne *gave before,*
And to the Parthians *and the* Ind's *extend*
His spacious Empire. At the Worlds fag-end,
Beyond the Ocean, and the starres beyond,
Out of the Starres and the Sunnes way, a Land
Doth lye, where Heav'n on Atlas *necke, thick set*
With Diamond starres, hangs like a Carkanet:
For feare of Him *the* Caspian fanes *resound*
With horrid Oracles; the Pharian Ground,
And seven-fold Nile *now hides his frighted head,*
Nor Hercules *so many strands did tread,*
Although the Erymanthian Boare he slew,
The brasse-hoov'd-Stagge, and Lerna's *Monster too;*
Nor Bacchus, *who discending* Nysa *checks,*
With Vine-leafe-reynes triumphing Tigers necks.

I must confesse *Sir*, I am now where I would be, and from whence I would not bee removed a great while, but for troubling Your Highnesse with unmannerly length; for this *Mirrour of Princes* I have above all others ever admired, not for his great *Victories* at home or abroad (these in themselves had been but *splendid Robberies*) but for *this*, that he directed all his *studies* and *actions* to *use*, and not to *ostentation* and *glory*; nor to his *own* use, but to the use and benefit of *Mankind*, whom it was more his Ambition to *civilize* and *make happy*, than to *subject* them to his Authority. Hence it was, that when he could have been easily *the Prince of Roman Eloquence*, he affected a *Plaine style*, both in speaking and writing, *and such as became a Prince. Hence*, that when he could have reach't the top of *Military Glory*, yet contenting himself with so much *Souldiery* as was sufficient to assert his succession to the Empire against *his Fathers Conspirators*, and to tye the hands of a *potent Mad people*, from doing farther mischief to themselves (for most of his forreign conquests he made by his Lieutenants) he chose to be *inferiour to Julius onely* in *Martiall Arts*, that *hee onely* might be *Superiour to Julius* in *Civill*. And *hence* it was, that he was heard often to deride the pride and folly of *Alexander the Great*, for enquiring after other worlds to conquer, and such like expressions; as if it were not more honour and content to a truly great minde to *governe one*, or a little part of one well, and to the felicity and content of the Subject; than to *subdue a hundred*. How dexterously and successfully *hee* for his particular acted this part, having beene but toucht upon in one word by *Virgill*, I must borrow Prose to explaine:

Nihil deinde optare a diis homines nihil, etc.

Thenceforth there was nothing that men could desire from the Gods, nothing that the Gods can bestow upon men; *nothing that can be conceived by our wishes, nothing that can be consummated with happinesse*; *which* Augustus (after his returne to the City) *did not bring to the People of* Rome, *and to the whole world. In the twenty yeare the Civill Warres were ended, forreigne buried, the fury of Armes every where laid asleepe*; *force restored to the Lawes, Authority to the Judges, Majesty to the Senate*; *the power of the Magistrate reduced to the former channell* (*onely to the Eight Pretors, two more added*) *the old and ancient forme of Government recalled*; *Culture returned to the Fields, Honour to things and persons sacred, security to mens*

Pat. p. 79. The publike happinesse under *Augustus*.

persons, to every one a certaine possession of his Estate, Lawes profitably amended, wholesomely made; Election of Senators without rigidnesse, not without gravity; Persons of quality, and such as had beene honoured with Triumphs, and gone through eminent Commands, by the Prince himselfe were invited to be Ornaments to the City.

When I reflect upon all these things, methinkes that Character which the same *Virgil* bestowes a little after upon the *Roman Nation* in generall, would have better *fitted*, and perchance also better *pleased Augustus*, then the former, as most insisting upon that excellency whereupon he valued himselfe *most*.

Excudent alii spirantia Mollius Æra, Vir. Æne.
Credo equidem: Vivos ducent de Marmore vultus, lib. 6.
Orabunt causas melius, caelique meatus
Describent radio, et surgentia sidera dicent.
Tu regere imperio populos, Romane, memento,
(Haec tibi erunt artes) pacique imponere morem,
Parcere subjectis, et debellare superbos.

Which I paraphrase to your Highnesse thus:

Others may breathing Mettals softer grave,
Plead Causes better, and poore Clients save
From their oppressours: with an Instrument
They may mete out the spacious Firmament,
And count the rising starres with greater skill,
Reyne the proud Steed, and breake him of his will.
Better their Sword, *and better use their Pen.*
Breton remember thou to governe men,
(Be this thy trade) And to establish Peace,
To spare the humble, and the proud depresse.

The Prince of Peace protect Your Highnesse most excellent life.

FINIS

Presented
TO HIS HIGHNESSE THE PRINCE OF WALES,
At his going into the West, *Anno* M.DC.XLV.
Together with *CESAR*'S COMMENTARIES

Sir,
Now that your Father, with the World's applause
Imployes your early Valour in his Cause,
Set *Cesar's* glorious Acts before your sight,
And know the man that could so *doe* and *write.*
View him in all his postures, see him mix
Terrour with *love*, *Morals* with *Politicks.*
That courage, which when fortune ebb'd did flow,
Which never trampled on a prostrate Foe,
Admire and emulate. Before hee fought,
Observe how *Peace* by him was ever sought:
How bloodlesse Victories best pleas'd him still,
Grieving as oft as he was forc'd to kill,
How most religiously he kept his word,
And conquer'd more that way then by the sword.
In whom was all wee in a King could crave,
Except that *Right* which you shall one day have.
Yet think (Sir) it imports you to make good
With all his worth the title of your blood.

Presented
TO HIS HIGHNESSE,
In the West, Ann. Dom. 1646

Grow *Royall Plant*, born for your Country's good,
The hoped cure of our great flux of blood.
That *Union*, and that peacefull *golden Age*,

Which to your Grandsire ancient *Bards* presage,
And we suppos'd fulfill'd in Him, appears
By Fate reserved for your riper yeers.
And *Thou*, self-hurt since that *half-Union* more
Then ever, *Britain*, thou hadst been before,
Raise thy dejected head, bind up thy hair
With peacefull Olive, all those things repair
Which fire and sword deface, and call agen
To their spoyl'd mansions thy fled Husbandmen.
They need not fear to come, this *Prince's* Starrs
Promise an end to all our *Civill Warrs*.
Never shall *English Scots*, nor *Scots* again
Infest the *English* with dire feuds, and stain
Their swords in brothers blood, thy Towns lay waste:
But their hands (prompt to War) henceforth make haste
To clasp in an eternall League. And *You*
(Blest Parents of a blessed Son) add to
His great *Birth* equall *Breeding*; *Civill Arts*
To *Arts of Warre*, and *Pietie* to *Parts*.
No Ship the Rudder so much turns and windes
As *Princes* manners do their *Peoples* mindes.
Not *Prisons*, *penall Lawes*, sharp *Whips*, severe
Axes, with all the instruments of fear
Can so constrain, as the dumb eloquence
Of *Vertue*; and the love and reverence
Of a well-govern'd Scepter shall perswade
Their wils, by *great Examples* eas'ly sway'd.
As when th' Arabian *Phoenix* doth return
From his perfumed cradle (his Sires Urn)
Where e're he flyes the feather'd people throng
With acclamations to salute the young
Admired King, not for his purple Seares
And golden Pounce (the *Regall marks* hee bears),
Nor that he's rarely seen; but 'cause he brings
His Fathers honour'd ashes on his wings,
And funerall odours, that it may be known
He climb'd not till his death his spicie throne:
(This *Pietie*, a Vertue understood
By brutes, attracts them: such a sense of good
Nature that heav'nly Steward doth dispense

Buchanan in his *Genethliacon* to King *James*, out of which this is taken.

To every living thing that hath but sense)
So do *the People* fix their eyes upon
The King; admire, love, honour *Him* alone.
In *Him*, as in a glasse, their manners view
And frame, and copie what they see *Him* doe.
That which the murdring *Cannon* cannot force,
Nor plumed Squadrons of steel-glittering *Horse*,
Love can. In this *the People* strive t'out-doe
The King; and when they find they're lov'd, love too.
They serve, because they need not serve: and if
A good *Prince* slack the reins, they make them stiffe;
And of their own accords invite that yoke,
Which, if inforc't on them, they would have broke.
And *Hee* again, with this more tender grown,
More *Father of his People*, on his *owne*
Shoulders assumes *their burthens*, beats the way
Which they must tread, and is the first t'*obey*
What he *commands*; to pardon *others* prone,
Inexorable to *himself* alone.
Neither in Diet, Clothes, nor Train will *He*
Exceed those banks should bound ev'n *Majesty*;
Nor rush like beasts to Venus, but confine
His chast desires to his own geniall *Vine*.
Who will with Silks his manly limbs un-nerve,
That sees domestick *Wooll* his *Soveraign* serve?
Who can the married bed too narrow think,
Which holds *a King*? Or drown himself in drink
Under a sober *Prince*? Who'l dare t' import
Beyond-sea vices to infect a Court,
And make his body with excesse and ease
A sink to choak his soul in, when he sees
A Monarch curb his pleasures, and suppresse
Those weeds which make a *Man* a *Wildernesse*.
Such golden *Tiber* saw the peacefull *Throne*
Of holy *Numa*, that of *Solomon*
Palmie *Euphrates*. 'Twas not the keen *blade*,
Or the thick quilted numerous *Legion* made
Those *Thrones* secure: 'Twas not the warlike *Steed*,
Nor the sythe-armed *Chariots* furious speed:
But *Wisdome*, *Mercy*, (which no harm will cause)

And *Majestie*, fenc'd with *unarmed Lawes*.
Whilest that great *Captain*, who the *World* had quell'd,
And those proud *Lords* that *Rome* in *bondage* held,
By *steel* or *poyson* ended their short date
Of pow'r, and blood with blood did expiate.
Frank *Nature* never gave a better thing,
Nor ever will to men, then a good *King*;
In whom his own true Image *God* doth place.
This, whether *Kings* shall in themselves *deface*
By ougly *Vice*, or other men by *wit*
Or *force demolish*, *God will punish it*
As a high Sacriledge, and will not see
Himself abused *in Effigie*.
So cruell *Nero*, fierce *Domitian* so,
And the *Sicilian Tirants*, whilst they throw
Dirt in their *Makers* face with their black deeds,
Are from the earth cut off, they and their seeds.
So those *rebellious servants* that durst joyn
Against their *Lords*, and impious *Cataline*
That strove to wrest the sword from *them* to whom
It was committed *by the Lawes of Rome*,
Pursu'd to fury and despair, did make
Hard shift by a most wretched death to shake
Their loathed lives off, leaving on their name
The blot and brand of never-dying shame.
These *lessons* let his tender yeers *receive*;
His riper, *practise*: And let him believe,
'Tis not so much both Indies to command,
As first to rule *himself*, and then *a Land*.

Selected Parts of Horace, *1652*

Selected Parts
OF
HORACE,
Prince of LYRICKS;

AND

Of all the Latin Poets the fullest fraught
with Excellent MORALITY.
Concluding
With a Piece out of AUSONIUS,
And another out of VIRGIL.
Now newly put into English.

Dux Vitae Ratio.

LONDON

Printed for *M.M., Gabriel Bedell, and T. Collins*,
and are to be sold at their shop at the *Middle-Temple-Gate*, 1652.

I, 1

That severall Men affect severall Things; That Himself is delighted with the Study of Lyrick *Verses*

Maecenas Thuscan Kings descent,
My Bulwark and sweet Ornament.
There are, that love their Charets spoak
With raisd *Olympick* dust should smoak:
And with hot Wheels the Goale close shaven,
And noble Palm, lifts Men to Heaven.
One, if the fickle Peoples blast
Redoubled Honors on him cast:
Another that delights to teare
With Plough Fields that his Fathers were;
If in His private Barnes He store
Whatever fruitfull Affrick bore;
The wealth of *Croesus* cannot gain
With trembling Keele to plough the Main.
Frighted with rough Icarian Seas,
The Merchant praises Home, and Ease:
But His bruis'd Vessel repairs straight,
Impatient of a mean Estate.
There is that neither scorns to taste
Old *Massique*, nor half days to waste
Under a Shady Poplar spread,
Or at a Bubling Fountains Head.
Some Drums and Trumpets Love, and War;
Which Mothers do as much abhor.

1–9] *Maecenas*, borne of Kings, my grace / And Columne; some affecte the Race, / Half choakt with dust Olympick; who / If with hot wheeles the Goale th'eschew, / And gaine the Palme, there is no odds / 'Twixt them, and the Immortall Gods. / One, if the windie People's blast, / Redoubled honours on him cast; / Another loving to manure *F*: Maecenas borne of Kings descent, / My pillar and sweet ornament: / There are that doe delight to rust / Their Chariots with Olympick dust: / Where the wisht Goale's as fast eschew'd / By the hott wheeles, as erst pursew'd, / And the victorious Palme conveys / To mortall men Immortall prayse. / One, if the windy People's blast / Doth treble honours on him cast: / Another that delights to plough *A*   10 Fields that] the fields his (altered in MS in Beinecke copy)   10–14] His fields, if on his threshing floore / A fuller Harvest he behold, / Then *Africk* beares, with all the gold / O'th'*Indies* cannot tempted be, / With brittle Barke to plough the sea *F*: His Fathers Land, but 'tis his now, / If in his private Barnes hee store / Whatever fruitfull Africk boare: / Not Priam's riches cann buy theise / With fearefull Ship to plow the Seas *A*

The Huntsman in the cold doth rome,
Forgetting his poor Wife at home,
Whether his Hounds a Stagg have Rowz'd,
Or Marsian Boar his Nets hath towz'd.
Mee Ivy (Meed of learned Heads)
Ranks with the Gods: Mee chill Groves, Treads
Of Satyrs with loose Nymphs, have show'd
A way out of the common Road;
Whilst kind *Euterpe* wets my Flute,
Whilst *Polyhymnie* strings my Lute;
Then write Mee in the Lyrick Role,
My lofty Head shall knock the Pole.

I, 2
To AUGUSTUS CAESAR

That all the Gods are angry with the *Romans* for the killing of *Julius Caesar*: That the only hope of the Empire is placed in *Augustus*

Enough of Hail and cruel Snow
Hath Jove now showr'd on Us below;

15–29] The Marchant compast with rough seas, / Tremb'ling commends his home, and ease / Yet his bruis'd ships repaires he strayte, / Impatient of a meane estate. / Some love to quaffe, and weare away / The relicks of a wearie day, / By a broad-shadie Beech-tree spread, / Or sacred Fountaine's bubling head. / Some Drummes and Trumpetts love and warre, / Which orphand mothers doe abhorre. / The Huntsman in the cold doth rome, / Forgetting his soft wife at home, / If his sure Hounds have rowzd a deere, / Or a wild Boare his Trammels feere. / Me Ivie, which the Poet loves, *F*: The Marchant 'frayd of Boreas' braves, / Wrast'linge with th' Icarian waves, / Commends the imbraces of a wife, / And quiett of a Country life. / But then repayres his shipping straight, / Impatient of a meane estate. / Some love to quaff, and weare away / The Relicks of a wearie day / Under a shady Poplar spredd, / Or at a sacred Fountain's head. / Some Drums and Trumpetts love, and Warr / Which tender Mothers doe abhorr. / The Huntsman in the cold doth rome, / Forgettinge his poore wife at home; / Whether his hounds a stagg have rows'd / Or Marsian Boare his netts hath tows'd. / Mee learned Ivy, Poets' Crowne *A* 30–6] Places in heaven; me shadie Groves / And Satyrs, with quick Nymphes advancing, / Withdraw from Townes, to view their dancing. / Whilst blithe *Euterpe* takes her flute, / And *Polyhymne* jerkes her Lute. / Then 'mongst the *Lyricks* ranke me thou, / I'le touch the Starres with my high brow *F*: Doth equall with the Gods renowne; / Mee, gloomy Woods, and Nymphs that dance / With Satyres, 'bove the Rout advance. / Because *Uterpe* lends her Flute, / And Polyhymny tunes my Lute. / Then putt mee in the Lyrick Rolle, / My lofty head shall knock the Pole *A*

1–3] Enough has Jove of cruell storme / Now sent; and with his flashing arme / Threatning to thunder steeples downe *F*, *A*

Enough with Thundring Steeples down
Frighted the Town.
Frighted the World, lest Pyrrha's Raign
Which of new Monsters did complain,
Should come again, when Proteus Flocks
Did climbe the Rocks;
And Fish in tops of Elm-Trees hung,
Where Birds wont build their Nests, and sung,
And the all-covering Sea did bear
The trembling Dear.
Wee, Yellow Tiber did behold
Back from the Tyrrhene Ocean rowl'd,
Against the Fane of Vesta powre,
And Numa's Towre;
Whilst the Uxurious River swears
Hee'l be reveng'd for Ilia's Tears;
And over both his Banks doth rove
Unbid of Jove.
Our Children through our faults but few,
Shall hear that We their Fathers slew
Our Countrymen: Who might as well
The Persians quell.
What God shall we invoke to stay
The falling Empire? with what Lay
Shall holy Nuns tire Vesta's Pray'r-
Resisting Ear?
To whom will Jove the charge commend
Of Purging us? At length descend
Prophetick Phoebus, whose white Neck
A Cloud doth deck.
Or Venus in whose smiling Rayes

5 Raign] tyde *A* 6] That turned the Creatures the wronge side *A* 7 Should come] Returne *F, A* 9–10] And Elmes the scalie fish did catch, / Where feathered fowle were wont to hatch *F*: And scaly fish the Elmes possest, / Where feath'red fowle were wont to rest *A* 12 trembling] fearfull *F, A* 17–20] Whilst his uxorious waters fight / His too revengefull wife to right / And swelling ore their margent rove / unbidd by *Jove F*: While to complayninge Ilia / He vows revenge (though Jove say nay) / Uxorious brooke; and his left shore / Stepps vagrant o're *A* 21 Children] Sonnes *F, A* through our faults] by our default *F*: whom we shall leave *A* 25–8] What God shall we invoke for Stayer / O'th' falling Empire? With what prayer / Shall *Vesta's* Nunnes tyre out her eares, / proof against prayers? *F*

Youth with a thousand Cupids playes:
Or Mars, if thou at length canst pity
Thy long-plagu'd City.
Alas, We long have sported thee,
To whom 'tis sport bright Casks to see,
And grim Aspects of Moorish Foote
With Blood and Soote;
Or winged Hermes, if 'tis you
Whom in Augustus Form we view,
With this revenging th' other Flood
Of Julius Blood.
Return to Heaven late we pray,
And long with us the Romans stay:
Nor let disdain of that Offence
Snatch thee from hence.
Love here Victorious Triumphs rather;
Love here the Name of Prince and Father:
Nor let the Medes unpunisht ride
Thou being our Guide.

I, 3

He prayes a prosperous Voyage to Virgil, Embarqued for Athens: and takes occasion from thence to enveigh against the Boldness of Man

Ship, that to Us sweet *Virgil* ow'st
(With thee intrusted) safe
Convey him to the Attick Coast;
And save my better halfe:
So *Helene's* Brothers (Stellifi'd)
And *Venus* guide thy Sailes,

41] Or *Mercurie*, if it be you *F*: Or, sonne of Maie, if it bee you *A* 42 Augustus Form] *Augustus* shape *F*: our Prince's shape *A* 43] Revenging thus that other floud *F*: Vouchsafing to revenge the Flood *A*

1–8] Shipp, which my dearest Pledge dost keepe / Deposited in thee; / Safe beare him through the azure deepe, / And save the half of me. / So *Hellen's* Brethren starrifyed, / And Venus drive thee on, / And *Eolus* accompanied / With Zephirus alone *F*: Ship that from us hast Virgill bore / With whom thou trusted art, / Safe sett him on the Attick Shore / And save my better part. / So pow'rfull Venus bee thy Guide, / And Laeda's Sonnes combin'd, / And Eolus accompany'd / With none but the right winde *A*

And the Wind's Father, having tie'd
  All up, but Vernall Gales.
Of Oake a Bosome had that man,
  And trebble-sheath'd with Brass,
Who first the horrid Ocean
  With brittle Bark did pass.
Nor fear'd the hollow Storms, that rore,
  The Hyades, that weep;
Nor the South-wind, which Lords it ore
  The Adriatick Deep:
What face of Death could him dismay,
  That saw the Monsters fell;
And wracking Rocks, and swelling Sea,
  With Eyes that did not swell?
In vain, the Providence of God
  The Earth and Sea did part,
If yet the watry Pathes are trod
  By a forbidden Art.
But Men (that will have all, or none)
  Still things forbid desire:
Iapetus bold Son stole downe
  The Elemental Fire.
Whence Leanness overspread the World,
  And Feavers (a new Race)
Which creeping Death on Mortals hurl'd;
  And bad him mend his Pace.
Daedale the Empty Aire did cut
  With Wings not giv'n to Men;
And *Hercules* the Gates unshut

9] His breast was wainscotted, and braz'd *F, A* 10] Who ventur'd first to plough *F*: That was the first did plow *A* 11–12] With brittle shipping unamaz'd, / The frowning Ocean's browe *F, A* 13–16] Though storming *Boreas* sigh'd his fall, / And weeping Hiadae, / And the South-winde, great Admirall / O'th'Adriatick Sea *F*: Unwarned by the sighinge winds, / And weeping Hiade, / And the rough South, that frees or binds / The Adriatick Sea *A* 25] But man, who dares do anie thing *F*: But men, that dare doe any thinge *A* 26] At things forbidd still aymes *F* 27] By theft did bold *Promethius* bring *F, A* 28] To Earth coelestial flames *F*: To th'Earth Coelestiall fire *A* 29] And Hellish too, the scalding breath *F*: On which ensu'd the firy breath *A* 30–32] Of feavers cover'd ore, / With ashie paleness, hastning death, / Which was but slow before *F, A* 33] The Ayrie Region Dedale cutt *F*: The empty Ayre did Dedale cutt *A* 34–5] With wings, not giv'n to men. / And *Hercules* the gates unshutt *F, A*

Of *Pluto's* dismall Den.
Nothing is hard to sinfull Man:
At Heav'n it self we fly;
Nor suffer *Jove* (do what he can)
To lay his Thunder by.

I, 4

To L. SEXTIUS *a Consular Man*

Proposeth the arrivall of the Spring, and the common Condition of death, as Inducements to Pleasures

Sharp Winter's thaw'd with Spring and Western Gales,
And Ships drawn up the Engine hales:
The Clown the Fire, the Beasts their Stalls forgo;
The Fields have cast their Coats of Snow.
Fair Venus now by Moon-shine leads a Dance,
The Graces after comely prance.
With them the Nymphs the Earth alternate beat,
Whilst Vulcan at his Forge doth sweat.
Now should we be with lasting Myrtle Crown'd,
Or Flowres late Prisners in the Ground.
Now should We sacrifice a Lambkins Blood
To Faunus in a gloomie Wood.
Death knocks as boldly at the Rich mans dore
As at the Cottage of the Poore,
Rich Sextius: and the shortness of our days
Fits not with long and rugged ways.
Swift night will intercept thee, and the Sprights,
They chat so of on Winter Nights,

36–9] Nothing is hard to *Man*; the fort / Of Heaven we scale like dolts / And with our crimes from *Jove* extort *F*: Nothinge is hard to man. Wee scale / The heav'n itselfe like Dolts: / And with our sinns from *Jove* ee'ne hale *A* 40] His patient thunder-bolts *F*, *A*

1–2] *Favonius* having thaw'd sharp Winter's ice, / Doth harbour'd Ships to Sea intice *F*, *A* 4] The Earth hath cast her coate of snow *F*, *A* 5] By Moone- shine now faire Venus leades a dance *F*: Now Cytherea leads a nightly dance *A* 9] Now thy sleeke head with Myrtle should be crown'd *F*, *A* 10 late Prisners in] now issu'd from *A* 11 Lambkins] fatling's *F*: youngling's *A* 12 gloomie] sacred *1652* [altered in MS in Beinecke copy] 18 on] in *1652* 18] Which, as they say, doe walke anights *F*: which old-wives say doe walke a'nights *A*

And Pluto's haunted Inn. Thou canst not there
Call for the Musick and good Cheere:
Nor in soft Chloris gaze away thy sight,
Her Sexes Envy, Our delight.

I, 5
To PYRRHA

*That those Men are miserable who are intangled in her Love:
That he is escaped out of it as from Shipwrack by Swimming*

What Stripling now Thee discomposes,
In Woodbine Rooms, on Beds of Roses,
For whom thy Auburn Haire
Is spread, Unpainted Faire?
How will he one day curse thy Oaths
And Heav'n that witness'd your Betroaths!
How will the poor Cuckold,
That deems thee perfect Gold,
Bearing no stamp but his, be mas'd
To see a suddain Tempest rais'd!
He dreams not of the Windes,
And thinks all Gold that shines.
For me, my Votive Table showes
That I have hung up my wet Clothes
Upon the Temple Wall
Of Seas great Admirall.

19 Inn] house *F* there] tripp *A* 20–2] There for a Lord's misrulership, / Nor cull soft Lycidas, that now enflames / The Youths, and shortly will the Dames *A*

1 Thee discomposes] thy waste incloses *F*, *A* 13–16] For me, my desperate plank, and dung-/ wett cloathes in *Neptune's* Temple hung; / Witnes I doe performe / My vowes, being scapt this storme *F*

I, 8
To LYDIA

He notes obscurely a certain Young Man whom he calls Sybaris, as undone with Love, and melted with Pleasures

Lydia, in Heavens Name
 Why melts yong Sybaris in thy Flame?
Why doth he bed-rid lie
 That can indure th'intemp'rate Skie?
Why rides he not and twits
 The French great Horse with wringled bits?
Why shuns he Tyber's Flood,
 And wrastlers Oyle like Vipers Blood?
Nor hath His Flesh made soft
 With bruising Arms; having so oft
Been prais'd for shooting farre
 And clean deliv'ring of the Barre?
For shame, why lies he hid
 As at Troy's Siege Achilles did,
For fear lest Mans Array
 Should Him to Manly Deeds betray?

I, 9
To THALIARCHUS

That being Winter, it is time for Men to give themselves to Pleasure

Thou seest the Hills candied with Snow
Which groaning Woods scarce undergo,
 And a stiff Ice those Veins
 Congeals which Branch the Plains.

5 and twits] carriers *F* 6] Curbing *French* steeds amongst his peers? *F* 9 soft] blew *F* 10–12] With Armes; who when the sledge he threw, / Or darte, such prayses gott? / Under a woman's pettycoate *F* 12 deliv'ring [MS annot. in Beinecke copy]] delivery *1652*: delivered *1652* 14] In Petticoats, as Pelias did *A*

1 the Hills candied] *Soracte* hoare *F* 2 groaning Woods] stooping Oakes *F* 4 Congeals] locks up *F*

Dissolve the Frost with Logs pil'd up
To th'Mantle-Tree; let the great Cup
Out of a larger Sluice
Poure the reviving Juice.
Trust Jove with other things; when He
The fighting Winds takes up at Sea,
Nor speared Cypress shakes,
Nor Aged Elme Tree quakes.
Upon to Morrow reckon not,
Then if it comes 'tis clearly got:
Nor being young despise
Or Dancings, or Loves Joies.
Till testy Age gray Hairs shall Snow
Upon thy Head, loose Mask, nor Show:
Soft whispers now delight
At a sett hour by Night:
And Maids that gigle to discover
Where they are hidden to a Lover;
And Bracelets or some toy
Snatcht from the willing Coy.

I, 13
To LYDIA

He complains that Telephus is preferr'd before Him

The Arms that Wax-like bend,
And Ivory henge, when you commend,
On which the Head doth turn
Of Telephus, ah, how I burn!
Madness my mind doth rap,
My Colour goes; and the warm sap

9–10] Trust *Jove* with th'other; when he charmes / The sea-provoking windes, nor stormes *F* 11 shakes] shake *F* 12 Elme Tree quakes] Pine-trees quake *F* 13–14] This onlie day thine owne accounte / 'Tis then cleare gaines what more doth mounte *F* 15 despise] reprove *F* 16–17] Balls, or the sweets of Love. / Till froward age have powr'd his snow *F* 18 Upon thy] On thy green *F* 20 a] the *F* 21 that gigle to] who gigling doe *F*

2 Ivory] Ivorie *F*: Iv'ry *A*: every *1652*

Wheesing through either Eie,
  Showes with what lingring Flames I frie.
I frie; when thy white hue
  Is in a Tavern brawl die'd blue,
Or when the sharp-set Youth
  Thy melting Kiss grinds with his Tooth.
Believe't, his Love's not sound
  That can such healing Kisses wound;
Kisses which Venus hath
  Made supple in a Nectar Bath.
O their Felicitie
  Whom a firm Cord of Love doth tie,
Unbroke with wicked strife
  And twisted with their threds of Life!

I, 18
To QUINTILIUS VARUS

That with moderate drinking of Wine, the Minde is exhilerated: with immoderate, Quarrels begotten

Of all the Trees, plant me the sacred Vine
In Tybur's mellow Fields, and let it climbe
Cathyllus Walls: For *Jove* doth Cares propound
To sober Heads, which in full Cups are drown'd.
Of Want, or War, who cries out after Wine?
Thee Father *Bacchus*, thee fair *Erycine*,
Who doth not sing? But through intemp'rate use,

10 a Tavern brawl] his drunken rage *A*   15–16] Rude man, as bath and rowl / Themselves in Venus' Nectar bowle *A*   17 their] the *A*   18] Of those whom a firme cord doth ty *A*

1] *Varus*, of all the fruits plumpe *Autumne* yeelds *F*: Varus, of all the trees the fatt Earth yeilds *A*   2] Plant me the Grape in *Tyber's* mellow fields *F*, *A*   3 *Cathyllus*] And on each *F*   *Jove*] God *F*   3–4] For God hath cares to sober heads allotted: / Which with a dash of sacred Wine are blotted *A*   5–6] Who talkes of want, or warrfare, after wine? / Who not of *Bacchus*, and thee *Erycine*? *F*, *A*   7–11] But least with *Liber* anie be too bold, / Thinke on the *Centare's* drunken fray of old; / And *Thracian* wives possest with wine; when, mad *F*: Thinke on the *Centaures*' fray fought in their Canns / And Evius cruell to Sythonians. / When they distinguish, by the difference *A*

Least **Liber's* Gifts you turn into abuse,
Think of the *Centaures* Brawle, fought in their Cans
With *Lapithes*: and to *Sithonians*
Heavy **Evous*, when their heated Blood
Makes little difference betwixt what's good,
And what is not. No, gentle *Bassareu*,
I will not force Thee: nor betray to View
Thy Vine-clad Parts: Suppress thy *Thracian* Hollow
And dismall dynn: which blind self Love doth follow,
And Glory, puffing heads with empty worth,
And a Glass-Bosome pouring Secrets forth.

Other names of Bacchus.

I, 24
To VIRGIL,

Who lamented immoderately the death of Quintilian

What shame, or stint in mourning ore
So dear a Head? Weep not, but rore
  Melpomene, to whom thy Sire
  Gave a shrill Voice and twanging Lire.
But does *Quintilian* sleep his last?
Whose Fellow, Modesty and fast
  Faith, with her Sister Justice joyn'd
  And naked Truth, when will they finde?
Bewail'd by all good Men, he's gone:
But, then Thee *Virgil*, more by none.
  Thou begst back (ah! pious in vain)
  The, not so lent, *Quintilian*.
If sweeter then the *Thracian* Bard,
Thou could'st strike Tunes by dull Trees heard,
  The Blood would never more be made
  To flow into the empty shade,
Which *Hermes* with his horrid Wand
(Inflexible to countermand

12] On their blinde lusts, the sence twixt good and bad *F*: Of their own eager Lusts, the slender sence *A* 13 And what is not.] They rooted-up *F*: Twixt right and wronge *A* 17] And Glorie blowing heads up with vaine worth *F*: And Glorie puffinge with Imagin'd worth *A*

Th'unevitable Doom of Death)
Once drove to the black Flock beneath.
'Tis Hard: but Patience makes that less,
Which all the World cannot redress.

I, 27
To his COMPANIONS

To his Companions feasting together, that they should not quarrel in their drink, and fight with the Cups themselves, after the manner of the Barbarians

With Goblets made for Mirth, to fight,
'Tis Barb'rous: leave that *Thracian* Rite,
  Nor mix the bashfull blushing God
  Of Wine, with Quarrels and with Blood.
A Cand-stick and Quart-pot, how far
They differ from the Cymitar!
  Your wicked noise Companions cease,
  And on your Elbowes lean in peace.
Would you have me to share th'austere
Falernian Liquor? Let me heare
  Megella's Brother, by what Eyes,
  Of what blest wound and shaft he dies.
No! then will I not drink: whatever
Venus tames thee, she toasts thy Liver
  With Fires thou hast no cause to cover,
  Still sinning an ingenuous Lover.
Come, thou maist lay it, whatsoere
It is, securely in my Eare.
  Ah Wretch! in what a Whirlpool tane?
  Boy worthy of a Better Flame.
What Witch with her Thessalian Rod
Can loose thee from those Charms? What God?
  Scarce *Pegasus* himself can Thee
  From this three-shap'd Chimera free.

I, 31
To APOLLO

He asks not Riches of Apollo, *but that he may have a sound Minde in a sound Body*

What does the Poet *Phoebus* pray
In his new Fane? What does he say,
  Pouring sweet Liquor from the Cup?
  Not give Me fat *Sardinia's* Crop,
Not hot *Calabria's* goodly Kye:
Not Gold, and Indian Ivory:
  Not Fields which quiet *Liris* laves,
  And eats into with silent waves.
Proyne, they that have them, Massick Vines:
In Golden Goblets carowse Wines,
  The wealthy Merchant, which he bought
  With Merchandise from *Syria* brought,
The Minion of the Gods: as He
That in one year the *Atlantick* Sea
  Three or Four times, unpunish'd past.
  Mine Olives, Endive my Repast,
And Mallows light. LATONA'S SON,
In Minde and Bodies health my own
  T'enjoy; old Age from dotage free,
  And solac'd with the Lute, give Mee.

I, 34
To HIMSELF

Repenting that having followed the Epicureans, he had been little studious in worshipping the Gods

I, That have seldom worshipt Heaven,
As to a mad Sect too much giv'n,
  My former waies am forc'd to balk,
  And after the old light to walk.
For Cloud-dividing-lightning-Jove
Through a clear Firmament late drove

His thundring Horses, and swift Wheels:
With which, supporting *Atlas* reels:
With which Earth, Seas, the Stygian Lake,
And Hell, with all Her Furies, quake.
It shook me too. God puls the Proud
From his high Seat, and from their Cloud
Draws the obscure: Levels the Hills,
And with their Earth the Valleys fills.
'Tis all he does, He does it all:
Yet this, blind Mortals Fortune call.

I, 37
To His COMPANIONS

Exhorting them to indulge their Genius for the victory of Actium. *Extols the magnanimity of* Cleopatra *in her dying*

Now let us dance, and *now* carowse,
Now out at Window throw the House:
Now is the time (Camrades) for Feasts,
To thank the Gods with Smoak and Beasts.
Before, from Grandsires Butts 'twas Sin
To draw the *best*, whilst the mad Queen
Prepar'd the *Empire's* Funerall,
And Ruine for the *Capitall*,
With her gelt Squadrons (a disease
Infamous) Violent as These,
A thing impossible to try,
And drunk with her Prosperity.
But almost all Her Navie burn'd,
Her Fury tam'd: and her Brain turn'd
With Fumes of Mareotick Juice
To true Fears CÆSAR did reduce:
With stretching Oars flying Her back
(As gadding Doves a long-wing'd Hawk;
Or Hunter in *Æmonian* Snow
Traces a Hare t'her Form) to throw
The Fatall Monster into Chains.
Shee (who to fall so flat, disdaigns)

Nor (Woman-like) feard Swords, nor fled
Into a Hole to hide her Head.
But with a look serene and bold
Durst visit her dampt Court, and hold
Dire Aspes unto her brests, thereby
A black and a swoln Corps to lie:
The *more* she ponderd, *more* unstirr'd;
An honour she could ill afford
Liburnian Ships; to waft a *Queen*
Led in proud *Triumph* to be seen.

II, 1
To C. ASINIUS POLLIO

He exhorts him to intermit a while, his writing of Tragedies, untill he have finisht his History of the Civil War of Rome. *Then extols that Work*

The Civil War from the first seeds,
The Causes of it, Vices, Tides
Of Various Chance, and *Our prime Lords
Fatal Alliance, and the Swords
Sheath'd but not yet hung up, and oyl'd,
The Quarrels fully reconcil'd,
Thou writ'st a work of hazard great:
And walk'st on Embers in deceit-
Full Ashes rak't. Let thy severe
Tragical Muse a while forbeare
The Stage: This publick Task then done
Thy Buskins high again put on,
Afflicted Clients grand Support,
And light to the consulting Court:
Whom thy Dalmatick Triumph Crown'd
With Deathless Bayes. Heark how the sound
Of thy brac'd Drums, awakes old Fears,
Thy Trumpets tingle in our Ears:

* *The Marriage of Caesars Daughter to Pompey; which occasioned, first the sharing of the Power of Rome, between them two by mutual Connivence: and afterwards again when that Bond ceased by the death of Julia childless: their falling out for the whole.*

How clattering Arms make the Horse shog,
And from the Horse-man's Face the blood.
Now, now amid'st the Common Heard
See the Great Generals fight, besmeard
With glorious dust: and quel'd, the whole
World, but unconquer'd *Cato's* Soul!
Juno, and whatsoever Gods,
To *Affrick* Friends, yeilded to th'odds
Of *Rome*; the Victors Grandsons made
A Sacrifice to *Jugurth's* Shade.
What Field, manur'd with *Daunian* bloud
Shews not in Graves, our impious Feud,
And the loud Crack of *Latiums* Fall,
Heard to the *Babylonian* Wall?
What Lake, what River's ignorant
Of the sad War? What Sea with paint
Of Latine Slaughter, is not red?
What Land's not peopled with our dead?
But wanton Muse, least leaving Toies,
Thou should'st turn Odes to Elegies,
Let Us in *Dioneïan* Cell
Seek matter for a lighter Quill.

II, 2
To C. SALUSTIUS CRISPUS

First He prayses P[ontius] *for his Liberality to his Brothers: Then shewes, that he who can repress his appetite, and despise Money, is only a King, only happie*

Salust, thou Enemie of Gold,
Mettles, which th'Earth hath hoarded, Mould,
Untill with moderate Exercise
Their Colour rise.
No Age the Name of *Pontius* smothers,
For being a Father to his Brothers:

1–2] *Salust*, thou foe of prized ore, / Silver, in Mines, looke dimme, before *F* 3 Untill with] With use, and *F* 4 Their] Its *F*

Surviving Fame on towring Wings
His Bounty sings.
He that restrains his covetous Soul,
Rules more, then if he should controll
Both *Land* and *Sea*; and adde a *West-*
Indies to th'*East*.
The cruel Dropsie grows, self-nurst,
The thirst not quencht, till the Cause first
Be purg'd the Veins, and the faint humor
Which made the tumor.
Vertue, that reves what Fortune gave,
Calls crown'd *Phraates* his Wealth's slave,
And to the Common People teaches
More proper speeches;
Giving a Scepter, and sure Throne,
And unshar'd Palmes to him alone,
That (unconcerned) could behold
Mountains of Gold.

II, 3
To DELLIUS

That the Minde should not be cast down with Adversitie, nor puft up with Prosperitie: but that We should live merrily since the Condition of dying is equal to all

Keep still an equal Minde, not sunk
With storms of adverse chance, not drunk
With sweet Prosperitie,
O *Dellius* that must die,
Whether thou live still Melancholy,
Or stretcht in a retired Valley;
Make all thy howers merry
With Bowls of choicest Sherry.

9 restrains] subdues *F* covetous] greedie *F* 13–15] Drink feeds the dropsie, whose dire thirst / Stints not, unles the cause gett first / Out of the bloud, and that faynt humour *F* 16 made] breeds *F* 23] Who can with eyes unfixt behold *F* 24 Mountains] Huge heapes *F*

Where the white Poplar and tall Pine,
Their hospitable shadow joyne,
And a soft purling Brook,
With wrigling stream doth crook;
Bid hither Wines and Oyntments bring,
And the too short Sweets of the Spring,
Whilst Wealth and Youth combine,
And the Fates give thee Line.
Thou must forgoe thy purchas'd Seats,
Ev'n that which Golden *Tiber* wets,
Thou must; and a glad Heyre
Shall revel with thy Care.
If thou be Rich, born of the Race
Of Antient *Inachus*, or Base
Liest in the street; all's one:
Impartial Death spares none.
All goe one way: shak'd is the Pot,
And first or last comes forth thy Lot,
The Pass, by which thou'rt sent
T'Eternall Banishment.

II, 4
To XANTHIA PHOCEUS

That he need not be ashamed of being in Love with a Serving Maid; for that the same had befallen many a great Man

To love a Serving-Maid's no shame;
The white *Briseis* did enflame
Her Lord *Achilles*, and yet none
Was prouder knowne.
Stout *Telamonian Ajax* prov'd
His Captives Slave; *Atrides* lov'd
In mid'st of all his Victories

10] Their shadeing armes lovingly twine *F, A* 11 soft] swift *F, A* 15 Wealth and Youth] Youth and Wealth *A* 17 forgoe] forsake *A* purchas'd] Parkes and *F, A* 21 If thou be] For be thou *F*: Bee thou *A* born] come *F, A* 25 All goe] There's but *F* 25–8] There's but one way with us. The Pott / Is shakt: and first or last our Lott / Comes forth, which is our Doome / To th'unreturninge Tombe *A*

A Girle his Prize:
When the Barbarian side went down,
And *Hector's* death rendered the Town
Of *Troy*, more easie to be carried
By *Grecians* wearied.
Know'st thou from whom faire *Phillis* springs?
Thou may'st be Son in Law to Kings;
She mourns, as one depos'd by Fate
From Regal State.
Believe't she was not poorly born:
Phoceus, such Faith, so brave a scorn
Of tempting Riches, could not come
From a base wombe.
Her Face, round Arms, and ev'ry Lim
I praise unsmit. Suspect not him,
On whose Loves wilde-fire Age doth throw
It's cooling Snow.

II, 8
To BARINE

That there is no Reason why he should believe her when she swears: For the Gods revenge not the perjuries of handsome Women

If any Punishment did follow
Thy Perjurie: if but a hollow
Tooth, or a speckled Naile, thy Vow
Should pass. But thou,
When thou hast bound thy Head with slight
Untwisting Oaths, art fairer by't:
And like a Comet spread'st thy Rayes,
The Publick gaze.
It boots thee to deceive the Ghost
Of thy dead Mother, and still host
Of Heav'n with their etern Aboads,

17–19] Assure thy self, she was not borne / Of low descent; such faith, such scorne / Of tempting guifts could never come *F* 22 unsmit] untoucht *F*

1 If any Punishment] *Julia*, if any curse *F*, *A*

And Deathless Gods.
Venus but laughs at what is done,
Her easie Nymphs, and cruel Son,
On Bloody whetstone grinding ever
His burning Quiver.
New Suitors daily are inrold,
New Servants come, nor do the old
Forsake their impious Mistress dore
Which they forswore.
Thee Mothers for their Wild Colts dread,
Thee gripple Sires, and Wives late wed,
Least wind-bound be, with thy sweet words
Their absent Lords.

II, 10
To LICINIUS

That Mediocritie, and Equality of the Minde in both Fortunes, are to be retained

The safest way of Life, is neither
To tempt the Deeps, nor whilst foul weather
You fearfully avoid, too near
The shore to steer.
He that affects the Golden Mean,
Will neither want a house that's clean,
Nor swell unto the place of showres
His envy'd Towres:
The Tempest doth more often shake
Huge Pines: and lofty Turrets take
The greatest Falls: and Thunder lops
The Mountain Tops.
A Minde which true proportion bears,
In adverse, hopes; in prosp'rous, fears

17] More servants too are still enroll'd *F, A* 18 Servants] lovers *F*: sutors *A* [21–4 from *Errata*, *1652*] 21 Wild Colts] Fillies *1652* 22 gripple] thriftie *F, A* late] now *1652* 23] Least thy bewitching Breath should fray *1652*: Least thy retarding breath should stay *F, A* 24] Their Lords away *1652, F, A*

9–10] The mightie *Pine* doth oftest shake / With windes: and loftie buildings take *F, A*

The other Lot. *Jove* Winters brings,
And *Jove* gives Springs.
It may be well, if now 'tis ill:
Sometimes *Apollo* with his Quill,
Wakes his dull Harp, and doth not ever
Make use of's Quiver.
In boyst'rous Fortune ply thy Oare,
And tug it stoutly to the shore;
Contract in too auspicious Gales
Thy swelling Sailes.

II, 13

To a Tree by whose Fall in his Sabine Villa, he was like to have been slain

That no man can sufficiently understand what to avoid; from thence he slides into the Praises of Sappho, and Alcaeus

A Planter with a [curse] was Hee
That with unhallowed Hand set thee,
A Trap for the succeeding Race,
And Ignominy of the Place.
He might as well have hang'd his Sire,
Or Practis'd all the Poysons dire
Medea temper'd, or have shed
His Guest's blood sleeping in his Bed,
Or if a worse Crime may be found,
As to place thee upon my Ground,
Unlucky Wood; Thee, stagg'ring Trunk,
To brain thy Master when th'art drunk.
No man knows truely what to shun:
The Punick Seaman fears to run
Upon some Shelf, but doth not dread
Another Fate over his head:
The Souldier, Shafts, and *Parthian* Flight:

1 (curse)] ( ) *1652* [reading from Beinecke copy of Brome's *Horace*, 1680. No annotator supplies the word in any copy of *1652*] 17 Flight] Fight *1652*

The *Parthian*, Chains, and *Roman* Might.
But Death had still, and still will have,
A thousand back-ways to the Grave.
  How near was I Hell's Jaundicd Queen,
And *Minos* on the Bench t'have seen,
And the describ'd *Elysian* shades?
And *Sappho*, of her Countrey-Maids
  Complaining on *Æolian* Wire?
And thee *Alcaeus*, with Gold Lyre
In fuller Notes thundring a Fight,
Ratling a Storm, flutt'ring a Flight?
  Both (worthy of a sacred Pawse)
The pious Ghosts hear with Applause:
But most the Fights, and Tyrants fears,
The shouldring Throng drink with their Ears.
  What wonder, when th'infernall Hound,
With three Heads, Listens to that sound?
The Furies snakes their Curles unknit,
Nor finde Revenge so sweet as it.
  'Tis Play-day too, with *Pelop's* Sire:
And Him that stole from Heav'n the Fire.
Orion ev'n his Hunting leaves,
And greater pleasure thence receives.

II, 14
To POSTHUMUS

That Death cannot be avoided

Ah *Posthumus*! the years of man
Slide on with winged Pace, nor can
    Vertue reprieve her Friend
    From wrinkles, age, and end.
Not, though thou bribe with daily Blood
Sterne *Dis*, who with the *Stygian* Flood
    Doth *Gerion* surround,
    And *Titius* Acres bound.

Sad Flood, which we must Ferry all
That feed upon this Earthly Ball,
From the King to the Poor
Beggar that howle at Door.
In vain avoid we *Mars* his Fury,
And breaking Waves that kill and bury:
In vain the sickly Falls,
Fruitfull of Funerals.
Visit we must the Sootie shore,
Of dull *Cocytus*, th'empty store,
Of *Daunus* wicked Stock,
And *Sisyphs* restless Rock.
Thou must forgoe thy Lands and Goods,
And pleasing Wife: Nor of thy Woods
Shall any follow thee,
But the sad Cypress Tree.
Thy worthier Heire shall then carowse
Thy hoarded Wines, and wash the House
With better Sack, then that
Which makes the Abbots fat.

II, 15

Against the Luxury of his Age

Our Princely Piles will shortly leave
But little Land for Ploughs to cleave:
Ponds out-stretch Lucrine Shores,
Unmarried Sycamores
Supplant the Elmes. The Vi'let, Rose,
With all the junkets of the Nose,

9–10] Sadd floud, which all of us must passe, / whom the Earth feedes with faiding grasse *F*, *A* 11 the King] Monarks *F* 12 howle] crys *A* 13] The blouddie warres we shunne in vaine *F* 14] And breaking waves of the hoarce Maine *F* breaking] wracking *A* 15 the sickly Falls] we flye with care *F*: the fruitfull falls *A* 16] The Autumn's aguish ayre *F* 17 shore] waters *F* 18–24] Of lazie *Styx*, dire Danaus daughters; / And *Sysiphus* damn'd ever / In toyling to persever. / Thou must leave lands, deare wife, and goods, / Nor shall one stick of all thy woods / Pursue their short liv'd Lord, / But *Cypresse* that's abhorrd *F* 25 worthier] wiser *F* 27 Sack] wine *A* 28 the Abbots] our Bishops *F*, *A*

1–3] Our sumptuous Piles will leave small space, / To plough ere long; our Pooles more place / will fill then *Lucrine* shoares *F* 5 The Vi'let, Rose] Myrtles and Roses *F* 6] Will for the feasting of our noses *F*

Perfume the Olive-Yards,
Which fed their former Lords:
And *Daphne* twists her Limbs to shun
The Suns rude Courtship. Not so done
By *Cato's* Precedent,
And the old Reglement.
Great was the Commonwealth alone;
The Private small. No wide *Balcon*
Measur'd with privat square
Gap'd for the Norths cool Aire.
Nor the next Turf might Men reject:
Bid at the Publick Charge t'erect
Temples and Towns, alone,
Of Beautifull new Stone.

II, 16
To GROSPHUS

That Tranquillitie of the Minde is wisht by all: But that the same is not purchased by heaping up Riches, or obtaining Honors, but by brid'ling the desires

Quiet! the trembling Merchant cries,
Into *Egean* Seas driv'n far;
When the Moon winks, and he descries
No guiding Star.
Quiet! in War the *Thracian* bold;
Quiet! the Medes with Quivers dight;
Not to be bought with Gems, nor Gold,
Nor Purple bright.
For 'Tis not Wealth, nor armed Troops,
Can Tumults of the Minde remove,
And Cares, which about fretted Roofs
Hover above.

10 The Suns rude] The Sons rude *1652*: Hott *Phoebus F* 12 Reglement] Government *F* 13–14] Small was their private; great alone / The Common-wealth; no wide Balcone *F* 17] Nor might they the next flint reject *F* 20 Beautifull new] faire selected *F*

His Little's much, whose thrifty Board
Shines with a salt that was his Sire's:
Whose easie sleeps nor fears disturb,
    Nor base desires.
Why in short Life eternall Care?
Why Changing for another Sun?
Who, having shun'd his native Aire,
    Himself could shun?
Take horse, rude Care will ride behind;
Embarque, into thy ship she crouds:
Fleeter then Stags, and the East-wind
    Chasing the Clouds.
Let Minds of any joy possest,
Sweeten with that whatever gall
Is mixt. No soul that ere was blest,
    Was blest in all.
The fam'd *Achilles* timeless di'd,
Old *Tython* did his Bliss out-live:
And Chance, what she to thee deni'd,
    To me may give.
A hundred Flocks about thee bleat,
And fair *Sicilian* Heifers lowe;
To thee large neighing Mares Curvete:
    In scarlet thou,
Twice-dipt, art clad. Indulgent fate
Gave me a Graunge; a Versing veine;
A Heart which (injur'd) cannot hate,
    But can disdaine.

II, 17
To MÆCENAS *Sick*

That he will not live after him

Why doest thou talk of dying so?
  Neither the Gods, Nor I'm content,
Maecenas, that thou first shouldst go,

23 then] them *1652*

My Pillar and great Ornament.
If Thee, the one half of my Soul,
A riper Fate snatch hence: Alas!
What should I stay for, neither whole,
And but the Dregs of what I was?
That day shall end Us both: Come, come,
I've sworn't; and will not break it neither:
March when thou wilt to thy long Home,
That journey We will make together.
Chimæra's Flames, nor (were he rise
Again) *Briareus* hundred hands,
Should keep Me back. 'Tis Justice, This,
And in the Book of Fate it stands.
Were I or under *Libra* born,
Or *Scorpio* my Ascendent bee
With grimm Aspect, or *Capricorn*
(The Tyrant of the Latian Sea:)
Our Stars do wondrously consent.
Benigner *Jove* repriev'd thy Breath
When *Saturn* was malevolent,
And clipt the hasty wings of Death,
In frequent Theater when Thee
Thrice the rejoycing People clapt,
A falling Trunk had brained Mee,
Between if *Faunus* had not stept,
The Gardian of Mercurial Men.
Pay thou an ample Sacrifice,
And build the Chappel thou vowd'st then:
For Me an humble Lamkin dies.

III, 1

That a happy man is not made by Riches or Honors, but by tranquillity of the Minde

I Hate lay-Vulgar: make no noyse,
Room for a Priest of *Helicon*:
I sing to noble Girles and Boyes
Such Verses as were never known.

Fear'd Kings command on their own Ground;
The King commanding Kings is *Jove*:
Whose Arme the Gyants did confound,
Whose aweful Brow doth all things move.
One Man may be a greater Lord
Of Land then other; This may show
A nobler Pedegree; A Third
In Parts and Fame may both outgo;
A fourth in Clyents outvye All.
Necessity in a vast Pot
Shuffling the names of great and small,
Draws every one's impartial Lot.
Over whose Head hangs a *drawn sword,
Him cannot please a Royal Feast:
Nor Melody of Lute, or Bird,
Give to his Eyes their wonted Rest.
Sleep, gentle sleep, scorns not the poor
Abiding of the Ploughman; Loves
By sides of Rivers shades obscure;
And rockt with West-Windes, *Tempe* Groves.
That Man to whom enough's enough,
Nor raging Seas trouble his Head,
Nor fell *Arcturus* setting rough,
Nor Fury of the rising *Kid*:
Not Hail-smit Vines and Years of Dearth;
Sometimes the too much wet in fault,
Sometimes the Stars that broyl the Earth,
Sometimes the Winter that was nought.
The Fish fear stifling in the Sea,
Damm'd up. The Master-builder and
His Men, the Land-sick Lord too, Hee
Throws Rubbish in with His own hand.
But Fear, and dangers haunt the Lord
Into all Places: and black Care
Behinde him rides: or, if on Board
A Ship, 'tis his Companion there.

* *This alludes to the known Story of* Dionysius *the Syracusian Tyrant, and* Damocles *one of his Flatterers: The scope thereof being to declare that no man can be truely called happy, who hath any terror hanging over his head.*

27 *Arcturus*] *Acturus 1652*

If Marble keep not Feavers out,
Nor Purple Rayment help the Blinde,
Nor Persian Oyntments cure the Gout,
Nor Massique Wines a troubled Minde:
With envied Posts in Fashion strange
Why should I raise a Stately Pile?
My *Sabine* vale why should I change
For Wealth accompani'd with Toyle.

III, 3

A Speech of Juno *at the Councel of the Gods, concerning the ending of the War of* Troy, *and the beginning which the Roman Empire should take from the Trojans*

An Honest and Resolved Man,
Neither a People's Tumults can,
Neither a Tyrant's indignation,
Un-center from his fast foundation;
Nor Storms that from the bottome move
The Adrian Sea, nor Thundring *Jove*:
If the crackt Orbes would split, and fall,
Crush him they would, but not appall.
Pollux, and wandring *Hercules*,
Gain'd Heaven by such ways as these:
'Mongst whom *Augustus*, leaning, sipps
Immortal *Nectar* with red lipps.
This way deserving *Bacchus* clombe
The high *Olympus*, with his own
Tam'd Tygers, which *Ambrosia* feed;
And *Romulus* on *Mars* his steed:
Pleas'd *Juno* speaking a good word
On his behalf, at Councel Boord.
Troy, Troy, (through mine, and Pallas *grudge)*
A fatal and adultrous Judge,
And forraign woman overthrew,
With its false King and damned Crew,
Because Laomedon *forsook*
The Gods, and brake the Oath he took.
The Spartan Strumpet's famous Guest

Is now no more jewel'd and drest:
No more doth Priam's *perjur'd House*
Resist bold Greeks by Hector's *Prowes*:
 And Wars, which I inflam'd, are done.
My Wrath then, and the Trojan Nun
's Abhorr'd Off-spring, here I give
To his Father Mars. *That He should live*
 In Bowres of light, suck Nectar-*Bowles*,
And be transcrib'd into the Rolls
Of quiet Gods, I will abide.
So long as spacious Seas divide
 Ilium *and* Rome; *so long as Beasts*
On Priamus *and* Paris *Breasts*
Insult, and (undisturb'd) the Wild
Whelp in their Tombes; Let the Exil'd
 Reign, Great, in any other Land:
The Capitol refulgent stand:
And awful Rome *with sev'n proud Heads*
Give Laws to the triumphed Medes:
 Rowzing her self let her extend
Her dreadful Name to the Worlds End:
Where mid-land Seas part Affricks *soyle*
From Europe, *to the Floods of* Nyle;
 More Valiant to despise hid Gold
(*Which wisely Nature did withhold*)
Then force it to Man's use, by Sack
Of Temples, or by Nature's Rack.
 What ever Corner would impeach
Her Progress, That, let her sword reach:
Visit the Stores of Snow and Hail,
And where excessive Heats prevail.
 Yet Warlike Romans *destinie*
On this condition I decree,
That they (too pious, and grown high)
Shall not rebuild their Mother Troy.
 With Troy, Troy's *Fate shall be reviv'd,*
And all her ominous Birds retriv'd,
When second Wars Our self will Move,
The Sister and the Wife of Jove.
 If Phoebu's *Harpe a Brasen Wall*

Should Thrice erect, Thrice it should fall
(Raz'd by my Greeks) The Wife, in chain,
Thrice mourn her Sons and Husbands slain.
  But whether saucy Muse? These things
Agree not with the Lute's soft Strings.
The words of Gods cease to repeat,
And with small Voice matters so Great.

III, 4

The Poet saith that he hath been delivered from many dangers by the help of the Muses: and that it hath gone ill with all who have attempted any thing against the Gods

Descend Thalia *with a Song*
From Heav'n; my Queen, I'de have it long
To the shril Pipe or to the Flute,
The Viol or Apollo's *Lute.*
  Do'st hear? Or do I sweetly rave?
I hear in yonder Trees, which wave,
Thy rustling Robe, and in that Spring
The tuning of thy Silver String.
  Me, am'rous Turtles (Poets Theam)
As by my native *Aufid's* Stream,
A Child opprest with sleep and play,
Under a Mountain side I lay,
  Fearless (for what hath he to fear,
Who from his Birth was Heavens care?)
With sacred Bayes and Mirtle Boughs
On which no Beast did ever browse,
  Covered, least Snake or ugly Beare
Should do me hurt as I slept there.
Which set the neighb'ring Fields at Gaze,
As wondering what should be the cause.
  Whether I mount the *Sabine* hill,
Or with cold Springs Preneste chill,
Or Me the healing Bath allures;
Where ere I am: Muses, I'me Yours.
  Friend to your Springs, with your Songs rapt;

At lost *Philippi* Field I scap't;
The fall of my own cursed Tree:
And Shipwrack in Sicilian Sea.
 Go you with Me, I'le (dreadless) try
The *Bosphorus* that threats the Sky,
And (travailing) defie the thirst-
y Sirian Sands to do their worst.
 Visit the Brittons, fierce to strangers,
The horse-fed Thracians bloody Mangers,
The Scythians whom no Sun doth warm:
And none of them shall do me harm.
 Great *Caesar*, you, with Martial Toile
Tyr'd out, and glad to breath a while
In Winter Quarters with his Men,
Refresh in the *Pierian* Den.
 You give him mild advice: And well,
From you, he takes it. We can tell,
The Giants selves for all their Troop
Of monstrous Bulkes, were Thunder-strooke
 By him that Townes, and dreary Ghosts,
Immortal Gods, and mortal Hoasts,
The Stupid Earth, and restless Maine,
Doth Govern with one equal raign.
 The horrid Band, and Brotherhood,
Who (whilst upon their terms they stood)
Pelion to heap on *Ossa* strove,
Gave not a little care to *Jove*.
 But what could *Mimas*, and the strong
Typhaeus, what *Porphyrion* long,
What *Rhaecus*, and with hurled Trunk
(Torn up by th'roots) the fury-drunk
 Enceladus, rushing against
Minerva's ringing Shield advanc't?
Here the devouring *Vulcan* stood,
There Matron *Juno*, and the God
 That never lays his Quiver by,
Bathes in pure dewes of *Castaly*
His dangling locks, haunts *Delian* woods,
Patros, and *Rhodes*, and *Xanthus* Floods.
 Uncounceld force with his own weight

Is crusht; a force that's temperate
Heav'n it self helps: and hates no less
Strength that provokes to wickedness.
This truth *Orion* understands,
And *Gyges* with the hundred hands:
He, purposing chast *Dian's* Rape,
Could not her Virgin Arrowes scape.
The Earth on her own Monsters throwne
(Thunderd to endless Night) doth grone
Over her Sons: *Ætna* doth rore,
Burning, and not consum'd. No more
Can *Tityu's* Heart in *Vulter's* Clawe
Or wast it self, or fill her Mawe.
Offended *Proserpine* restraines
Perithous in three hundred Chaines.

III, 5

The Praises of Augustus, *the dishonour of* Crassus, *the constancy of* Regulus, *and his return to the* Carthaginians

Jove governs Heaven with his Nod:
Augustus is the Earthly God;
Bold Brittons to the Empire bow'd,
And Persians, with late Trophies prowd.
Could *Crassus* Soldier lead his life
Yoakt basely with a barbarous Wife?
And with Foe Father-in-law grow gray
In Arms, under a Medians Pay,
(O Fathers! And degenerate shame!)
His *Blood* forgotten and his *Name*,
Eternal *Vesta*, and the *Gowne*,
Whilst there was yet a *Jove*, and *Rome*!
This fear'd wise *Regulus* his mind,
And so the base Accord declin'd,
Weighing the Consequence, unless
The Captive *Youth* died pittyless.
I saw (quoth He) *Our Ensignes stucke*
In Punick *Fanes, without a stroke*

Soldiers disarmed, Citizens
Their free hands bound behind with Chaines.
And the Ports open, and that Field
Which Romans had incampt on, till'd.
All This I saw. Redeem'd with Gold
They'l grow, belike, in fight more bold.
Buy not Iniquity. As staine
White wool 'twill never white again:
So, if true Vertue fall, despair
To stop her till the lowest stair.
A Hind out of the Tramels free,
And make her fight then so will He
That rendred to a faithles Foe,
And Carthaginians overthrow
In second War; That tamely took
The lash, and (Death but named) shook,
Why these (forgetting whence they came)
Confounded War with Peace. O shame!
Great Carthage! *Thou hast overcome*
The Vertue (more then Troops) of Rome.
His chast Wife's kiss, and his small Fry
Of Babes, he's said to have put by
(As being a slave) and not t'have took
From Earth his sterne and manly look:
Till he th'unwilling Senate brought
To Vote the Thing that he had sought:
Then through his weeping Friends he went
Into a glorious Banishment,
Though well he knew what Torments were
Ready prepared for him there
By Barb'rous Men. Yet brake through all
His Kindred, and the Crowded Hall
To beg of him He would not go,
No otherwise then He would do
From Clyents Swarms, after the end
Of a long Tearm going to spend
In sweet *Campania* the Vacation,
And give his mind some Relaxation.

III, 7
To ASTERIE

He comforts her, being sad and sollicitous for the absence of her Husband

Asterie, why dost thou mourn
For *Gyges*, shortly to return
On wings of Vernal air,
Rich in Sicilian Ware,
 More Rich in Faith? He by a Blast
After long Storms on *Epire* cast
His widowd Nights steeps there
In many a watchful Teare.
 Yet *Chloe's* subtil Messenger
Shewing what sighs it pulls from Her,
Whilst in thy Flame she fryes,
A thousand waies Him tryes.
 She tells how the fals Woman wrought
On credulous *Pretus*, till she brought
A cruel Death upon
Too chast *Bellerophon*.
 Of *Peleus* neer his fatal hower
Whilst He shuns Love that's arm'd with Power:
And (cunning) rakes from Dust
All Precedents for Lust:
 In vain. For Deaf as Rocks to Prayre
He's yet unmov'd. But take thou Care
Enipeus at next Door
Do not thy love procure.
 Though none with better skill be seen
To weild a Horse in *Mars* his green:
Nor with more active Limbs
In Tiber's Channel swims.

2] For *Gyges*, who will now return *F*: Giges, that will in Spring returne *A* 3 Vernal air] gentle Aires *A* 4 Ware] wares *A* 9 subtil] smooth-toung *F*: cunninge *A* 10 Shewing] Telling *F* pulls] drawes *F*, *A* 12 thousand] hundred *F* 15 cruel Death] cruell fate *F*: fatall doome *A* 17] Of Pelius like to have bin slayne *A* 18 shuns] scornes *F* 18] Whilst pow'rfull Love hee doth disdayne *A* 19 (cunning)] subtle *A* 20 All] Great *F* 25 skill] grace *F* 27 with more active] none with quicker *A*

Shut to thy Gate before it darken,
Nor to his whining Musick hearken:
And though he still complain
Thou'rt hard, still hard remain.

III, 9

A Dialogue of Love and Jealousie, betwixt Horace *and* Lydia

The Original of this Ode is that which Scaliger *writes he had rather have been the Author of, then to be King of* Persia.

HO. Whilst I possest thy love, free from alarms,
Nor any *Youth* more acceptable Arms
About thy Alablaster Neck did fling:
I liv'd more happy then the *Persian King*.
LY. Whilst Thou adord'st not more another face
Nor unto *Chloe Lydia* gave place;
I *Lydia*, (soaring on the wings of Fame)
Eclipst the *Roman Ilia* with my Name.
HO. *Me, Thracian Chloe* now rules Absolute,
Skill'd in sweet Layes, and peerless at her Lute:
For whom to die I would not be afraid,
If Fates would spare me *the surviving Maid.*
LY. *Me, Calys* (rich *Ornitho's* Heir) doth scorch
With a reciprocal and equal Torch:
For whom I would indure to die twice over,
If Fates would spare me *my surviving Lover.*
HO. What if old *Venus* should her Doves revoke,
And curb Us (stubborn) to her brazen Yoke:
If bright-trest *Chloe*, I would henceforth hate,
And to excluded *Lydia* ope the Gate?
LY. Though *He* be fairer then the *morning Star*;
Thou, lighter then a Cork, and madder far
Then the vext *Ocean*, when it threats the Skye:
With *Thee* I'de (gladly) *Live*; I'de (willing) *Dye*.

29] shut too the gates when it growes darke *A* 30 hearken] harke *A*
5 adord'st] ador'st *1652*

III, 11
To MERCURY

That he would dictate to him a Song, wherewith to bend Lyde.
The Fable of Danaus *Daughters*

O Mercury (for taught by you
Deaf stones by th'Ears *Amphion* drew)
And *Shell*, whose hollow Belly rings
With seven Strings:
Once mute and graceless, now the Tongue
Of Feasts and Temples: lend me a song
To thrid the maze of *Lyde's* prayre-
Resisting Eare.
Who like a three years Colt doth fetch
A hundred Rings, and's hard to catch:
Free from a Husband, and not fit
For backing yet.
Thou mak'st stiffe Forrests march, retreate
Prone Rivers: *Cerberus* the Great
Porter of Hell to Thee gave way
Stroak'd with a Lay,
Though with a hundred snakes he curle
His head, and from his nostrils hurle
A filthy stream, which all bedrops
His triple Chops.
Ixion too with a forc't smile
Did grin. The Tubs stood dry a while,
Whilst with thy musick thou didst please
The *Belides*.
Tell *Lyde* That: That Virgin-slaughter,
And famous Torment, the vain water
Coozning their Urnes through thousand drains,
And posthume pains.

1] *Hermes* (for thy sweet Art being taught *F* 2 Deaf] Dull *F* drew] brought *F* 2] The senceless stones Amphyon drew *A* 3] And thou, deare Shell, whose concave rings *F* 7 prayre] eare *F*, *A* 8] Proof against prayer *F*: Perverse to heare *A* 11 Free from a Husband] Kicking at husbands *F* 14 Prone] Swift *A* 22 Did grin] Lookt grimm *A* 25 Tell *Lyde* That] Lett Lyde heare *A*

For cruel Maides laid up in store,
Cruel. For what could they do more,
That could with unrelenting Steel
Their Lovers kill?
One onely worthy Hymens Flame,
And worthy of Immortal Fame,
Her perjur'd Father (pious Child)
Bravely beguild:
Who said to her young Husband; *Wake,*
Least an Eternal sleep thou take
Whence least thou look'st: deceive my Sire,
And Sisters dire,
Who like so many Tigers tear
(Alas!) the Prey: I (tenderer)
Will neither slay, nor keep thee thus
I'th Slaughter House.
Me let my Savage Father chain
Because my Husband is unslain,
Or into farthest Africa
Ship me away.
By Land or Sea take thou thy flight,
Cov'red with wings of Love and Night:
Go, go, and write when thou art safe
My Epitaph.

III, 16
To MÆCENAS

That all things flye open to Gold. Yet Horace *is contented with his own Condition, in which he lives happy*

DANÆ in Brazen Towre immur'd,
From night-adulterers, Doors barr'd,

30 Cruel] Wicked! *A* 31] Wicked that could with barb'rous steele *A* 34 Immortal] perpetuall *F*, *A* 37] Wake (sayd she to her Sweet-hart) wake *F* 37 Who] That *A* Husband] Bridegroome *A* 41–2] Who (ah) their Lords as fiercely teare, / As wolves the prey. I tenderer *F*: That like so many Lyonesses / Teare each of them their prey to peeces *A* 43 *slay*] kill *F* 43–4] I softer will not strike thee deare, / Nor coope thee here *A* 45 *Savage*] rigid *F*: angry *A* 50 *Cov'red*] Shrowded *F* 51–2] Goe safe, and write upon my hearse / A thankfull verse *A*

And of fierce Doggs a constant Ward
Would have sufficiently secur'd,
If *Jove* and *Venus* had not fool'd
The Gaoler of the Cloystred Maid,
(Though of his own shadow afraid)
Turning his Godship into Gold.
Gold, loves to break through armed Guards,
And Castles that are Thunder-proof.
The *Grecian Augur's* sacred Roof
Was undermined by rewards.
Gifts, were the *Macedon's* Petar,
With which he blew up City-Gates,
Subverted Rival Kings and States,
And laid aboard their Men of War.
With growing riches cares augment,
And thirst of greater. I did well
To shrink my head into my shell,
Maecenas, Knight-hoods Ornament.
The more a man t'himself denies,
The more indulgent Heav'n bestowes.
Let them that will side with the I's:
I'me with the Partie of the No's.
A greater Lord of a small store,
Then if the fruitful Crops of all
Appulia I mine own did call:
In mid'st of so much Plenty Poor.
My little Wood, and my pure Stream,
And corn that never failes; makes me
A Man more truely blest, then he
That wears rich *Affrick's* Diadem.
Though neither *Corsick* Bees produce
Honey to Me, Nor Clothing fine
Segovian Flocks: Nor *Massick* Wine
Mellow in Barrels for my use:
Yet Pinching *Povertie's* away.
Nor, wisht I more, wouldst Thou deny't.
Who, with contracted Appetite
May easier my Tribute pay,
Then if deputed *Egypts King*.
Large issues follow large supplies.

He, to whom Heav'n nothing denies,
Owing an Account of every Thing.

III, 24

He enveighs against covetous men, who continually joyn Houses to Houses, Building in the very Sea it self: when in the mean time no buildings can free them from the necessity of dying. He saith the Scythians *are happy who draw their Houses in Waggons, and till the Fields in Common. Moreover, denies that corruption of Manners, and license of sinning to be amongst these, which is amongst the* Romans. *But for the rooting out of these Evils, together with the depraved desire of increasing Riches, affirms there is need of a more rigid Discipline*

Though richer then unpoll'd
 Arabian wealth, and *Indian* Gold,
Thou with thy works shouldst drain
 The *Tyrrhene* and whole *Pontick* Main;
Thou couldst not, when Death layes,
 On *Thee* his Adamantine Mace,
Thy *Minde* from *terrour* free,
 Nor *Body* from *Mortality.*
Wiser the *Scythians*,
 Whose Houses run on wheels like waines;
And frozen Getes, whose field
 Unbounded doth free *Ceres* yeeld:
Nor is't the custome there,
 To sow a land above a year;
And when that Crop is borne,
 The rest relieve it each by turne.
There women mingle not
 For Son-in-Laws a poyson'd pot;
Nor *Govern*: on their Dow'r
 Presuming, or Adultrers pow'r.
Their Dow'r's *To be well bred*:
 And *Chastity*, flying the bed

9–10] Better those Vagabonds / (That draw their wand'ring Mansions) *A* 14 a land] one Land *F* 15 that Crop] its brunt *A* 17 mingle] temper *A*

Of others, their own trust
  Perswading, and the price of Lust.
Oh! he that would asswage
  Our blood-shed and intestine rage,
If he would written have
  His Countries Father on his Grave;
Let him not fear t'oppose
  Unbridled Licence to the Nose:
So shall he gain great praise
  In after times; since (wo the daies!)
We envy living worth,
  But miss it when it's laid in Earth.
For what do our Laws stand,
  If punishment weed not the Land?
What serves vain Preaching for,
  Which cannot cure our lives? If nor
Those Lands which flames imbrace;
  Nor where the Neighb'ring *Boreas*,
Shuts up the Ports with cold,
  And snows fast nayl'd to the free-hold,
The Mariner repel?
  If crafty Merchants learn to quell
The horridst Seas? the fear
  Of that crime (*Want*) making them bear,
And do all things, and balke
  Severer vertues narrow walke.
Would Heaven wee'd carry all
  Our wealth into the Capital!
Or in the next Sea duck
  Our Jewels and pernicious muck,
Fewel of all that's naught!
  If we repent us as we ought,
Strike at the root of ills;
  And mould we our too plyant wills
To rougher Arts: the Child

31] The wonder and the prayse *A* 32 In] Of *A* 33 living] present *A* 39 Lands] parts *F*, *A* 43–6] Repell the Marchant? feare of shamefull want makeing him beare *A* 45 The horridst] Ev'n horrid *F* 53] The matter of all nought *A* 56 plyant] tender *F*, *A* 57 Child] chitt *A*

Of Noble Linage cannot wield
A bounding Horse of War,
Nay fears to hunt, more skill'd by far
To stride off the Greek bowle,
Or the forbidden Dice to trowle,
The whilst his perjur'd Father
Deceives his Partners trust, to gather
For one that hath no wit.
So ill got wealth grows fast, and yet
Something still short doth come,
To make it up *An even Summe*.

III, 27
To GALATEA going to Sea

He deters Her principally by the example of Europa

Let ill presages guide the Ill,
A screeching Owle, or from a Hill
A She-wolf mad upon the Flocks,
Or pregnant Fox.
And a Snake shaft-like shot athwart
Their Horses way to make them start,
Their Journey stop. What place is here
For provident Fear?
Before the Tempest boading Foul
Descend into the Standing Pool,
My prayre shall from the *Orient* stir
The Kings Fisher.
Be blest, wherever thou wouldst be,
And *Galatea* think of me;
No ominous Pye thy Steps revoakes,

58 Noble] Honour *F*: gentle *A* Linage cannot] knowes not how to *F* wield] sitt *A* 59 A bounding] Upon a *A* 60 Nay] And *A* hunt] him *1648* skill'd] learned *A* 64] Cozens his dearest friend, to gather *F* 65–7] Wealth for a thriftless Child: / So wicked riches grow like wild, / Yet ever something lacks *A* 68] To make-upp the uneven Summe *F*: To make up the uneven sacks *A*

1 Let ill presages] Ill-boading screech-owles *F* 2 A screeching Owle] Or crossing Haires *F* 5 And a Snake] Or Adder *F* 15 thy Steps revoakes] doth thee revoke *F*

No Raven croakes.
Yet pale *Orion* sad descends:
I know too well what it portends
When black I see the *Adriatick*,
Or white th' *Japick*.
Let our Foes wives, and all they love
Thc rising *Kids* blind Anger prove,
And the vext *Ocean* when it roares
Lashing the shores.
Europa so, trusting her soft
Side to the ticing Bull, skreekt oft,
The Rocks and Monsters to behold,
Though she was bold.
She that late pickt sweet flowers in Medes,
And wove meet Garlands for *Nymphs* heads,
In a clear night could nothing spy
But Sea and Sky.
In populous *Crete* arriv'd soon after,
O Sire (quoth she) *left by thy Daughter*
And duty in my feeble brest
By Love opprest,
Whence, whether rapt? One death's too small
To expiate a Virgins fall.
Do I (awake) true Crimes lament,
Or (Innocent)
Doth some false Dream put me in pain?
Was't better through the horrid main
To rove far off: or with my Father
Fresh Flowrs to gather?
Had I that naughty Bull now here,
How with my nailes I could him tear,
And break the Horns about the Pate,
So lov'd of late!
Shameless I left my Sire's Aboads:
Shameless I pawse on death; ye Gods,
(If any hear) show me the way
Where Lions stray,

16] No Ravens croake *F* 22 *Kids*] Kid *1652*: Kidds *F* 23 vext] black *F* 30] And Garlands wove for the Nymphes heads *F*

Ere my fair skin grow tand and loose,
And of the tender prey the juice
Run out; whilst I am plump I wou'd
Be Tigers food.
Dye base Europa (*whispers me*
My Sire) behold yon beckning tree!
The zone from thy chaste waste unknit
To thy neck fit.
Or if sharpe Rocks delight for speed,
This hanging Cliff will do the deed:
Unless (being come of Royal Kin)
Th'adst rather spin,
And be a barbrous Mistris Thrall,
Her Husband's Trull. Venus heard all
And *Cupid* falsely laughing now
with unbent Bow;
At length she said, *This rage forbear*;
That naughty Bull thou shalt have here:
Prepare thy self 'gainst he returns
To break his Horns.
Jove is thy Bull. *These fountains dry*;
Learn to use greatness moderately:
Thy Thirds *oth' World shall called be*
Europe from thee.

III, 29
To MÆCENAS

He invites him to a merry supper, laying aside publick Cares

Off-spring of *Tyrrhene* Kings; I have,
Waiting thy leisure in my Cave,
Of Mellow Wine an unbroacht But,
With Spicknard and Rose buds, to put
Upon thy Haire. Break off delay:
Do not moist *Tibur* still survay,
And *Æsula's* declining Hill,

53 *fair*] sleeke *F* *tand*] wanne *F*

And his that did his Father kill.
  Leave fulsome plenty, and thy proud
Palace whose head is in a cloud:
Respite the love of smoak, and noys,
And all that wealthy *Rome* enjoyes.
  Rich men are mostly pleas'd with change,
And cleanly meales in a poor grange,
Without their Tapestries, unplough
The Furroughs of a careful Brow.
  Andromed now peeps with his star,
Now *Procyon* shews the *Dog* not far,
He barkes, and *Phaebus* kindling Raies
Haste to bring back the sultry daies.
  The Shepherd now with his faint Flock
Looks, panting, for a gushing Rock,
The horrors of a gloomy wood;
And no Air stirs to crispe the Flood.
  Thou mind'st affaires of State and (fraught
With fears for *Rome*) busiest thy thought
What *Scythians*, what the *Bactrians* think,
And those that distant *Tanais* drink.
  Wise God hath wrapt in a thick cloud
What is to come: and laughs aloud
When Mortals fear more then their share.
Things present manage with due care:
  The rest are carried like a stream,
Which now runs calm as any dream
Into the *Tyrrhene* Sea; anon
(Beyond all limits overflown)
  Sweeps with it houses, herds, and flocks,
And Trees intire, and broken rocks,
Making the woods and mountains roar,
That man has happiness in store
  For a hard winter, that can say
Unto his Soul, *I liv'd to day.*
To morrow let it shine, or rain,
Yet cannot this the past make vain,
  Nor uncreate and render void

15 Without] Whithout *1652*

That which was yesterday injoy'd.
Fortune that knows the Mistris part
To use her servants with proud Art,
Her fickle favours now bestows
On Me, now on Another throwes.
If she stay, best: If she will pack,
I give her all her presents back,
(Like Wooers when a match is broke)
And wrapping Me in my old Cloke,
My Vertue, marry the next hower
Chast Poverty without a Dower.
When North Winds bellow, 'tis not I
Run scar'd to wretched pray'rs, and cry
Let not my Spice, my Silkes increase
The Riches of the greedy Seas.
When Men may be in Oars convayde
Through Pontick storms, then I wil trade.

III, 30

By Writing Lyricks he saith he hath provided better for the immortality of his Name, then if He had procured Brazen Statues, and Pyramides to be erected to him. And intimates that His chief praise would be, that he was the first of the Latins *who in this kinde of Verse imitated the* Greeks

A Work out-lasting Brass, and higher
Then Regal Pyramid's proud Spire,
I have absolv'd. Which storming Winds,
The Sea that Turrets undermines,
Tract of innumerable daies,
Nor the rout of Times can raze.
Totally I shall not dye,
And much of me the Grave shall flye.
Posterity my name shall boast,

Headnote. imitated] intimated *1652*

When *Rome* her self in *Rome* is lost.
Where like a King loud *Aufid* reigns,
Where *Daunus* (poor in Stream) complains
To neighb'ring Clowns: I shall be sed
The Man, that from an humble head
T'a Torrent swoln did first inspire
A *Roman* Soul in *Grecian* Lire.
I labour with deserved praise:
Crown, Crown Me (willing Muse) with Baies.

IV, 2

To *Antonius Julus*, the Son of *Mark Anthony* the Triumvir

That it is dangerous to imitate the ancient Poets

Who thinks to equal *Pindar*, tryes
With waxen wings to reach the skyes,
Like him that (falling) a name gave
  T'his watry grave.
As a proud stream that swoln with rain
Comes pouring down the hils amain,
So *Pindar* Flowes, and fears no drouth,
  such his deep mouth:
Worthy the Bayes, whither he powre
From unexhausted Springs a showre
Of lawless *Dytherambs*, and Thunders
  In bolder Numbers:
Or sings of *Gods*, and *Heroes* (seed
Of Gods) whose just swords did outweed
The *Centaures*, and *Chimera* stout
  Her flames put out:
[Or whome the *Pythian* Palme for Prize,
Or Horse-race wonne, half deifyes
Records; and him with verse embalmes,
  Worth twentie Palmes.]

1 thinks] strives *F* tryes] flyes *F* 2 to reach] into *F* 3] Like *Icarus*; his name t'ingrave *F*, *A* 4 T'his] On's *F*, *A* 13 and *Heroes* (seed] and Kings proceeded *F*: or Kings the seed *A* 14] Of Gods, who with their swords out weeded *F* 17–20 [Not in *1652*; in *F* and *A*. In Latin text of *1652*. Restored from *F*.] 20 twentie *F*] forty *A*

Or mourns some Youth, from his sad Spouse
Unkindly torn, whose strength and prowes
And golden minde he lifts to th'sky,
And lets not dye.
This *Theban* Swan, when he will sing
Among the Clouds, raises his wing
On a stiff Gale. I like the *Bee*
Of *Calabrie*,
Which (toyling) sucks beloved Flowers
About the Thymie Groves, and Skowrs
Of Fount-full *Tibur*, frame a terse
But humble Verse.
Thou *Anthony* in higher strains
Chaunt *Caesar*, when he leads in Chains
Fierce *Germans*, his victorious Browes
Crown'd with Bay-boughs.
Then whom a greater Thing, or good,
Heav'n hath not lent the Earth, nor shou'd
Though it refin'd the Age to th'old
Saturnian Gold.
Thou shalt sing too the publick playes
For his return, and Holy-dayes
For our prayers heard, and wrangling pleas
Bound to the peace.
Then I (if I may then be heard)
Happy in my restored Lord,
Will joyn ith' close, and O! (Ile say)
O Sunshine day!
And (thou proceeding) wee'll all sing,
Io, Triumph! And Agin
Io, Triumph! At each Turning
Incense burning.
A Hecatomb's requir'd of Thee,
And weaned Calf excuses Me,

30] Skowrs [*sic* in *1652*, *F*, *A*] 39] Although it did restore againe *F*, *A* 40 *Saturnian*] *Suturnian 1652* 40] The Golden Rayne, *F*, *A* 46] Frantick with joy to see my Lord *F* 46 restored] returned *A* 47 O!] then *A* 48 Sunshine] blessed *A* 53] Ten Bullocks, with their Heyfers, thee *F*: Ten Bullocks thine, as many cowes *A* 54 And] Excuse *F* excuses Me] quitts me *F*: shall pay my Vowes *A*

In high grass fat and frisking now:
    To pay my Vow.
Resembled in whose shining Horns
Th'increasing Moon his Brow adorns;
Save a white Feather in his head
    All Sorrel red.

IV, 3
To MELPOMENE

That he is born to Poetry, and by the benefit thereof hath obtained immortality and glory

Whom thou *Melpomene*
    Hath smil'd on in his Infancie,
Him neither *Isthmian* Game
    Shall ever for a wrestler fame;
Nor stout *Olympick* steeds
    Victorious draw: nor Martial deeds
Shew to the *Capital*
    A Lawrel-Crowned General
For taming Kings: but floods
    Which wash rich *Tibur*, and green woods
Their bushy locks grown long,
    Make big with an *Æolian* song.
Queen *Rome* hath noted me
    Of her own sacred Quire to be,
Where sweet-tongu'd Poets sing;
    And now I fear not envies sting.
O *Muse*! Whose sugard words

55] which in high grasse is fatting now *F*: That in high grass doth friske and play *A* 56] Against that day *A* 57 Resembled] Decypherd *F* 58 his] whose *A* 57–8] Fronted like the horned Tire / O'th' Moone, when shee renews her fyre *A* 59–60] And (being els as black as night) / One starre of white *F*: And, save an eye of white in's head, / All over redd *A*

1–2] On whome thou once has smil'd, / And rockt his Cradle, being a child *F* 2 Hath] Once *A* 3 neither] not the *A* 10] Which wash rich Tybur's feet: and woods *F*: Fat Tyber wash, and careless Woods *A* 11 Their] Whose *F* grown] grow *F*: left *A* 12] Innoble with Alkaick song *A* 13] Queen *Rome* by votes chose me *F* 15–19] Queen Rome of speciall grace / Hath given mee a Lyrick's place, / 'Mongst Poets' lovely Press: / And envious teeth now bite mee less: / O Muse that dost inspire / With dulcet noise the golden Lyre; / Who, if it please thee, can *A*

Are married to the golden Chords:
Who, if thou touch their tongues,
Giv'st to mute fishes swan-like songs:
'Tis (all) thy Boon, that I
Am pointed at as I pass by
Romes Lyrick: thine it is,
I *live*, and *please*, if I do *This*.

IV, 4

He celebrates the Victories of Drusus Nero (*who was Son-in-law* to Augustus Caesar) *over the* Rhaetians *and* Vindelicians. *Also commemorates certain valiant deeds of* Claudius Nero

As th' *Armor-Bearer* of great *Jove*
(Made King of all that soars above
For stealing him from *Troy*
The *yellow tressed Boy) **Ganymed*
Youth whilom and his native courage
Drew from his nest ere he could forage:
And now soft winds (being fair)
Teach him to form ith' Air
Unwonted steps: Anon more bold
With hostile force assaults a fold;
Resisting snakes anon
For fight and prey sets on:
Or such as Kids a Lion view
From tawny mother weaned new,
Ready in Pastures sweet

20] Inspirst mute *Fish* with swan-like songs *F*: change a mute fish into a swan *A* 21 Boon] gift *A* 21–2] For thy sake I ore heare / Men say, *Rome's Lyrick passes there F* 23–4] Thou makst my journies short, / And if I'me lov'd, I thanke thee for't. *F*: The Lyrick there doth goe: / Thyne, that I breath and please (if so.) *A*

1 As] So *F* 1] Such as the bird that beares the thunder *A* 2 King] Queene *F* soars] flyes *F* 2] Whom Jove the winged flocks putt under *A* 6 he] she *F* 7 soft winds (being] the weather *F* 8] Calme windes doe frame i'th'ayre *F* 9 Unwonted] Her timorous *F* 10] Foe-like she flyes upon the Fold *F* 12 fight and prey] prey and fight *F*, *A* 13 Or such as] And so the *F* 15–16] Readie with curdled bloud, / To yeeld him first strong food *F*: Ready with their warm youth / To flesh his Infant tooth *A*

To hansel his first Teeth:
  Such *Rhetians* did behold and fly
Drusus beneath the *Alpes*, who why
They carry at their backs
An *Amazonian* Ax,
  I list not to determine here:
Perhaps nor can. But this is clear
Their long Victorious Bands
Subdu'd by a Boy's hands,
  Felt what a minde right got, and true-
Bred under lucky roofs could do,
What *Caesar's* Fatherly
Care of the *Claudii*.
  A valiant man gets men of spirit;
Ev'n Beasts their fathers minds inherit;
Nor doth the Bird of *Jove*
Get a degenerous Dove.
  But *Learning* inward strength thrusts forth,
And *Princely breeding* confirms worth:
Still where good precepts want
Goods Plants turn recreant.
  What unto *Nero's* ROME thou ow'st,
Speak *Alpes*, and *Asdrubal's* red Ghost,
And that bright day to *Thee*
The black Clouds made to flee:
  The first, since the dire *African*
Through the *Italian* Cities ran
Like fire throug Piny Woods,
Or storms on *Thuscan* Floods.
  Thenceforth thy *Youth* with prosperous pains
Still grew; and thy religious Fanes,
Sackt by the *Punick* sword,
Had their chac'd *Gods* restor'd;

21 determine] entreate of *F* 23 Bands] land *F*, *A* 24] Now quelled by a yong hand *F*, *A* 30] Their fathers' mettle Colts inherit *F* 30 Ev'n Beasts] And colts *A* 31 Nor doth the] And the fierce *F*, *A* 32] Begetts not a faynt Dove *F*, *A* 33–4] Yet inbred sparkes are blowne by Arts; / And vertuous breeding confirmes harts *F*: Butt thewes the inbredd sparks excite: / And learned Love confirmes a spright *A* 36 Plants] slipps *F* 37 unto] to the *F*, *A* 39–40] And that bright day to *Rome*, / The thick Clowdes overcome *F*, *A* 45 thy *Youth*] our State *F*, *A*

And perjur'd *Hannibal* 'gan say
At length; *Poor Sheep (of Wolves the prey)*
We worry, whom to fly
Were a great Victory.
The Nation that through flames of Troy,
And Tyrrhene Billows did convoy
Their Gods, and Babes, and hoare
Sires, to th' Ausonian *Shore,*
Like a dark Oak on the rich top
Of Algidum, *which Hatchets lop,*
Growes by its loss, and takes
Strength from the very Axe.
Not mangled Hydra *more increast*
Under Alcides, *nor that Beast*
Jason, *or he subdu'd*
Of Thebes, *more lives renew'd.*
Plunge them ith'Sea; they swim (fresh) out:
Foyle them, with doubled force they'l rout
The Conquerour: and fight
As in a Mistris sight.
Now shall I send no more proud Posts
To joyful Carthage. *Lost, O! Lost's*
(*Now* Asdrubal *is slain*)
The Glory of our Name.
What is't but *Neros* can effect,
Whom Heav'ns with prosperous Stars protect,
And their own prudent care
Clews through the Maze of War.

50 *Sheep*] Hindes *F* 51 *worry*] follow *F* 65–8] Ducke them; th'are Bladders; fling them downe, / Strayte thou shalt see the thrower throwne; / The dead himself survives; / They'l fight, to please their wives *F*: Duck them, they'l rise the fresher for't / Cast them, they'l foyle in gallant sort / The untoucht Conquerors: / And fight like Emperors *A* 71–2] The fortune of our Name; / Now Asdrubal is slaine *F, A* 76 Clews] guides *A*

IV, 5
To AUGUSTUS

That he would at length return to the City. Describes the peace and happiness which Italy *injoyed under his Government*

Heav'ns choicest gift, *Rome's* greatest stay,
Now thou art too too long away:
The holy Senate urge thy word
    For soon Return, Return. Afford,
Like day, thy presence: like the spring
Give a new life to every thing:
The first (good Prince) our night will chace,
    The second will prolong our daies.
As a fond Mother for her son,
Whom, having over Seas been gon
Above a year, the envious wind
    Keeps back from her embraces kind;
And now she eyes the Vane, and prayes,
And from the crooked shore doth gaze:
So, with a loyal Passion strook,
    The People for their *Caesar* look.
For now the Oxen walk in Peace;
Corn, and white Innocence increase;
The cleared Main the Sea-men Sail;
    Faith promises, and dares not fail;
The married bed unsoil'd remains,
Custom and law preventing stains;
Babes, like the Father, praise the Mother;
    Punishment is Sin's Twin-Brother!
Who fears cold *Scythians*? Who, the *Medes*?
Fierce Sons of *Germany* who dreads?
Whilst *Caesar* doth in safety raign,
    Who is afraid of Wars with *Spain*?
Each man his proper field doth till,
And hides the Sun behinde his Hill:
Returning then to sup with Glee,
    His second course is praising Thee.
For Thee he prayes, to Thee propines,

Thee with his Houshold Gods he joynes,
As, for like reason, thankful *Greece*
Did *Castor* and great *Hercules*.
Long last these Golden Holy dayes!
Thus *Italy* for thy life prayes:
Sprinkled at night, not chang'd at Morn,
When to dry labour they return.

IV, 7
To L. MANLIUS TORQUATUS

Proposing the arrival of the Spring, and the equal necessity to all men of dying, without hopes of living again, and proposing likewise the change and Vicissitude of all things, he invites to lead a merry and pleasant life

The Snows are thaw'd, now grass new cloaths the earth,
And Trees new hair thrust forth.
The Season's chang'd, and Brooks late swoln with rain,
Their proper bankes contain.
Nymphs with the Graces (linkt) dare dance around
Naked upon the ground.
That thou must dye, the *year* and *howers* say
Which draw the winged *day*.
First *Spring*, then *Summer* that away doth chace,
And must it self give place
To Apple-bearing *Autumne*, and that past
Dull *Winter* comes at last.
But the decays of Time, *Time* doth repair:
When *we* once plunged are
Where good *Æneas*, where rich *Ancus* wades,
Ashes we are, and shades.
Who knows if *Jove* unto thy life's past score

1 Snows are thaw'd, now] snows are vanisht *F*: snow is vanisht *A* 2 thrust] putt *F*, *A* 3] The times are chang'd, and their owne banks containe *F* 4] The Brookes, late swollen with rayne *F*: Within their bounds contayne *A* 5] The *Graces* with the *Nymphes* dare dance a Round *F*, *A* 15 *Ancus*] *Tullus F*, *A*

Will add one morning more?
When thou art dead, and *Rhadamanthus* just
Sentence hath spoke thee dust,
Thy Blood, nor eloquence can ransome thee,
No nor thy Piety,
For chast *Hippolytus* in Stygian night
Diana cannot light:
Nor *Theseus* break with all his vertuous pains
His dear *Perithous* chains.

This Ode hath a tang of that Heresie, which being sprinkled in other parts of Horace, *He recants in the 34. Ode of the first Book of Songs, and wherein he is generally concluded to have followed the* Sect *of the* Epicureans; *though for* Epicurus *himself, he disavows the Doctrine in an Epistle by him written to* Herodotus, *in which he saith as followeth*: *Viz.* When we affirm pleasure to be the *chief Good*, we intend not the pleasures of Luxurious men, nor those which are placed in the Taste, (as some either ignorantly mistaking, or maliciously wresting our words do suppose) But not to feel pain in the Body, and to enjoy Tranquility of the Minde and freedom from perturbations, we affirm to be that good. For not eating and drinking, not enjoyment of women and boyes, not the use of fish and other delicates which a more exquisite Table affords, beget a sweet life—But a sober Reason; and that sifts into the causes and reasons of Things, why any thing is to be chosen, or declined; and avoiding those controversial disputes, by which minds are (for the most part) wrapt farther into Error, and engaged in Animosities. *Thus he explains himself: and in this sence our Poet was an* Epicurean, *even after his reformation, and in the sounder part of his Book which is almost the whole, having had no clearer light to follow, then that of Nature and reason; and yet how far that was able to carry him the Reader of it may discern.*

[after 18, not in *1652*] What 'mongst thy friends thy bounteous hand doth share / Shall 'scape thy gaping Heyre *F*: What 'mongst your Frends, with bounteous hand you share / Shall 'scape your greedie Heire *A* 19] When once th'art dead, when *Minos* hath with just *F* 19 thou art] once th'art *A* 20 hath spoke] pronounc't *F*, *A* 21 Blood] Birth *F* 21] Not then thy blood, nor Tongue cann ransome thee *A* 25–6] Nor Thesus the Infernall chaine discuss / From deare Perithous *A*

IV, 8
To MARTIUS CENSORINUS

That there is nothing which can mak Men more immortal, then the Verses of Poets

My Friends, I would accommodate
With Goblets, *Graecian* Tripods, Plate
Of *Corinth*-Brass: and, *Censorine*,
The worst of these should not be thine:
That is to say, if I were rich
In those same antique Pieces, which
Parrhasius and *Scopas* fame;
He skill'd to paint, in stone to frame
This, now a God, a Mortal now.
But I have not the means; nor Thou
A mind, or purse, that wants such knacks.
Verse thou dost love. Thou shalt not lack
For Verse. And hear Me what 'tis worth.
Not inscrib'd Marbles planted forth
To publick view, which give new breath
To great and good men after death:
Not the swift flight of *Hannibal*,
And his threats turn'd to his own wall:
Nor perjur'd *Carthage* wrapt in Flame,
By which Young *Scipio* brought a Name
From Conquer'd *Affrick*: speak his praise
So loud, as the *Pierian* Layes.
Nor, were Books silenc't, could'st Thou gain
The Guerdon of thy Vertuous pain.
What had become of *Ilia's* child
She bare to *Mars*, had darkness veil'd
The merits of our *Romulus*?
From *Stygian* waters *Æacus*,
Vertue and fav'ring Verse assoiles,
And consecrates to the blest Isles.
A man that hath deserv'd t'have praise,
The Muse embalms. She keeps Heav'ns Keyes.
Thus *Hercules* (his labours past)

With *Jupiter* takes wisht repast:
The Sons of *Leda* Stars are made,
And give the sinking Sea-man aid;
Good *Bacchus*, crowned with Vine-leaves,
His drooping Votaries relieves.

IV, 9
To LOLLIO

That his writings shall never perish: Vertue without the help of Verses is buried in Oblivion. That he will sing Lollio's *praises, whose vertues he now also celebrates*

Least Thou shouldst think the words which I
(By sounding *Aufid* born) compile
To marry with the Lute b'a skill
Never before reveal'd, shall die:
  Though *Homer* lead the Van, the Muse
Of *Pindar*, nor *Alcaeus* heights,
Grave *Stesichore*, nor *Caean* sighs,
Are silenc't, or worn out of use.
  Nor what of old *Anacreon* plaid,
Hath time defac't: *Love* lights his Fire,
And with his Quiver weares the Lyre
Of the yet fresh *Æolian* Maid.
  Helen was not the onely she
A curled Gallant did enflame,
The Splendor of his Royal Traine,
And Gold and Pearles Embroyderie.
  Nor *Teucer* first that drew a strong
Cydonian Bow. *Trojans* had fought
Before: nor that age onely wrought
Deeds worthy of the *Muses* song.
  Nor valiant *Hector*, and the brave
Deiphob, were the onely men
Receiv'd deep wounds upon them then,
Their Children and chast Wives to save.
  Men slasht ere *Diomed* was made:
But all are in oblivion drown'd,

And put unmourn'd into the Ground,
For lack of Sacred *Poets* Aide.
Vertue that's buried, and dead Sloth,
Differ not much. Un-understood
Thou shalt not die; nor so much good
As thou hast acted feed the Moth.
Lollio Thou art a man hast skill
To fathome things: that being tride
In either Fortune, couldst abide
In both up-right, and *Lollio* still.
Of covetous Fraud a scourge severe:
On whom the All-attracting Gold
Could with its Tenters ne'r take hold:
Nor Consul of one year. When ere
A vertuous Magistrate, and true,
Shall call good, gain, bid Bribes Avaunt:
Upon Opposers bellies plant
His conqu'ring Flags: *Lollio*, That's You.
He is not happy that hath much:
But who so can his minde dispose
To use aright what Heav'n bestows,
He justly is accounted such:
If he know how hard want to bear:
And fear a crime, more then his end.
If for his Country, or his Friend
To stake his life he doth not fear.

Epode 1
To MÆCENAS

He offers Himself to accompany Maecenas *going to the War of* Actium, *not for any help he can bring him by his presence, but because being present he shall have less apprehensions for him*

Thou go'st now our Fleet's General,
Our Fleet, the Empires Wall:
To take thy Sov'raigns danger, prest

1 go'st now] goe now *F* 2 Empires] Kingdome's *F* 3 thy] our *F*

Upon thy willing brest.
I, to whom life in thine is sweet,
But bitter without it,
Shall I (though bid) mine ease pursue
(No ease if wanting you)
Or else with courage Masculine
Make one in the designe?
I will: and Thee ore *Alpes* I'll follow,
Through Lands unseen b'*Apollo*,
And to the farthest Western part,
With an undanted heart.
Thou't ask, what serves my going for,
Weake and unapt for Warre?
I shall fear less, if I be there;
Absence augmenteth fear.
So Birds, divorc'd from their raw young,
Fear more the snake's forkt tongue:
Whereas (alas!) if they had staid,
They could have lent no aid.
This and all warfares I'd embrace,
Onely to gain thy Grace:
Not that my galling Ploughs may vex
A hundred Oxens necks;
Nor that my Flocks when the Dog raigns,
For hills may change the Plaines:
Nor that my In-land *Seate* may reach
To the far-distant Beach.
Thy bounty hath o'reflow'd my measure.
I would not mass up Treasure
To bury with the Miser's Care,
Or Squander like his Heire.

4 thy willing] your loyall *F* 5 thine] yours *F* 19–21] As Birds, which their raw young have left, / Dread more the snake's sly theft: / And yet, alas! although they stayde *F* 22 have lent] extend *F* 28] May change the hills for Plaines *F* 33 bury] burie't *F* 34 Squander] fool't away *F*

Epode 2

He comprehends in this Ode divers Praises of a Countrey life: Commending it chiefly from the Tranquillity and Frugality thereof

Happy is He, that free from Mental Toil
(Like the old *Mortals*) ploughs his *Native* soil
With his *own* Oxen; out of *debt*: Nor leads
A *Soldiers* life, still in Alarms; nor dreads
Th'enraged *Sea*: and flies at any Rate
From *Law-Suites*, and the proud Porch of the *Great*.
What does he then? *He* lofty Poplars joyns
Unto adult and marriageable Vines;
And the Wild branches with his Sickle lopt,
Doth better children in their rooms adopt:
Or in a hollow Valley, from above,
Beholds his lowing *herds* securely rove:
Or, his best *Honey* (which he means to keep)
Puts in clean pots: or sheares his tender *sheep*.
Or, when plump *Autumn* shews his bending head
With mellow Apples beautifully red,
With what a Gust his grafted *Pears* he pulls;
And *Grapes*, the poor mans Purple! Whence he culs
The fairest, for thee *Priap*; and for thee
Sylvanus, Guardian of his Husbandrie.
Under an aged Oake he loves to pass
The *Heates*; or lolling on the matted grass.
Between deep Bankes a *River* rowls the while;
The *Birds*, they prattle, to the *Trees* that smile;
A purling *Brook*, runs chiding all the way:
Which gentle slumbers to His eyes convey.
But when rough *Winter* thundring coms, to throw
The treasures open of the Rain and Snow:
Eyther with dogs, behinde him and before
He drives into his toiles the tusked *Boare*:
Or spreads his thinner Nets beside some Bush,
An Ambuscado for the greedy *Thrush*:
And (*dear delights*) inveigles in his snare

The Travailer-*Woodcock*, and the Coward-*Hare*.
Who at these sports, evades not all those darts,
With which loose *love* assaults our vacant hearts?
But if a vertuous *Wife*, that bears sweet fruit
Yearly, to one; and guides the house to boot:
(Such as the *Sabine*, or the Sun-burnt Froe
Of him that was chose Consul from the Plough)
Build of old Logs, 'gainst her good man comes home
Weary, a *Fire* as high as half the room;
And shutting in knit hurdles the glad *Beasts*,
With her own hand unlade their swagging Breasts
And drawing this year's *Wine*, from the sweet But,
Dainties unbought upon the Table put:
Your *Lucrine* Oysters cannot please me more,
Nor a fresh Sturgion frighted to Our shore
Nor any rarer Fish. No Pheasant Hen,
Or Quayle, go down my Throat more sav'ry; Then
An *Olive*, gather'd from the fattest Bough;
Coole *Endive*, wholsome Mallowes; or allow
A *Lamb* upon some mighty Festivall;
Or *Kid*, from the Wolfe's jawes; *That's worth them all.*
Amid'st these *Feasts*, how sweet 'tis, to behold
The well-fed *Sheep* run wadling to their Fold!
To see the wearied *Oxe* come trayling back
Th'inverted *Plough* upon his drooping neck!
And the Plough-Boyes (the swarm that makes us thrive)
Surround the shining *Hearth*, content and blythe!
All this the Us'rer ALPHEUS having sed,
Resolv'd (*what else*?) a Country Life to lead;
At *Michaelmas* calls all his Moneys in:
But at *Our Lady* puts them out agin.

Epode 7
To the People of ROME

An Execration of the Second Civil War waged after the Death of Julius, *by* Brutus *and* Cassius *on the one side; on the other by* Octavius, M. Antony, *and* Lepidus

Why, why Your sheath'd Swords drawn again?
  Whether rush Yee, impious Brood?
Have not the *Earth* yet and the *Main*,
  Drunk enough of *Latin* Blood?
Not that proud CARTHAGE burnt might be,
  Rivall of the ROMAN STATE:
Nor the chast Mistress of the Sea
  BRITAIN on Our Triumphs waite.
But that the Thing the *Parthians* crave,
  ROME, may make Her Self away.
Lions and *Wolves* this Temp'rance have,
  On their *Kind* they will not prey.
Is't a blinde Rage, or force more strong,
  Or *Crime*, drives You? *Speak*. They look
As pale as Death, and hold their tongue,
  As their Souls were Planet-strook.
'*Tis so*: dire Fates the ROMANS haunt,
  And a *Fratricidall* Guilt:
Since Blood of *Remus* innocent,
  On the cursed Ground was spilt.

Unconquered, though twice attempted by the rude Courtship of *Julius Caesar*.

Epode 14
To MÆCENAS

That his love to Phryne, *is the Cause why he doth not finish his promised Iambicks*

Tis Death (my sweet *Maecenas*) when so oft
  You ask me, why a soft

1–2] You kill me, Sir, asking so often, why / A sloathfull Lethargie *F*

Sloth stunns my sense, as if with thirsty Draught
I had together quaft
Lethe's oblivious Lake into my Blood.
It is a God, a God,
Forbids Me finish my Iambicks, Though
Promis'd thee long ago.
Besotted thus, *Anacreon* was 'tis said
Upon the *Samian* Maid:
Who sobb'd his Love out to a hollow Lyre
With stumbling Feet. That Fire
Consumes Thee too. If fairer burnt not *Troy*
Besieg'd, in thy lot joy.
Mee a Bond-Woman, such a one torments,
As no one Man contents.

Epode 16
To the People of ROME

Commiserating the Common-Wealth, in respect of the Civil Wars

Now Civill Wars a second Age consume,
And *Rome's* own Sword destroys poor *Rome.*
Whom neither neighbouring *Marsians* could devour,
Nor fear'd *Porsenas* Thuscan Pow'r;
Nor *Capua's* Rivall Valour, Mutinies
Of *Bond-slaves*, Treachery of *Allies*;
Nor *Germany* (Blue-ey'd *Bellona's* Nurse)
Nor *Hanniball* (the Mothers curse)
Wee (a blood-thirsty age) our selves deface,
And Wolves shall repossess this place.
The barb'rous Foe will trample on our dead,

3 Sloth stunns my sense] Creepes through my minde *F* 13–16] Consumes thee too; but since a brighter Dame / Did not sackt *Troy* inflame, / Rejoyce: a bond-mayde tortures me, and one / Not pleas'd with one alone *F*

1] Another Age now wasts in Civill Brall *A* 2 destroys poor] unbowells *F* 2–5] And Rome on her owne sword doth fall. / Whom nor the bord'ring Marsians could devowre, / Nor dread Porsenna's Tuscan Powre: / Nor rivall Capua, nor bold Sparta's might *A* 6] Of slaves; nor falsnes of Allies *F*: Nor trecherous Allobrogite *A* 7] Nor blew-ey'd Germans with their curled hayre *A* 8 curse] feare *A*

The Steel-shod Horse our Courts will tread;
And *Romulus* dust (clos'd in religious Urne
From Sun and tempest) proudly spurne.
All, or the sounder part, perchance would know,
How to avoid this *comming blow.*
'Twere best I think (like to the *Phoceans*,
Who left their execrated Lands,
And Houses, and the Houses of their Gods,
To Wolves and Bears for their aboads;)
T'abandon all, and go where ere our *feet*
Bear us by *Land*, by *Sea* our *Fleet*.
Can any man better advice afford?
If not, in name of Heav'n *Aboard*!
But you must swear first *to return again*,
When loosned Rocks float on the Main,
And be content to see your Mother-Town,
When *Betis* washes the Alpes crown;
Or *Appennine* into the Ocean flies,
Or new Lust weds Antipathies,
Making the Hind stoop to the Tygers love,
The rav'nous Kite Cuckold the Dove;
And credulous Heards, t'affect the Lyons side,
And Goats the salt Sea to abide.
This, and what else may stop our wish'd return
When all, or the good part have sworn,
Fly hence! Let *him* whose smooth and unfledg'd breast
Misgives him, keeping the rifled neast.
You that are men, unmanly grief give o're
And sail along the Tuscan shore,
To the wide Ocean. Let us seek those Isles
Which swim in plenty, the blest Soyles:
Where the Earths Virgin-womb unplow'd is fruitfull,
And the unproyned *Vine* still youthfull:
The *Olive Tree* makes no abortion there,

12 Steel-shod Horse] bounding Steed *A* 13 dust] bones *A* clos'd] shutt *A* 14 Sun] winde *A* tempest] weather *A* 15] All, or perchance the better part, would know *A* 17 'Twere best I think] I think 'tis best *A* [21–2 not in *A*] 25 you must] let us *A* first *to*] wee will *A* 28] When Padus laves Matinus' crowne *A* [32 not in *A*] 45 makes no abortion] never miscarries *F* [45–6 not in *A*]

And Figs hang dangling in the aire;
Honey distills from Oakes, and *Water* hops
With creaking feet from Mountain tops.
The gen'rous Goats without the *Milk-maids* call,
Of their full bags are prodigall;
No Evening Wolf with hoarse Alarums wakes
The Flocks; nor breeds the up-land Snakes.
And (farther to invite us) the plump Grain,
Is neither drunk with too much rain,
Nor yet for want of mod'rate watring drie:
Such the blest *temper* of the Skie.
Never did *Jason* to those Islands guide
His Pirat-ship, and whorish Bride.
Sydonian *Cadmus* never toucht these shoares,
Nor false *Ulysses* weary Oares.
No murrain rots the *Sheep*, no star doth scorch
The *Cattell* with his burning Torch.
When *Jove* with brass the Golden-age infected,
These Isles he for the pure extracted.
Now Iron raignes, I like a Statue stand,
To point *Good Men* to a *Good Land.*

52 nor breeds the up-land] nor swells the Land with *A* 53 (farther to invite us)] for our farther comfort *F*: which is yett more wond'rous *A* 54–5] Of neither fortune doth complayne; / Not drunk with too much Moysture, nor yett dry *A* 56 the blest] is the *A* 59] Nor Cadmus ever rested upon theise shoares *A* 61] Nor scabb infects the flock; Nor starr doth skorch *A* 65 I like a Statue stand] So I (a prophet) stand *F*: from which good men are sent *A* 66 *Good Land*] safe land *F* 66] By mee to happy Banishment *A*

Satire I, 6
To MÆCENAS

He reprehends the vain Judgement of the People of Rome *concerning Nobility, measuring the same by Antiquity of Pedigree, not by vertue, nor willingly admitting to Magistracy any but such as were adorned with the former. That there was no reason to envy him for the friendship of* Maecenas, *as for a Tribuneship: since that was not given by Fortune, but acquired by the recommendations of Vertue. Lastly, shews his condition in a private life to be much better, then (if he were a Magistrate) it could be*

Horace being the Son of a Manumised Slave in the borders of *Appulia*; was nevertheless (for the eminent qualities that were found in him) received into the familiar Friendship of *Maecenas*, and (by his Mediation) of *Augustus* also: By whom he was moreover invited to the nearest Trusts about his person. But, as on the one side, he did not a little please himself in that value which he saw set upon him by persons as *Good* as they were *Great*; so on the other (in respect of his poor Birth, and Philosophicall inclinations) he declin'd the envy and trouble of those high Employments: putting really in practise that happy Moderation, which himself both professes and recommends in this, and other parts of his Book.

Not that the *Tuscans* (who from *Lydia* came)
Have nothing nobler then *Maecenas* Name;
Nor, that thy Mother's, and Sire's Grand-sire were
Gen'rals of old, makes thee as most men, sneer
Thy nose up at poor folks, and such as *me*;
Born of a Father, from a slave made free.
When thou affirm'st, *It skills not of what kinde*
Any is come, if of a noble minde;
Thou deem'st (and right) that before *Tullus* raign
(Who was a King, yet not a Gentleman)
Many a Man of no degree, no Name,
By Great Atchievements to Great Honors came.
Levinus contrary (*Valerio's* Sonne,
By whom proud *Tarquin* was expeld the Throne)
Him worthless, Ev'n the People (*whom you know*)
They scorn'd; Those Fools that Honors oft bestow
On Undeservers; Doating on gay men,
Dazled with shields, and Coronets. What then
Shall we do, lifted far above their Sphere?
The People to *Levinus* did prefer

A new man *Decius*; yet now, should I
Stand for a place, hoarse *Appius* would cry,
Withdraw! 'cause I'm no Gentleman: and shall,
When *Horace* meddles farther than his Naule.
But *Honor* takes into her golden Coach
Noble and base. *Tullus*, what hast to touch
The Purple Robe (*which Caesar forc't thee quit*)
And be a Tribune? Envy thou didst git
Thereby, by whom ith' dark thou'dst neer been spide:
For when the People see a strange face ride
Up to the ears in Ermins, and a List
(Or more) of gold; strait they demand, *Who is't*?
What was his Father? Just as when some youth,
Sick of *the Fashions* (to be thought, forsooth,
Handsome) inflames the fairer Sex, to call
His face in question, Hair, Teeth, Foot, and Small.
So when a man upon the Stage shall come,
And say; *Give me the reines that govern* Rome,
I'll manage Italie, *the State shall be*
My care, I, and the Church likewise: Ods me!
It forces every Mortal to enquire
And know; *Who was his Mother? Who his Sire*?
Shall then the Off-spring of a Minstrel dare
Displace this General, condemn that Peere?

This *Tullus* had bin *Praetor*, whom nevertheless being of obscure Birth, and having bin of *Pompey's* party, *Caesar* degraded from all dignity. But, *Caesar* being dead he resumed his former State: therefore this *Envy*.

Novius was one Hole lower. Being the same
My Father was, you'd think from *Brute* He came.
But if two hundred Draies obstruct a street;
Or with their Trumpeters, three Funerals meet;
Louder then all, he chafes with brazen Lungs:
And this is something to awe Peoples tongues.

A Slave set free.

But to my self, the Son of the freed Man.
O (envy cries) *The Son of the Free'd Man*!
Maecenas, now, Because thy Guest: before,
Because a *Romane Tribune's* charge I bore.
These Two, are not alike: I may pretend,
Though not to Office, yet, to be thy Friend.
Thou being chiefly in this case so choice;
Not guided by Ambition, popular Voice,
Or by a chance: *Virgil* his Word did pass
For Me, Then *Varus* told thee what I was.

When first presented, little said I to thee,
(For Modestie's an Infant) did not shew thee
A long-taild Pedegree; I did not say,
I bred Race Horses in Appulia:
Told what I was. As little thou replid'st,
(Thy mode) I go: at nine months End, thou bid'st
Me, of thy Friends, be one. Of this I boast,
That I pleas'd *Thee* (Who to *distinguish* know'st)
Not Noble, but of fair and Crystal thoughts.
Yet, if except some few (*not hainous*) faults,
My Nature's straight (as you may reprehend
In a fair Face, some Moles) If (*to commend
My self*) I am not given to Avarice;
Not nasty, not debaucht, not sold to vice;
Lov'd by my friends, obedient to the Lawes:
Of all these things my Father was the cause.
Who (though but Tenant, to one smal lean Farm)
In *Flavio's* School would never let me learn,
When great *Centurions* sent their great boys thither,
Their left armes crampt with stones, hung in a leather-
Bag, with a counting-board; But boldly parts
With me (a child) to *Rome*: T'imbibe those Arts
A *Knight*, or *Senator*, might teach *His* Boy.
That who had seen my cloathes and my Convoy
Of Servants, cleaving through a press, would swear,
Some wealthy Grandsire did my charges bear.
Himself (*the carefull'st Tutor*) had his Eye
Over them All. In short My Modestie
(Vertue's first bloome) *so* watring from *this* Well;
He both preserv'd my *Whiteness*, and my *Smell*.
Nor fear'd, least any should in time to come,
Blame Him He had not bred me still at Home
To his own Trade: or I my self complain:
(*The more His Praise, my Debt*) if I have brain,
Of such a Father now shall I repent,
Like some that quarrel with their own descent,
Because their blood from Nobles did not flow?
Reason, as well as Nature, answers; No.
For, if I could unweave the Loom of Fate,
And chuse my self new Parents, for my State,

In any Tribe: Contented with mine own,
I would not change to be a Consul's Son.
Mad, in the Vulgar's judgement; But, in Thine,
Sober, perchance: because I did decline
An irksome load I am not us'd to bear.
For I must seek more Wealth straight, if that were;
And, to beg Voices, many a visit make,
Must at my heels a brace of servants take;
For fear my Honour should be seen, alone,
To go into the Country, or the Town.
There must be Horses store, and Grooms thereto;
A Litter's to be hir'd too; Whereas now
'Tis lawful for me, on a Bob-tail Mule,
To travail to *Tarentum*, if I wull;
My cloak-bag galling her behind, and I
Digging her shoulders. Not, with Obliquy,
Like *Tullus, when in *Tiber*-Road hee's seen
Attended with five Boys, carrying a skin
Of Wine, and a Close-stool. Brave Senator,
More decently then Thou, and thousands More,
I could do that. Where e'er I list I go,
Alone, the Price of Broath, and Barley know;
Crow'd in at every *Sight*, walk late in *Rome*:
Visit the *Temple* with a Prayer: Then home
To my Leek-Pottage, and Chich-pease. Three boyes
Serve in my supper: Whom to counterpoyse
One Bowle, two Beakers on a broad white slate,
A Pitcher with two Ears (**Campanian* Plate.)
Then do I go to sleep: securely do't,
Being next morning to attend no suite
In the *Great-Hall* (where *Marsya* doth look
As if lowd *Nomio's* Face he could not brooke)
I lie till Four. Then walk, or read a while;
Or write, to please my self; Noint me with oil:
(Not such as *Natta* pawes himself withall,
Robbing the Lamps.) When neer his Vertical
The hotter Sun invites us to a Bath
For our tir'd Limbs, I fly the Dog-Stars wrath,
Having din'd onely so much as may stay
My Appetite: Loiter at home all day.

The same TULLUS abovementioned, who it seems was no less sordid then ignoble.

Earthen.

These are my Solaces: this is the life
Of Men that shun ambition, run from strife.
Lighter, then if I soar'd on *Glorie's* wing,
The Nephew, Son, and Grand-Son to a King.

Satire II, 1

He dilates upon the advice given him by Trebatius *to write the Actions of* Augustus, *rather then Satyrs, (as things that are dangerous to meddle with) and shews why he cannot obey him*

Some think I am too sharp a Satyrist,
And that I stretch my Work beyond the List.
Others, what ere I write is nervlesse say,
And that like mine a thousand Lines a day
May be spun. What wouldst Thou advise Me now
(*Trebatius*) in this case? *Sit still.* As how?
Not to write Verse at all, dost thou aver
As thy Sense? *I doe.* Let me never stir,
If 'twere not better. But I cannot sleep.
For that, swim Tyber (*noynted) Thrice: or steep*
Thy Brains at night in Wine. If thou must needs
Write, dare to write unconquerd CÆSAR'S *deeds,*
Great Rewards following. Father, That being it
I'de fain be at, my Will exceeds my Wit.
Not ev'ry Pen can paint in horrid Field
Thick Groves of Pikes, Spears broke in French-men kild,
And a hurt Parthian dropping from his Horse.
His Justice though thou maist, and his Mindes force:
As wise LUCILIUS *those of* SCIPIO.
Ile not be wanting to my Self, if so
Occasion serve. The passage must be clear
When *Horace* words pierce *Caesar's* serious Ear:
Whom, stroaking, if we think t'approach: 'ware heels!
Is not that better, then in verse that reels
To jeer this Gull, that Prodigall, when each
Man, thinks he's meant (though quite from thy thoughts reach)
And hates thee for't? What should I do? Being hot
Ith' head, and seeing double through the Pot,

Milonius frisks. CASTOR on *Hors-back* fights:
The Twin of the same Egg in *Clubs* delights.
As many thousand *Minds*, as *Men*, there be.
I, like *Lucilius* (Better then both We)
My words in Meeter love t'enclose and bind.
His way was, in his Books to speak his Mind
As freely, as his Secrets he would tell
To a tride Friend: and took it ill, or well,
He held his Custome. Hence it came to pass,
The old Man's Life is there as in a Glass.
His steps *I* follow, whom you neither can
Of *Luca* call, nor an *Appulian*.
(For the *Venusian* both their Borders ploughs,
A Colony of *Rome*, as old Fame shows,
The *Sabells* thence expell'd, to stop that Gate,
And be an Out-work to the *Roman-State*.)
Yet I'de not harm a Chicken with my will:
For shew, and countenance bearing my Quill,
Like a Sword sheath'd: which, why should I draw, not
Set on by Rogues? with Rust there may it rot
O *Jove*, Father and King: and none bereave
The Peace I seek. But if there do, believe
Me, they will rew't; when with my keen Style stung,
Through the whole Town they shall in Pomp be sung.
Servius, the penall Statutes (angerd) threats
Canidia to Witch them, 'gainst whom she sets:
A mischief *Turius*, to all those wage Law
Where *He*'s a Judge. That every one doth aw
Them whom He fears, with *that* where His strength is,
And *that*, by Natures Law, appears in this:
Wolves smite with Teeth, Bulls with the Horn (This must
Be taught them from within.) With *Scaeva* trust
His long-liv'd Mother: my Head to a groat,
His pious hand shall never cut her throat.
Not his? No more then an Ox bite, a Bear
Kick thee: But she shall die of poyson. There
Now lies his Skill. Me, whether (in effect)
The quiet Harbour of old Age expect,
Or Death with sable wings hover about:
Rich, Poor, at *Rome*, or by hard Fate thrust out

Into Exile; in whatsoever way
Of life, I must write Verses: that's my play.
O Child! Thy Taper's neer the end I doubt,
And that some Great Man's Brave will puffe thee out.
Why? When *Lucilius* durst begin this way
Of writing Verses, and the skins did flay,
In which the outward-fair disguis'd their shame;
Were *Laelius* and *He* that won a Name
From *Carthage*-raz'd, offended with his wit?
Or did *they* winch, *Metellus* being hit?
And *Lupus* stript and whipt in Verse? Yet *Hee*
Spouted his Ink on men of each degree:
None spar'd, but *Vertue* and her friends. Nay when
Retir'd were from the Stage, and Croud of Men,
Scipio's exalted Vertue, and the mild
Wisdom of *Lelius*: Till the Broth was boild,
They Both would play and toy with Him, ungirt.
Though *I* in wit, and in condition, short
Am of *Lucilius*: Envy shall confess
Against her will, I've liv'd nevertheless
Amongst *great Men*: and (thinking to have stuff
Here, for her rotten Teeth) finde I am *tough*,
If learn'd *Trebarius* take Me at *my* rate.
Nay truly, I can finde nothing to bate.
Onely I warn thee, least through ignorance
Of setled Laws thou come to some mischance:
If any write base Verses against other,
It bears a Suite. If *base*, I grant: but Father,
If any write *good* Verses, that Man's prais'd,
Caesar the Judge. If I the street have rais'd
By barking at a Thief, my self being none,
The *Bench* with laughter cracks, *I* (freed) go Home.

Satire II, 6

He saith he lives content with what he hath, and wishes no more. Then compares the Commodities of the ease he injoyes in the Countrey, with the discommodities of businesses and troubles which accompany the City Life

This was my wish, *a moderate Scope of Land,*
A Garden with a plenteous Spring at hand:
And to crown these a Plump of Trees, Heav'n gave
Better then this. 'Tis well, no more I crave
Good *Mercury*: make but these things indure:
If neither by ill wayes I did *procure,*
Nor by ill wayes shall *wast* them: If I scape
Longings: *O that yon Nooke, which doth mishape*
My Field, were added! O that I might find
A pot of Gold! *As* (Hercules *to Friend*)
He did, who, hir'd to delve Anothers Ground,
Bought the same Land he digg'd, with what he found:
If what I have please me: If thou incline,
When I pray; *Make my Flock, and all that's mine*
Fat, but my wit; and as Th'ast ever done
Stand my Great Guardian. Therefore (when being flown
Out of ROME 's Cage into the Woods, I put
Discourses in rough Verse, and horse my Foot)
Nor Feavers kill me, nor Ambition's Itch,
Nor sickly Autumnes making Sextons Rich.
FATHER MATUTE: *or* Janus (*if that style*
Affect thee more) From whom their Births, and Toyle,
According to the Julian *year men date*:
With thee I auspicate my Work. When straight
Thou thy self hurriest me away to ROME,
To be a Surety: *quick: lest some one come*
Before, that's more officious. Rain, or Blow,
And though the Colds shrink day to nothing, Goe
I must: and *after*, wrastle through a Crowd,
And crack my Lungs, t'undoe my self aloud:
Injure, who ere is slower. *Name of Mars*!
What mean you? *Whose Solicitor*? (Thus curse
Those men, upon whose Corns I tread) *O! You*

Hasting to serve Maecenas, *care not who*
You run ore. I'le nere lye; This grieves me not:
'Tis Musick. But anon, when I have got
Esquiliaes misty Top, Thousand Affaires
Of other men flie buzzing in mine eares,
And sting me back and sides. *Roscius requests*
To morrow, Two, you'd help him i'th' Requests.
The SECRETARIES *pray you'd not forget*
A Businesse that concerns the Publick, Great,
AND NEW, TO DAY: *stay Quintus, get this Bill*
Sign'd by Maecenas: If I can, I will.
Nay, Thou canst doe't: and presses me. 'Tis now
A seven years past, *Maecenas* doth allow
Me of his family, only t'advise
Whom He should take into his Coach in Journeys,
To whom commit his Meddals: *What's a' Clock*?
Which Fencer will beat (*think'st thou*) *or which Cock*?
'Tis a hard Frost: *wil't bear another Coat*?
With such like Trifles as are safely put
In Leaking Ears. This Prentiship have I
Serv'd under Envy's lash, more and more dayly.
Our Friend bowl'd with Maecenas *th'other day*:
I and they sate together at the Play:
(*Some men have Fortune*!) Blows there through the street
A bleak news from the Change? Streight all I meet;
Good man: (For thou being neere the Gods must know)
Dost hear ought of the Dacians? In sooth, No.
Thou'lt nere leave jeering. Hang me, if I do.
The lands then which the Emperour promis'd to
The Souldiers, in SICILIA *shall they be*
Allotted to them, or in Italy?
Swearing, I nothing know: *Well, goe thy wayes*
For a deep pit of Secresie! and gaze.
Mean while my Taper wastes: scarce time to pray:
O Fields! when shall I see you? O! when may
I, rowl'd in Books, or lull'd in sleep and ease,
Opium life's cares with sweet forgetfulnesse?
When shall I taste the *Pythagorean* Bean
With sav'ry broth, and Bacon without lean?
O nights! and suppers of the Gods! which I,

And mine, consume in my own Family;
Where my Clowns, born within doores, tear the feast
I tasted to them; Where the lawlesse guest
Dries the unequall Cups, as his Complexion
Askes soaking showres, or moderate refection.
Then talk we not of buying lands, nor school
Other mens lives: nor whether *Caesar's* Fool
Dance well, or not: but things of more concern,
Are our discourse, and which men ought to learn:
Whether to happinesse do more conduce
Vertue or Wealth? If we our Friends should chuse
For Ends, or Honesty? What's understood
Truly by Goods? and which is the chief Good?
My Neighbour *Cervius* interweaves his old
Fables, as thus: *Arellius* wealth extold,
(Forgetting with what cares it tortures him)
I'le tell you a tale (quoth he) *Once on a time*
The Countrey Mouse receiv'd in her poor House
Her ancient and good Friend, the Citie Mouse.
A mightie Huswife, and exceeding nigh,
Yet Free in way of Hospitalitie.
In short, the Chich-pease she had laid for hoard,
And unthrasht Oates she setts upon the Board,
Brings scraps of Bacon in her Mouth, and drie
Barley; desiring with Varietie
(Had it been possible) to have o'recame
The stately nicenesse of the City-Dame.
When the Good Wife herselfe on her strawe-bed,
(Leaving the best) on Chaffe and Akorne fed.
At length, her Guest: Friend, how canst thou indure
To live in this Rocke-side, moapt and obscure?
Wild Woods preferr'st Thou to a Towne, and Men?
Come Goe with Mee. Since All shall die, and when
Wee goe, our Mortall Soules resolve to dust,
Live happy whilst thou mayst, as one that must
Bee Nothing a while hence. *Drawne by this spell,*
The Countrey Mouse skips lightly from her Cell:
And Both their way unto the City keepe,
Longing by Night over the Walls to creepe:
And now 'twas Midnight, and her Foote each setts

In a Rich House: Where glittring Coverletts
Of Tyrian die on Ivory Beds were cast,
And many Offalls of a great Feast past
Lay in the Pantry heapt. Her Rurall Mate
Prayd to repose under a Clothe of State.
The City-Mouse, like an officious Hoast,
Bestirs her selfe to fetch bak'd, boyl'd, and Roast:
And playes the Carver, tasting All she brings,
Shee thinkes the World well chang'd; and Heavens good Things
Stretching, injoyes. When Streight ope flyes the Roome,
And tosses Both out of the Wrought Couch, plomme,
Running like Things distracted, but much More
When with Molossian Doggs the high Roofes roare:
Then said the Countrey Mouse: No more of This,
Give Mee my Wood, my Cave, and Roots with Peace.

Epistle I, 1
To Maecenas

He sayes he dismisses his trifling studies, and embraces those that tend to vertue: yet so as not to swear to any Masters words. And that these studies are such, that there is none but may be bettered by them, if he but lend a patient eare thereunto. In the end he reprehends the depraved judgement of men placing Vertue after Wealth and Honours, and caring more for the things of the Body then the things of the Mind

Maecenas mention'd in my Odes, to be
Mention'd in all I write; Thou would'st have me
(Enough seen, and applauded on the Stage)
To the old sport; I have not the same Age,
Nor the same Mind. Upon *Alcides* post
His Arms hung up, ere his won Fame be lost;
The *Fencer* that is wise, retires. I heare
A voyce sound dayly in my cleansed eare,
Free an old Horse, lest he (derided) lagg,
And, broken-winded, in the last act flagg.
Therefore Love-songs, and all those toyes, Adieu:
My work is now to search what's *Good*, what's *True*:

I lay in precepts, which I straight may draw
Out for my use. If thou demand, *Whose Law*,
What Guide I follow: Sworn to no mans words,
To this and that side I make Tacks and Bords.
Now plung'd in billows of the *Active* life,
At vertues Anchor ride contemplatife,
With ARISTIPPUS now yeild to the stream,
More studying to *get* wealth, then to *contemne*.
As *Nights* are long to them their Mistress fails:
To Hirelings, *days*: To curbd Wards *years* are Snails:
So *slow* and so *unpleasant* my Time flowes,
Till seriously I *act*, as I *propose*,
That which alike boots *rich* and *poor*, if done,
Alike hurts *young* and *old*, if let alone.
It rests, these Rules I to my self apply.
Thy eyes will never pierce like *Lynceus* eye,
Scorn not to noint them though if soare they are:
Nor, of a Wrastlers strength if thou despaire,
Neglect to salve the knotted Gout. If more
's deny'd, 'tis something to have gone thus furre.
Revenge and Avarice boil in thy heart:
There's words and sounds will cut off a great part
Of thy disease. Swell'st thou with love of praise!
There is a Charm too which this Devil lays;
Reading a good Book thrice devoutly over.
The Envious, Wrathful, Sluggish, Drunkard, Lover:
No Beast so wild, but may be tam'd, if Hee
Will unto Precepts listen patiently.
'Tis Vertue, to fly Vice: and the first Staire
Of Wisdome, to want Folly. With what Care
Of Mind, and Toil of Body, we *avoid*
Mean wealth, and honours *hunt* (Ambition's God?)
Th'unwearied Merchant runs to farthest *Ind*,
Through Fire, through horrid Rocks, Riches to find:
What thou thus fondly doat'st on, to despise,
Sit, learn and hear from those that are more wise.
Whose sword hath won him Honour in *true* Fights,
Dusty *Olympick* Lawrels, that Man slights,
(Above those Toyes, and in his own self rowld)
Gold excels silver, Vertue *excels Gold*.

O *Romans, Romans*, first seek *Money*; Then
Vertue. This drops from every Scriv'ners Pen.
This is the Doctrine old and young men preach,
Carrying a black Box dangling at their Breech.
If *of *Sesterces* fourty thousand lack,
Six or seven thousand only, though you make
It up in Vertues, Courage, Eloquence,
Faith, and the like; you'r a *Plebeian*, Hence
But playing in the streets, the children sing
Another song: *He that does well's a King.*
Be this a wall of Brasse, to have within
No black Accuser, harbour no pale Sin.
Now (sadly) which is better, *Otho's* Law
Or the Boyes Song, which gives a Regall aw
To him does well? A song oft sung of old
By manly *Curii*, and *Camilli* bold.
Counsels he better, that says, MONEY GET,
If thou canst, well: but if not, get it yet,
That thou some piteous Play may'st neerer see?
Or he that bids thee, *Brave, erect, and free,*
To face proud Fortune? If ROME 's people now
Object, *Why plac't on our Bench vot'st not Thou*
The same with us? Abhor'st not what we hate?
Affect'st not what we love? My Answer's, That
The slie Fox once to the sick Lion made:
The Footsteps that way all, make me afraid,
And from thy Den that I perceive no treads.
The people, 'Tis a Beast with many heads.
What, or *whom* should I follow? some by-places:
Some for rich Widowes trade with Beads and Glasses,
And feed old men with Gifts, like Fish with bread,
That they on them may afterwards be fed.
Many grow fat with Usury. But well,
Let sev'rall men have sev'rall minds. Now tell,
How long will any in the same mind stay?
Baiae? The World hath not a sweeter Bay,
The *Rich man* cryes: when streight the Sea and Lake
The joy of their arriving Lord partake.
Who, if an ominous Hare (forsooth) come thwart
To morrow; *Smiths unto the* THEANUM *Cart*

This alludes to the Lex Roscia, *the Law made by* Roscius Otho, *that he who was worth* 40000 *Sesterces (a certain* Roman *coyn) should be a Knight of* Rome, *and admitted to those Benches in the Theater appointed for that Order: otherwise not.*

The *Iron *work.* Has he at home a wife?
No life (he sayes) *like to the single life.*
If not, *None blest* (he swears) *but married men.*
What knot can hold this changing *Proteus*? Then
The poor Man (laugh) alters his eating-room,
His Barber, Bed, and Bath: and sick of *Rome*
As much as Rich-men that keep Barks, to float
Upon the water, goes and hires a Boat.
If thou meet one, by an ill Barber notcht,
Thou laugh'st: If one in Scarlet breeches botcht
With Frize, *thou laugh'st.* But what if my *Mind* fight
With it selfe? *Seek* that which it *slighted, slight*
That which it *sought*? all Rules of Life confound?
Turn like the Tyde, build, raze, change *square* to *round*?
Thou think'st me mad in *fashion*, and *laugh'st not*,
Nor that I need to have a Doctor got,
And to be plac't in Bedlam by the Mayre:
Though th'art my Patron, and consum'd with care
At the least fingers aking of thy friend
That honours thee, and doth on thee depend.
In summe, *A wise man's only less then Jove*:
Rich, free, fair, noble: last a King, above
The common rate of Kings: But chiefly sound,
That is to say, *Unlesse his spleen abound.

* *To build there, which he intended at Baiae.*

* *Deriding the Stoicks who say A wise man is happy though he be sick.*

Epistle I, 2
To LOLLIO

He says Homer *in his Poems teaches fuller and better what is honest, then some* Philosophers; *bringing arguments to prove the same. That in the Iliad, what are the incentives of War to foolish Kings and Nations, is described: and in the Odyssee, by* Vlysses *example, what vertue and wisdom can do, is shown. Then exhorts to the study of Wisdom, as that which will heal the diseases of the mind, which he reckons up. But teaches withall, that men must from their tender age accustome themselves to such like precepts*

Whilst thou (Great *Lollio*) in *Rome* doest plead,
I, in *Praeneste*, have all HOMER read:

Who, what's our *Good*, what *not*; what *Brave*, what *Base*,
Fuller then *Crantor* and *Chrysippus*, says.
Why I think thus, (unless thou'rt busie) hear.
The Lines, that tell how *Greeks* and *Trojans* were
Involv'd in a long War for *Paris* love,
Rash Kings and Nations foolishness reprove.
Antenors Counsell was, to send the Cause
Of the War back. PARIS sayes, *No: what Lawes*
Compell Kings to be safe? NESTOR, to peece
The diffrence, runs, betwixt the King of *Greece*
And *Tethy's* Son: *One* boyling with Love's Flame,
With Anger *Both*. The PRINCES, *They*'re to blame,
And the poor PEOPLE smart for't. Mischief, Strife,
Fraud, Rage, and Lust in *Town*, and *Leaguer* rife.
Again what *Vertue* and what *Wisdom* can,
He shews us in th'Example of the *Man
Of *Ithaca*: who (*Troy* in Ashes laid)
The Towns and Manners prudently survay'd
Of many Lands: and through the *Ocean* vast,
Returning Home with his Companions, past
Many sharp Brunts, not to be sunk with Storms
Of adverse Chance. Thou know'st the *Sirens* Charms,
And *Circe's* Cups: which had he greedily
And fondly tasted with his Fellows, He
Had serv'd a Whorish Dame, and liv'd a Dog
On his own Vomit, or mire-wallowing Hog.
The Suitors of *Penelope* were meer
Puppets, made only to devour good Cheer:
Raskals, who minded nothing but their skin,
And, that perfum'd and sleek, to sleep therein
Till it was Noon; then thought it brave, to wake
With the same Lutes with which they rest did take.
Doe Thieves sit up all Night to kill and steal?
And cannot we rise to intend our Weal?
But if in health, thou wilt not stir about,
Hereafter thou shalt run (though with the Gout)

* *Ulysses*,

14 to] too *1652*

To a Physitian: and unless thou knock
For Candle, and a Book, with the first Cock:
Unless to Studies, and to honest Things
Thou bend thy Mind, with Love's or Envy's stings
Thou'lt lie awake tormented. If a Fly
Get in thy Eye, 'tis puld out *instantly*:
But if thy *Mindes* Ey's hurt, day after day
That Cure's deferr'd. Set forth, thou'rt half thy way.
Dare to be wise: Begin. He that to rule
And square his Life, prolongs, is like the Foole
Who staid to have the River first pass by:
Which rowles and rowles to all Eternity.
Money is sought, and a Rich Wife for Brood,
And a sharp Culter tames the savage Wood.
Let Him that has enough, desire no more.
Not House and Land, nor Gold and Silver Oare,
The Body's Sickness, or the Mind's dispell.
To rellish Wealth, the palat must be well.
Who fears, or Covets: House to him and Ground,
Are Pictures to blind men, Incentives bound
About a gouty Limb, Musick t'an eare
Dam'd up with filth. A vessell not sincere
Sowres whatsoere you pour into't. Abstain
From pleasures: Pleasure hurts, that's bought with pain.
The Cov'tous always want: your pray'rs designe
To some fixt mark. The Envious man doth pine
To see another fat: Envy's a Rack:
Worse, no *Sicilian* Tyrant ere did make.
Who cannot temper wrath, will wish undone
What, in his haste, he may have done to one,
To whom he (possibly) would be most kind,
Anger is a short madness: Rule thy mind;
Which reignes, if it obeys not: fetter it
With chains, restrain it with an Iron bit.
The Quiry moulds the Horses *tender* mouth
T'his Riders will. The Beagle from his *Youth*
Is train'd up to the woods, being taught to ball
(A *Whelp*) at the Bucks heads naild in the Hall.
Now Boy, in the *white* paper of thy breast
Write VERTUE: Now suck precepts from the Best.

A pot, well season'd holds the primitive tast
A long time after. If thou make no hast,
Or spur to over-run me, *I* am One
For none will stay, and will contend with none.

Epistle I, 5
To TORQUATUS

Hee invites Torquatus *to supper, which He sayes shall be a frugall one. Exhorts him (bidding farewell to Cares, and the desire of Riches) to give himselfe to Mirth; and (seeming a little light-headed with the joy of Augustus his Birth-day) lashes out into the Prayses of drinking, Names three things whereof he is studious in His Entertainment, and the first of these, Cleanlinesse*

If Thou (a Guest) on a joyn'd-Stool canst sup,
And in a small Mess all the Broath sup up:
I shall at home expect thee by Sun-set.
Wine thou shalt drink of middle age, and wet
Minturnae's growth hard by. If thou hast ought
That better is, command it to be brought,
And treat thy Host. Already the Logs burn,
And the scowr'd Pans shine, on thy score. Adjourn
Light Hopes, and Riches strife, and *Mosco's* Cause
To morrow; CÆSAR's Birth-day gives a Pawse
To Toil, and leave to sleep. Without offence
We may spin out with chatting Eloquence
The Summer night. What doe I care for wealth,
Unlesse to use? 'Tis a mad kind of stealth,
For one to rob himself, t'enrich his Heire.
I'le quaffe, and sprinkle Roses, and not care
Though I'me thought wilde for this. The rare effects
Of Wine! Love, hid in Blushes, it detects:
Hopes it ensures: It makes the Coward fight:
Learned the Ignorant; The sad Heart light.
Whom have not flowing Cups Eloquent made?
Whose debts (though nere so great) have they not paid?
I am the Man: and my charge I will make it,

(Willing, and not unfit to undertake it)
To have the Forms clean-rubb'd: The Napkins such
As may not curl our Noses up to touch:
That in the Platters thou maist see thy Face:
That no false Brother carry from the Place
Ought that is spoke: That all of a Suit, bee
Septimius? *Brutus*? sure Cards, These. Let's see:
Then (if not taken up with better chear,
Or by his Girl) *Sabinus* shall be here.
Each Guest may bring his shadow. But the sweat
Will be offensive, if too close we set.
Thy Number, write: and (all things laid aside)
Thy Clients bobb'd, out at the back door glide.

Epistle I, 10
To FUSCUS ARISTIUS

He praises to Fuscus Aristius *(a lover of the City) the Country-life, with which himself was delighted, and recounts the severall Commodities thereof. Withall deters him from ambition, which accompanies the City-life, not that of the Countrey*

To *Fuscus*, the *Towne's* Lover, health I wish
That love the *Countrey*: diffring much in *this*,
In all *else* Twins. Both like, dislike, what *either*:
A pair of old Doves bred of Eggs together.
Thou keep'st the Nest: *I* love to flye abroad,
To haunt sweet Brooks, the mossie Grott, and Wood.
What wouldst thou have? I live and reign, when *I*
Have shun'd those things *thou* praisest to the sky.
And like a Comfit-maker's Prentice fled,
Cloyd with *Preserves*, am better pleas'd with *Bread*.
If one would live with all conveniency's,
And first in building the Foundation is,
Where doth frank Nature thrust out such a Breast
As in the Countrey, with all good things blest?
Where is it that the Winter's warmer? Where
To cool the Dog-starres byte, is fresher aire,
And the fierce Lyon's rage, when all his heat

Th'exalted Sun poures in, to make it great?
Where does lesse envious care our sleeps dispell?
Doe Floores of *Parian* Marble look or smell
Like Flowers? The water when it heaves to burst
The leaden Pipes with which in streets 'tis forc't,
Runs it so pure, as when melodiously
It quavers in the Rivers Falls? Ev'n Hee
Affects t'have Trees, who in the *Citie* builds,
And that his house should but survey the fields.
Drive Nature with a Pitch-fork out, shee'l back
Victorious (spite of *State*) by'a secret Track.
He that wants skill right Scarlet to descry
From counterfeit, will not more certainly
Be cosend in a Shop, then he shall be
That knows not true from false Felicitie.
Him, whom a prosp'rous State did too much please;
Chang'd, it will shake. What thou admir'dst with ease
Thou canst not quit. Fly great things: In a Cell,
Kings, and the Friends of Kings, thy Life may excell.
The *Stagg* superior both in Arms and Force,
Out of the Common-Pasture drove the *Horse*:
Untill the vanquish'd after a long fight
Pray'd *Man's* assistance, and receiv'd the *Bit*:
But, having beat the Victor, could not now
Bit from his *Mouth*, nor *Man* from his *Back* throw.
So He that fearing *Poverty*, hath sold
Away his *Liberty*, better then Gold,
Shall carry a proud Lord upon his back,
And serve for ever, 'cause he could not lack.
Who fits not his Minde to it, *his* Estate
If *little*, pinches him: throws him, if *great*.
Wisely (ARISTIUS) thou wilt like *thy* lot,
And wilt chide Me, if *mine* content *Me* not:
If more I cark for, or if more I crave.
Who ere has Money, either 'tis his Slave,
Or 'tis his Master, as when two Men tug
At a Ropes ends: W'are dragg'd unless we drag.
*Giv'n in Vacation, at that *Goddess Cell:*
Save that I have not Thee, perfectly well.

* The *Romans* adored *Vacation* as a *Goddess*, by the Name of *Vacuna*.

AUSONIUS *His ROSES*
Edyl. 14

'Twas *Spring*; and (bitter-sweet) the Saffron *Morn*
  Blew hot, and cold from *Amalthea's* Horn.
A brisker gale usher'd *Aurora's* Ray,
  And bad her Steeds out-strip the winged day.
Between the Gardens water'd beds I went,
  Apollo's growing fury to prevent.
On the bent grasse I saw congealed drops,
  And Crystall pendants on the pot-hearbs tops.
Broad Cabbages from leaf to leaf distill'd
  The Orient Pearle, and all their bottles fill'd.
The hoarie Fruit-trees here and there a Gem
  Had candi'd ore, to melt with the first Beam.
The Rose-trees in their *Pestan* Scarlet laught,
  And with red lips the *Mornings Nectar* quaft.
'Tis doubted whether HESPER borrowed,
  Or lent, that paint, and dy'd the *Roses* red.
One deaw, *one* colour, *one* Celestiall power
  Of *both*: For they are VENUS *Star* and *Flower*.
Perchance *one* odour too: but *That* being high,
  Expires ith'aire: *This*, throws her Incense nigh.
The PAPHYAN Mistresse of the *Flow'r* and *Starre*,
  Bade *both* her servants the *same* Liv'ry weare.
The moment came when on opposed Banks
  The flowrie Squadrons plac'd themselves in Ranks.
One lay conceal'd in her Leaves close green-hood:
  Another peeping through the Lattice stood.
This opes her first aspiring Pyramed,
  And ends it in a crimson poynted head.
That looz'd her garment (gather'd in her lap)
  And in her native silks her self did wrap;
Uncovers, *Now*, her laughing Cup, and showes
  The golden Tuft which in her bottome growes.
She, that but now shone drest in all her haire,
  Stands *pale*; forsook ev'n by those leaves she bare.
So sudden change I wondered to behold,

And Roses in their *Infancy* grown old.
Whilst I speak *This*, those envy'd Beauties shed
Their glorious locks: earth cover'd with their *dead.*
So many kinds, *so many* births of Flow'rs,
One day discloses, and *one day* devours.
NATURE, why mad'st thou fading Flow'rs, so gay?
Why shewd'st us gifts, to snatch them streight away?
A day's a Roses Age. How neere do meet
(Poore Bloome!) thy *Cradle*, and thy *Winding-sheet*?
Her whom the rising Sun saw newly born,
He sees a witherd corps at his return.
Yet, well with them: Who, though they quickly dye,
Survive themselves in their posterity.
Gather *your* Roses *Virgins*, whilst they'r *new*:
For, being *past*, no Spring returns to *You*.

VIRGIL'S *BULL*

Out of his Third Book of Georgicks

A Beauteous Heyfer feeds in a great Wood:
For whom two Bulls exchange thick wounds: black blood
Flowes largely from them both; and their sharp horns,
Whil'st either bearing on his Rivall turns,
They drive in with huge groans. The bellowing ground,
And the *Celestiall* Bull, report their sound.
Nor is't the fashion when the War is done,
For these stout Combatants to live in one
And the same Field. The vanquish't quits the place,
Exil'd in parts far off: his own disgrace
Lamenting deep, and the proud Victors blowes,
Also the *Love* he (unreveng'd) did lose:
And, casting back a ruefull look, is fain
To leave the Pastures where his Sire did raign:
With all care therefore he doth exercise
His strength, and nightly on the hard stones lies
Without his Litter, feeding on rough boughs,
And on sharp Flags penuriously doth browze:

And tries himself, and practises on Oaks
To clash with horns, provokes the wind with stroaks:
And, spurning up the sand with angry feet,
Before the fight doth flourish, having knit
His slackend Nervs, he doth his Trumpet blow,
And rushes headlong on his secure Foe:
As when a Billow in the midst o'th' *Maine*
Began to Foam, and gathers a long Train
Advancing through the *Deep*: and rowld to Land
Roares in the Rocks, nor overlays the Strand
Less heavie then a Mountain: but boils up
With curling Whirlpools to the *Ocean's* top,
And throws high Works up of black Sand.—

La Fida Pastora, *1658*

LA FIDA PASTORA.

Comoedia Pastoralis.

Autore

FF. ANGLO-BRITANNO.

Adduntur nonnulla varii argumenti
Carmina ab eodem.

Dux VITAE RATIO.

LONDINI,

Typis *R. Danielis*, Impensis *G. Bedell* & *T. Collins*,
apud quos veneunt proxime ianuam Templi Mediani
in vico dicto *Fleet-Streete*. *1658*.

AUTHOR

ad Opusculum

Prodi, *Libelle*; fiat periculum si qua possim, domi naufragus, super hanc *Tabulam* enatare; suffragii nonnihil apud Exteros (nam quid dissimulem?) aliquantulum patrocinii, obtinere. Ecce autem primo limine, LA FIDA PASTORA! Invidiosus Titulus, idemque heterogeneus, tanquam extorta ansa Æmulationis altissimae. *Icare*, quo volas? non jam ut Nomen tuum pereundo perpetues, sed ut pereas usurpando alienum. In promptu Clypeus est. Hanc tibi Appellationem (non ego) celatam imposuit *Autoritas*; a qua recedere neutiquam debeo. Casu an Consilio id egerit, non constat: nec qua illa dictabat Anglice, succurrit mihi ab *Antiquis* vocabulum quo reddam Latine. Hinc necessitas. Enimvero quanti ego aestimo GUARINUM, et quantum veneror, illum ipsum testor *Pastorem Fidelem*, qui ut semper fuit apud Italos celeberrimus, *Italumque* Fontem petentes; sic nunc apud Nostrates etiam, vel bis coctus, et me Interprete, numeratur in deliciis. Quod si ejusdem GUARINI aliorumque externas merces Anglici Portus benigne receperunt, et indies recipiunt (de Scriptis et Linguis loquor) externos portus, saltem qui liberi nuncupantur (certe *Sermo Latinus* est *Sermo Mundanus*) Anglicis quoque mercibus aperiri quis vetat? Profecto si quae multa inter angustias Borealis Insulae propter linguae insolentiam continentur diviniora Poemata, usitatarum aliqua ab initio fuissent conscripta; aut si ipsorum animae in earum quamvis, felici furto, *Pythagoricaque transmigratione*, etiam nunc prodirent, non video *in Anglicanis Musis* (praesertim Scenicis) quid despicere possit, vel *Francia*, vel *Hispania*, vel (ut amplius nihil dicam) antiqua aut nova *Italia*. Sed quo rapior, *Patriae* plenus? ad Te redeo: Prodi, LIBELLE.

4 limine] limimine *1658* 8 celatam] celata *1658* 22–3 etiam nunc] etiamnum *1658*

LA FIDA PASTORA

PERSONAE DRAMATIS

CLORINDA	LA FIDA PASTORA
SATYRUS	*Frugi*
SENEX PASTOR CUM COMITATU PASTORUM ET PASTORARUM	
SACERDOS DEI PANOS	
PERIGOTTUS	*Amator* Amorettae
AMORETTA	*Amatrix* Perigotti
AMARYLLIS	*Deperiens* Perigottum *aequivocans* Amorettae
PASTOR MELANCHOLICUS	*Nequam*
CLOE	*Lasciva*
THENOTTUS	*Deperiens* Clorindam
DAPHNIS	*Pastor pudibundus, Amator* Clois
ALEXIS	*Audax, et ille Amator* Clois
DEUS FLUVII	

[LA FIDA PASTORA]

Actus primi Scena prima.

Intret CLORINDA Pastora *in Viridario ubi sepeliverat* Amatorem *suum.*

Salve, sancte Lapis, gelidis qui amplecteris ulnis (p. 1)
Pastorem, quo nemo Gregi constantior unquam
Pinguia Thessalicis indulsit pabula campis.
Sic tua busta colo, sic matutina reporto
Vota, negant madidum neque lumina nostra tributum
Nunc quoque dilecto cineri: sic (libera) flammae
Aeternum maledico novae, maledico sagittae.
Nunc omnes lususque, voluptatesque, jocique,
Queis Pastoribus est mos indulgere, valete.
Laevia non posthac juvenili haec tempora serto
Cingentur, laetas ducam nec ut ante Choreas:
Non jam formosas vegeto fulgore puellas,
Aut ego Pastores hilaris comitabor ovantes:
Dulcis-acuta sonans non fistula valle profunda,
Qua frondes recreant Venti cava sibila, me nunc
Exhilaratura est. Procul haec, procul omnia sunto;
Nam procul es, cujus quoties vicina sedebam
Dilecto lateri rosea Regina corona,
Cum circumfusa est Plebs pastoralis in herba.
Concolor, et picto (qui spernit Sceptra) bacillo;
Pendula deque humeris meliori pera cadebat
Per costas ex pelle caprae? Sed tu periisti,
Ex periere mihi, periere haec omnia tecum:
Omnia mortua sunt, tenebrisque sepulta, nisi unum
Hoc, meminisse Tui; quod dulce manebit in aevum;
Contingetque Tibi, post propria vivere fata,
Fistula donec erit, vel ament alterna Camoenae.
Et nunc prona tuis tam sancti in amoris honorem (p. 2)
Ossibus haerebo, meliorem oblita dierum
Gaudia quos niveis mihi distinxere lapillis;
Sola memor Medicae, teneram quae me imbuit, Artis,
Plantarum scrutantem animas, viresque latentes.
Huic operam dabo, tam gratis hanc deinde datura,
Quam gratis dedit hanc qui donat et omnia gratis.

Omnia nota novae mihi sunt medicamina plagae,
Sitve Hominum, Pecudumve; malo noceantur ab angue,
Cantibus an magicis, an Amoris tabe fatiscant;
Vel cerebri morbo nimio fervore laborent,
Auribus aut oculis obducto humore gravatis.
His largimur opem: Virtus ea pollet in Herbis,
Virginea tractante manu. Mihi praebet inemptas
Haec fera Sylva dapes; baccas, poma aurea, quaeque
Sole rubent depicta genas; et vertice raptum
Procerae pinus penetrantem nubila fructum.
His beor, ingenua contenta quiete, fruique
Te, vel in hoc Thalamo, cum Nox caecaverit Orbem.

Intret SATYRUS.

SAT. Illam planitiem per aestuosam
Quae curvat tremulo Mari lacertos,
Hoc et spissicomum nemus cucurri,
Cui numquam jubar ima basiavit
Ex quo Ver cupidum auspicatur annos.
Ut *Pani* (domino meo) placerem,
Huc illuc sine fine cursitavi,
Fructus propter eum legens, rogata
Cui multa dape proximis tenebris
Ipsius Domina est, corusca *Syrinx*.
Sed quiddam video magis serenum! *Stat attonitus.*
Per te, lampadis aemulam diurnae,
Una ex Angelico choro videris,
Altum Coelituum genus Deorum;
Nam plus Nobilitatis, et verendae
Majestatis, inest tuis ocellis,
Quam mortale potest genus tueri (p. 3)
Impuris oculis et imbecillis,
Nec mox inde mori. Genu profundo
Hanc terram ergo premens colo, tuumque
Demissis oculis adoro Numen.
Acceptum manibus meis referto
Quicquid dulce solum sinu feraci
Frugum parturit elegantiorum;
Et (si sit *Satyro* fides habenda)
Per famosa fluenta pulchriores

Ad praesens (Dea) nemo vidit usque,
Nec gratas magis innocente succo.
Sunt Uvae, vegetus perenne quarum
Sanguis dat lepidis decus Poetis;
Huad unquam melioribus coronam
Texebat sibi pensilem *Lyaeus*.
Est Nux plurima, concolorque dente
Frangenti sibi corticem sciuro:
Aequi candida consulas, bonique.
Has propter Dryope, nigris ocellis,
Iussit me genibus subire plexis.
En ut nobile Tempus inquinavit
Fuso turgidulas genas ab ostro;
Quali pingitur et tuum labellum!
Has Regina potest vorare baccas;
Sunt quaedam virides, rubraeque quaedam.
Hic est et cibus ille delicatus
Quem PAN ipse solet Deus comesse.
Haec, et quicquid habet Nemus comatum,
Aut Mons pendulus, aut profunda Vallis,
Affectu tibi dono liberali;
Et mox plura dabo, daboque pluris.
Supplex te interea rogo valere,
Ne PAN maximus exuat soporem,
Fissura qui jacet illius Vireti
Sub Fagi patulae supinus umbra.
Currendum mihi nunc, mihi volandum,
Ignes ocyus excitante Sole.

Exit.

CLORIN. Atque mei tecum fugiant quicunque timores. (p. 4)
In me quae virtus, quae vis occulta moratur,
Ut mihi sic humilis rudis hic sit virque caperque?
Sum pol mortalis, Pastoris filia, (nec non
Is mortalis erat) mortali matre creata.
Punge meum digitum, sanguis manabit ab illo:
Febris, et agnellos quae crispant flamina, quassant
Me quoque. Mortalem timor arguit. Attamen olim
Audivi (mater mihi dixit, nunc quoque credo)
Virgineum si cura mihi servare pudorem
Castum, illibatum, pulchrum, maculaque carentem,

Non Lamia, Umbra, Lemur, Daemon, Faunus, Satyrusve,
Si quid et est aliud Sylvarum numen, habebit
Me male, nec fatuis seducet in Avia flammis,
Nec voces media mea nomina nocte sonantes,
Quas coeno peritura sequar, segnive palude.
Hoc sine, cur rudis hic, morum inscius, atque politae
Doctrinae, cuius vel se truculentior ipso est
Et magis asper amor, mihi sic, mihi poplite flexo
Arrepat? certe magno hoc in nomine (*Virgo*)
Numen inest, omnes rudioris Sanguinis undas
Compescens; omnes, qui rumpunt fraena, calores.
Ergo mihi tu forte scutum fortissima rerum
Sis pudor: hic etenim vivam sub paupere tecto
Strenua in oppositos Fatique Erebique furores.

[I. ii]

Intret SENEX PASTOR, *cum quatuor paribus* Pastorum *et* Pastorarum.

SEN. PAS. Nunc, magno quia Festa Deo solemnia nostro
Egerimus, Ritusque eius celebravimus omnes,
Ignibus ingenuis incorruptisque vacate;
Sic, ut cum sancta vobis riget ora *Sacerdos*
Atque potente manu,
Velle malum cedat, calidusque libidinis ignis,
Fluminibus lustralis aquae. Jam flectite Turba,
Flectite Turba genu; *Panos* venit (ecce!) Sacerdos.

Intret SACERDOS.

SAC. Sic purgans abigo (gregum Magistri)
Quicquid praeteritus dies, vel iste (p. 5)
Festivus, dedit haud boni, quod inter
Vestro sanguine miscuit pudico.
A succo calido rebellis uvae,
A segni validi cibi vapore,
A desideriis libidinosis
Queis accenditur hinc et inde pectus,
Vos hoc flumine sanctiore lustro:
Pulchri estote dehinc, dehinc lavati.
Vestris interioribus medullis,
Sit quicquid meditemini politum,

Aura castius, et magis serenum.
Nunquam flamma dehinc libidinosa
Purgatos petat impetu meatus,
Aut ruptae fidei querela coelum,
Aut versus facilem impudicus aurem.
Ite omnes (maculis vacatis) ite.

Surgunt et cantant in laudem Panos.

Cantio

I

Qui nostros redimit Greges periclo
Pana canamus,
Nostrorumque Ovium Patrem; catena-
tisque lacertis
Cunctatim moveamus in rotundum,
Dum Tellus cava proximi Vireti
Implet murmure Musicam profundo.

II

O Pan, *magne Deus, modo Tibi* Pan
Psallimus isto.
Tu, qui nos retines magis pudicos
Vere recente,
Laudes perpetuo tuae sonentur,
A cunis rubicunduli diei,
Ad Solis moribunduli sepulchrum.

Exeunt omnes praeter PERIGOTTUM et AMORETTAM.

PER. Fronte potens *Amoretta*, mane, generosa Puella:
Te rogat ille tuus Pastor (Formosa) manere,
Cui vita plus chara sua es. (p. 6)
AMO. Dic age, plena tibi est indulta licentia fandi:
Lingua eadem sit, ut ante, tibi, tam nescia fraudis
Quam quae Aulam nunquam gustavit blanda, nec Urbem:
Sis semper verax.
PER. Quam non tuus esse, vel ignes
Incipiam puros miscere cupidine turpi,
Ante meas PAN linquat oves, quas Rege remoto
Aut Lupus, aut Hyemis rigor, Æstatisve calores

Et sitis absumant, vel adhuc sine nomine morbus;
Et mea communem comitentur fata ruinam.
AMO. Non optes generose, precor, tibi talia, Pastor;
Fido tibi: tam difficile est mihi credere falsum
Te, quam difficile est tibi me non credere pulchram.
PER. Pulchrior (O) longe es, castos fundente rubores
Aurora; pulchro tu sidere pulchrior illo,
Quo ducente Fretum secat anceps Nauta profundum;
Rectior erecta super alta cacumina pinu;
Candidiorque recens nudato lacte, sub ortum
Solis, ab extentis utero pendente mamillis
Nostrarum pulchrarum Ovium: Tibi crinis, ut aurum
Crinis Apollinei.
AMO. Pastor, te perdere noli;
Littora tu nostrae liquisti pone loquelae
Iam longinqua nimis.
PER. Quod non ego solus amarem,
Non mihi dixisti quondam? tot vota, precesque,
Iuramenta, Faces, fore non ludibra Ventis,
Quot sparsi ad Coelum? donasti non mihi dextram
Pignus? eam niveam? transferre negaveris ulli
Quae mea Tu primo fecisti gaudia pacto.
AMO. Virginis in quantum pudor audet dicere Verum,
Sum tua rursus ego; rursus tibi porrigo dextram.
Effuge tu semper Zelos, grave crimen Amoris. (p. 7)
PER. Summum tango bonum, petiturus id amplius unum,
Ulterius nostri quo confirmentur amores,
Formoso ut luco mox conveniamus in illo
Nocte hac felici; quo praemia ferre laborum
Longorum fidis mos est Pastoribus olim.
Dic, mea mella, sedet?
AMO. Veniam da (Pastor amice)
Si dubium mihi fit, quid Nox taciturna, diei
Juncta calori hujus, juvenili in sanguine possit.
'Omnia tuta timet virgo: neque lotus es omnis.
Ito, lavandus adhuc; haeret labecula cordi.
PER. Suspiciosa tibi non sit mea semper honesta
Veraque simplicitas: tam puri a faecibus ipse
Et mea flamma sumus, quam quae ardent nocte dieque
Virgineae taedae prope magnae Altare *Dianae*.

Id solum mihi mentis erat, cum talia suasi,
Foedus inire novum castis amplexibus ambo,
Inque manu posuisse manum solenniter illic.
Sacro etenim luco sacer est fons insuper illo,
Florea cui lepidis circundant ora choreis
Alipides Lemures Lunae pallentis ad ignem,
Surreptos pueros tingentes saepe, rigescat
Unde caro, fragilisque necem Natura repellat.
Multus ad hunc fontem juravit Pastor amoenum,
Multaque pacta fides, quam Fors, neque livor iniquus,
Nec potuit Tempus rescindere dente vetusto;
Cum multis quoque suavioli, quae casta dabantur,
Blanda Voluptatis venturae pignora: Fontem
Plurima ad hunc gelidum suffuso Virgo rubore
Flore coronavit iam olim Pastoris amati
Tempora diverso; dum felix ille canebat
Dilectae Paeana suae, charisque catenis.
Omnis ibi crescit quae planta salubrior apta est
Discinctis flammis brutali in parte premendis,
Objurgans venas, intestinumque calorem
Ocyus extinguens, qui mox ab origine parva
In deplorandos aliter prorumperet ignes.
Tam sacer ille locus. Crede ergo, et cede, et utrumque
Est generosi animi: nec avara audire fideli
Cum Pastore tuo, Faciei convenit illi. (p. 8)
Praeterea—
AMO. Vicisti; valeas: ventura hac nocte pudicam
Sera coronabit tibi spem, sed certa Voluptas.
PER. In caput ipse tuum PAN haec benefacta refundat
Hunc in Pastorem vestrum collata misellum,
Virgineae virtutis inexaequabile germen.
Cum cesses stupor esse meus, magnumque pudoris
Exemplum, rabidi merear miserabile nomen
Semi-caprique viri; vel me domet igne secundo
Foemina quae plures generavit publica morbos
Quam calidis *Sol* pronus equis, cum *Sirius* urget
Per stellata *Canis* furibundum Regna *Leonem*,
Lethiferum eructans irata fauce vaporem,
Inferius replens et peste et morte *Rotundum*.

Exit AMO.

Intret AMARILLIS.

AMA. Sum, Pastor, dictura quibus pudibunda, licetne
Mi sperare fidem?
PER. Licet, O formosa puella.
AMA. Tunc (sed ad auriculam) sic est; Amo te, Perigotte:
Gauderemque magis redamari, quam vegetum Ver
Terra gelata diu niveis amplectier ulnis.
Horres? non facias, nec me mirere rogantem
Tu, qui flos juvenum nostrorum, qui Gregis audis
Pastoralis apex his luxuriantis in umbris.
Quis vel ocellus hebes, semperque rebellis Amori,
Aut te luctantem vidit, cursuve natantem,
Ingenuove volans dantem molimine saxum,
Quin scintillavit subito, caecamque per omnes
Circumvicinas dispersit lampada venas?
Quis te cantantem audivit, qui rettulit illam
Quae concessa tuae est libertas aurea Voci?
Tunc vitio ne verte mihi (dulcissime Pastor)
Auferri tanta commiscerique caterva
Me quoque, si nullus vidit Te liber ocellus.
PER. O miseranda mihi, sed non redamanda Venustas,
Dulci corda tuae clauserunt Fata querelae.
Quicquid opis nostrae est prior occupat altera, meque (p. 9)
Spesque meas; frustra conceptum extingue calorem.
Mutet Amor sedes, ubi Fors et libera colla
Igne levent ignes, et mutua flamma resultet.
AMA. Merces ergo meum tam nulla manebit amorem,
Crudelis? si forsan Anus deserta rogarem,
Donaremve genis naturam ex arte secundam,
Communisve forem Pastorum flamma quod usquam est,
Aut revocare meam possem tam prompta, Puella
Quam nonnulla suam; poteras me spernere, Pastor.
Sed soli tibi sum. Non sit tibi ludu abuti
Ignibus innocuae, Pastor generose, Puellae.
PER. Uteris his verbis (frustra Pulcherrima) frustra.
Quippe scias, hesterna prius retroflectere possem
Tempora, vel remoram venienti ponere Nocti,
Quam flammas revocare meas, aut perfidus esse.
Pascere te vana spe nescio: convenit ista

Nocte, puellae illi pulchrae simul atque pudicae
(Quae cordis Regina mei est) fieri obvius illo
In luco, nostros ubi consummemus Amores.
Jam nimis ipsa diu te decipis; elige rursus:
Pastores alios habet haec vicinia multos,
Me, cum liber eram, gratos magis atque venustos.
Me praetermittas, et in hos hunc confer honorem.
Tu felix fias flamma meliore. Valeto.

Exit.

AMA. Crudelis! magis icta tua cado mortua Voce,
Quam si pallentes adigat me fulmine ad umbras
Jupiter iratus. Nolo desistere amore;
Non possum: non, non... Puber, Te utcunque fruemur;
Quamvis spes nostras interponantur et illud
Mille pericla. Habitat prope Funda palustria Pastor,
Cuius vita tulit prae se plus semper acerbi
Quam frons *Saturni* cum stat nascentibus arctans
Triste supercilium; qui solis carpitur agris, (p. 10)
Nec fruitur semet, nisi rumpens sacra duarum
Pacta voluntatum; qui quicquid ubique venusti est
Luxuriosus avet, nunquam veneratur Amator,
Sit licet ingenuo Facies magis aucta decore
Plurima quam *Phoebe*, laevisve juventa *Lyaei*;
Cui male nutritus scabie Grex semper inundat,
Et corrumpit Oves, quibus una pascitur, omnes;
Cuius postremi nascuntur, et ubere matrum
Non depulsi Agni moriuntur; cujus, ut ipse,
Sic macer et Canis est, scabraque rubigine plenus,
Nec voci domini, nec acutae auritus avenae.
Hic, bene lactatus, mirandum quid dabit, aptam
Discludens portam longis erroribus actae.
Ocyor (en!) votis venit opportunus is ipse.

Intret MELANCHOLICUS PASTOR.

MEL. Ne rudis appeller, quod sic (Formosa) recessus
Interrumpo tuos: Amor, intolerabile vulnus,
Me tulit huc aegrae quaerentem Balsama menti.
Non sis, Pulchra, ferox: tales ferus ipse *Cupido*
Insectari olim juravit vindice dextra.
Credas ergo meis, quibus induor undique, flammis;

Sic ut ego votis, jam antiquis, perfruar, et Tu
Igne leves ignem, cujus mea vita sit esca.
AMA. Certa forem si, Pastor, uti tua verba videntur,
Esse tibi sanum sic Cor; tibi forsitan in me
Suppeditaretur longi medicina doloris:
Nam gravis illa nimis, nimis aspera poena juventae,
Nunquam grata mihi, qua carpitur aeger amore.
Illico ego contenta forem tibi ferre quietem,
Officium si Tu facias mihi graviter unum.
MEL. Ingens illud opus mihi pandito: sitve periclum,
Quodve vel Ars humana potest, Industria, vel vis;
Sique tibi factum penitus non reddo, ratumque,
Nunquam iterum Solis radios orientis adorem.
AMA. Ain'? Te probo sic: Hoc ipso Vespere (Pastor)
Qui nobis tacitis illabitur humidus Alis,
Nobile par aequa pepigit concurrere flamma; (p. 11)
Idque nemus locus est, illorum ubi Corda manusque
Aeternum jungenda forent. Tu destrue pactum
Hoc, stabilemque fidem; tuaque, et post fata, manebo.
MEL. Nomina fac noscam; tunc si mea magna potestas
Ipsorum centrum non deturbarit amorum
Esse suo fixo, nunquam post inde calescam
Dulcibus his oculis quos tam devotus adoro.
AMA. Veneris, inque via dabitur tibi scire quod optas:
Insuper, unde regas opus hoc, documenta dabuntur.
Exeunt.

[I. iii]

Intret CLOE.

CLOE. Quomodo temporibus nocui, Sectaeve Virorum,
Quod sic praetereant ignotam haec tam sacra *Festa*,
Inque salutatam? Non sic frigere solebat
Pastorum, primo ridentum flore, Catervae.
Non bene tunc oluit vegetam miscere juventam
Sanguine multifluo tardum, pinguem, sine motu
Humorem, atque *Hominis* (natu sociabilis) hostem,
Dico pudicitiam, stupidam vereque gelatam.
Vix videor formosa (puto) nimiumve senesco,
Sumve parum propensa, meo vel non ab Ovili

Duco gregem magnum satis, alliciatur avarus
Quo Pastoris opes solum sectantis ocellus.
Sed formae satis est, aliis mihi credere si fas;
Nec nimis apellent, modo dicant vera, severam:
Plurimus est mihi Grex, et pascua plurima tondent.
Frigoris illorum, non nostri culpa pudoris
Ergo sit, aeternas quod moerens fundo querelas.

Intret THENOTTUS.

THE. Quis, quod vult, nolit; cui mens arrideat Axi
Fixa suo; et quis non, nisi non redamatus, amare
Audeat aut vellet, si quaeritur; Ecce misellum!
CLOE. Pastor, non abeas, non, (quaesumus:) unde venis nunc?
Aut quo vadis? ubi viret hac magis horrida Sylva?
Spirat et hic, qua nec melior nec mollior aura est,
Laevis ubi *Zephyrus* faciem lascivus oberrat (p. 12)
Crispatam labentis aquae; floresque quot ulla
Vere novo producit Humus, totidemque colorum.
Quod placet hic omne est; gelidi fontesque lacusque,
Arboreaeque domus plumatis flore Corymbis,
Antra, lacunosique apices. Horum elige quid vis.
Ipsa tuo cantans lateri concreta sedebo;
Hosve legam juncos (digitis tibi vincula longis:)
Crebraque Amoris erit pro Te mihi Fabula; pallens
Ut primum vidit sylvis venando *Diana*
Endymiona, bibens oculis labefacta Puelli
Aeternos ignes, et non medicabile vulnus;
Molliter ut conduxit eum, gremioque refusum,
Atque soporifero redimitum tempora flore
Ad *Latmi* caput antiqui, quo devolat illa
Omni nocte, aurans fraterno lumine Montem,
Basia mille datura genis quas deperit.
THE. Absint
Ista poetarum quae vinum atquae otia gignunt
Somnia: decretum est: et amare, et amarier, aeque
Dedidici. Versus, Hymni, laetaeque choreae,
Sunt aliena mihi, quae mulcent saepe Puellas.
Pectora sola procul mirari casta remansit:
Haec neque flos Aevi, neque dulcis lingua, nec aurum,
Expugnare (simul) potuerunt; tam bene formam

Accepere sui: Tali me servo Puellae.
Illa mihi forma est; moveo, sto, spiro, per illam:
Sola potest miserum me reddere, sola beatum.
CLOE. Fas est ignotae, bone Pastor, noscere divam
Cui tantum debes, quam tam devotus adoras?
THE. Fas: et ad exemplum discas componere tantum
Vitam, Nympha, tuam. Nam pulchra audire, nitere
Nec virtute pari, solummodo pascet ocellos
Pomposi juvenis, flammamque foventis inanem.
Ergo velim NEMORIS noscas ea VIRGO vocatur:
Hoc quoniam castos olim sepelivit amores,
Et nunc busta colit, capitisque cupidine functi
Devovit strictum se Virginitatis in Album.
Hanc tantum admiror: leviori sanguine nulla,
Nec nova forma placet. *Exit.*
CLOE. Pastor miserande, valeto,
Non mea materies: subitis mihi mentibus usus, (p. 13)
Libera queis effrons sermo maturet in Acta.
Sit mihi, qui prima facie simul ausit amare,
Solicitare simul.

Cantio

Venite, Pastores, actutum,
Venite, venite,
Dum statis in flore vitae;
Nemus viride est mutum,
Et nunquam feret illa cocleata
Ulli Basia; blandulis nec illos
Nodos innumerabiles lacertis
Qui dantur: mera suavitas, Pacesque,
Queis accenditur impotens senectus,
Et sanguis quoque virginis rebellet!

Tunc, si unquam,
Nunc, aut nunquam,
Sumite gratis
Id quod ego
Nulla nego
Quando petatis.

Intret DAPHNIS.

CLOE. En Alter! meliora mihi Tu, Numen in ipso
Sanguine qui regnas. Sed (ni male nota legenti,
Quam cerno, Facies) hic est pudibundulus ille,
Ille salutator tantum, non oscula ferre,
Non cantare bonus, non alternare loquelas,
Arte susurrandi palpare, nec illud amatum
Poscere non timide propter quod nascimur omnes;
Qui vultu procus est, foret et contentus amari,
Ni audendo detur: Spes hac mihi friget in umbra.
Quem nisi quod trudent huc fata, virum mihi mallem
Ex nive confectum, vel in usus sumere nostros
Eunuchum. Sed sic, quia venit, molior illum.
Vir peramande, adsis acceptatissimus Illi
Quae, nisi Te propter, jamdudum vivere nollet:
Accipe (cur dubitas?) nostram pro pignore dextram,
Hanc, data quae nulli fuit ante; sedetoque tantum
Colliculum super hunc juncosum, floribus orbo
Dum ramos ego virgineis, aut illico carpo
Quicquid praecipui prato constellat in illo, (p. 14)
Unde coroneris, mollive ligere catena,
Languida vel subter sternantur membra, Voluptas
Cum sensus nobis omnes captivet. Ut harum
Conspectus, laevi surgentum flore, genarum,
Me meminisse facit pubentis *Adonis* olim,
Cum, fastu turgens et dulci sorte, jacebat
Inter stringentes *Ericinae* mobilis artus!
Fortius est oculis (si cerno) loquacibus istis
Incantamentum, majorque hac fronte moratur
Dulcedo, quam pictores praebere tabellis,
Quas et ament, possint. Non insociabilis ille,
Qui se deperiens lachrymarum evenuit imbre,
*Silvani*ve rubens Puer, aut bis rapta Puella,
Quam propter *Pyrrhi* ceciderunt *Pergama* dextra,
Aequiparandi aliter tibi sunt, quam mortua plantae
Arbor oliviferae.

DAPH. Mihi cor quod possit amare est;
Sed piger effari, ne sim nimis inde futurus
Infelix.

CLOE. Felix dicas: non, *Daphni*, rubescas;
Si tibi (chare puer) lux est inimica tuisque
Mollibus igniculis, venientem sumito noctem;
Omnibus illa favet: Nemus exspatiabor in illud,
Omnis cum tenebris oculus claudetur amicis.
Convenit? Ah! nimium certe pudibundus es; Aude:
Dic, Sedet.

DAPH. Aio quidem: nec fallam, dummodo fas sit
Te sperare mihi (pulcherrima Pulchra) fidelem.

CLOE. Vota tibi cedunt.

DAPH. Tenerissima Virgo, valeto.
Heus! rogo (me quoniam jussisti nocte venire)
Soli ne metuas occurrere sola: nocere
Nam licet ipsa velis, nollem tibi, si mihi mundus
Sit pretium sceleris: Pacto stes firmiter ergo.
Fervescant alii venali sanguine; noster
Purior est anima quam fulcit, et usque pudicus.

Exit.

CLOE. Pauperior nunc sum quampridem. Nonne stupendum est,
Inter tot calido vernantes sanguine, solos (p. 15)
Me reperire viros, queis venae, fluminis instar
Languentis quia fonte procul, sunt semper eadem,
Tardae, stagnantes, cursu motuque carentes,
Si conjurati pulsent latus undique venti?
O vos felices, quibus *Hymen* cognitus unquam,
Notaque quae sitio genialis gaudia lecti!
Insideatque Tibi gravius Tempusque dolorque,
Tu, qui ignave mihi poteras succurrere Pastor,
Quam cui perpetuo lacerat praecordia rostro
Vultur edax.

Intret ALEXIS.

ALEXIS. Proprione potest haec forma vagari
Tuta satellitio, nec praetereuntis ocellos
Attrahere aut cupide conspectae, avideve cupitae;
Dum Labyrinthea melior vertigine rapta
Pars contemplatur, dans votis, totaque Venae
Fraena laboranti?—Nivis aemula Nympha Rosaeque,
Fasne mihi causam vestri penetrare recessus,
Cur ita sola meas? potior (me judice) campus,

Pastorumque chorus juventum magis aptus inani hoc
Incultoque loco: Non Tu *deserta* frequentes,
Hasque venustates oculis ne deme Virorum,
Quae nos Pastores inter sunt vivere natae.

CLOE. Pastor, habes votum; nunquam conspeximus ullum
In quo plura micent animae solamina, quam Te.
Dicere plus possem, si libertatis ademptae
Spes foret inde mihi. Totum mihi cede ruborem,
TITHONI *croceum linquens*, AURORA, *cubile*,
Semper Virgo.

ALEX. Mihi (plus quam suavissima rerum)
Isti si spirant flores, dic vota, tenesque.
Dirige tu linguam (melior mihi daemon) amicam,
Trude meum nomen dubitantis in ora pudica,
Ut sit quod primo verbum producat.—

CLOE. *Alexi*,
Cum Sol decedens vitreo dabit oscula Ponto,
Thetidos et niveis somno litabit in ulnis, (p. 16)
I nemus in sacrum; Me, Pastor, habebis in illo.

ALEX. Si morer, aeternus torpor, ventusque volando
Flumina qui claudit *Rheni Volgae*ve, calentis
Dum solis radius redit irritus inde, refraenet
Me quoque, nec glacie exaequet mea frigora tanta.
Ut juvenesco, furens! ut transeo totus in ignem!
Migrandum est.

CLOE. Signum *Cloe* sit.

ALEX. Fuge lux, fuge *Phoebe*.
Exit.

CLOE. Triste foret mihi nunc, si fallat uterque puellam.
"Carbasa mutabit Vento qui navigat omni.

Actus secundi Scena prima.

Intret SENEX PASTOR *Campanam pulsans, et* SACERDOS *Panos sequens.*

SAC. Pastores, et amabiles puellae,
Omnes claudite mox Greges Ovili:
Condensatus enim nigrescit Aer;
Magnum nunc quoque Sol iter peregit.
En ut stillula basiat caduca
Quicquid rideat herbulae per Agros,
Florum pendula sericis coronis,
Ut Crystallinus ordo fibularum!
En nubes gravidas Polo ruentes!
En Noctem Styge *Vesperum* vocantem!
Qua surgente, subit gravis saluti
Caligo, vapor, humidique flatus
Lascivam faciem super volantes
Horum ala trepidante Pascuorum;
Qui, quacunque cadent, ibi innocenti
Nec flori neque gemmulae favebunt.
Tantis protegat illico periclis
Unusquisque suas oves amatas;
Atque extra jaceant canes soluti,
Ne de monte ruat lupus propinquo,
Ut fur nocte latens, et ante lucem (p. 17)
Aut agnum sibi rapiat, vel haedum;
Aut latrociniis opima vulpes
Incautas dirimat dolo phalanges.
His tuti satis esse si velitis,
Securi nimis esse nesciatis:
Sit lumen vigil alterum vicissim,
Dum dulces capit alterum sopores.
Pastores ideo boni futuri,
Pastorumque (nimis) Deo potenti
Gens dilecta, levis sopor, quiesque
Dulcis, mellifluum velut poema,
Vestris sensibus incidant. Valete.
Vespertinam ita clauda cantilenam. *Exeunt.*

[II. ii]

Intret CLORINDA Pastora, *herbas separans, et explicans earum qualitates vel virtutes.*

CLOR. Nunc videam mea quid generosa scientia fecit,
Magna noctivagae virtute adjuta *Dianae*,
Tunc cum tota micat. Vos, non impia Terrae
Progenies; Solis, Vos, quies datur inclyta virtus;
Almae debentes rerum majora Parenti
Quam vel *Homo*, dilectus ei super omnia, et Haeres;
Vos sinite ut venerer: Vos, est quibus aequa potestas
Et Necis et Vitae, producentes breve stamen
Aurae vitalis longo per tempora tractu;
Vos, quae hae carpsere manus multo ante diei
Ortum; nomina mi date vestra, mihi date vestras
Moxque potestates occultas. Aurea *Clote* haec;
Marrubium hoc nigrum est; ovibusque oviumque; magistris
Dente venenato rabidi Canis acriter ictis
Ambo salutifera. Hi rami sunt mollis *Acanthi*,
Qui si vestibulis aut postibus affigantur,
Unde fores pendent, incantamenta repellunt
Omnia, pestiferae fuerint licet illa MEDEÆ,
Quae laedunt homines pecudesve. Remedia certa
Haec rabiae neque lenta ferunt: *Absynthium* amarum,
Salvia, *Solsequium*, humanae saluberrima genti.
Haec *Tormentilla* est, data cui suprema potestas
Mortiferum quodcunque fugandi a corde venenum.
Haec est *Narcissi radix*, lenire tumores
Optima; *Lysimachus* flavus, pastoris ocellis (p. 18)
Defessi dulcem bonus accelerare soporem,
Occidens ubicunque venit culicesque molestas,
Omnigenamque volat quae non sine murmure muscam:
Celandina leprae contraria, cum *Calamintha*,
Et *Lolio*, quibus est virtus purgare meatus
Sanguinis humani, sic ut non purior hoc sit
Halitus infantis, vel aquae crystallinus haustus.
Hic aliaeque duae, sed earum noxia virtus
Non venit apta mihi, quarum est natura rebellis.
Vos igitur, *Cynosorchi* salax, *Terebinthina* turpis,
Me simul atque meis procul este sodalibus, ambae;

Vos quae pellicitis venas, sufflatis in illis
Civilem flammam, Rationis scanditis Arcem,
Decipitisque ducem visis, mentisque chimaeris
Lascivae, donec satietur anhela libido,
Devia eunte anima, divinae lucis egena.
Tu quoque, tu facilis stimulans ad gaudia mentes,
Et risum sine lege, levis *Verbena*, sequeris.
Non ego te gelidis tingam de more fluentis,
Et ramos aspergam omnes omnemque columnam
Vivificante tuo succo, Pastoribus implens
Laetitiaque domos, et vanis ora cachinnis.

Intret THENOTTUS.

THE. Haec domus est frondosa, sui qua gloria sexus,
Maxima quae spiravit adhuc, laterive datura est
Unquam Pastoris felicem exinde calorem,
Una se digna existens, sibi vivit et uni.
Stella beata, Tibi grates pro lumine reddo;
Tu, cujus radiis Noctis caligo profundae
Exula a Terra; cujus vice triste tuentis
Fax tua casta subit, faciem diffusa per aegram
Totius mundi, crispans fraternum callida lumen,
Deque *Chao* dans usque diem, prae qua sine luce est
Quae *Jovis* augustam *Via lactea* ducit ad Aulam.
Tuque pudicitia salve Dea castior ipsa,
Quaeque micas stella noctu quoque pulchrior illa:
Omnis feminea Constantia quae fuit unquam,
Unquam feminea quae gente futura sit, omnis:
Cui pulchris oculis ignis sacer evolat ille (p. 19)
Quem desiderii matrem dixere Poetae,
Omne per ingenuum pectus, generosius omne,
Infundens meliorem animam, magis atque beatam,
Quam quae *Hominem a Bruto* distinguit coelitus orta.
CLOR. Quomodo Tute locum venisti Pastor in istum?
Nulla hic trita via est, gramen viridantius omne,
Quod Ver ediderat, nullo pede colla reclinat:
Solum picta cutem, procul a rumore tremendo
Curvati cornu, dama haec arbusta frequentat.
THE. Castior Aurora, non huc erroribus actus
Deflexi gressum, forti vel imagine lusus;

Te, Te quaesitum veni, pulcherrima cujus
(Crede mihi) est magnis gravidus virtutibus aer,
Fortiter atque gemit, dum Fama resultat ab Astris
Pastoresque ferit stupefactos, posse virilis
Virtutis tantum sexu esse minore virili.
CLOR. Si qua mihi virtus, Ars si qua occulta medendi,
Quae te vel morbo levet, antiquove dolore,
Unde (recens quod hiat, vel quod radicitus haeret)
Judicio alterius sit non medicabile quiddam;
Ausim adhibere manum.
THE. Non est cruciatus hic extra,
Quem patior; Non est nimio quae sanguine vena
Colluctans infesta vehit contagia cordi;
Ulcus Apollineae non est in corpore toto
Artis egens; animae gravior dolor incubat isti
Quam sanaverunt unquam medicamina, cuique
Tu (Virgo formosa) potes, Tu sola mederi.
CLOR. Pastor (amabo) tuam fac me cognoscere poenam:
"Pandere quem non vis, non est medicina dolori.
THE. Ergo (nimis Formosa) scias; *Amo te*—
CLOR. Nihil addas,
Pastor; honorati stuprasti limen Asyli,
Sacrilegumque nefas istius in ossa patrasti
Dulce quiescentis gremio Telluris opaco:
Quae nisi vis surgant, fugite hinc velocibus Alis (p. 20)
Tuque tuique simul fatui ignes, ne sera Mortis
Vindictaeque lues animam tibi terreat ipsam
Horribili Facie.
THE. Numeros perfecta per omnes,
Non mea sancta fides mereatur dedecus istud.
CLOR. Aude'n stare, effrons, haec donec Terra cadaver
Parturiat divisa suum? quod nempe futurum est,
Si tu lascivo perrexeris igne sacratum
Hunc temerare locum: resipiscas ergo, et abito;
Laudibus intera Manes placabo sepultos
Illius, hoc sine, qui Te quid foret esse doceret
Aemulus aeternae flammae quam servat in urna.
THE. Non candore gena rubor intertextus in illa
Te veneraturum poterat mihi flectere pectus;
Non oculus tuus, extensus licet atque serenus;

Frons augusta, humero *Pelopisque* simillima laevis
Nec qui fossiculis latet illis risus, *Amantes*
Capturus faciles; longi digitique manusque
Distincti venis opulenter; nec tua lingua,
Dulcior illa chely quamvis vel *Arionis* esset;
Pendulus aurato productus stamine crinis,
Innumerabilibus satagens involvere nodis
Errantes animas; totius Corporis atque
Fabrica justa tui, quod purius esse vel ipsis
Virgineo Alpinis nivibus candore videtur:
Haec unita, mihi (tua si constantia abesset)
Non aliter placitura forent, quam nigra procella
Sit misero nautae per caerula regna vaganti.
Hoc sed honorifico dum sis tu septa rigore,
Quamvis tot pestes, utero quod in aeris amplo
Nox inimica serit super hac cervice rotarent,
Has ego discuterem, fragiles ut ab arbore guttas,
Et circumfusis securus amabo periclis.
CLOR. Mene sepulchrales (demens) excire favillas
Olim defuncti muta in Tellure Mariti
Quas cinit abscondit gelidus?
THE. Charissima rerum,
Non ausim petere hoc, tibi nec concedere fas est.
Strenua sta voto, nec sis labefacta; memento (p. 21)
Quam fuit ille tuus, sisque id quod ab omnibus audis.
Velle, nec ille Deus mulierum dira Cupido,
Fraena dehinc rumpant; non desidera longo
Exilio revoces, abjuratoque calores:
Stes veluti rupes frustra pulsata procellis
Irati Coeli, pontique sequacibus undis.
Si cedis, nostros extinguis funditus ignes.
Ille fidelis amor, cineri quem solvis humato,
Ille est quem stupeo, quem sic prostratus adoro.
Attamen est aliud quiddam quod vota requirunt,
Si me audire velis; sed non (precor) annue votis.
O PAN! incerto mea spes ut fluctuat aestu!
Ocyus hinc elinget enim, si mansero, vitam
Haec mihi flamma duplex.
CLOR. Fac hod quod dicis; et illud
Hora terat, cui non Ars et Natura medentur.

THE. Virtus ipsa, vale; longosque beere per annos;
Dum mecum miser ipse moror. Sed figere sedem
Me prope te (pretiosa) sinas; mihi fiet id Antrum
(Lugubri umbratum Taxo moestaque Cupresso)
Dulce palatiolum; quo primo mane, priusquam
Phoebus ab irriguis nectar libaverit herbis,
Dura et iniqua nimis super impendentia plangam
Vertice fata meo.
CLOR. Tibi dent pia Numina, Pastor,
Tum properata feri, tum certa remedia, Morbi.

Exeunt.

[II. iii]

Intret MELANCHOLICUS.

MEL. Non amo, quae mihi nunc est convenienda, Puellam;
Nam meus inconstans oculus non hauserit ullam huc
Usque venustatem, quamvis et suavior illa,
Pulchrior et sit flore novo, cum spirat in ipsum
Aut *Zephyrus* levis, aut rosei lux prima diei,
Cum matutina facie nant mille rubores:
Haec, concinna aliqua mihi praesentata figura,
In me vel minimum nequeant accendere amorem;
Velle ingens possent, subitumve libidinis ignem.
Femina qualiscunque mihi venit aequa, sit illa
Nigra vel alba cutem, mixtive ab utroque coloris;
Virgo, virumve satur: quaecunque est, vota coronat. (p. 22)
Juro, perjuro, fleo: nemo frequentius ista;
Virginis instillat Mel nemo mollius auri;
Narro et ei quam fortis amem, quam antiquus adorem;
Crudelem voco, marmoream:
Offero ei quodcunque meum est, ut sit mihi praedae
Gemmula quae teneris, est tam pretiosa Puellis:
Mox odi, et fugio. Quid sorte beatius ista?

Intret AMARYLLIS.

AMA. Pastor ave; PAN servet oves oviumque magistrum,
Tu quia promissum servas mihi.
MEL. Pulchra Puella,
Perquam grata venis; tuus in te vota retorquet

Pastor amans eadem, cui, praesens tempus adusque,
Nunquam oculus luxit, qui me torquere lacertos
Cogeret, assidueque mori languore recente.
Nunc age; connexas ipsorum quomodo flammas,
Et quando, dirimemus? ei dementiar illum?
Ficta quod est, jurabo, fides; amor ejus, ubique?
Dicam, ludibrio quod eam tibi nuper habebat;
Quod vero simile est, te confirmante, futurum:
Nam tanti est candoris ea, et tam simplicis, ut cum
Nesciat ipsa, putet mentiri posse nec ullum.
Aut *Amorettam* Illi infectar, castamque videri,
Sed non esse, aiam? Mecum jurabo fuisse
Inter obumbrantes hesterno Vespere Ficus;
Et dulcem sudisse animam, sanctumque pudorem,
In gremium mihi; lascivum struxisse cubile
Horibus et foliis, ubi se mihi tota premendam
Indulsit, stravitque volentia membra per herbas:
Ejus ibi multa jam nomen in Arbore sculpsi,
Atque meum, citius quo credi haec fabula possit.
Dametam nostin', vetuli Pastoris *Amolpi*
Haeredem? Hunc multos inter secernere visum est,
Complicitos qui se nos invenisse, suoque
Adventu nostros turbasse referret amores:
A me sunt puero promissa crepundia multa,
Mendacis merces; et (munera grata) volucres
Capturi laquei, cumque Arcu tundere telum (p. 23)
Utile saltantes inter Virgulta sciuros,
Parque Cothurnorum, mollisque, Capillus ut ejus,
Agnus, olorino vel pectore pluma minuta.
Hoc feci Te propter ego, mihi parte futurum
Jucundum duplici: donat Discordia vitam.

AMA. Pastor amate, Tibi grates: Pastoribus istas
Forsan inexpertis poteras obtrudere technas
Non huic; cujus amor stabili fundatus in axe
Nec folio possit, nedum radice, moveri.
Strenuiore manu, qua murus ahenus iste
Corruat, utendum est: Tu tantum inventa secundes,
Et tua semper ero.

MEL. Meque experiaris, et illa.

AMA. Hoc par Pastorum felix mox inde coibit,

Palantes simul atque Greges cum sole reponant,
In spisso Nemoris collem quod proximat illum
Cui lateri insculpsit Fontem Natura petroso;
Nec, nisi qui lepidis celebratur ubique Poetis,
Huic par ullus erat. Crescunt latera ardua juxta
Omnes quae magicis miscentur cantibus herbae;
Omnes, quae donant mortem, donantve salutem;
Quicquid odoriferi Nubentum Festa coronat,
Sive colorati; manet illic *Maia* perennis;
Omnia nascuntur, juvenescunt, atque virescunt.
Grabem ibe nullum est quo frigida decidit unquam
*Autumni Brumae*ve manus: Tam plena caloris,
Plena vigoris humus, fontem quae circuit istum,
Qui, de monte cadens, lento pede rumpit in amnem;
Dum vallis scatet omnis aqua, piscesque ministrat
Multorum generum, pastorum pabula genti.
Huic mihi saepe sacro narravit Anicula fonti
(Incantamenti, dum vixit, conscia multi)
Esse potestatem formas quascunque creatas
In nova mutandi quae corpora jusserit ille
Qui demittet eas ter in imo vortice mersas,
Carmen et hoc repetet mihi quod moribunda reliquit;
Et docuit quae, quoque modo, medicina ligetur
Illius Fronti, cui stet variare figuram,
Ante soporandi ter, quam credatur Abysso huic. (p. 24)
Haec mihi cuncta: simul, secreto hoc jussit ut ejus
Uterer, invito si quando *Cupidine* amarem.
Pastor, hoc experiar: quae tradidit omnia sunt hic
In promptu mihi nunc, tingique audebo vel ipsa.
Tristibus his herbis, agedum, mea tempora cinge;
Cumque sopore gravem me videris, imbue me ter,
Fac et ut ex lymphis emergam *Amoretta*: reique
Me dimitte meae, redituram (deserat ante
Quam terras lux alma) mei Pastoris in ulnas.
Tunc me redde mihi; quam protinus accipe totam,
Intensumque tuae restingue cupidinis ignem.
Et tibi ni quadrem, neque tu mihi denique quadres.
Hujus inauditi sitio miracula Fontis.

Exeunt.

[II. iv]

Intret DAPHNIS.

DAPH. Hic morer, haec etenim statio est umbratilis a te
Assignata, *Cloe*: Deludere nolis amantem,
Clara oculos virgo: venias, mea Pulchra, venito:
Non timor insipiens, nec honoris frigida cura,
Te (Formosa) tui teneat pastoris ab ulnis.
Aegrius inducar qui castae robora mentis
Impugnare tuae, quam Sol extinguere Lucem,
Aut illud magnum dare passus retro *Rotundum*.
Ingenuus meus error erit, plenusque decori,
Sermo labe carens, mea ut est sine labe juventus;
Nec meditabor ego, facilis quod fluminis instar
Non circumscriptum sensim prorumpat in aequor
Exiguo de Fonte.
ALEXIS (*intus*). *Cloe!*
DAPH. Vox ipsius haec est.
Respondebo, *Cloe!* Quam crebos quamque tenaces
Amplexus dabimus, castas sanctasque catenas
Confusis manibus? Venis, quotcunque subestis,
Mando meis (per quas et sanguis et halitus errant)
Clave repugnantes vestros cohibete calores;
Et votis inferte obices, ne magna rebellent:
Insanire ultra nolite, modestia quam sit
Rubra genas tolerando. (p. 25)
ALEXIS (*intus*). *Cloe!*
DAPH. Peramabile nomen
Rursus in aure sonat, cui protinus obvius ibo—

Intret ALEXIS

Sed quis hic est? aliquis Pastor; non dormio certe:
Quid velit hoc aenigma sibi? remanebo seorsim
Ut plus ediscam.
ALEX. Jecur hoc, meus ignis, ut uris?
Responde formosa mihi. *Cloe. Alexis, Alexis,*
Strenuus, elatus, florentis prodigus aevi,
Invocat usque *Cloen*. En, hospita brachia tendo
Fervidus aureolem jam tacturientia fructum,
Qui pendendo diu nimirum tentavit avara

Lumina! Rumpe moras. Centrum qui ducit in illud
Hic Labyrintheus mihi totus obibitur error,
Dum refrigerium inveniat mea adusta libido.
Crudelis, venio. *Exit* ALEXIS.

DAPH. Mea tantum tristibus umbris
Mens inimica sibi est, credam haec ut vera, fidemque
Dem posthac oculis? aut apparentia tantum?
Puraque nunc etiam mihi labis habebitur illa?
Caecus ut erret amor fixo de tramite, saepe
Talia sunt sane phantasmata, et ante fuerunt.
Sed procul a me sit curare haec somnia: frustra
Exclamata *Cloe*, mihi Te sedet esse fidelem.
Audi, Pulchra *Cloe*.

CLOE (*intus*). Quis me?

DAPH. Nolae instar acutae
Non sonat ista virum nova vox: O femina certe!
Praeteritum mihi redde sonum, peramabilis Echo.

Intret CLOE.

CLOE. Hic.

DAPH. O, quae crux est, nos tam prope flectere nostros
Nec conferre gradus?

CLOE. Pastor, convenimus: altum
Subtrahe te in lucum, ne qui cadit humor in herbas
Reptilibus guttis, lentae caliginis instar,
Humectat soccos tibi.

DAPH. Formosissima rerum,
Inventa es? Qui sic erraveris, ut melior pars
Hujus felicis transiverit irrita Noctis?
O mea vita! Tibi vehementer ut obvius ire
Ardebam! niveis ut basia serre lacertis!
Sortem ut inire bonam quam donat amabilis illi
Vox ea, qui vestram laeta bibit aure loquelam! (p. 26)
Sed nimis esse rudis videor, nimis esse protervus,
Et prope lascivus, qui tecum moribus utor
Tam caldis, ubi sanctus honos, ubi curor decori,
Atque meus pudor, atque tuae reverentia famae,
Dicere quaeque potest frater sine labe sorori,
Debuerant nostram potius compescere linguam.
Sed melior (mihi crede) sub isto cortice mens est;

Ne doleas igitur (semper mitissima) primus
Quod meus Aggressus sapiat leve pectus, et audax;
Protinus evado sermonem mutus ad omnem
Qui tibi non castisque tuis sonet auribus aptus.
Basiolum certe te poscere nolo, minutos
Nec torquebo tibi digitos; supplexve rogabo
Astra ea fixa duo mihi subridere beata;
Omnis fraus juvenum, stratagemataque; omnia, *Amantum*;
Lascivum omne mori sine morte; aliena futura
Sunt mihi: virtuti tantum sum Victima vestrae
Aeterna.

CLOE. Primo (Pastor) agam grates, quod amamur honeste:
Proxima cura mihi est ut amor sit magnes amoris.
Non—Puer infelix: nimio Tu frigore torpes,
Haud mihi quadratus; Tibi nobile sanguinis aurum
Desinit in plumbum. 'Non est pudor inscius esca
"Femineae mentis; nec qui jam sponte favores
"Respuit oblatos, reduces post inde meretur.
Evigilone, videns juvenem talique figura,
Quemque creaturam pulchram appellare solemus.
Tam segnem? quantum pretiosae perderet Artis,
Hunc partes egisse viri quae cogere vellet?
Ipsa sed abjiciam, quem non retinere valebo.
"Audaces *Fortuna* juvat, juvat atque *Cupido.*
Daphni, secundo adeo quoniam convenimus astro;
Et nunc sors eadem, manet idem casus, utrumque;
Hoc super inde velim, votis utrinque sacratis, (p. 27)
Et nexis manibus, nunquam rumpenda pacisci:
Dextram carpe viam; meditans dum talia mente
Devota, carpo non eminus ipsa sinistram.
Hos postquam, nemorum perque alta silentia noctis,
Solverimus ritus, et debita sacra: revertens,
Invenias quercum veterem, cava cujus utrumque
Complecti nostrum possint; I protinus illuc,
Valle stat adversa.

DAPH. Stet. *Exit* DAPH.

CLOE. Conveniemus ibidem
Nunquam—stulte pudor.

ALEXIS (*intus*). *Cloe!*

CLOE. Vox illius haec est.

Quem magis audacem fore spero.
ALEXIS (*intus*). *Cloe!*
CLOE. Bene verti
Maxime nunc mihi PAN *Syringis* propter amorem.
Exit CLOE.

Actus tertii Scena prima.

Intret PASTOR MELANCHOLICUS *cum* AMARYLLIDE *dormiente.*

MEL. Has herbas tibi fronte sic revello,
Ut non discutias jubens soporem,
Sacris vorticibus quousque Fontis
Illius, magico potente versu
Verbis horrisonantibus referto,
Ter demissa mihi, ter extraharis.
Hoc ligamine Cannabi perusti,
Luna jam rutilante perplicati,
Sic corpus tibi stringo somnolentum:
Nascentum caput ad diem reflecto,
Ad Solisque tuos pedes sepulchrum:
Dextrum verto tuum Noto lacertum,
Et stellis Borealibus sinistrum:
Corpus tollo tuum solo execrando,
Hac mortaliter extasi sopitum:
Nunc hos in latices sacri fluenti
Forti labere pensilis lacerto.
Hanc Fons accipias sacer puellam
Totis fluctibus intimoque fundo:
Tingo perspicuis tuis in undis,
Sic cum pace tua, pedes minutos;
Sic hanc do latici profundiori,
Ut Tali quoque sentiant liquorem;
Sic profundius, ut genu puellae
Haustus Nectareos utrumque gustet.
Non ultra: fuge protinus, quod usquam
Felices radios amat diei.
Unius pia *Veritas* figurae,
Hoc sit Carmine te loco repello.
Anguis, qui renovas cutem quotannis;
Inconstante, *Camelio*, colore;
Sexum qui varias, *Lepus*, quotannis;
Proteus, pluribus et malis figuris;
Nocturnis, *Hecate*, Sacris triformis;
Lymphis induat haec Puella santis
Humescens *Amorettulae* figuram:

Carmen, *Cinthia*, tu meum secundes.
Te sic extraho liberam periclis
Isto Fonticulo sacro: resurgas
Par illi, simul exuas soporem.

Expergiscitur.

AMA. Pastor, ad externam sum (dic) *Amoretta* figuram?
Defuit aut aliquis Magica tibi ritus in Arte,
Cujus defectu me deficiente, retecti
Esse modi possint quos tanto struximus astu?
MEL. Per Lunam, nisi quod sto cespite fixus eodem,
Cujus adoptivam te fecit sumere formam
Halitus hic, cujusque manus demisit in undas
Te siccam, madidamque statim retraxit ab illis;
Ipsa *Amoretta*, mihi quoque, comparitura fuisses:
Omnia tam similes, vestem, vocemque, coloremque,
Et gestum: ut non vos sensus distinguere possit.
AMA. Tunc haec techna potens, hic inevitabilis error,
Meque datura tibi est, et ab illa dividet illum.
Huc illa est ventura, fidem si servat; et ille
Nunquam ita cultus erat, foret Autor ut ipse puellae
In Nemus umbrosum, cum nox incumbit et horror,
Obviam eundi illi, neque nosceret ante venire
Esse suum: venienti autem causabor Amoris
Me festinantem pennis venisse priorem,
Nec cessisse loco: Tunc sylvae ambagibus illum
Ulterius ducam; sed tu hic remanebis, et huc si
Ejus eum verus quaesitum venerit ignis,
Per diversum aliquem facias abcedere callem,
Quem dicas calcasse recens ipsius *Amantem*:
Non procul hinc abero. Quin si sit forte necesse,
Hic aliud mihi, quo nebulae demantur ocellis,
Incantamentum est, ad Lunae incendia lectum;
Meque quod in propriam faciat transire figuram.

Intret PERIGOTTUS.

MEL. Subtrahe te, *Perigottus* adest; qui firmus Amator,
Cernere gestit eam cujus geris ipsa figuram. (p. 29)
PER. Hic pulchra est *Amoretta* locus; nondum appulit hora,
Hic omnis delectatur Sylvana potestas
Illum ferre sacrum circum vestigia fontem,

Carmine quem multo multumque potente bearunt;
Devius obscura nam nunquam nocte Viator
Incidit huic, pecudesve vagae; sed lumine cassi
Invenere viam veram, ducentibus Illis:
Tam sacer hic locus est.
Quaerere sed libet ulterius, ne prima *Amoretta*
Appulerit, sic sola diu petat avia gressu.
Mi *Amoretta, Amoretta!* *Exit.*
AMA. Meus *Perigotte!*
PER. Meum Cor!
AMA. Cor tibi curro meum. *Exit.*
MEL. Nunc votis illa potita est,
Nec minus optatis longis ego perfruar illa.
Jamque corusca micat velut ostentando *Diana*
Exiguo hoc Luco jubar omne quod exit ab illa

Intret AMORETTA.

Endymioni alicui, quem deperit illa secundo.
En *Amorettam* aliam! quid ab illa discrepat istam?
Fictitiam secum si non *Perigottus* haberet,
Hanc ego rerer eam. Plantae, Sylvaeque, lacusque,
Quanta scatet vobis vis, si constaret ocellis!
AMO. Hanc noctem vix esse reor; non ipsa tremisco
(Per nemus hoc errans) ursam, saevumve leonem,
Tempore quorum alio tremui vel nomina, quando
Fabellans eorundem aliquem lacerasse Puella
Sub sylva stantum par nobile dixit *Amantum.*
Nullos esse puto Lemures; Hominesque quod aiunt,
Alipedes Dryadas lucos errare per istos,
Somnia vana: adeo crevit mihi robore pectus,
Quod, *Perigotte*, Tibi cupidis feror obvia plantis.
Mi *Perigotte*! (quis ille?) meus *Perigotte!*
MEL. Puella!
AMO. Hei mihi! Tu non es *Perigottus.*
MEL. De *Perigotto*
Sed tibi porto novi quiddam: Sub vertice nigro
Arboris illius solidam duravit in horam,
Te reboans tortis iterumque iterumque lacertis;
Et dixit lachrymans, cur sic *Amoretta* moraris? (p. 30)
Tunc descendebat callem properando per illum,

Errasses ne forte viam: spectabilis esset
(Tam prope sertur adhuc) si lux foret ista diei.
AMO. Grates Pastor ago generose, pigetque morarum,
Tramitis ambigui mihi quas dilemmate feci.
Quam cito me tenerae (quas nulla industria lasset
Quae disquirat eum) poterunt conducere plantae,
Hunc sequar; et (tanti pretium non vile favoris)
PANA precor, tua te pariter dilecta sequatur.
MEL. Quam formosa fuit! quam fulsit amabilis illa!
Relligio fuit in talem peccare juventam.
Substrinxit vestes, capreaeque evanuit instar;
Quin et virgineo pro me candore precata est
Qui malefeceram ei. Dum praesens esset, ab illa
Ire videbatur quicquid tenebracula noctis
Lucis inaurabat, visa est dare Cynthia nullam
Quae non ejus erat. Cum solo sola manebat,
Si mihi sic placuit, cur tunc non ejus amorem
Ambivi? certe mihi succubitura fuisset:
"Femineum pectus, *vir* non, *occasio* vincit.
Finge negavisset, potuissem cogere solam
Fortior esset uter nostrum contendere lucta.
O hebetem stultumque nimis, cui excidit ansa
Tam pretiosa manu! sequar et nunc: sanguis inundat,
Nec fluctus retinere queo. Venio, alma *Amoretta*.

Intrent ALEXIS *et* CLOE.

Sed quinam sunt hi? duo Amantes? cesserit illam
Ille mihi: "pulchra est flagrante libidine quaevis.
ALEX. Qua requiescemus? nisi quod meus ardor in illa est,
Jam dudum defessa *Cloe* migrando fuisset.
CLOE. Hic requiescamus, si sit securus (Alexi)
Angulus, atque omni procul a Pastore remotus;
Nam mihi nosse datum, multos hac nocte vagari
Has circum sylvas: aliquis locus ergo petatur,
Nos ubi furtivo sine teste fruamur Amore.
ALEX. Hic ergo audacter: nulli patet iste virorum
Conculcandus apex; sacer est undique cespes;
Nulla vagas hic quaerit oves, aut virgo juvencam; (p. 31)
Hunc Fauni Dryadesque locum, Satyrique tuentur:
Hic secura igitur complectere, et ocula fige;

Nullaque defuerit, fraenata timore, voluptas.
CLOE. Tunc lateri conjunge latus; quantum ocyus illud,
Tardius aspiciet nostram lux postera culpam.
MEL. Solve meam: si non, sydus tibi juro per illud
(Quo Gens Pastorum nihil audet dicere majus)
Hic, ubi (contemptor divum) sub Robore sacro
Hanc temerare paras, dabitur tibi triste sepulchrum.
ALEX. Si PAN ipse ruat sylvestribus horridus Antris,
Faunorum Satyrumque fera comitante caterva,
Et dicat mihi, *Solve meam*; duo *Sydera* juro
(Hujus fatidicos oculos) absistere nollem.
MEL. Protinus a gelida nunquam tellure resurges;
Sed simul amittes vitam dulcemque puellam.
CLOE. Pastor Amice, manum reprimas.
MEL. Pastorcula pulchra,
Tu venias mecum; nec te minus ardeo et ipse
Hoc sine fronte viro, qui te sperabat ineptus
Anticipare mihi, meriti cui gloria major.
ALEX. O! mihi non adimas, illam cum sanguine; meque
Ipsius annexum lateri permitte perire.

Intrat SATYRUS, *fugiunt* ALEX. et CLOE *diverso tramite.*

SAT. Nunc, dum Luna regit corusca coelum,
Stellarum quoque lumen imbecillum
Noctem pallidula serenat umbra,
Magno me Domino jubente PANE,
Hoc totum nemus ambulo, reducto
Ejusdem gremio (pedem profanum
Quo mortale nihil ferebat unquam)
Dum tripudiat ipse, Musicamque
Convivae, atque epulum dat, eleganti:
Huic imbrem pluit in sinum Rosarum
Illo vel *Zephyro* suaviorum
Cujus flamine leniter movebant;
Uvas; multiplici sapore baccas;
His nunquam similes dapes videbam.
Sed pensum vocat: Hic mihi manendum est,
Ut si quis pede deviat protervo

155 fatidicos] fatisicos *1658*

Mortalis, videam; simul misellum
Falso lumine, splendide dolosus,
Verae per tenebras viae reducam.
Rimandum quoque si quis innocentem (p. 32)
Jam jam viribus opprimat puellam;
Torto protinus insusurro cornu,
Omnes cum Lemures repente current,
Ad Lunam pariter tripudiantes,
Atque illum tenus ossa vellicabunt
Donec renibus exulet libido.

ALEX. O Mors!

SAT. Hoc iterem solum: videtur
Vox audita hominem mihi sonare;
Hoc te Carmine vincio potente,
Hujus te laticis sacri vigore,
Te Lunae rutilantibus Pyropis,
Humana species, loquare rurus.

ALEX. Oh!

SAT. Mortalis ibi jacet, soporem
In terra capiens: Iners, resurge.
Intermortuus angiter misellus,
Ejus vulnere purpurantur herbae,
Et sordent tepido cruore vestes:
Formosae Nemoris Deae, meaeque,
Quae puris manibus dabit salutem,
Qua tantum caret, auferam misellum.

Reintret CLOE.

CLOE. Cor micat, hirsutum vidi ex quo territa monstrum,
Serpentemque novum rubus omnis habere videtur;
Sed Natura redit, vicitque cupido timorem.
Est alicunde mihi Pastor nonnullus habendus:
Una deest certe saltem mihi causa timoris,
Nam me posse rapi prohibet propensa voluntas.
Hic super hoc clivo dilectum ex corde reliqui
Sanguine purpureum proprio de vertice ad imum.
Essera sed donec me fecit abire Figura,
Saucius ille licet, mihi restitit attamen unus;
Nunc ambo periere mihi: vel fare, moveve,
Si tibi quid vitae est, etiamnum noster *Alexi*.

Mortuus est, clivo vel ab alto debile repsit
Spectrum infame timens. Ubi tu confossor Amantis
Ergo mei? maneas, et agas Pastoris adempti
Ipse vices: Tunc justus eris, mihi floribus exhinc,
Et designatis illi decorande Corollis. (p. 33)
Dura tibi strictis ambibo colla lacertis,
Si superesset adhuc, foret amplectendus ut ille:
Sed tu fugisti; quae spes mihi denique restat?
Ad te, *Daphni*, cava qui clauderis Arbore, curram;
Ludere quem mens ante fuit; licet inde supersit
Spes tenuis, tentanda tamen, ne nulla supersit:
Forsitan aut Natura ejus, nostrive calores,
Aut utrique simul, doceant quid oportet et illum.

Exit.

Intret MEL.

MEL. Hic locus est, nec erat nisi vis obtusa videndi,
Mixta horrore mei facti, noctisque tenebris,
Quae mihi mille metus struxit (fugiendo) figuras,
Unguibus et pulchram fecit me solvere praedam.
Sum solus (responde Ovium generosa magistra)
Ipseque amandus amo. Sed me indignata reliquit;
Qui, cum mortiferum dederam ejus vulnus Amanti,
Inde metu turpi fugi solamque reliqui.
Hinc quoque sanguineum properantius (ecce) cadaver
Abstulit exanimis, quem sic dilexit, Amici.

Intret PERIGOTTUS *et* AMARYLLIS *forma* AMORETTAE.

Sed fugite haec mentem, fugite haec phantasmata nostram
Me latitare decet; juvenis venit huc *Perigottus*,
Tuque *Amarylli*, dolis, *Amorettae* et imagine, tecta;
Fac, Amor, ille cadet.

AMA. Charissime mi *Perigotte*,
Nidum ostende aliquem quo quaestu membra reponam
Lassa tui, solidam qui continuavit in horam
Ante tuum adventum.

PER. Culpo vestigia lenta:
Te super hoc sancto clivo, formosa, repones;
Cespite non super hoc lethalis nectitur Anguis
Retibus ipse suis, neque pascit Bufo venenum:

Hic sparsas ostende manus, exempta timore;
Nulla venenoso dabit illis pustula succo
Herba, nec audacem callem limosus arabit
Per faciem Testudo tuam, dum languida dormis;
Garrulus hic nunquam cuculus sua sputa reliquit;
Nunquam Stella cadens est ausa refundere dirum
Pus super hoc clivo: tua stragula texta sit iste;
Hic, mea, qui violis distinguitur alter ut astris.
AMA. Non me, non *Perigottus* amat.
PER. Formosa Puella,
Dicere saepe AMO TE me saepe negando lacessis.
Haud dubio, haud dubitas, (p. 34)
AMA. Facio, mihi crede.
PER. Quid hoc est?
Esse proci rursus nunc incipiemus? Amantem,
"Ludere cum capto, mille est involvere nodis.
AMA. Testor PANA Deum, mihi quod *Perigottus* amatur.
Teque, per hanc Lunam, me neutiquam opinor amare.
PER. Testor PANA Deum (sique hunc perjurus adoro,
Ille meas non servet oves; Vulpecula glubat
Agnos primigenas; Lupus ipse, sopore soluto
Me, ruat in reliquos; Gregibus gravis ingrue, Tabes)
Plus amo te, foetum quam Capra annosa recentem,
Aut Ovis aegra sum; materni utrumque coloris:
Diligo te, plusquam maternam Agnella papillam,
Qua fruitur rapta: Lupus irruat agmine facto
Nostrum in Ovile furens, et gressus torqueat ad Te,
Turba voret cunctas, vetulas simul atque tenellas,
Tu mihi vita, tibi vellem succurrere Soli.
AMA. Credere me verbis, videam cum facta, jubebis?
Parte jaces alia, latus hoc procul effugis ultro.
PER. Id fuit in testem casti nos inter Amoris,
Solum cum sola quantumvis contigit esse.
AMA. Non: *Perigottus* avet sit in illo quanta potestas
Cogendi fessam licet, impetuose *Amorettam*
Sede movere sua monstrare, et in ejus abire.
En *Amoretta*! tuam stringas, et basia figas.
PER. Quid mea Lux sibi vult?
AMA. Fieri id quod amantibus usu,
Queis, bene velle, frui est. Nulla est hac valle Puella

Oscula libandi luculentior Arte, nec ulla
Lascivis magis apta modis.
PER. Charissima, mitte
Scrutari an purum mihi cor: non vivere mallem
Vivere quam sine lege, tuumve offendere honorem.
AMA. Ergo pudicitiam muliebri existere sexu
Sentis adhuc? Sylva nulla est, *Perigotte*, Puella
Sola rogata viro, quae vellet abire puella.
Ne tibi credulitas puerilis adhaereat aevi;
Utere temporibus: cur surgis?
PER. Saeva, necasti
Fidum pectus.
AMA. Humo polite, *Perigotte*, resigam.
PER. Solvas me, Serpens, mihi pectoris ima penetrans
Calliditate tua; non tu jculariter ista? (p. 35)
AMA. Chare recumbe puer.
PER. Quoniam hoc spectare supersum
Meque Gregesque meos aliquis Notus afflet acerbus.
AMA. Velle meum facias: jurasti me quod amabas.
PER. Denuo sis quod eras, et eris mihi denuo chara.
AMA. Sum quod eram, quod & est omnis, Mulierque futura est
Mille viros faciles licet Artibus infatuemus.
PER. Tunc meus hic finitur Amor quicunque, novoque
Me mea credulitas ne forsitan implicet igne,
Te coram, cujus Facie mea capta juventa eat,
Finitur mea vita: caput cruor illud inundet.
AMA. Siste manum! tua te, tua te hic *Amoretta* precatur.
PER. Haud male consultum; prior es moritura *Amoretta*,
Aeterni quae causa mali mihi sola fuisti.
AMA. Siste manum!
PER. Ferrum hoc lascivum cor tibi punget.
Currit post ipsam.

Intrat propere MELANCHOLICUS PASTOR, *et ei solvit incantamentum.*

MEL. Herbas hic & ubique, susque deque,
Purgatrice manu sero per auras:
Hinc, hinc, vester odor repellat omnes,
Quae menti nebulam creant, vapores.

294 polite] pol te *1658*

Plantae, Flumina, queis latens potestas
Visum decipit, innovant figuras,
Infectum facitote, me jubente,
Quod factum prius est, jubente memet:
Evadat, fugiat, volet per altum,
Reddatur propriae suae figurae.

Intret AMARYLLIS *propria sua forma.*

AMA. Te teneas; erras; ovium generose Magister,
Fugit ea in silicem quam sectabare, viamque
Transversata tuam cholerae succedo paratae,
Cujus et ipse timor prope jam mea fata peregit.
PER. Condones, Formosa, mihi; Nox iraque junctae
Caecarunt simul externos et mentis ocellos.
Absit at o longe, Sylvae per amoena vagantis
Ut cruor innocuae maculet me tela puellae.

Exit AMA.

Intret AMORETTA.

AMO. Innumeros passus callem sus deque per illum
Infelix *Amoretta* dedi, Te sedula quaerens,
Te *Perigotte*, meam neque vox tua venit ad aurem:
Mi *Perigotte*, vocat quae Te super omnia valde (p. 36)
Diligit.
PER. En ubi stat! Quam nunc quoque pulchra videtur;
Illius aethereas tamen halitus inquinat auras.
AMO. Mi *Perigotte*!
PER. Hic sum.
AMO. Felix.
PER. Miserabilis ictum
Libo tibi primum, mihi restat acerbior ictus.

Vulnerat eam.

AMO. Te teneas, mea Lux, injustus es, o *Perigotte*.
PER. 'Justa libidinibus mors est et debita merces.

Exit PER.

MEL. Illorum sane jam rescindentur amores,
Ictam etenim fonti injiciam, ne forte viator
Nocturnus plagae cura medicetur honesta.
In mortem Te, Nympha, pares.
AMO. Nihil amplius oro:

Tu mihi non poteris dare vulnus amarius isto.
Illi qui dedit hoc (dedit hoc ipsius Amanti)
Non corpus dicas, animam penetrasse sed ipsam;
Dicas, hanc animam fruituram pace quieta
Post obitum, si me putet ille suisse pudicam.

Praecipitat eam in fontem.

MEL. Hic tibi pro tumulo sit fons; tam nescia fraudis,
Femina tu certe non designata fuisti;
Vivam impossibile est emergere, namque serenum
Longa Caverna premit fontem tellure sub ima,
Donec per latus id, quod lumine spectat amico
Sol matutinus, luctans aqua rumpit in Amnem.

Exit.

Surgit DEUS FLUVII portans AMORETTAM *in brachiis.*

DE. Quod Carmen Magicum potens reducit
Antiquis mea fontibus fluenta,
Sic ut non potuit Deus Tridente
Ter percussa meo, ter increpata,
Notis finibus illa continere?
Ripas pisciculi mei sagittant;
Non unus manet et cibum capessit;
Omnes se viridi tuentur alga.
En mortalem anima fere vacantem,
In nostri caput alvei caducum
Tot sic carminibus sacratum ab aevo,
Ut delapsus eo sit ante nemo!
Est (pol) femina, limpida est puella,
A Raptore aliquo data in Barathrum: (p. 37)
En in Pectore vulnus innocente,
Cui nulla hactenus applicatur herba!
Etjamnum tepet, et fibrae laborant,
Signum est igniculum subesse vitae.
Virgo si cluis integri pudoris,
Praesens est manibus meis medela.
In vulnus bibe guttulam a Capillo
Humectante meo, rotundiorem
Ex conchis Orientis unione,
Et quam ferre potest caro impudica,
Ignitam magis atque puriorem;

Spirat languida, sanguinisque porta
Flumen jam calidum recenter exit:
Impolluta stat undiquaque Virgo:
Fluxus sanguinis est tenendus iste.
Ripis ipse meis
Florem hunc carpo manu sacra, potentem
Et sanare simul, simulque virus
Plaga dissinuare. Pulchriorem
Mortalem his oculis videre nunquam
Concessum fuit. Excutit soporem
Nunc, nunc, mortiferum: Loquare, Virgo.
AMO. Quis mihi me reddens vitam dedit Arte novellam,
Mortis et ex gelidis luci prodire lacertis?
DE. Plagis contuli ego tuis medelam.
AMO. Eheu!
DE. Non medicum tuum timere.
Sum fontis Deus istius, tumescunt
In rivum inferius mea fluenta,
Ripas perque duas, ubi ordinantur
Quae gaudent salices locis in udis,
Inter prata ruunt amoeniora,
Et tentant iter huc rotis et illuc
Qua est aequissimus alveus per herbam.
Quod si grata velis abire mecum,
Mortalem fugiens sodalitatem,
Undis in gelidis jacebis usque,
Immunisque malis, ut ipse, cunctis:
In pastum tibi praeparabo nullum,
Qui caeno soleat latere, piscem;
Sed Trutem, et Lucium, qui amant natare
Qua de margine multiplex arena (p. 38)
Undas per vitreas potest videri.
Gemmas ex Oriente, quae decerent
Reginam, dabo, queis tuus vicissim
Aquiratur amor, daboque concham
Qua serventur eae: meis in undis
Nullus piscis erit, tuis ocellis
Qui non mox veniat domesticatus,
Ad nutum et properet tuum silendo,
Muscam ut de nivea manu reportet.

Et, quo tu melius videre possis
Fluctus ut mihi sint mei audientes,
Bullas ejicient canente memet
Fonte argenteolo suaviora.

Cantio

Plantas non timeas tuas, Puella,
Nudas ponere limpidis in undis;
Morsurum tibi non pedem colubrum,
Bufonemve putes, hirudinemve:
Nec surgens aqua, dum vadum penetras,
Singultus tibi flebilesque questus
Causet: Sed mihi sis comes perennis,
Et fluctus tibi neutiquam dolebunt.

AMO. Quae sacros regis hos latices, aeterna potestas
Si bene me novi, sum non ego digna videre
Te mihi, Dive, procum; quae jam sine numine vestro
Naturae fragilis specimen moriendo dedissem:
Praeterea, sanctis (jurante utroque) sigillis
Ante dicata fui Pastori propria, cujus
Formosam faciem scio me aemula Numina posse
Efficere ut videam desistere, non ut amarem.
DE. Is perstet pariter tibi fidelis;
Formosissima Virgo, nunc valeto:
Laxandae mihi sunt aquis habenae,
Ne mox aridus alveus queratur,
Et fontem pecudis meum petentes
Impoti redeant calente Sole;
Quod nolim, quia nuper universus
Ad ripas populus meas sedebat
Vicinus, niveos duos et agnos,
Queis complere datum dies vigenti,
Ad nostras pius immolavit aras: (p. 39)
Annum propterea per hunc vacabunt
Saevis diluviis, leves arenas
Quae dum praetereunt serunt per herbam:

434 Praeterea] Paeterea *1658*

Sudabunt nimio nec imbre prata,
Cum gramen jaceat modo secatum.
AMO. Ob tantum mihi praestitum favorem
Nunquam a marginibus tuis, procellae
Vi, transversa tuis feratur ulla
Arbor fluctibus, opprimens euntes:
Nunquam, Bellua, quae venis bibendum
Ripas dirue cornibus protervis:
Nemo, piscibus abditis tyrannus,
Ripas amputet, ut fluenta siccet.
Nulla stans gelidis tuis in undis
Uxor nudipes, aut puella Pagi,
Cum spes littore splendeat marina,
Tundat spermata cannabum lavando.
DE. Grates, Virgo: mihi petendus imus
Fons est denuo, neutiquam dolorem
Donabit tibi plaga; ne stupescas
Quod te tam subito reliquit ille;
Est imposta super manus sacrata.
Exit.
AMO. At solis mihi luctibus creatae,
Qui memet fugit, insequi necesse est. *Exit.*

Actus quartus Scena prima.

Intret PERIGOTTUS.

PER. Est falsa, inconstans, dura est; evanuit illa,
Inque suum est resoluta nihil; *Notus* intonet altum,
In montes et turbet aquas; si qua audeat Arbor
Illius implicitis ramis contra ire furori,
Non stabili stet dura loco: cava repat in antra,
Et quatiat mundum, veluti solet, actus in orbem,
Ad monstri natale novi; constante manente
Me interea, fidum dextra amplectente, cadente
Sic et in hoc jaculum.

Intret AMARYLLIS *currens.*

AMA. Dextram, furibunde, teneto
Funestam, nimis ipse tibi (mihi credere si vis) (p. 40)
Succenses, Pulcher: morere, et non quotquot opaca
Nubila dimittunt imbres purgare reatum
Turpem et femineum, tibi qui imminet inde, valebunt.
Fortis adhuc dilecta tua est, sine labe remansit:
Crede mihi, pariter numerari possit arena
Atque ea mutari. Nugari nescio, Pastor;
Per Lunam cunctasque faces (quas ecce!) minores,
Quae, *Perigotte*, tibi dixi sunt omnia vera.
Reddaris tibi tu, mala desperatio cesset,
Dirum et velle mori; frontem erige leniter, albam
Vel sub nube sua: sis qualis ab ubere pendens
Quum tua primaevam ceperunt lumina flammam.
PER. Hei mihi! bis moritur, cupiens qui credere, nescit;
Non bene, quod remoram morienti ponis, ut hic sim
Cum fociis multo pejoribus: atra sed o Mors,
Non sic incaleo bullae vitalis amore,
Hanc ut non ausim difflare: haud poena forato
Pectore, nec longos fila extendenda per annos,
Esse voluntati poterunt obstacula nostrae:
Non ego me, tu vociferas *Amoretta*, TRUCIDA.
AMA. Paulisper maneas, unam paulisper in horam;
Etsi tunc herbis verbisque potentibus, ipsa
Nocte magis nigris, tibi non monstravero memet,

Quatenus ad speciem externam, vestram ipsam *Amorettam*
Ejusdem chlamydem propriam pictosque cothurnos,
Insculptumque tua bacculum quem gestat ab arte,
Scriptum litterulis utriusque ex nomine, et infra
Signatum multis, Labyrinthi more, figuris;
Sertum flore novo, variatis cingula bullis,
Annulum et aureolum, tua munera dulce canenti,
Mundumque omnigenum quo se vestire solebat;
Prima tui patiar chalybis male vindicis iras.

PER. Sum contentus ego, mihi copia siqua supersit
Me spe lactandi breve tempus in unius horae;
Vade, sub illius rediens me tegmine fagi
Invenies, mixta sic credulitate timentem.

AMA. Coram PANE prius mihi tu pro pignore certo
Des animam, Te nolle tibi, vesane, nocere, (p. 41)
Donec ego redeam.

PER. Per PANA, per atque duellum
Harmonicum, *Phoebo* rivali, judice *Mida*
Aurimano, nolo. *Exeunt.*

[IV. ii]

Intret SATYRUS *portans* ALEXIM *saucium.*

SAT. Furtivo pede promovens, ut Amnis,
Hoc cum pondere luctibus gravante,
Pernoctis taciturna somnolentae,
Ductus vermiculi micantis igne,
Huc tandem venio; Vireta multa
Perfluxi.
Me frondes tremuere palpitantes;
Dumus quem tetigi timebat omnis
Avi prodere me levi, tenello
Super vimine dulce dormienti;
Nec repit, stimulum vibrante cauda,
Per terras animosus ille vermis,
Qui si me videt, ut ratis, natantem,
Me vento magis impigro volantem,
Me praeter nebulas leves euntem,
Non abdat tenerum caput, vel intra
Rimas arboreas, vel Acciarum

Semen parturientium maniplo.
A lecto pedibus meis cieri
Nec lepus poterit meticulosa:
Non votum volat, aut secat profunda
Piscis marmora tam repente (post se
Nec vestigia nec sonum reliquens)
Quam, libans pedibus solum citatis,
Longam conficio viam brevi hora.
Felix arboretum sed ecce tectum,
Quod curam mihi sublevabit istam,
Sacrataque animam manu reducet
Istius miseri, Necis lacertis
Colluctantis adhuc! Opem fer illi
Coelum, PANque potens. Tu, Vireti
Lux, et rustica pulchritudo, Salve!
Heri candidior mei puella! (p. 42)
Fas vestrae Deitatis impetrare,
Hunc quae faucibus eximat sepulchri
Mortalem miserum, manum juvantem,
Parcis nunc acuentibus bidentem
Cultellum. Viden', ut chalybs cruentus
Disclusit jecur!

Intret CLORINDA.

CLOR. Quis tu qui sacris revocas me ritibus audax,
Mortis et horrisonis teneras rumoribus aures
Terrificas? nomenque tuum, jussumque reclude.
SAT. Non nosti *Satyrum*, tuum replevit
Qui jam primitiis sinum beatum;
Cum fructus iterum legat, daturus
Plures, et tibi pluris estimandos.
Vel nunc, haud vacua manu revertor;
En ex Arbore flosculus! Sed illum
Quae carpsit pereat manus scelesta,
Quique excerpsit eum sagax ocellus
Inter vere novo tot elegantes;
Pastoralis enim suaviorem
Gens ostendere neutiquam valebit,
Nec Regum sata, divitium nec horti,
Et quod spargitur undiquaque pagis:

Illo (conspicin?) angulo repertum
Vinxi molliter in meis lacertis,
Huc et mortifere tuli sopitum,
Plagis flentibus in modum dolentis
Quod talis poterit juventa nasci
Cum nascente Die, cum moriente mori.
CLOR. *Satyre*, Te vocitare rudem est injuria summa:
Sis licet externe rigidus suscique coloris,
Morum par dulcis, Tibi par est candor, et illi
Qui se cunque effert haeredem ex asse quod unquam
Extitit ingenui. Plagam monstraveris; herba haec
Stricta Orificio compescet sanguinis aestus,
Internasque simul poenas quas frigidus Aer
Impulit in vulnus; putrefactum exinde cruorem
Haec trahet.
SAT. Prosint, Numina vos precor superna!
CLOR. Molli dilue dextera cruorem:
Sustentes parili virum, quousque (p. 43)
Sacris Fontibus irrigem imbecillo
Multum tempora; torqueas eum bis
Ad Lunae cava, vellices ter ipsum,
Sensim ut spiritus exuat laborans
Eclipsem gravidam.
SAT. Movere vidi
Ejus nunc cilium.
CLOR. Capessat auram.
Hem! quodvis gelidae necis periclum
Nunc evanuit; hac ab unctione
Emplastroque malire pullulantis
Omnem in secula dissipo timorem.
SAT. En se colligit, incipitque lucis
Haustus quaerere languidis ocellis!
Nunc suspiria ducit oscitando.
Ut venas repetit cruor, fuerunt
Quae nuper vacuae!
ALEX. O mei lepores!
O mi chara *Cloe*, charissima semper *Alexi*!
Poena meum penetrat latus, intolerabile quiddam
Viscera transadigit, quod et anguis acutius oestro est.
PAN, succurre mihi! Quid es? per illum

Non nocere mihi; meae fidelis
Sum *Cloi*, fugiat licet fidelem,
Huic et mortifero relinquat astro:
Illic stat, niveam movere dextram
Nec vult molliculam periclitanti.
Toto coelo erro; facie illa namque pudicae
Plus virtutis inest; majestatisque severae,
Jurgantis magis, et magis verendi,
Quam nostra his oculis, adusque praesens,
Concessum fuit in *Cloe* videre.
O, mi poena, redis acerba multum.
Cedo salutiferam, per *Amati* lumina, dextram!
CLOR. Pastor, nequaquam potes obdormire, priusquam
Eradicetur contemplativa libido,
Unde Cupidineus sufflando renascitur ignis;
Cesset ocellorum lasciva cohaesio, sanguis
Strenuus, ejusdemque sequi mandata voluntas:
Haec purgare decet candescat vena quousque; (p. 44)
Tunc rescipisce, pia magnum prece PANA fatigans
Te a simile servare malo, tibique ipsa salutem
Promitto facilem; latus haec tibi xeria rodet
Interea tenerum; dextram mihi porrige surgens:
Satyre, sustineas non firmo crure labantem.
ALEX. Amissus mihi sanguis est abunde.
(Lucro apponito) sanguis inquinatus.
Pastor, perdetuam salacitatem:
Sit quaedam in coitu licet voluptas,
A tergo stimulum sui relinquit;
Experto magis, hoc magis patebit.
CLOR. Intus (age) hunc, ubi sit mihi commoda cura; caveto
Quum fueris sanus, sanetur et ipsa libido.
SAT. Mortalis metitur quid osculando?
Per nostrum melius caput deesset.
Si, pulcherrima, quid novi supersit
Quo servire tibi queam, sine omni
Figmento faciam; licet juberer
Ventum prendere retibus volantem,
Labentes viridi sato vel umbras,
Reginae aut Lemurum throno sedenti
Omnem ut surripiam suum decorem,

Fiet, tam reverenter incalesco
Illis sydereis tuis ocellis.
CLOR. Reddo tibi grates, bone *Satyre*; si quis alius
Cujusvis planctus morbo vel vulnere laesi
Te trahat huc, operam des sodes ducere et illum.
SAT. Fiet: cumque Tibi (favente coelo)
Escas sidere rivuli placebit,
Hamum argenteolum feram, feramque
Filum textile serici politi,
Et lacti calamum parem recenti
(Fraudes Pisciculis:) simul valere
Te, Virgo, jubeo; precorque, semper
Aestas hoc habitet super vireto,
Et ver perpetuum. *Exit.*
CLOR. Vale, sodalis. *Exit.*

[IV. iii]

Intret AMORETTA *quaerens suum* PASTOREM.

AMOR. Hic locus est infaustus, ubi mihi demptus *Amator*,
Et mea vita fere est, omnesque exinde pererro (p. 45)
Has Sylvas; nullum specus hic, non Angulus ullus
Quo vel parvus avis, vel bellua magna moratur,
Quin ibi eum quaeram; mons nullus fronte superba
Pendulus, aut fissura canoro pervia vento,
Non viridis clivus, vel qua pastoribus usu est
Aut aenigmatibus vel arundine ludere dulci,
Vel sibi forte pares assumere, gratior umbra
Praetermissa mihi, dum nomen amabile clamo.
Quo me fugisti, nimis asper tu *Perigotte*?
Quo te contuleris? in te committere tantum
Quid potui? aut nostri sunt tam grave crimen Amores?
Contemptus sequitur? tali mercede quiesco.
Sed, Pastor, te scire velim (nec nesciat hoc nunc
Dulce nemus) tam pura manet deserta *Amoretta*
Ignis adoptitii, quam non violabile coelum
Mixturae externae, aut felicis lucis Abyssus:
Haec quoque vera scias, et quod fatale dedisti
Pectore in hoc vulnus, me non meruisse, sed esse

14 Contemptus] contemprus *1658*

Suspitione tua factum, caecoque furore.
Hic ergo quoniam vitam, Solamen, Amicum,
Perdiderim, super hoc Tragicum florensque Theatrum,
Quod primum nobis fecit divortia, tanti
Scena doloris erit mox, ut viduetur ocellus
Omnis fonte suo assidue, mea stamina rupta
Ante diem plorans.

Intret AMARYLLIS.

AMAR. Oculis non capta quod erro,
Quodve creat formas sibi mens inimica, videtur
Haec *Amoretta* mihi; Ratio me linquat, et omne
Quod non vel stupor est, majorve stuporibus horror.
Hujus enim parili, nunquam *responsa* dederunt
Phoebeiae fortes; transcendit somnia, quaeque
More fluunt Rivi, refluuntque amentis ideas.
Vix hora elapsa est (vocemque his auribus hausi) (p. 46)
Ex quo clamavit, *Miserere mei, Perigotte*:
Dum ferus ille puer pectus sulcavit inerme,
Quod percussit humum sine sanguine, et absque calore;
Atque *Melancholicus Pastor* (si vera feruntur)
Exanimem validis captam excussamque lacertis
Fontis ad ima sacri dedit insuper, humida claustra
Usque habitaturam; sed ea est, eadem est *Amoretta*,
Vivaque; tam puram nequeunt pia numina ferre
In cinerem ire facem. Guttas deterge doloris,
Virgo graves, et adhuc crescentem rumpe procellam,
Quae nisi sit depressa, prius quam lassa quiescat
Et cordis rumpet fibras, et stamina vitae:
Ille tuus *Perigottus*—
AMO. Ubi est, et quis *Perigottus*?
AMAR. Illic languet humi (testor pia Numina) multum
Te plorans, sortemque tuam; solamina latum
I misero, invenies solum sub margine denso
Pinibus aequoreis, montem qui circuit illum.
AMO. Non eo, sed curro: da coelum rursus *Amantem*
Hunc mihi lucrari. *Exit* AMORETTA.

Intret MELANCHOLICUS.

MEL. Siste, *Amarylli*, mane: nimium cita curris, ad horas

Usque duas nox est: Sedeamus (jussa peregi)
Sanguine collidens et sanguis inebriet artus,
Donec vivida vis ad mollia suscitet Arma.
AMAR. Pastor, acris nimis es; surgens Aurora videbit
Abstineas paulisper.
MEL. Et hoc paulisper in aevum est.
AMAR. Te teneas, Pastor, teneas; deludere noli:
Non prius illorum pepigisti rumpere amores?
MEL. Feci, inquam, Virgo.
AMAR. Nequaquam: irrupta remansit
Copula, concordes rediere, nec aegrius illis
Dividitur certe labes a sindone pura.
MEL. Dico quod arte mea dirimuntur, tamque remoti
Ut redituri una sint nunquam.
AM. Fallere, Pastor;
Nam tantum subeas ad pendula montis, ibique (p. 47)
Crede tuis oculis.
MEL. Semper mihi nectis inanes
Nugas, atque moras; pudor ergo gelate, valeto,
Inque decore viris: sic te, impia virgo, saluto.
AMAR. Sic et ego te invito sequi: Cape, si poteris, me.
Exit.
MEL. Et si non capiam, dicas minus esse viro me.
Exit persequens eam.

[IV. iv]

Intret PERIGOTTUS.

PER. Furtim ne fuge Nox, et fortiter utere fraenis,
Queis pigros moderaris equos ferrugine captis.
Plaustra gelata retro vertas, Auriga *Bootes*,
(In se flexa rotis) noctemque afferto secundam,
Quae celit veniente meos a luce dolores.
Non humana meum mirentur lumina vultum,
Et mea fata legant; latebras concedite nigras,
Quo nunquam radium jaculavit *Apollo* salubrem,
Unde sedens miseram fundam cum murmure vitam
Instar euntis aquae, nunquam redeuntis ad ortus
Cum de rupe ruens sonus ejus abivit in auras.

Intret AMORETTA PERIGOTTUM *quaerens*.

AMOR. Hic locus est; mihi responde si forsitan hic sis:
Mi *Perigotte!* tuum tua multum chara *Amoretta*
Nomen dulce vocat.
PER. Vetitas quae, femina, calcas
Absque timore vias; ubi Mors et cura morantur
In facie tenebrarum,
AM. Ego sum, tua lux *Amoretta*;
Huc ades, O positure modum languoribus istis;
Sursum oculos, bone vir; memini non Vulneris ipsa,
Et dulcis quem te propter sum passa doloris;
Rursus et esse tui contenta revertor Amores.
Cur crines lacerasti auri, queis saepe pependi
Cingula purpureasque Rosas, et saepe refudi
Vim bene olentis aquae, ne non superentur ab illis (p. 48)
Florea nupturam decorant quae serta puellam?
Brachia cur nectis? Facies cur prona, duobus
Coeliculis istis tellurem flens super, imbres
Majores pretii, nitidos magis atque rotundos,
Quam quae pallenti pendent de fronte *Dianae*?
Siste, Puer, questus; eadem quae semper eram, sum:
Priscus amor rediit, vetus indulgentia: certe
Condonare tibi possumque (nec ante rogata)
Et volo quod possum.
PER. Sic, sic mea Pulchra locuta est:
O vos qui Terram circumvolitatis, Aquamque,
Aeraque, sterilemque ignam, miracula vestra
Occulti fontis cur hos tribuistis in usus?
Talis erat Facies, tam pulchra vigensque *Amorettae*;
Talia verba suis, tam blandula, tamque novella
Fluxerunt labiis; erat ipsi talis ocellus,
Talis et ex illo scintillula, cuspidis instar
Sanguinei, peracuta volans: Eadem omnia ad unguem;
Et vestis, pictumque pedum, pictique cothurni,
Aptaque totius compages corporis. O me!
O *Amoretta!*
AMOR. Quid hoc tibi vis aenigmate, Pastor?
Quae maga me memet tantum disjunxit, ut ipsa
Nunc ego non ego sim? Viden', hic est Annulus ille

Ipse mihi quem Tu dederas; circumque lacertum
En pretiosa comis armilla micantibus illis
Per te texta! Sat est? agnoscis nunc *Amorettam*?
An novus igniculus te non meminisse coegit
Antiquae fidei?
PER. Magis est mea vita, magisque:
His ipsis verbis stabilem me saepe probavit;
Sic stupor et vultu, sic saepe vocatus, inhaesit;
Multaque signa dedit capitisque, manusque, silendo
Vociferans, Pastor, quondam haec meminisse pigebit.
AMO. Sumne ego non *Amoretta*? loco quo perdere memet
Contigit? est Coelum, Tempusque, Hominesque, et eorum
Maxima pars fluitans? Quo sancta fides abiisti?
Omnia vota jacent defuncta, et federa, corque,
Extensaeque manus, exoptatique Hymenaei? (p. 49)
Nullum horum superest? pars nulla? "Scit ergo (probatum est)
"Maxima te virtus, Constantia, nemo virorum.
PER. Sorte virum nihil orbe fuit felicius unquam,
Donec livida Parca creavit vos et Amorem:
Vos, fatale genus, vestros quotcunque supino
Ore bibunt risus, duplici quibus omnia fronte
Aequivocant, plenis fraudum: lepus ut mala fidos
Ante canes, quae mille rotas, quae devia mille
Nectit, et huc cursum saltando torquet, et illuc,
Ne pateat vel odore sui.
AMO. Vim nempe, dolosque,
Imbellis queis praeda foret, fugitura virorum;
Gentis inexpleti jecoris, magis atque ferini
Quam fuerint ipsaeve ferae, piscesve fluenti.
PER. Hi cuncti simul, et plusquam Natura volebat
Cuncta creans, es tu; fera gaudia, risus amarus,
Intensissimus ignis, at hic qui durat in horam,
Frigidior subito quam somniserumve venenum,
Aut mare, cui sedet in rugis aeterna Pruina:
Quicquid agis, nullo contentum limite semper,
Aut gyaris restrictum arctis; ut "nemo vel alta,
"Vel vada, femineae possit cognoscere mentis.
AMO. Aetas ulla, diesve, vel hora, aut lingua virorum,
Esse potest tantae culpae rea, quanta puellae
Verba Columbinis dare moribus? *O Perigotte*,

Omnis heri probitas, omnis sine crimine, quicquid
Et genus humanum solet appellare beatum;
Fons in quo rudior sese speculata juventus,
Siquid ab inde boni successit, id hauserit ex te:
Tu, qui semper eras justus, semperque coruscans
Nobiliore fide; virtutis alumnus ab ipso
Ventre vocabaris, quam Tu cum lacte bibebas;
Omnibus unus *Amor* mortalibus (ista fuisse
Quanta ruina sonat, nunc unicus esse vicissim
Nequitiis, omnesque doli superare Magistros?)
Quin ut ego vivens hoc in me sentiam, et abs Te,
Quem pluris feci propriis oculisve, vel ipso (p. 50)
Virgineae vittae, quem sit jactamus, honore;
Pluris, hirundineo quam sit lux primula nido,
Cervisequaeve cani laeti taratantara Cornu;
Pluris, erit (nova si qua juvet) quam proxima flamma,
Et multo pluris, tibi quam fuit altera; pluris,
Quam vel tu potes esse tibi, licet ardeat in te
Omnis amor proprius, qui cum puero fuit illo
Indignabundo extinctus, qui nunc brevis est flos,
Quem rigat innumeris lachrymis miserabilis Echo?
Et sic digna fero tam purae praemia flammae?
Sic et ego mereor lascivae nomen *Amantis*?
Ergo veni, deserta salix, mea tempora cinge,
Atque obiisse meos fac tu sciat orbis Amores.
Deseror, infausto feci naufragia portu,
Ut sedet ignavo quicumque in littore, dicat,
Inconstans erat, atque levis, citiusque vel istis
Nubibus, aut gelidis evanida sole pruinis.
Dic, tua numquid adhuc *Amoretta* revivet amata?
PER. Tu non digna cluis tam sancto nomine, crimen
Quam mihi nosse foret: lascivam projice flammam,
Qua levior sanguis ficto sermone calescat,
Et personatis affectibus. I, mala; nunquam
Infidus *Perigottus* erat, dignabitur aut nunc
Mentitae facilem descendere frontis ad escam.
AMO. Tunc me Coelum, audi, justas cui spargo querelas;
Quaeque coronatis radianta sydera Noctem;
Et tu, Terra parens, hujusque silentia sylvae;
Et moestae lentis itis quae passibus Horae;

Meque audite Umbrae, quibus est habitare voluptas
Horrentes tenebras, et Numina tristis Averni,
Quos efflo moribunda sonos:
Illa ego sum virgo, fida hactenus illa *Amoretta*,
Prodiga quae, fraudumque amens ignara virorum,
Huic juveni donabam animam, qui nunc vocat effrons
Me ignotam, non persona, non moribus, ipsam:
Et sic multa fides propriis me perdidit armis.
Illa ego sum Virgo, quae dilatando, negando,
Et quasi spernendo cunctorum lusit amores,
Istius exceptis; licet (haud ignota recordor) (p. 51)
Me multi petiere pari fervore, parique
Affectus anima: Quotus et mihi Balteus et Nux,
Annulus atque quotus, puero veniebat ab illo,
Occidua qui pascit oves in Valle? Columbas
Daphnis et agnellos, cyathos mihi misit *Alexis*:
Quae mox transmisi tibi cuncta; nec illa, nec illos
Curavi, aut memori posui vel mente, vel arca.
Sed cur certa mori non sum, si certa dolere?
Felix ille foret, mihi si mortalis et esset,
Plaga tuae dextrae: nunc illa parte jacerem,
Omnis qua liber captivus, pectus et omne,
Quod vivens nutrit curas, requiescet: et illuc
Infelix *Amoretta* volo.

PER. Volitabis. Ocellis,
Sicut ego, propriis ecquis tam incredulus unquam?
Tam similisve sibi fuit ullas, ut haec *Amorettae*?
Quam propter promitto tibi, si volvitur in te
Intus agens Daemon, sic solvere Corpus ab illo.

Rursus illam vulnerat.

AMOR. Nunc actum est: Tu vive, vale, constantior illi
Quae mihi succedet.

Intret SATYRUS, *fugit* PERIGOTTUS.

SAT. Nascentis Rosa germinat diei,
Et lux ejaculatur instar ignis
Subtilis radii; gelatque ventus,
Aurora faciente se patentem.
Nunc dulces avis excutit sopores,
Et ramos tremit insuper sciurus,

Ut fructus rapiat nucesque saltu:
Matutina tacens modo Cylindrix,
Surgenti modo garrulat diei
Multos versiculos, modosque multos:
Meis excubiis modus sit ergo,
Ne Pastor vagus incidat periculo,
Et se nesciat explicare.

AMO. Vae mi!

SAT. Quicquid tu fueris, loquare rursus;
En promptum tibi me! loquare, dico. (p. 52)
Per primum rosae jubar diei,
Per mysteria Noctis atque PANOS,
Te conjuro loqui ad vicem secundam.

AMO. O memet magis omnibus misellam!

SAT. Plus dum sanguinis? Audeam Nerones
Istos dicere saucios cerebro.
Ausa est ulla manus, ferum vel ullum
Huic aequale nefas jecur patrare?
Per Lunam (sine luce quae refugit,
Quum tantum scelus esset executum)
Huic nunquam faciem parem videbam!
Ducam hanc ad Dominae meae viretum,
Et multis precibus piam rogabo,
Aut vitam miserae det, aut sepulchram.

Exeunt.

[IV. v]

Intret CLORINDA.

CLOR. Me, dum securos intus capit una sopores,
Altera cura foras furtim facit ire per umbram.
Tu sponsi mihi nunc ignosce cadaver humati
Quod latere ipsa tuo tam praesto abscedere possim:
Constans semper ero, spatium nec in unius horae
Me sine solus eris: Cum faedera prima resolvam,
Me laceret nemoris *Fera* maxima saepe cruentis
Faucibus, inferiasque tuam super immolet urnam:
Ingenio sanare vocor grave vulnus Amoris,
Nulla quod herba potest; hoc mox reditura peracto.

Exit.

Intret THENOTTUS.

THEN. Infelix Pastor, jaceas hac semper in umbra,
Clorindaeque tuae contemplans limen, obito.
O Amor infelix, qui redditus, illico cessas!
Parvulus utque infans exclamat, et anxius arctat
Molle super cilium, quum (torquens lumina) vidit
Forte micans aliquid prope se, quod vellet; at ipsum hoc
Si datur, actutum abjiciet, petiturus eadem
Anxietate aliud quo ludere: sic mea flamma
Currit ad objectum fugiens, fugeretque prehensum.

Intret CLORINDA. (p. 53)

CLOR. En ubi prostratum! Fuit unquam, hunc praeter, amavit
Qui mulierem ullam, quia constans haesit *Amanti*
Defuncto, quod (quicquid id est) cessare priusquam
Huic superinduci possit nova cura necesse est;
Ipseque subvertat causam quam propter amavit
Ante, perinde liquet; quam flectere possit *Amatam*?
Infelix Pastor, mihi dent pia Numina posse
Solvere Te poenis, et me servare fidelem.
Sursum oculos, Pastor!
THEN. Tua gloria caecat; adultus
Sic poterit *Phoebus* subjecto dicere Mundo,
Aspice me! Tua sic constantia fulget, ut aegra
Non ausim radiis opponere lumina tantis.
CLOR. Cur te perdis amore mei?
THEN. Cur par tibi nulla est?
CLOR. Audi te propter (bone Vir) Clorinda qui audet
Jam tua.

Is surgit propere.

THEN. Siste gradum, constans *Clorinda*; remansit
Si tibi feminei tantillum, quo levis unquam
Esse potes, meditare prius quam solveris ora.
CLOR. Audi quam sanctum te propter ego abrogo votum.
Illa ego jamdudum fama super aethera nota,
Quod sic defunctum constans venerarer.
THEN. *Amantis*
Chara prioris adhuc *Clorinda* memento, fuisset

Quamque tibi fidus, si tardior isset ad umbras.
CLOR. Te propter tamen haec nihili mihi cuncta.
THEN. Memento,
Quantum laudetur super omnia femina constans.
CLOR. Cespite et hic super hoc tibi me quam prompta resigno;
Juris fio tui.
THEN. Cur corde incendis in ejus
Plus rabiae contra muliebrem (perfida) Gentem,
Qui sexum totum praeter Te exoderat ante?
Dulcior O quantum Mors, te constante, fuisset,
Quam vita est, mutante, mihi! Si sana, redibis;
Chara redibis adhuc: in te non femina vincat.
CLOR. Ne nunc insulta, cunctando occide nec illam,
Omnem te propter quae venum exponit Honorem.
THEN. Non venum exponis; certum tibi dedecus emptum,
Execranda tuo sexu, quia nunc liquet omnes (p. 54)
Vos semel in vita perjuras esse futuras.
Ut te nunc odi! Redeas dum.
CLOR. Sis mihi justus:
Me simul, atque meam vin'tu me perdere famam?
THEN. Nulla tibi fama est, sed rumor; et id quod agebas
Instar honorifici, fuit impetus hac vice qui Te
Impulit in melius transversam: Ut ventus apertam
Turbine qui perflat Turrim sus deque suapte
Res jacit, at proprio poterit rem forsitan unam
Ferre loco; Sic velle tuum, non zelus, acervo
Unum aliquod pepulit bene te confundere casu.
Vertere adhuc.
CLOR. Tentas me tantum an linquere possim
Nexus (chare) tuos nexus ob Amantis humati,
Si superesset adhuc; sed non hac parte timendum.
THEN. Nunc Te contemno, nunc figere lumen, et ausim
In te ferre gradus; majestas namque severa,
Quae stetit hoc vultu, mihi nunc extincta videtur,
Tuque aliarum instar: perjura puella, vedeto
Quae merces servata levi est. *Exit.*
CLOR. PAN magne, per actum est.
Laus tibi, quod fuerat qui non medicabilis Herbis,
Convalet ingenio.

Re-Intret THENOTTUS.

THEN. An resipiscis adhuc, an adhuc ingrata redibis,
Arboreo claustro Sponsi devota sepulti.
CLOR. Tecum vivere amo, tecum sit dulce sepulchrum.
THEN. Nemo sciet pulchrum te commaculasse rigorem,
Sancta fereris adhuc, egoque hac recubabo sub ulmo
Denuo, tabescamque tuo moriarque rigore
Laetius, instabilem quam te nunc cerno dolenter.
CLOR. Te fruar, et quovis vivam sub cardine coeli.
THEN. Es mulier; satis hoc in se complectitur: Hujus
Spes sexus postrema, vale; quarum bona donec
Una videbatur, timui maledicere et uni.
Sed quia nunc omnes ejusdem cerno farinae,
Ut mos et aliis, oculo mihi deinde placebo. (p. 55)
Exit.
CLOR. Laus tibi quod dederis tam promptam, Dive, medelam,
Conatusque meos tam felix meta coronet.
Femina sim quamvis, malo maledicere cunctis
Dignum laude virum, quam ut me moribundus adoret. *Exit.*

Actus quintus. Scena prima

Intret SACERDOS, *et* SENEX PASTOR.

SAC. Expergiscimini gregum Magistri;
En Aurora latus senile linquens,
Rimatur pudibunda per fenestras;
Dum Sol culmine Montium potitus,
Valles succiduas inaurat omnes
Flammis exorientibus, gradatim
Quae crescunt, ut in altra scandit ille!
Ignavi Pueri, resuscitate;
Et peram simul ac utrem replete.
Strictum pallia cingulum coarctet,
Ne cedant Borealibus procellis.
Vos appellite Virgines, simulque
Quae lecto magis haeserit, notate;
Ut tota careat die hac Amico.
Mercedem canibus: subinde PANA,
Vos omni tegat a malo, rogate:
Clausos solvite tunc oves, et ite.

Papae! nullus adhuc produit per compita Pastor;
Sive nimis molles lectos sensere jacentes,
Aut nova sic humiles perfundere gaudia cellas,
Ardoresque novos, ut eorum oblivio mentes
Ceperit esurientum ovium, natique diei.
Ut reminiscantur, quam turpem incuria labem,
Pastorisque ferat titulo socordia, pulses.
SEN. Frustra erit, hac nullus sua dormitoria nocte
Cognovit, jacuitve intra Mapalia, Pastor.
Hos Nemus, aut aliquis circum vicinia Pagus
Dulcia cui patulo junguntur Pascua Monti,
Intentos ludis traxit juvenilibus illuc,
Aut errabundus qui spirat Cinnama potus,
Quem circum glomerant omnes pueri atque puellae, (p. 56)
Dum mulcet bibulas Tibicen amabilis aures.
SAC. Peccantum miserere Deus! qui ducit ubivis
Esse solent, monstrato viam mihi comis.
SEN. Ad amnem
Haec, Nemus illa.

SAC. Mihi jacet acceptatior ista;
Pastor, amabo, mihi ne tu comes ire recuses.

Exeunt.

[V. ii]

Intret CLORINDA *in Arboreto suo, comitante* ALEXI.

CLOR. Nunc mens pura tua est fere, tuumque
Corpus stat parili gradu salutis,
Omnem ex pectore pelle vanitatem,
Ne rupta cute rursus ulceretur.
ALEX. Aeternas grates tibi reddo, sancta puella:
Errantes nostrae fuerant quae mentis ideae
Consilio prudente tuo quasi sentio fixas,
Externumque tuis coalescere vulnus ab Herbis.
Et vertus vitiumque tui patet hac vice sexus;
Altera consolidat, quam fecerat altera, plagam.
CLOR. Plus ultra tua poena mitigetur:
"Morbus pessimus est redire morbum.
Sit quicquid mediteris usque castum,
Sano in corpore Mens eritque sana.

Intret SATYRUS *cum* AMORETTA.

AMOR. Sis ferus, atque feras inter saevissimus omnes,
Qui me sic proprio rapis huc in sanguine mersam,
Exanimemque, scias hoc, me non posse noceri:
Sum virgo, nomen mihi murus aheneus hoc est.
SAT. Me, pulcherrima virgo, ne timeto,
Qui te fortibus in meis lacertis
Sanandam veho, non veho nocendam:
Sunt nobis Homines magis ferini.
En sylvam (Dea pulchrior supernis)
Novo sanguinis imbre purpurarunt!
Huic vir pol aliquis sinum foravit,
Tam mollem, tremulumque, candidumque,
Ut non ulla *Fera* hanc, vigil vel esset,
Ausit laedere, vel gravem sopore;
Tam dulcem, ut *Coluber, Ptyas*, vel *Aspis*, (p. 57)
Quo totus calesiat, a lacerto
Per mammas jacuisset ad lacertum

In noctem solidam, calensque recta
Isset, nec stimulasset hanc iturus.
Herbas protinus applica Mamillis:
"Est quaedam species *Homo* Ferarum.
CLOR. Par pectus super, innocente dextra
Has herbas sero quae creant soporem:
Et donec redeat salus manebunt,
Ambo si sumus integri pudoris;
Sed si non sumus, excident ab illo.
En! a vulnere decidit. Puella,
Tu non integra, tu libidinosi
Plena es sanguinis.
SAT. Ecquis hoc putasset
Tam pulchram faciem?
CLOR. Huic id imputandum est.
AMOR. Sint licet (ut reor) haec, quae dico, novissima verba,
Sic me PAN juvet, ut sum vita, et pectore, castis.
CLOR. Et sic PAN juvet hanc meam medelam,
Ut quicquid meditor pium et pudicum est.
Haud longe hinc aliquid latet scelesti,
Quod nostras facit irritas medelas.
Praesto! *Satyre*, quid sit explicato.
SAT. Ni fallor, subolet mihi per inde;
Adhuc fortius; Hic (io!) latentes,
Hic, hic, arboris in cavo retexi
Mortales stolidos duos.
CLOR. Fer illos
Me coram; solido carent valore.

Intret CLOE *et* DAPHNIS.

SAT. Sic vos per digitos traho retortos;
Sic vos sisto Deae meae ad Tribunal;
Frustra obnitimini: venite comes.
Non dixi, *Subolet*? 'libido putet.
CLOR. Ne plus, *Satyre*: nunc vitrum hoc capesse,
Totum sparge locum sacro liquore,
Purges aera ab halitu impudico,
Hanc ut surripiam neci puellam;
Immotusque mane, quousque plagae,
Ne crescat dolor, applicentur Herbae.

SAT. Hoc ex vitriolo pluo liquoris
Guttam perspicui super cacumen (p. 58)
Omne hic gramineum, duasque florum
Effundo super omnium coronas.
Fumus prodeat. Aeremque reddat
Fragrantem et salubrem, putum et beatum,
Hujus vulnere virginis patente.
CLOR. Intus, Satyre, transfer imbecillam.
SAT. Sic non ponderat, innocens ab omni
Est, per PANA puto, haec iniquitate:
Frondes te super has leves repone.
Angores sopor efficax levare
Mortales, oculos tuos coronet,
Et poenam premat illicoque casset.
CLOR. Pastorem mihi (Satyre) ut probemus
An sit pectore moribusque castis.
SAT. Adsis, Pastor.
DAPH. Amo, sed absque labe.
CLOR. Tanto tu melius potes probari.
Ipsius digitum plica hunc ad ignem,
Cui, si sit veneri datus, nocebit,
Flamma; sin minus, innocens recurret,
Carnem laedere respuens pudicam.
En retro fugit! Aufer hunc; valeto
Mortalis; quod es, esse perseveres.
SAT. Cur formosa fugis gradu citato?
Nobis et tua Castitas probanda est.
Hic est quae quatitur manus timore,
Haec certe minus innocens videtur.
CLOR. Ipsius digitum plica hunc ad ignem:
Laudem, aut dedecus, inde consequetur.
SAT. Stare haec judicio timet severo,
A flamma teneram manum revellens;
Et fax sanguineas vibrans sagittas
Perstringit digiti cutem tenellam.
Intus tu maculis scates, habesque
Mentem, si nihil amplius, protervam.
ALEX. Annon illa *Cloe* est? meus est ipsissimus ardor.
Cloe pulchra!
CLOE. Quis est? *Alexi!*

ALEX. Certe.
CLOE. Stringam te cupidis meis lacertis.
CLOR. Sensu hic ne viduetur, aufer istam.
ALEX. Non, Non; vita prius mihi auferatur.
CLOR. En rupta cute vulnus ulceratum!
Hanc Sylva teneas in hac propinqua,
Hoc dum obstruxero sanguinis fluentum.
Si menti dedero prius levamen,
Et membris propere dabo salutem.
Hoc interposito repello velo
Crudos Aeris halitus acuti.

Intret PASTOR SENIOR *et* SACERDOS.

SAC. Aeternum periisse puto; labor irritus esset
Quaerere solicite multum, multoque labore,
Quos ardor maturus agit, praecepsque voluntas,
Ut nisi peccati, fugiant consortia cuncta.
Quid nunc consilii? Redeundum est denique nobis?
Propositumve animi servabimus usque priorem
Quaerendi constanter eos?
SEN. Cuncteris, amabo;
Matutina meos etenim nisi fallit ocellos
Caligo, jam certe ovium distinguo Magistrum
Unum ex hac reducem genio indulgente Caterva.

Intret THENOTTUS.

SAC. Nonne pudet te, Pastor, in his juvenilibus annis
Desidiae esse reum, pecudesque relinquere solas,
Idque sequi quod sanguis iners, quod dira Cupido,
Sensibus obtrudit calidis sub imagine Recti;
Oblitus, quae lingua potest narrare futuris
Temporibus Mundo, te defecisse, querique
Ut tibi sit neque cura boni, neque cura pudoris,
Non virtutis amor, famaeve ex inde sequentis;
Et desperanti similis (cui gloria in hoc est)
Qui magni sibi virus emit, moriturus ab illo;
Sic tu Luxuriam; cui merces unica Morbus
Faetidus, et dolor est, atque immatura Senectus,
Et mors ante diem? Venis ardentibus illis
Hi crescunt fructis, quae non nisi ad otia pulsant

Excogitanda sibi, seque igne fruuntur in ipso,
Aspirant molles tumide, lauteque superbae.
THEN. Non novi, reverende parens, hac nocte quid esset
Blanda voluptatis facies, licuitve videre (p. 60)
Lascivi quicquam: Mihi Musica, Festa, Quiesque,
Quod stomacho de Febre malo Medicina, fuerunt.
Non ludus, quem ex ungue scio: non ulla puella,
Lingua volubilior sua si pede Temporis esset;
Forma aeterna simul, divinaque Carminis instar
Intonuit felix noster quod *Tityrus* olim;
Non, licet illecebris penum superaret opimum
Frugiferae Aestatis, cum porrigit Arbor onusta
Sponte viatori dulces, quas esurit, escas:
Haec mihi non essent aliud quam fulmina Lauro,
Quorum possit eam circundare noxius ignis,
Non ramis haerere sacris: Sic protegor ipse
Contra feminei metuendum fulgur Ocelli.
SAC. Cur tunc errasti?
THEN. Votum seduxit in agros
Me nocte hesterna; quo jam sine fraude soluto
Vado domum versus, nova pabula mane daturus,
Ut vivant, ovibus.
SAC. Bona pol est Musica, Pastor,
(Si sit in hac cordi sua pars) et dulcis in aure.
Ast ubi sunt reliqui?
THEN. Prato convenimus ex quo,
Vespere praeterito, gregibus de more locandis,
Nullum horum vidi: tamen hoc Nemus omne cucurri,
Et pernoctavi vetulae sub frondibus ulmi;
Sed neque Pastorem vidi per opaca vagantem,
Nec natam Pastore, meis aut auribus hausi
De vivente sonum, nisi tu, *Philomela*, fuisses
Inter spissicomi Nemoris virgulta canoro
Sola sedens planctu, totamque in murmura noctem
Convertens; aut Bubo; vel insatiabilis hostis
Ile gregum, gelidum usque ululans ad lampada Lunae.
SAC. Ito, cavens ne deinde cadas.
THEN. Pater, est mihi curae.

Exit THENOTTUS.

Intret DAPHNIS.

SEN. En alter vagabundus adest! reus esse videtur
Hic juvenis Pastor. *Daphnis*? (p. 61)
DAPH. Sic.
SAC. Parte relicti
Qua tibi sunt socii?
DAPH. Multum reverende Sacerdos,
Tu—me—re—spi—rare sinas paulisper inhorrens,
Donec quae vidi, possim quoque visa referre,
Qualia venerunt nullam Pastoris ad aurem:
Hei mihi! cor geminas, dicturo talia, motu
Scinditur in partes. *Clorindae* cella pudicae
Ignota est nulli, cujus vis magna medendi
Saepe homines, pecudes donavit saepe, salute;
Illic quae promissa fuit *Perigotto Amoretta*,
Pulchra perornato, vitam cum sanguine fundit.
(Fatalis quod macro aliquis, quod ferrea dextra
Patravit) juvenisque illi conjunctus *Alexis*.

Intret AMARYLLIS *fugiens* MELANCHOLICUM.

AMAR. Siquis vicinus sis rivulus, aut cava quercus,
Accipe me gremio, pateas mihi porta salutis;
Terga libido premit. Semper sis justus et aequus
O Tu Pastorum Numen PAN, illius ergo
Quae gaudet ripis fluvialibus, ac tremit et nunc
Frigida commemorans cursum Te urgente calentem:
Talis arundo Ego sim per secula, mutaque nutem
Ad casum modulantis aquae, dum me levis omnis
Per virides canit aura comas vixisse pudicam.
SAC. Haec nox horrorum est: animere *Amarylli*; Deorum est
Ulcisci tales, ulciscenturque querelas.
AMAR. Vir dilecte DEO, et campis deus alter in istis,
Audi me, servaque meum tenus hac sine labe
Virgineum florem a macula sine fine; per omnes
Illa coronarunt usquam quae tempora, myrtos;
Perque tuum castum officium, lectumque jugalem (p. 62)
Quem tu sole beas, per nostro quotquot habemus
Debita sacra Deo, quotque ardent ejus ad aram
Virgineas taedas; ne me permitte priore
Degenerare statu, quod nulla oblitteret Aetas,

Stigmate signandam. Non jam lasciva *Amaryllis*
Illa ego sum: Coelo, Pater hic reverende, Tibique
Concipio votum, Nocti si forte supersim
Huic infelici, sic ut concludere possim
Virgo diem, non me laturam exinde loquelas,
Aut impurorum consortia vana virorum.
Jam venit: O tege me!
SAC. Pone hoc te pone rubetum,
Iste Puellarum quoad innotescat adulter.

Intret MELANCHOLICUS.

SAC. Infamis juvenum.
MEL. Super omnia chara *Amarylli*,
Passum siste tuum; sine pigrior insequar ut te,
Nec totis velis, gravioribus utere pennis.
Ah! tibi ne auratos lacerarit spina cothurnos:
Pastorem visura tuum post terga, reflecte,
Robustum, blandum, quacunque ex parte potentem.
Non sum (Virgo) pudens; possum cuicunque placere
Vel prima facie; possum te arctare lacertis,
Oscula mille tibi dare succida, plena caloris,
Ut quae maturis Sol imprimit aureus uvis,
Malorumve genis, quae mittet *Persia*, rubris;
Sum laevis rugaeque expers *Neptunus* ut, antris
Indignabundos cum comprimit *Aeolus* Euros:
Sic et inexhaustam possum vibrare juventam.
Cur fugis amplexus nostros? *Amarylli*, memento
Te propter juvenem manus haec occidit *Alexin*;
Te propter *Perigottum* inter fidumque *Amorettam*
Pectus ei, aeternae jeci fundamina rixae:
In puteum detrusi illam Te propter eandem,
Quo, donec Tempus cessaverit esse, manebit.
Verte igitur, pansis verte amplexura lacertis
Omnia Pastorem qui gesserit ista fidelem.
Verte, reverte, inquam; non sum ludendus Amator.
SAC. Te teneas, monstrum; Pestis, qua vesceris, aurae (p. 63)
Et quam respiras; Vermis, cor omne pudicum
Suffodiens rixis; Tu, cujus adusta pepercit
Ira viro nunquam, nunquamque libido Puellae;
Hanc quoque, Virgineas quae Virgo cucurrit ad aras,

Peccatrice manu trepidantem avertere tentas.
MEL. Exponas pia Simplicitas ex arte, fuissem
Si nudus nudam amplexus, quid ab inde pericli?
Quae spectanda forent exhinc miracla?
SAC. Libido,
Ustaque mens.
MEL. Ultra; Juvenescere possit ut usque
Mundus, et humanam per secula ducere gentem,
Non rerum dixit Mater Natura, necesse
Et dulce esse simul, similes generare sibi omnes?
SAC. Doctior es caedis, pravaque libidinis Arte,
Me fateor longe: nunc virginis antra petamus;
Et simul haec meritas ut solvat Bellua poenas.

Exeunt.

[V. iv]

Intret PERIGOTTUS *manu sanguine cruentata.*

PER. Hic matutino te, dextera, rore lavabo,
Quem stillat super omnem herbam floremque minutum,
Imbre argenteolo, rutilo Dea praevia *Soli*.
Est *aqua lustralis*, multumque his usibus apta:
Purgari negat ista manus. Mea laesa Voluptas,
Si tuus aereis etiamnum spiritus errat
Castus in exiliis, hunc desuper aspice mitis,
Qui reus hic stat adhuc soleas de vertice ad imas,
Purpureamque tuo sustendit sanguine dextram;
Et licet immeritum dederim tibi perfidus ictum,
In caput Autricis justos vertisse furores
Extenuet factum quod suaserat error iniquum;
Hoc et rore meam possim depellere labem.
Mundari negat; O, sacro cui denique fonti,
Qui me sanguineo lavet hoc a flumine, curram?
Has inter platanos humili *Clorinda* moratur
Sancta casa, sectis cui pendent culmina ramis;
Fert et opem cunctis. Hanc quaeram, illique fatebor (p. 64)
(Illacrymando) meae temeraria facta juventae:
Forsitan arte manum, precibusve potentibus, illa
Reddiderit, casto pollutam sanguine, pulchram.
Ipse strui parvam post inde sub arbore cellam

Non procul hinc aliqua faciam; quia mortua nunc est
Quam veneratus eram, postponam ibi gaudia curis,
Exemploque tuo vivam, *Clorinda*, severo.

Exit.

[V. v]

Sipario deducto, apparet CLORINDA *in Arboreto sedens, latus ejus claudente hinc* AMORETTA, *illinc* ALEXI *et* CLOE, *astante* SATYRO.

CLOR. Jam sanguis tibi sistitur secundo;
Exemplo sape Virginis, vir, hujus
Quae te consequitur prior salutem:
Tam vix est medicabilis libido.
Tunc ne lumina torqueas caveto
Has in candidulas libidinose;
Et tu, Nympha, cave ut trahas volentem
Ipsius, vagulis tuis, Ocellum;
Non torto digitove vellicato,
Aut risu impuleris levi labantem.
Numquid verus adhuc, et est pudicus,
Sic et semper Amor tuus futurus?
ALEX. Desideria vana dereliqui,
Ignes et fatuos, et impudicos.
"Est sincerus Amor vapor benignus,
"Pulmones modicus fovens, nec urens.
CLOE. In me nobilior creatur ignis,
Qui nec fluminis indiget, nec escae.
CLOR. Tactu jungite dexteras pudico,
Et semper maneatis id quod estis.

Intret PERIGOTTUS.

PER. Illius illa casa est, vocitans in aprica Puellam
Eminus hic stabo; nec enim prope limina sacra
Ferre meam dextram (cupiens) audebo profanam.
Prodi, *Clorin*; opem misero *Clorinda* clienti
Fer tempestivam.
CLOR. Quis tu mea nomina clamas?
Porrigit auxilium cunctis *Clorinda*: propinques. (p. 65)
PER. Non ausim.
CLOR. Videas, amice, quis sit

Qui me flebilis orat ut juvarem.
SAT. Quidam Pastor ibi stat in propinquo
Tendens sanguineam manum per auras.
PER. O *Clorinda*, veni; simul, haec manus unde lavetur,
Lustrales purasque tuas adduxeris undas.
CLOR. Qualia, praeterita miracula nocte fuerunt!
Extendas juvenis manum cruentam;
Illam tu pariter laves fricesque.
PER. Semper tu pluis, at manus quod ante est.
CLOR. Intret (*Satyre*) fac in Arboretum,
Utendum est aliis aquis potenter.
SAT. Mortalis, dubio procul, pudicae,
Qui sic inquinat, est cruor puellae.

Ductus a SATYRO *in Arboretum, aspicit ibi* AMORETTAM, *quae in genua lapsum* PERIGOTTUM *agnoscit.*

PER. Quicquid tu fueris, Umbra ejus, an una Dearum.
Quam juvat ipsius Nemus hoc errare figura,
Condones misero *Perigotto.*
AMOR. Sum tuus Ardor,
Ardor sine carens, *Amoretta* tuissima: nudum hoc
Percute pectus adhuc, et adhuc te hoc pectus amabit.
Si me diligeris vel nunc, quam praesto volaret
Praeteritus de mente dolor.
PER. Sic gaudeo quod Te
Nunc video vivam, ut me nulla cupido fatiget
Scire modum—est et adhuc tibi condonare potestas?
AMOR. In quantum vel amare tibi, mihi vivere vel sit;
Gratior adveniens nunc, quam si tramite nunquam
Errasses.
PER. Et cum sine me torquebere gratis,
Mors mihi contingat, vel Tabes pejor eadem. (p. 66)
CLOR. Nunc labes tua forsan abluetur;
Qui sanguis modo carnibus cohaesit
Cum lympha simul en cadit cadente!
Omnis denuo flectitur potestas,
Hoc et propitia est recente nodo:
Dextras jungite, a solo virenti
Surgentes; pariter referte grates
PANI, qui tulit huc (favens) utrumque.

Intret SACERDOS *et* SENIOR PASTOR.

CLOR. Quicquid Tu fueris, nisi quod mediteris honestum,
Purum, et virgineum est, torque vestigia retro;
Non sacram calcaris human. Cape, *Satyre*, dextram
Ejus, eumque probes propere.
SAT. Mortalis adesdum.
Donec constiterit, probante flamma,
Num sis cui pede libero sit istum
Fas calcare locum, manum elevato:
Hac nunquam caro purior! vir iste
Est (Pulcherrima) sanctitate plenus.
CLOR. Tu nefari audacter, quid in hac statione requiris?
SAC. Primo, inhiare tuam faciem (veneranda Puella)
Omnis ubi probitas scatet; explorare secundo
Verane fama meas nuper veniebat ad aures,
Pastores illi quos sors peracerba secuta est
(Consiliis pravis, et deterioribus usos
Moribus) ecquid adhuc quae gestant vulnera crudum
Aera ferre queant, an adhuc speranda medela est;
Postremo, quae poena manet, quae digna misellos
Criminis authores tanti vindicta, videre:
Huc etenim (pia Virgo) tuli genus omne scelestum,
Cur intentarunt alienam et quomodo mortem
Audaces, ultro fassos.
CLOR. Spargantur odores,
Lustrales spargantur aquae, ad dextram atque sinistrum;
Repit enim patulas contagio tetra per auras; (p. 67)
Fervet adhuc magis atque magis: cape vascula thure
Plena pio myrrhaque duo, neque frigida desit
Camphora: Tu partes, bone *Satyre*, curre per omnes;
Caepit enim sudare locus, Factisque laborat
Peccantum horrendis: Procul, O procul este, prophani!
Plenae etenim Lepra, flamma et prurigine plenae
Sunt quoque vestrae animae; sic, ut terra ipsa gemiscat,
Pondus inauditi nequiens tolerare veneni,
Nec centro stet fixa suo.
Sancte vir, acceleres; Hominumque simillima Monstra

71 Tu nefari] tunc fare *1658*

Stirpe fuges casta, norint haec pascua nunquam
Rursus, at ante diu quam Sol redivivus Eois
Exoriatur aquis, oculis ea deme, simulque
Abscondas animis obliviscenda pudicis.
Hoc age, ne ruptis renoventur vulnera pannis.

Exit SACERDOS.

PER. Chara *Amoretta* nimis, "felix par illud *Amantum*
"In quibus aeternum brevis ira creavit Amorem,
"Quem neque livor edax, neque vis, neque tempora laedant!
Ut sentis plagas? eheu! miseranda Puella,
Quam plane deceptus eram; mihi cede dolorem,
Est nam jure meus.
AMOR. Credo; sat, Amice, superque est:
Mitte queri, nostrasque manus jungamus, ut ante,
Cordaque nostra iterum, fato irascente fruentes.
PER. Promptius, aestivis quam solstitialibus unquam
Frigida quaesivi languens Crystallina fontis
Queis avidam placare sitim. Sit nodus in aevum hic;
Audi nos, Coelum.
AMOR. Stabilis sis.
PER. Si modo non sim,
In caput infidum PAN fulminet aequus ab Alto
Vindictam duplicem, consortia nosse Virorum
Non ausim, aut oculos posthac mirarier illos.
AMOR. Pastor, basiolo moritur lis omnis ab isto. (p. 68)

Intret SACERDOS.

SAC. Illustris Virgo, sum functus munere; Pastor
In quo tanta fuit rabies, et tanta libido,
Conformes dedit infamis, te judice, poenas:
Sola puella manet, vultu praesaga futurae
Virtutis; culpam flet plurima. Pulchra, potensque,
Arbitrium revoca, sperans meliora, severum;
Quorum sponsor ego: curvatam pondere mentem
Illius erigito, quae jam prope mersa recumbit
Æternis curis, et se torquentibus ipsas.
CLOR. Condono facilis, fac intret; purior Aer
Manat, et intensum coepit laxare calorem:
Quanta procelloso succedit gloria Coelo!
Satyre, vade cito, dextramque ipsius in isto

Fortiter igne proba; si pura sit atque pudica,
Semper et esse quod est sedet illi firmiter, ipsis
Diis dignum superamus opus.

SATYRUS *introducit* AMARYLLIDA.

SAT. Prodi, femina, delitere noli,
Nec celet faciem dolor pudorque;
Nunc, nunquamve, tibi parato nomen
Quod te sublevet, eluatque quicquid
Impuri latet in tuis medullis.
Flammis admoveas manum, puella;
Si sis moribus undiquaque castis,
Aut te strenua voveris futuram,
Hic ignis tibi pallidus favebit:
En fax lurida parcit innocenti!
I felix, violet tuum deinceps
Nec labecula sanguinem; referto
Diis grates, et (honesta) perseveres.
CLOR. Nunc quia Virgineo, Pastorcula, redderis Albo,
Sis eadem, maneasque tuae pro tempore vitae;
Te nisi castus Amor Pastoris fidi alicujus (p. 69)
Compulerit mutare statum, cui sis quoque fida:
Sic vitam degas, ut tu post funera possis
Vivere, non vitii sed magni exemplar *Honesti*.
Sancte vir, hos poena vacuos, plenosque salute,
Trado tibi rursus; simili defende periclo;
Acturis prope sis; doceas purgare maligna
Suspicione viam, quae spinis longa terenda est:
Prospice ne faciant, neque quid patiantur iniqui:
Et labor, et parcus luctet cum sanguine victus:
Rivulus, aut avidam restinguat proxima Fontis
Gutta sitim: Faetis non lugeat Arbor ademptis,
Undique lascivis quae pendet onusta racemis:
Nosse (nisi in Sacris) vinum Pastoribus esto
Religio: Bone vir, tibi sint haec omnia curae.
Parcere peccato peccans Clementia nolit:
Et memor auge illum, qui (pascua providus augens,
Fructificansque gregem) multum sudavit et alsit:
Pastores procul ignavos ab Ovilibus arce,
Qui sua floriferis pascunt armenta genistis,

Virginibus glaciem obducas, ut semper earum
Florentem timeant pueri tentare juventam.
Exulet ingenuo cedens Sycophantia vero
Omnis Pastoris jecore, et sermonibus omnis;
Nulla sit ars illis, persuasio quanta libebit.
Sic tibi, sic istis, exopto (Sancte Sacerdos)
Cunctaque praesentis bona vitae, et cuncta futurae.

OMNES. Cunctaque quae Coelum dederit Mortalibus usquam
Gaudia, nos petimus, Cellam exonerentur in istam.

SACER. Unusquisque genu Pastor jam flecte, potente
Dum benedico manu vestris gregibusque gregumque
Pastibus; Et culpa PAN vos defendat et ira:
Illis vos tueatur a periclis
Quae votum quoque proprium sequuntur:
Vos finaliter instruat, quod omnes
Vestrae divitiae, quod omne robur,
Non servare valent pedes cadentes
Vestros a fovea libidinosa,
Quae Templis etiam subest et Aris;
Donec *Optimus* Ille, *Maximusque*, (p. 70)
Menti cuilibet auream superne
Pacis fulguret, et quietis, horam.
Vobis prospiciens, refraenet ille
Quicquid pestiferi, vel ulcerati,
Vel quocunque modo dolentis, aut vos
Posthac inficiat, gregesve vestros.
Affectus alios det unicuique,
Humoresque novos, novosque mores,
Ut sitis sine termino fideles.
Surgite nunc, et abite, piaque canatis euntes
Voce Gregum Divo felix id carmen, honestus
Quod panxit *Dorus*; *Dorus*, qui mens fuit altae
Et Deus Harmoniae.

Cantant Omnes.

Cantio
I

Vos quotquot Nemora, Arbores, Vireta,
Virtutesque vagae, potentiaeque,

Aut stagnis habitatis in profundis,
Aut Dumis, titubantibusve rivis;
Vos pede nostrae
Plaudite voci,
Dum sonat omnis
Proxima vallis
Ejus nomine laudibusque, noxa
Qui nostros redimit greges ab omni.

II

Ille est omnipotens, et ille justus,
Et semper bonus, et modo hoc colendus.
Narcissis, violisque, liliisque
Dilectis, simul ac Rosis utrisque
Undique jactis,
Vociferemus
Sancte per aevum,
Sancte per aevum,
Et semper juvenis, verende semper;
Sic PAN *Maximus indies canetur.*

SAT. Terrae pulchrior incolis, beata,
Perquam candida Virgo, praepotensque,
Dilectissima Diis, et absque fraude,
Stellatis oculis, pari capillo
Phoebeis radiis; mihi explicato (p. 71)
Quid digni super arduique quid sit,
Quod praestet tibi *Satyrus*: volabo
Per Regnum celer Aeris secundum,
Et nimbi (potis) impetum rotantis
Sistam? fortiter occupabo Lunam,
Et blande dominam rogabo Noctis
Pallentem, tibi mutuum det Astrum?
Immergar penetralibus profundi,
Ut rubrum tibi colligam Corallum,
Discludens tumidas viam per undas
Tanquam velleribus Nivis cadentes?
Vis (Charissima) capreas fugaces,
Aut muscas capiam, quibus per alas
Æstas texuit Iridis colores?

Aut pina alta legam? Polove furer
Vatis Threicii lyram vetusti?
Cuncta haec, plusque, tui probabo causa;
Quam cunctae hae flexo venerantur vertice Sylvae.

CLOR. *Satyre*, prospicias tantum (nihil amplius oro)
Hos circum lucos, ne gens innoxia noxam
Aut damnum capiat.

SAT. Puella Sancta,
Per totum Nemus hoc tripudiabo,
Surgentis celer ut jubar Diei;
Saltus perque ferar, per atque valles,
Alis Ventimolae magis citatus.
Tu nunc ut valeas precor, simulque
Quod solaminis uspiam invenitur,
Phoebi quale solet creare lumen,
Et te prosperet, et tuum viretum.

CLOR. Et tu sis Domini tui voluptas.

Exeunt.

FINIS

Prose Works

By His Highnesse the Prince of Great BRITTAIN, *Duke of* CORNWALL *and* ALBANY, *Highest Captain Generall of all His Majesties Forces raised and to be raised within the Kingdom of* England, *Dominion of* Wales *and Town of* Berwick, &c.

A PROCLAMATION,

For all persons within Our Quarters in the County of *DEVON* able to bear Arms, not being otherwise imployed by His Highnesse, or dispenced withall, to attend His Highnesse now advancing in Person to meet the Rebels.

AS ALSO

For a Generall Supplication to be made in all Churches of DEVON and EXETER, on Sunday the 4 of *January*, for Gods blessing on His Highnesse, and His Forces.

Whereas, upon the motion of the Enemy on this side *Exeter*, We have resolved in Our own Person to repair to Our Army, and to that end We resolve with all possible expedition to advance with Our Forces, hoping, by the blessing of God, to expell the Enemy from this County, We have thought fit to publish and declare this Our resolution, desiring and requiring all Loyall and able men of what degree or quality soever within Our Quarters in that County as well those of the Trained-Bands, as all others able to bear Arms, who are not otherwise imployed or dispenced with by Us, to repair to Us very speedily in person, to Our assistance, with such Arms as they can bring; And We must professe that We shall impute the absence of any person, not so imployed or dispenced with as aforesaid, to want of Loyalty, or want of Courage, both which at so important a time, and upon so important an occasion, We hold equally odious. And for the procuring a blessing from God upon this Our first enterprize, which We undertake for his Service, and for the procuring a blessed Peace upon this miserable Kingdom, towards the which Our entreaties and earnest desires of mediation have been rejected, We desire that on Sunday next a general Supplication may be made in all the Churches within Our Quarters for Gods blessing upon Us and Our Forces, intending also to see the like Supplication solemnly made by the whole Army, when We shall have drawn it into a body. And the High-Sheriffe of

Devon is to cause this Our Declaration and Proclamation to be speedily publisht in all Market-Towns and Publike Meetings in Our Quarters there, and read in all the Churches and Chappels within the said County, We having directed the like to be done in Our Dutchy of *Cornwall*, and hereby likewise directing the like to be done in the City of *Exeter*.

Given at Our Court at *Tavistoke* the 29. of *December* 1645.

CHARLES P.

By His Highnesse Command
in Councell

Rich: Fanshawe.

Imprinted at *Exeter* by ROBERT BARKER, and JOHN BILL, Printers to the Kings most Excellent Majesty, 1645.

A MESSAGE
FROM HIS HIGHNESSE
The Prince of Wales,

DELIVERED

To the right Honorable the Lord Baron of Inchiquin Lord President of Mounster, in a Councell of War at Corcke the 28. of November, 1648. By Richard Fanshawe Esquire, imployed by his Highnesse into Ireland.

Printed at Corck, in the yeare 1648. and are to be sold at Roches building.

A MESSAGE FROM HIS HIGHNESSE THE PRINCE OF WALES, etc.

His Highnesse gave me Letters of Credence to my *Lord Lieutenant*, Commanding mee to assure his Excellencie of his great Affection to, and high esteeme of him, as the principall Person by whom hee shall be advised in what concernes this Kingdome of *Ireland*, and that his said Highnesse shall upon all occasions contribute whatsoever is in his power towards the assisting him in the great worke hee hath now in hand, of setling this Kingdome in his Majesties obedience, with a due care of the Protestant Religion, and the English Interest: which I have accordingly done.

He commanded me to give these his other Letters of Credence (*here read*) to your Lordship my *Lord President* of *Mounster*, and to assure your Lordship of his good affections to, and confidence in you, as a Person who hath performed very eminent services to the King his Father. Hee commanded mee to let your Lordship know that hee hath a very just sense of the streights you are in, and of the sad Condition your Army is reduc'd to, for want of Moneyes and other supplyes, and that hee will use his utmost endeavours for their reliefe in such manner as he hopes will shortly prove effectuall, and to that degree, as not onely to preserve them from such wants as might enforce them to submit to dishonorable or unworthy Conditions, either with *Irish* or *Independents*, but to enable them to be the happy Instruments (as his Highnesse is persuaded they are by Devine Providence reserved to be) for the bringing both the one and the other to Termes of Reason, and for the rescueing of his Majesties and his Subjects Rights from the usurpation of either.

Upon this occasion his Highnesse commanded me to enlarge my selfe in severall perticulars, to show a greater probability hereof then may appeare at first sight against the opposition of so many visible enemyes; provided his Highnesse may be so happy as to have entire and faithfull obedience from this Army in order to those ends. As First, that this Fleet (which [he] is sending hither victuall'd for three Moneths and payd for six) is a much greater then ever was applyed to the service of this Kingdome, the opportunity of the Ports whereof (perticulerly in this Province) for Trade, for Defence, for Offence, and indeed to make it every way considerable both to Friends and Enemyes, though much more potent then it selfe, the world hath hardly the like of, in any one Kingdome or dominion. All which Advantages have hitherto laine buried like

Gold in Mines, (which likewise for ought I know may be found here indeed: Silver here is, and courser Mettalls in great aboundance) for want of such a Navy Royall to draw them forth, and improve them perhaps also for want of the presence of an active Prince amongst you. Upon which occasion I may adde to this Branch, that which, if it had beene absolutely resolved upon before I came out of *Holland*, would of it selfe alone have beene the greatest Consideration whereupon to ground the hope of successe in your Loyall undertakings; which is, that his Highnesse the *Duke of Yorke* is certainly to come along with the Fleete; and I doe verily believe, that the Prince himselfe will be here likewise; either with it, or not long after, his strength peradventure being not yet recovered since his Highnesse late sicknesse at the *Hague*; by which meanes you will have the Countenance of persons borne and form'd for Command, both by Land, and Sea, and growing every day more capable thereof; and together with them you will have the hearts, and perhaps the hands likewise, and purses, of many thousands of people, who will be more enflamed, and more readily engage in his Majesties cause, when they shall see it coupled with the personall defence of his Royall Offspring, so hopefull and so innocent Princes. Which will carry a double benefit along with it; first, here will be a Sanctuary for so many honest men, with so much of their Estates as they can save out of the hands of those that oppresse them; and then in the second place, the addition of these persons, and their stocks will be so many more helpes to defend and improve a Kingdome so capable of improvement and defence as this.

Severall good Ports there are elsewhere still remaining in his Majesties Obedience, and opportunely situate to assist you, and offend your enemies as if they had been placed there on purpose to tosse the ball from hand to hand: and God will send more. For the second Consideration which his Highnesse commanded mee to ground a hope upon of your successe in so pious an undertaking, is, That by the providence of God the Affections of his Majesties people of *England* are in the view of all the world more deepely rooted in them towards his Majestie, at this very time, then ever; and this his Highnesse is well assured you will ere long see some effects of, if the Treaty in the Isle of *Wight* succeed not; for then the paint of the *Independent* designes will be washt off, and the beauty of his Majesties gracious disposition for the welfare of his People will appeare in fresher Colours.

A third Consideration whereupon to ground a hope of your successe (you will thinke that strange) is from the very successe of the *Independent* Army in what they undertooke. His Highnesse (as young as he is) hath seene enough of the world to know that the nature of Man (impatient, either of hot, or cold fitts) is too apt, either in great prosperitie, or in great adversitie, to thinke there can never be a period of the one, or the other; Whereas in truth *Hee* who alone is *everlasting*, and *who spurnes downe the loftie, and raises up those that are low*, hath placed the greatest instability of all upon those Pinacles and extreames of Fortune. But this is not the thing. Because you cannot certainly foresee the end of these Men, his Highnesse desires you to looke back upon their Beginning, what they attempted, and atchieved, with an Army not very much greater, nor at that time any whit more victorious then yours, and despised (as much as any bodyes folly can doe yours) by the Contrary partie, which consisted of almost all the visible power and acknowledged authority of the three Kingdomes; both by land and sea; themselves in the meane time having no shipping, no Treasure, no Prince, or great Men in the head of them, and few friends. They entred by force of Armes the City of *London* (whose wealth principally had maintained them) [triumphant, with Lawrell in their hatts:] They dismembred [both houses of the Parlia]-ment of *England* under whose Commissions they served; and they over-threw the Armies, and Decrees of the *Parliament of Scotland*, with which they had solemnly Covenanted; besides other remarkable successes. Whence all this? Or to what cause (besides a tough resolution, which you know how to put on as well as they) may we impute so great effects? you will find these *Men of Warre*, were their Arts Masters, who to make their Approaches as securd as unsuspected, hung out the Kings Colours, casting forth many halfe words, and doing as many actions with two handles, to make the world (which was prone to believe what they wisht) swallow an opinion, that they marcht up, and strengthened themselves, with a purpose to worke the freedome, and restauration of his Maiestie, who was then in an eclypse at *Holdenby*; with other specious matters, whereby they inveigled the people, some to be Newters, some to be Assistants, all generally to be well-wishers to them. Thus, and in this disguise, like *Jacob*, *They came with subtilty and tooke away their elder Brothers blessing*, whose intentions were cleerer then theirs; And this it was which gave them their first Rise. But *hath our Father but one Blessing? can hee not blesse Us, even Us also?* They have had their Time; and may yet (if it please them to sound a Retreate) rise great Gainers. But in case no reason will satisfy them, why may not your turne be come? If *His Maiesties Name* though but softly and hollowly spoken, was such a charme upon the people, and proved so auspicious and usefull to the Independents for the accomplishment of their vast designes (this now is that which his Highnesse commanded me to inculcate to you) why should not you, with the helpes I have mentioned, and backt with all the Authority which a free King and Parliament could give, be as able to compasse your honest and moderate ends, being the same in reality which they but pretended?

His Highnesse is verily perswaded in his mind, that you are the Men in whose power it is (though you had no helpers) to pull that Independent partie, from the height of their designes, only by a firme union and combination among *your selves*, and a rough expostulation with *them*, according to their own way with Parliament, (your swords in your hands) what in the Name of God they intend to doe, with our Protestant *Religion*, our good *King*, our wholesome *Lawes*, and poore *Countrey*, in such manner, as that they may plainly perceive you have set your hearts, and brests, upon the righting of them all, so as never to sheathe those swords till you see it done. Not long after which his Highnesse doubts not, but that, upon cooler blood they will renew and conclude the Treaty of Peace with his Majestie, how scornfully soever they may reject it at this time, you being under God the happy Authours of it, and including therein your owne Arrears, and whatsoever other just demands, with the generall applause and thanks of all men. What glory will it be then for this Army and Countrey, if the *Prince of Mounster*, as *They* may call him, (perchance prophetically in respect of that additional Title which he may hereby acquire to himselfe and the Heires of *England* for ever) shall recover from hence, by your valour and Fidelitie, the *Crowne of England*? Why not, as well as the *King of Diepe* (so tearmed in *derision*, but afterwards, *in good earnest*, *Henry the Great*) did from that poore Towne alone, wherein likewise hee was besieged, recover *the Crowne of France*? His *Highnesse* Person, and Youth, promise no lesse then his; and, if these things run in a blood, hee is his owne Grandchild (the thing was no longer a goe.) Or if you should but stand here as meere spectators for a few months of the issue of things England and whether those enemies (in the[ir] minds they a[re, eit]her through mislead opinions, or, for the present invincible, because guilty, apprehensions) of an ancient and Glorious Monarchy, can as easily agree, and find the way to *build up*, as they have done to *pull downe*; His Highnesse thinks that this alone would goe neere to produce the same effect; And that you will soone be courted, not underhand, but in an open and honourable way by the best, and also by the prowdest there, when they shall find a necessity of the ancient Government of *England*, if they have any Bowells towards their Countrey; and although they should have none, yet when they shall see that after they shall have tost and tormented *themselves* and the People (*their patients*) with many costly experiments, they shall but *dispute in a Circle*, and must come to *that* againe at last. This (I say) provided there be that firme unity and harmony among your selves which is recommended. For in this Case (as in your Battailes and Skirmishes) it matters not whether *you* or *the prevalent party in England*, are the *greater*, or the *stronger*; but which of the *two* is like to *route* first; now you have *the Sunne*, and *the Wind*, on your side; I meane, *THE PRINCE* to rise in *their* Faces; and *THE LAW* to rally you. Adde; That, if you can hold your hands from disturbing of them, in *England*, which they will be affraid of, whilst they are busy in dividing the spoile, you shall never need to feare their troubling of you here; for in case they [should attemp]t it, will the Princes Fleet (thinke you) doe nothing the while? and then, whom will they leave behind to guard their *Prisoners*? Believe it, they are a very vast number; His Highnesse conceives *the whole people of England* in their present thraldome understand themselves to be such.

Some of these perticulers were not fully ripe as yet for publike knowledge, I having had commission to speake them only to my *Lord Lieutenant*, and Your Lordship; but herein I obey Your Lordships Command, not doubting of my Masters approbation thereof, the rather, because it is suitable to that gracious disposition which I have alwayes observed in his Highnesse, that, *the prevalent Partie in England* (which thinks to roule the world before them for ever) should be *warned*, as well as *his Friends incouraged*, thereby: and that *They*, as well as *You*, should see, and know, that *Lawes with Charitie are the onely Bond of Peace*; and that *the King* (the common Father of his People, and his *Lawes*) is *the only possible Ciment of the three Kingdomes*, so happily united *in his Person*. That therefore *They* (whatever they may be apt to flatter themselves) can never have any *Peace* in their *Habitations*, no more then *that* of a *good Conscience*, or the Blessing of *God*, or the *People*, untill they shall conclude a *well-grounded Peace* with *his Majestie*. But that, two hopefull and insur'd *Princes*, a strong and resolv'd *Fleet*, severall well-placed and fortified *Islands*, and a faithfull and couragious *Army*, (I summe up only what is *in the hand*, his Highnesse reckoning much more upon what is *in the Bush*, from *Him* who spake to *Moses* out of it; for *Truth is great, and will prevayle.*) that all these, I say, will be perpetually [up]on their skirts, will be as so many continuall goades in their sides, till they come to honorable Conditions with *his Majestie*. Which if his Highnesse shall be driven to contend for to this extremitie, and that it shall please *God*, through your assistance, to give him Victory in that unhappy, yet necessary contention; He assures you, *in the word of a Prince*, hee will make no other use thereof, then, what *his Majestie* hath alwayes publisht to be his intentions; and *You* also to be the ends of your *Armes*, being specified in *your owne Declaration*.

Eight Unpublished Letters

[1. To (Sir) John Heath]

[Collection of Robert H. Taylor, Esq., Princeton: uncatalogued]

Honest Jacke,

I have newly received yours of the 14th of November by Nol Jephson, and give you many thankes for your Newes, and your double pitty of Me in respect of my approaching Losse both of my M[aster] and M[istress] at once. But for the first I will not despayre of Him whilst he is in Mr. Lowes hands; And for the second, She is preferd if the other fall. Agayne, I was armed agaynst the first losse a Priori, having long agoe forecast the worst, and considered Him in somewhat more then a possibility of falling both from the Princes favour, and the Peoples opinion (in which He then stood fayre enough) when I did consider him Great, and Active: Agaynst the second a Posteriori, For though I confesse I rusht too confidently upon my hopes of her, and without due foresight climbd too high, yet it hath been my good fortune to meet with so many boughs in my Fall and to be so long in falling by that meane that (I thanke God) I am not much bruised with it, somewhat I am. So that (to speake in my Warre phrase) I had a Breast-Plate agaynst that Evill which I was manly to encounter, and a Backe-Peice agaynst this which I was to overcome by flying. neyther perhaps would it prove so ridiculous as safe for you (who are going on upon the like Enterprise as I am come off from) to put my Backe-Peice now upon your Breast, with this Word (if you please) *Tamquam abiturus*. For such is the Nature commonly of those delicate Creatures that We may be certayne never to have them when once they are certayne that they can never loose Us. which may be the cause of that Advantage peradventure observed by Mrs Stampe on the side of the Merry Wooer, that mirth being a signe that he layes nothing greatly to heart, and therefore not his M[istress.] For mine, He or She who wishes her more joy and happiness than I doe must wish her in Heav'n allready. And so I conclude that Poynt.

For your Verses I must confesse I received them before in sommer, but cannot yet determine in so nice a Controversie, and indeed am loath to proceed to judgement in a Cause where both yours are at Stake. the Copies are both very good in earnest, and I could wish the matter were taken up freindly between you. If that may not be I shall hereafter deliver my opinion, in the meane time I shall consult our Bookes in the Case.

And though I knowe it is a requiting Evill for good, yet I have so little Conscience as to send you herewith for them some torne blotted Papers

of mine owne, the issues of those few idle howers which I have had in this Kingdome, on which you may revenge your selfe if you please for their Intrusion upon your Studies. Pray make Mr Lowe tend his Businesse diligently at the Towre. So I rest
your faythfull Freind
Richard Fanshawe

Dublin the 26 of
decemb: 1640

[Docket on verso:] For Mr John Heath
from Dublin 26. december. 1640.

[2. To Sir Richard Browne] [Eve.]

Sir,
I hope my cutt of Armes done by a Herold secundum actum came very long agoe to your hands, I having sent it to Mr Sambourne of Rouen inclosed to you in a letter and returning mee answeare therupon that he had sent to you by a safe hand.

Being bound this day back for England I have left here for you a peice of folly of mine owne (a Translation of pastor fido) there be 3 more, one for my Lady Dalkeith, another for Mr Harding, and a 3d for Cheife Justice Heath's son, which I desire your favor to have delivered accordingly when they come to your hands, staying to be sent when some trusty person that passes that way will take the trouble of them. they are left with Dr. Henchard at my Lord of Bristol's. I am

Sir

your most affectionate and most faythfull humble kinsman and servant

Richard Fanshawe

My wife and I present our most affectionate service to you and your Lady, and allso to your fayre daughter to whome we wish much joy.

I Besech you doe mee the favor to give the first conveyance to the inclosed.

Caen 15 of Aug:
1647 styl: no:

[3. To Sir Richard Browne] [Eve.]

Sir,
I give you many heartie thankes for your care of my Seales which I perceive by yours of the 22d present, and doubted not before. Neither doe I make any question but that the 2 Cornelians formerly sent are safe all this while though I heard not of them till now, nor of the letter you mention to have sent with them. Whereat I wonder not at all because it was very difficult for your Servant to hearken mee out, whom it concerned to live as privatly as possibly I could, being not qualifyed to stay in London.

I question as little the safe winning of your Saphyre to Mr Boothes hands with such care as you are pleased to take, to whom I have sent directions whether to send it for mee together with some other small things of mine concerning which I have intreated his favor in the same kind. When you shall doe mee the favor to imploy mee in something wherein I may be capable to serve you, I shall then believe you have forgiven this great trouble from

Sir

your most affectionate Kinsman and humble Servant

Richard Fanshawe

Aug 19 stylo vet: [1647, London]

I beseech you present my humble [service] to your Lady, and my faire cosen. My Wife would say the same to you all if she were with me.

[4. To Sir Richard Browne] [Eve.]

Calais 19 Novembris 1650

Sir,

I am very glad to find by your letter you are as commodiously, though not so magnificently seated as formerly. May you long injoy it or a better. Mr. Wyndom went from this Forward, full of the care of you, and resolved to make it his buisinesse to serve you, and his master in you. I shall be inquisitive of him how his indeavours therein have thrived when I see him, which I presume will be suddaynly, being this very day bound towards him.

The news of the Prince of Auranche his death hath strooke us all dead heere. And no lesse hath the boasts of the London-diurnalls touching the Scotts treating with Cromwell (though contrary to advertisments from many others) occasioned our melancholy.

My Wife, Sister, and Favourite, went the last Sunday to England much your Servants, leaving many affectionate Services for you and yours. They intended to have taken a solemne leave of you by a joynt letter, but were snatched from that purpose by a suddayne faire opportunitie (as we thought) of a passage, allthough it proved otherwise, a terrible storme rising at their very landing hower, which kept them a whole night in the Downes, in extreame Danger, and sufferance: But God be thanked they landed well and safe.

My poore Tutor Doctor Beale's death in Spaine requires a teare apart: good man! nudus in ignota! it was often his owne sad expression when I saw him there, but I little thought it so profeticall as it hath fallen out.

I beseech you doe me the favour to address the inclosed.

With my humble service to your selfe, my Lady, and my Cosens all, I remain,

Sir,

Your very affectionate and faythfull humble Servant

Ric. Fanshawe

[5. To John Evelyn] [BL, Add. MS 28,104, ff. 6–7]

Tankersley 27th of Dec: 1653.

Noble Cosen,
Yours of [ ] instant together with a manuscript which your modestie is pleased to intitle an essay upon the first Booke of Lucretius, found mee out in this remote Corner. Whereby I perceived, a Friend (how clowded soever with absence, and misfortune) can no more bee hidden to your kindnesse, then the most abstruse Author to your Apprehension or (by that time you have done with him) to any man's else. Yet Absence alone is a death: not that it uses to kill Freinds, but Freindship. The Spaniard calls it, putting of Earth between, so both Death, and Buriall too. and hee hath a Proverb that tells us, *A Muertos y aydos no ay Amigos.* the crossing whereof is the thing I now take so kindly at your hands. Then (to evidence that no further whatsoever can stand in your way) I knowe not where you could have made so crabbed a Choyce as you haue done, though for intrinsick value an incomparable one, and well quitting your paynes. on my word (Cosen) this Peice is *The taming of the shrew.* What shall I say more? Hauing (as skillfully as I could) confronted his Latine with your English, they appeare to mee *Lifes* both: or rather both Pictures of one *Life*, the features beeing exactly the same in each, only yours (as the younger, so) the smoother. It puts mee in mind of the two *Amphitruo's* in Plautus, where the Translation was taken for the Originall by her That should best haue knowne which mistake had probably not hapened, if the divine Counterfett could not haue spoke the Husband's Thought as well as indued his shape. And if that Metamorphosis made a long Night, this of yours I am sure makes the day short. But I injure it with the name of a Translation. It is *Lucretius* himselfe. A judged Case in a certaine Italian Comedie. Thus. A Bondman of Naples is apprehended in open street. no running away now: no denying the fact for which he is accused. what then? hee changed his language, facing both the officers and his Prosecutors downe in perfect Spanish (a concealed qualitie he had) that hee is not the man they take him for, nay not so much as of the Nation. in this manner feines for good space against them All. (the Scene is not unpleasaunt) but doe you thinke it seru'd his turne in the end? no, nor would haue done, though he had for his better disguize shifted himself into a gew-like habit, and garbe. And so shall wee knowe *Lucretius* in your Booke, though it retaine neither his Voyce, nor yet his Hayvinesse;

since it hath both his Soule, and his Lineaments. Nor haue you in my conceipt (however I find it difficult to explaine) so much put him into your Cloathes, as out of his owne person.—*sic prauis componere pulchra solebam.*

One thing I must needs acquaint you with: and it is, that this came to my hands just when I had made an end of reading a posthumous Translation, by Mr or Doctor Bathurst lately printed at London (I presume you have seen it) of *Spenser's Shepheards Calendar* into Latine; as if opportunely to prevent my idolizing that Language: to the advantage wherof above ours, I doe not now impute that admirable worke, which (unlesse my Augury deceive mee) I will, where it's true origine shall be unknowne, passe for a Native of ould Rome, and that as farr, as the utmost bounds extend of the Commonwealth of Learning. For if the great wonder there bee, how a Poem, which the Author made it his businesse to cloathe in rugged English, could be capable of so smooth Latine; certainly it is no lesse a one heere, how so rugged a Latine Poem (rugged in spite of your Author's teeth, through the stubbornesse of the stuffe and povertie of words as himselfe confesses) can be rendered in so smooth English. And, if Mr Bathurst by that exported commoditie doe more honour to England Abroad: You, by this imported, will more inrich it at home: making our Income proportionable to our Expense.

Thus (since you will make a Countrey Felow a Judge) I have parted the Apple between you, all though it is true the other Gentleman's Cause is not before *Mee*; yet, because his merits are. But That which I give you intirely to yourselfe, is

Sir

Your very affectionate Kinsman and humble servant

Richard Fanshawe

I returne here with your Booke, addrest to Mr Radcliffe for you. my wife and I say our Very humble services to your selfe, and my good Cosen your Lady. Likewise to my Lady Browne, if in those Parts: For heere wee are ignorant of every thing.

[6. To Lady Fanshawe] [V, Uncatalogued]

Toledo. Munday morning 18th of January [1666]
style of the place.

Dearest life,
Hitherto (God be thanked) all well, the ayre and motion agreeing exceedingly well with mee, as I believe it will with thee and the children as often as the weather shall prove favorable. God bless us all, and send us soon and happily to meet, wherof I am allready mett with something of a good omen, as lodged in the House now belonging to a rich Portugues, and in a Citty most interested of any in Spaine in, most greedy of, a peace with Portugal in respect of their Trade. For which reason they expresse among the wise great joy at my passing through in order to that End, for sufficiently publike it is every where. Once more and ever God blesse us all.

Dearest only Love

Thine owne ever

Ric. Fanshawe

I doe not know if I left any thing forgott there. Services to all Freinds.

[7. To Lady Fanshawe] [V, Uncatalogued]

Merida Sunday 28 of February 1666.

My dearest deare,
By the date of this (informing thy selfe) thou will find I draw neare thee as fast as I can having never in my whole life more longd to bee with thee, and that is a prowd one. Till then I am silent, but very well and comfortable as to our perticular, however the publike shall determine of their owne concerns, wherunto no indeavors of mine have or ever shall be wanting neither.

Thine by the 3rd post I read in my way at Estremos and was very wellcome.

Sir Ro[bert] Southwell comes with mee, I wish Don Patricio Hodser would meet at Casa Rubias to tell what is provided as to him. I reckon I shall be there (at Casa Rubias) on Saturday or Sunday next at night. God blesse us all. The Duke bestowes to mee high commendations on Dick. This night I lodge at Medellin.

Dearest life

Thine ever

Ric. Fanshawe

I have this last expresse from the Duke still with mee, and shall dispatch him too two or 3 days hence with advice of my neerer Approach and more certain time of my arrivall.

[8. To Lady Fanshawe] [V, Uncatalogued]

Para mi muger Doña Ana Fanshawe que dios garde muchos anos.
Oropesa Friday morning. 3 of March 1666.
At night in Talauera de la Reyna. 6 leagues.
Saturday night at St. Olalla. 6 leagues.
Sunday night at Casa Rubias. 6 leagues.
Munday night at Madrid. 7 leagues

My dearest life, this is only to tell thee what is allready above sayd, and that my selfe (I thank God) and all my companie are and have continued hitherto in perfect health. hoping to find thee and all at home with the like, so remaine

my only deare love

Thine ever

Ric. Fanshawe.

Oropesa Friday morning
ready to put foot in litter for Talavera.

COMMENTARY

Fanshawe's Earliest Translations

General Notes

The surviving evidence suggests that, apart from one student poem in Latin, Fanshawe's first English works were all translations. The earliest work would appear to be a translation of the verse portions of Boethius' *De Consolatione Philosophiae*; translations of Psalm 45 and of selected *Epigrams* of Martial appear to have followed soon after. It is also possible that Fanshawe's first versions from the *Odes* of Horace were being made concurrently. These Horatian versions evolved gradually over 20 years into the nucleus of *1652*, a collection which includes many *Odes* in versions which are substantially those which Fanshawe made as a young man. Only one mildly libertine *Ode* appears to have dropped out of the collection between the compilation of MS A and the compilation of MS F.

This choice of originals for his first works implies that Fanshawe had a clear attitude towards himself as a poet, and from the beginning certain characteristics of the mature Fanshawe are present: the modesty of the translator, the belief that poetry has a moral as well as an aesthetic dimension. Fanshawe's earliest poems work contentedly within the limits defined by the previous generation. The choice of Martial is dictated perhaps by convention; while that of Psalm 45 is not without significance: the use of an intermediate neo-Latin version (that of George Buchanan) suggests that Fanshawe was already aware of that neoteric tradition to which he was to make a considerable contribution. This first exercise in celebratory and political verse foreshadows the sensitive adaptation of past originals to present circumstances which is a distinctive feature of the collection of *1648*.

It is clear that Fanshawe greatly admired Spenser and the traces of Spenser's influence are frequent in his earlier poems. Ben Jonson is also a guiding figure in his early work: there is no record that Fanshawe associated with Jonson, but there are recurrent Jonsonian elements in his early poems. At this early stage in his career, there is no record of Fanshawe frequenting literary circles in London: his only contact with the world of professional letters seems to have been a friendship with Thomas May (cf. John Aubrey, *Brief Lives*, ed. A. Clark, Oxford, Clarendon Press, 1898, ii. 55).

His literary friends seem rather to have been amateurs like himself (cf. MS Eg. for evidence of such a friendship with John Heath, and also Fanshawe's letter to Heath (pp. 329–30)).

There are two further literary influences which require notice in this context: Fanshawe appears to have been drawn to some late Elizabethan lyric poetry, of the sort which is to be found in *The Phoenix Nest* of 1593 (ed. H. E. Rollins,

Cambridge, Mass., Harvard University Press, 1931). Fanshawe's 'What 'tis he loves in his Mistresse' (pp. 39–41) is particularly indebted to the *Phoenix Nest* poems. It also appears from internal evidence that he attended the playhouse during his first years in London and that he either remembered what he heard or else bought play-books, for his later works have a number of distinct dramatic echoes.

Ad... Almam... Cantab... (p. 2)

There are verbal parallels throughout with the first Elegy ('Ad Carolum Deodatum') of Milton's *Elegiarum Liber* (*The Poetical Works of John Milton*, ed. H. Darbishire, Oxford, Clarendon Press, 1955, ii. 236–8).

l. 10. *languet Amor.* Milton, l. 12, 'laris angit amor'.

l. 12. [*vir*]*gineosque Choros.* Milton, l. 52, 'Virgineos videas praeteriisse choros'.

l. 14. *Barbara Rura.* Milton, l. 32, 'Detonat inculto barba verba foro.' The rhythmic similarity of the lines is clear.

l. 16. *chara.* Milton, l. 1, 'chare' as form of address.

The first eight lines of the text are too lacunose to supplement with any certainty. Fanshawe seems to be making Cambridge a parting gift of a poem before he leaves the University to practise law at the Middle Temple, pleading for his gift to be accepted. Lines 9–12 can be reconstructed with a fair degree of certainty, thus:

Nec dum etiam L[ethes na]tantibus undis
  Vester in in[genio defessus] languet Amor
Saepe ego sub noc[tem sopor cum] deprendat Amantem
  Ad musas pr[opero vir]gineosque Choros.

and thereafter the poem is complete for a further ten lines.

Translation:

Fostering parent, now I am leaving your [ ] fields but even if I have left behind the [pleasant] waters of the Granta, or even after swimming in the waters of the [Lethe], my [tired] love for you lies dormant in my [soul.] Often [when sleep] takes hold of lovers at night, I myself hurry to the Muses and their virgin chorus. For this reason, none of the Muses is worthy of indulgence: that the wild countryside does not wear the flowering laurel [desire] take up the relics of the laws and the verses which are rustic and enfeebled, and conceal them in your dear bosom. It is necessary to set before profane eyes things which were previously unseen: may it be right to recount sacred things truly to the vulgar. And it was mine to wish to set in motion Latin verses, and to give what is mine to say by the law. Our own tongues do not know peaceful ease, and rage lays waste the neglected work.

Translations of Boethius

General Note

The poetical part of Boethius' *De Consolatione Philosophiae* is an unsurprising choice for Fanshawe's earliest translations. There was a strong English tradition of interest in Boethius, who had been translated into English by King Alfred in the ninth century and Chaucer in the fourteenth, and who was translated by Queen Elizabeth herself (*Queen Elizabeth's Englishings*, ed. Caroline Pemberton, London, Early English Text Soc., 1899), subsequently flowering in the highly successful version by 'I.T.' which was published at London in 1609 (Boethius, trans. 'I.T.', *Consolation of Philosophy*, ed. W. Anderson, Arundel, Centaur Press, 1963).

The interest of these translators seems to have focused on Boethius' exposition of the paradoxical goodness of God and of the irrelevance of worldly prosperity. In Europe, however, the poetic portions of *De Consolatione* were receiving particular attention for their own sake, for the diversity of possible Latin verse-forms which they include. In 1610 Tanius published an edition of the poetical portion divorced from its philosophical setting which was printed at Milan and enjoyed a wide distribution. Fanshawe seems to have been interested by the poetic part of *De Consolatione* both for its content and its form. The variety of verse-forms would have constituted a powerful attraction to a young man who wished to put himself through a serious poetic *cursus honorum*.

In finding English equivalents for the diverse verse-forms of his original, Fanshawe is, to an extent, following the example of 'I.T.' Without being part of the late sixteenth-century movement which attempted to write classically quantitative verse in English, Fanshawe makes a clear attempt to echo the shape of the stanza of his original in equivalent lines of rhymed English iambics: thus, in his version, the elegiac couplets of Boethius I, 1 are echoed in alternating iambic lines of ten and eight syllables and the adonics of I, 7 are matched in a tumbling iambic metre of two feet in the line; in the same way the long lines of V, 5 are imitated in a sluggish iambic with six feet to the line.

Fanshawe's translation as it stands appears to date from before 1630, and only one piece (I, 1) was revised, possibly in the early 1640s. There is, however, no firm evidence to suggest that the revision was prompted by a perception of the relevance of Boethius to an England which was sliding into conflict. What Fanshawe did do, albeit unwittingly, was to anticipate a revival of interest in Boethius, directly prompted by the disturbances which attended the Civil War. The most remarkable of these is to be found unpublished in Bodleian MS Eng. Poet. f. 16. Its translator, John Polwhele, a Cornish clergyman who completed his translation in 1649, produced a version which suggests that Boethius' work had become a real and personal consolation. It seems possible that Polwhele had seen at least parts of Fanshawe's translation.

Apart from the problematic revision of I, 1, Fanshawe's moral interest in Boethius' *sententiae* on the endurance and celebration of adversity can have been only a general one, in accordance with a prevailing theoretical stoicism, rather than an attempt to reflect on contemporary events.

The revision displays a certain progress into poetic individuality; it displays a conscious effort to remove the Spenserian vocabulary and phrasing which dominate the first version. This took its tone from the winter poetry of Spenser, but lacked any sense of personal involvement. It also has an elusive resemblance to ll. 16–17 of Ralegh's 'Conjectural First Draft of the Petition to Queene Anne' (*The Poems of Sir Walter Ralegh*, ed. Agnes Latham, London, Constable and Company, 1929, p. 96). The second version is altogether tougher and more nervous.

In the first version there are strong echoes of 'I.T.', whose cadence Fanshawe adopts, as the brief quotations following demonstrate. 'I.T.' 's rendering of ll. 3–6 (p. 27),

My work is fram'd by Muses torne and rude,
And my sad cheeks are with true teares bedew'd
For these alone no terrour could affray,
From being partners of my weary way

has clearly provided Fanshawe with a tone as well as some specific words for

The Muses with torne hayre indite to mee,
And true teares blott my Elegie,
These yette no feare nor terror could prevent
From followinge to banishment.

The images of the seasons which Fanshawe introduces into his first version of ll. 7–8, together with the use of 'whilome', recall the December Eclogue of *The Shepheardes Calender*, in which Colin Clout laments his fall from the happiness of his youth, echoing most specifically ll. 19–20: 'Whilome in youth, when flowr'd my joyfull spring, Like Swallow swift I wandred here and there' (Spenser, p. 464).

In his revision Fanshawe removed this echo, although another Spenserian echo is introduced in l. 11 of the re-working, 'My head bloosms early Snow', which recalls l. 103 of the December Eclogue, 'My boughes with bloosmes that crowned were at first' (Spenser, p. 464), although the recollection is more on the level of unconscious catching of sound than deliberate imitation. If Fanshawe had continued to revise along these lines his finished work might well have resembled Polwhele's sombre and nervous reading of his original; but even as they stand these Boethean versions give in some instances a clear promise of Fanshawe's future accomplishment as a translator.

The Metres *from Boethius'* De Consolatione Philosophiae

[I, 1] (p. 3) l. 11. Cf. Spenser, *The Shepheardes Calender*, i, ll. 33–4 (p. 422).

ll. 15–16. Cf. 'I.T.' 's version of the same lines (p. 27), and also the same lines in the unpublished version by John Polwhele, 'But oh! he's deafe to miserable cries, / The tyrant will not close up weepinge Eyes' (Bodleian Library, Oxford, MS Eng. Poet. f. 16, f. 15r).

[I, 3] (pp. 4–5) ll. 7–8. Cf. 'I.T.' 's version (p. 30) and also Polwhele's, 'But if bold Boreas blow those mists away / And breake the prison of the day' (MS cit., f. 16v).

[I, 5] (pp. 5–6) ll. 27–39. The translation of these lines makes no allusion to the condition of England, of the kind which would later be developed by Polwhele's version of 1649 (MS cit., f. 18r):

Due to the guiltye punishments
Inflicted on the innocents
The ostro-Gothes doe tread uppon
Most sacred necks to mount the throne.
Patricians in exile hide,
Att home true Patriots have died
For treason.

[I, 6] (p. 6–7) l. 6. Cf. Spenser, *Virgil's Gnat*, ll. 206–7 (p. 489).

[II, 3] (p. 9) ll. 1–4. Cf. Polwhele's version (MS cit., f. 21v):

When Phoebus in Aurora's coach
Drawes on the blushinge morne
The wearied stars at his approache
Appaled look forlorne.

l. 5. *teemeing*. Cf. Shakespeare, *Sonnets*, 97, ll. 6–7 (*Shakespeare's Sonnets*, ed. Stephen Booth, New Haven and London, Yale Univ. Press, 1977, p. 84).

[II, 4] (p. 10) ll. 21–2. Cf. 'I.T.' 's version (p. 50).

[II, 6] (pp. 11–12 nn) ll. 10–12. Cf. Spenser, *The Faerie Queene*, I. xi. 31, ll. 1–4 (p. 60).

[III, 2] (pp. 14–15) l. 37. *To period.* To end.

[III, 3] (p. 15) l. 3. *Erithrean.* Of the Persian Gulf. This is a paraphrase of Boethius' 'Oneretque bacis colla rubri litoris', probably derived from Martial, *Epigrams*, V. 37, ll. 3–4.

ll. 5–6. Cf. Polwhele's version, 'Yet biteing care shall vex thee till you dye / Then ebbing wealth slides from your company.'

[III, 7] (p. 16) ll. 1–2. Cf. 'I.T.' 's version of these lines (p. 70) and also the unpublished version by Nicholas Bacon, 'Al pleasure hath this property, / Those who enjoy it it doth stray' (Bodleian Library, Oxford, MS Tanner 306, f. 312v).

[III, 9] (pp. 17–18) ll. 5–6. Fanshawe omits nine lines of philosophical disquisition on the nature of the soul. Cf. the version of 'I.T.' (p. 74).

[III, 10] (p. 18) ll. 17–18. Cf. Polwhele's version, 'Compar'd to this Angelick lighte / Snow, swans and sun-beams are not white' (f. 31r).

[III, 12] (pp. 19–20) ll. 46–7. Cf. Fanshawe's 'A Friend's Wedding', ll. 23–6 (p. 97).

[IV, 1] (p. 21) ll. 11–12. *sentinel perdu.* One placed in an advanced and dangerous position. In Renaissance cosmology, Saturn is the farthest of the planets, on the edge of the stars.

[IV, 4] (p. 23) Fanshawe's version is written in innocence of the political applications which Polwhele was to find (MS cit., f. 36r):

That a sad glory 'tis to muster bands
  Daring combat Fate with our owne hands!
Death is a volunteer, if it you'll have,
  He keeps short stages posting to the grave.

Those lives Lyon, Tyger, Beare, Boare shake
The more invenom'd brutish sword will take.

[IV, 5] (p. 23) ll. 9–10. Fanshawe alters the original image which speaks only of packed drifts of melting snow, 'Neo nivis duram frigore molem', via a recollection of Shakespeare, *The Tempest*, IV. i, ll. 170–4.

[V, 5] (p. 26) l. 6. Cf. Spenser, *The Faerie Queene*, III. iv. 49, l. 9 (p. 164).

PSALM 45 (pp. 26–8)

This version is in a small minority amongst seventeenth-century versions of the Psalms, in that it is conceived in terms of words to be read or spoken rather than to be sung. Those numerous Psalm paraphrases which followed the influential work of Sternhold and Hopkins (Thomas Sternhold and John Hopkins, *All such Psalms of David, as T. S. did in his life tyme drawe into Englishe metre, together with seven by I. H.*, London, 1594) are united in their adaptability for singing and their use of lyric verse-forms. The versions by the Sidney family, by Henry King, and by Carew all conform to this style (Sir Philip Sidney, *The Poems*, ed. W. A. Ringler, Oxford, Clarendon Press, 1962; Henry King, *The Poems*, ed. Margaret Crum, Oxford, Clarendon Press, 1965; Thomas Carew, *The Poems*, ed. R. Dunlap, Oxford, Clarendon Press, 1949).

The nature of Fanshawe's verse militates against singing: it uses long phrases, complex sentences, frequent enjambements. Although considerations of date preclude any notion of direct influence, Fanshawe's style in his version is not unlike that of George Sandys, whose *Paraphrase upon the Psalmes of David* is also designed for the speaking rather than the singing voice (George Sandys, *A Paraphrase upon the Psalmes of David*, London, 1636). Another comparable Psalm paraphrase, which expands the original in verse intended for the speaking voice, is Crashaw's version of Psalm 23 (Richard Crashaw, *The Poems, English, Latin and Greek*, ed. L. C. Martin, 2nd edn., Oxford, Clarendon Press, 1957, pp. 102–4).

The process by which Fanshawe made his version is simply explained: it is a faithful translation of a Latin paraphrase by the Scottish poet George Buchanan (George Buchanan, *Psalmorum Davidis paraphrasis poetica, nunc primum edita*, Paris, 1566). Fanshawe was again to draw on Buchanan for the second poem to the Prince of Wales published with the 1647 edition of *Il Pastor Fido* (pp. 143–6).

Fanshawe's translation requires little commentary: he proceeds line by line; he takes mood, tone, and feeling directly from Buchanan. Very few lines need be quoted to indicate how closely the English runs in parallel with the Latin:

Cor micat, exultant trepidis praecordia fibris,
Eructantque; novum gravido de pectore carmen:
Certat lingua animum fando, manus aemula linguam
Scribendo exaequare, meo nova carmina regi
Dum cano . . .

(p. 7[2])

is rendered, with no significant departure in tone or vocabulary, in Fanshawe's:

My heart boyles o're with what I shall rehearse,
And my full bosome bubbles out new verse.
My tounge my minde, my hand would match my tounge
In expedition, whilst I sing a song
Touching the King.

In Fanshawe's translation, it is clear that he is using Ben Jonson as a model in inventing a ceremonial register. It is not possible to establish whether Fanshawe had personal contact with Jonson at the time when this translation was made, but there can be little doubt that Jonson's verse provided him with a model. The diction of this translation is very close to that of Jonson's court poetry, particularly of his masques; the only direct English echo in the poem is of a Jonsonian masque. Fanshawe's poem concludes,

but I'le bequeath thy fame
To late Posterity, where it shall runne
As farr, and as unweary'd, as the Sunne.

which imitates ll. 350–3 of Jonson's *Oberon*:

'Tis he, that stayes the time from turning old,
And keepes the age up in a head of gold,
That in his owne true circle, still doth runne;
And holds his course, as certayne as the sunne

(Ben Jonson, *The Works*, ed. C. H. Herford, Percy and Evelyn Simpson, Oxford, Clarendon Press, 1941–7, vii. 353).

Epigrams of Martial

General Note

The translations of the *Epigrams* of Martial which are found in MS A represent one of Fanshawe's least successful attempts at translation of a Latin text. Possibly the most significant aspect of these versions is that he felt compelled to make them at all. His early poetic choices would not naturally lead him to the translation of sophisticated, bitter, and frequently scatological originals. The epigram was, however, a form which enjoyed high prestige throughout the first half of the seventeenth century, a prestige which was reinforced by the success of Jonson's collection of 1616. Fanshawe's friend John Heath was, at this time, on the evidence of MS Eg., working on translations from Martial, apparently with Fanshawe's collaboration.

The chief influence on Fanshawe's versions of Martial was that of Thomas May, who published his *Selected Epigrams of Martial* in 1629. Aubrey refers to the friendship between Fanshawe and May in the *Brief Lives*, when he writes of May's circle,

Amicus: Sir Richard Fanshawe. Mr. (Emanuel) Decretz was present at the debate at their parting before Sir Richard went to the King.

(John Aubrey, *Brief Lives*, ed. Andrew Clark, Oxford, Clarendon Press, 1898, ii. 55.)

In the preface to his translations, too, May himself appears to be making allusion to gentleman translators such as Fanshawe:

The Second reason is, because it is more than probable that divers Gentlemen have exercised and pleased them selves in translating some of these, and may therefore peruse mine with a more rigid censure.

(Thomas May, *Selected Epigrams of Martial*, London, 1629, sig. A6v.)

The style of Fanshawe's translation is very close to May's: both are generally faithful to the literal sense of the original and neither translator makes any consistent attempt to modernize or localize his version in the London of the seventeenth century. (Jonson's *Epigrams*, in contrast, are focused on contemporary London and they frequently appropriate passages from Martial.) Only in his version of *Epigram* V, 62 does Fanshawe make any attempt to report English fashions in English slang. He makes occasional gestures towards a Jonsonian rewriting in contemporary terms, but no consistent scheme of modernization is carried through to the end of any single poem: *Epigram* X, 19 contains one unconvinced reference to London, but the overall content remains securely Roman.

The selection of *Epigrams* made by both Fanshawe and May focuses on Classical Rome: satirical epigrams are sparsely represented and are rendered with a patent lack of enthusiasm. May is drawn to the civic celebrations of the *Liber Spectaculorum*; Fanshawe is drawn to 'moral' epigrams, to epitaphs, and to poems on literary matters. It is possible that Fanshawe's interest in this aspect of Martial had been awakened by his schoolmaster, Thomas Farnaby, whose edition of Martial's *Epigrams* was published in 1615. There is nothing in Fanshawe's versions of Martial to suggest that he did not use this edition as his source text. May and Fanshawe, however similar their attitude to Martial, only have three *Epigrams* in common in their selections (VIII, 3, X, 2, and X, 26), but the degree of resemblence between their version of *Epigram* X, 26 establishes the influence beyond doubt. Fanshawe's text (p. 33) bears more than a slight resemblence to May's,

Varus, which as Rome's Tribune didst command
An hundred men, renowned in Aegypt's land,
Now as a stranger Ghost thou dost remaine
On Nilus' shore, promis'd to Rome in vaine...
Yet in my Verse eterniz'd shalt thou bee,
Of that false Aegypt cannot cousen thee.

(Thomas May, *Selected Epigrams of Martial*, London, 1629, sig. G2v.)

The positioning of 'Varus' is common to both versions; the rhyme of the first couplet is the same; the phrase 'stranger Ghost' is common to both; the shape of the concluding couplet is similar in both versions, and both use the phrase 'false Aegypt' in the same position in the concluding line.

This debt to May is interesting; as well as providing Fanshawe with a model for his versions from Martial, May must also have awakened in the younger poet's mind an awareness of the possibilities of Roman poetry as a means of making a reticent commentary on contemporary events. Fanshawe's first published poem was a tribute to May (Thomas May, *Supplementum Lucani*, Leiden, 1640, sig. *6r–*7v): this tribute was published again in *1648* and *1658*, after the Civil War had estranged the two poets.

Epigrams *of Martial*

[I, 62] (p. 28) l. 1. Cf. Fanshawe's version of Horace, *Epode* 2, ll. 38–40, (p. 209).

[VIII, 55] (pp. 30–1) Fanshawe worked on this translation with great care; the cancelled version is heavily reworked in A; the final version, on A, f. 47r, is in the poet's autograph.

[X, 20] (p. 32) ll. 20–2. Cf. Herrick, 'When he would have his verses read', ll. 9–10 (*Poems*, ed. L. C. Martin, London, OUP, 1965, p. 7).

[XII, 48] (pp. 34–5) l. 11. *Reader*: Lecturer in Law at the Inns of Court.

[*Epigram*] (p. 35) This is not by Martial. The Latin is probably Fanshawe's own pastiche of elements from Horace, *Satire* I, 5, ll. 34–5.

[Horace, *Ode* III, 20] (pp. 35–6) This *Ode* is found neither in F nor *1652*.

Fanshawe's Unpublished Poems, 1630–48

General Note

This grouping of poems is an editorial arrangement of those poems dating from the earlier part of Fanshawe's career which he chose to exclude from the first published collection of his works, *1648*. They were written concurrently with those poems which were selected for publication in *1648* and *1652*, and with the translation of Guarini's *Il Pastor Fido*, which is outside the scope of this edition.

It is difficult to give firm dates for the poems which Fanshawe wrote during these years, although reasonable conjectures may be made. The latter years of the period are the most easily comprehensible: after his return from Spain in 1636, Fanshawe appears to have composed and revised his two complimentary poems to the daughters of Lord Aston, and to have made a number of translations from the Spanish, some of which were published in *1648*. At the same time he was working on *Il Pastor Fido* and on those poems published with it. From the years before his departure to Spain in 1632, his years in the Inner Temple, there survives a small group of original poems. Perhaps the most interesting of these is the 'Oade', a personal poem in which Fanshawe considers the worth and possibilities of his own career.

An Oade. Splendidis longum valedico nugis

The subject of this poem is Fanshawe's own state of mind during his years in the Inner Temple: his feeling that his real talent was for literature and not for that *cursus honorum*, civic or legal, for which his training was preparing him. The first section is a renunciation, a farewell to poetry headed by a motto which seems to have been popular in the early seventeenth century for poems of renunciation and farewell. The second part negates the thesis of the first. Lady Fanshawe's *Memoirs* confirm that the dichotomy expressed in the poem was one which Fanshawe felt acutely at the time (p. 112):

He was admitted into the Inward Temple, but it seemed so crabbed a study and disagreeable to his inclinations that he rather studied to obey his mother than to make any progress in the law.

The whole 'Oade' hinges upon the ambiguity inherent in its Latin motto or subtitle 'Splendidis longum valedico nugis': this motto (its source still unidentified) was used by a number of writers, either directly or in translation, as part of a poem of renunciation. It comes at the end of Sir Philip Sidney's *Certain Sonnets*; it is the motto to Henry King's 'The Farewell'; it is appended to the Epistle at the beginning of Sir John Denham's 1668 *Poems and Translations* (Sir Philip Sidney, *The Poems*, ed. W. A. Ringler, Oxford, Clarendon Press, 1962, pp. 161–2; Henry King, *The Poems*, ed. Margaret Crum, Oxford, Clarendon Press, 1965, p. 60; Sir John Denham, *The Poetical Works*, ed. T. H. Banks, New Haven and London, Yale Univ. Press and Oxford Univ. Press, 1928, p. 68). The motto also appears on the flyleaf of Bodleian MS Rawl. Poet. 148 with John Lilliat's translation, 'Fowle vanities to you / for evermore adue.' And it is also translated by the opening of the popular (and variously attributed) lines which begin 'Farewell you gilded follies, pleasing troubles' (cf. Henry King, p. 251).

The Latin line is metrical (a Sapphic hendecasyllable) which suggests a poetic source; but no such source has yet been discovered, although the motto was clearly well known in the late sixteenth and early seventeenth centuries. There are some lines of George Buchanan which come near to it, but these may in themselves constitute a variation on a pre-existing source: 'Ite leves nuge, sterilesque valete Camenae, Grataque / Theorbo Castalis unda choro' ('Quam misera sit conditio docentium literas humaniores Lutetia', ll. 1–2; George Buchanan, *Poemata*, Edinburgh, 1615, sig. B12v).

The only further clue as to the origin of the line is given in Bodleian MS Tanner 465, where a copy of 'Farewell you gilded follies, pleasing troubles' is titled 'An Hermite in an Arbour with a prayer booke in his hand, his foote spurning a globe, thus speaketh', which points towards an emblem source; but if this is the case, it remains untraced.

Amongst the group of poems which use the motto, Fanshawe's 'Oade' has least in common with 'Farewell you gilded follies . . .' which is a simple farewell to the world; but it does have affinities with King's and Sidney's poems.

Sidney's concluding sonnet, 'Leave me o Love, which reachest but to dust', is, in its argument at least, a more straightforward poem of renunciation than

Fanshawe's renunciation of poetry in the 'Oade'. Sidney's farewell is to earthly love, to transient and human attachments. The simplicity of his imagery of light, pleasure, and riches is not simple-minded: it is a hard-won simplicity at the close of a sequence which has faced the complexities and distractions of earthly life.

Henry King, in 'The Farewell', is also writing a poem of withdrawal from the world, a farewell which verse by verse takes its leave of the world's attractions before leaving the world itself. It is a poem of withdrawal into an hermitage as distinct from Sidney's sharp perception of an alternative reality. Unlike Sidney's poem of hope and resolution, this is one of ambiguous remorse for the past expressed in an image of farewell. King's aim in quitting the world is not illumination or reconciliation with God: he is seeking a Stoic quiet, an Horatian freedom from disturbance.

Fanshawe's poem, like King's and unlike Sidney's, ostensibly seeks a temporal security through renunciation: he is less grave than either King or Sidney, and his renunciation of poetry functions as part of a rhetorical stratagem, as the second part of the 'Oade' is an exposition of the reasons which make such a farewell unnecessary.

In the first part of the 'Oade', Fanshawe is close to King in personifying poetry as a mistress who is urged to leave the poet for another, as King urged Love to go and seek another 'Patient'. There is also an echo of Jonson's epigram 'To My Muse' in which poetry is personified as a mistress who is urged to seek a wealthier protector (Ben Jonson, viii. 48).

In ll. 5–8 of the answering second part, Fanshawe gives an impulsive representation of the strength of his feeling, conveyed in emotive language ('rapt', 'dreames') and with an echo of a poem of John Fletcher's which seems to have had considerable personal significance for him: the 'melancholic' song in *The Nice Valour*. This song, from Act III sc. iii of the play, is prefixed by a speech of renunciation by the Passionate Cousen, very much in the 'Splendidis longum' tradition. The echo is unmistakable, from Fletcher's,

> Fountain heads and pathless Groves,
> Places which pale passion loves . . .
> Then stretch our bones in a still gloomy valley,
> Nothing's so dainty sweet, as lovely melancholly.

(John Fletcher and Francis Beaumont, *Comedies and Tragedies*, London, 1647, p. 157) to Fanshawe's 'Through Hills, through Dales, by tumbling streames, / (Places which sadd fancy loves) / And silent Groves?'

An Oade. Splendidis longum valedico nugis (pp. 36–8)

l. 43. The reading 'lother' is clear in A. The sense might be related to a version of the marriage service, quoted in *OED*, 'for fairer, for loather'.

l. 44. *kept*. In the intransitive sense of living in a set of rooms.

Upon the report of fowre Kings dead at once (p. 39)

The year must be 1632, including, by reckoning the new year from 25 March, the January to March of 1633, in which time died the Elector Frederick of Bohemia (November), Gustavus Adolphus, King of Sweden (November), Sigismund III of Poland, and Landgrave Maurice of Hesse (January–February 1633). Frederick V, King of Bohemia, Elector Palatine, husband of Charles I's sister Elizabeth, had been attempting since 1620 to recover his lost kingdom. In 1630 Gustavus Adolphus entered Germany against the Holy Roman Emperor Ferdinand II. On 16 November 1632 the Imperial forces under General Wallenstein were defeated at Lützen, in which battle Gustavus Adolphus was killed.

There are poems on the subject by King, Carew, and Randolph. Randolph's poem is copied on ff. 35v–36r of A.

l. 1. Cf. Crashaw's 'Upon the Gunpowder Treason', ll. 1–2 (Richard Crashaw, p. 387).

l. 4. *Mournevell.* A hand of cards containing four Aces, Kings, or Queens.

What it is he loves in his Mistresse (pp. 39–41)

This poem is hard to date: it is not included in A and may predate the making of that collection. A Platonist tradition of focus on the beauty of the soul would have been familiar to Fanshawe as it is represented in the work of Spenser, particularly in *An Hymne in Honour of Beautie*, which contains the significant lines 'For of the soule the bodie forme doth take: / For soule is forme, and doth the bodie make' (Spenser, p. 591, ll. 132–3) and in the poem by Thomas Lodge, 'Faine to content, I bend myself to Write' which contains the line 'My inward mind, your outward faire admires' (*The Phoenix Nest,* 1593, p. 58). Fanshawe takes the opportunity to extend the conceit outwards: his poem opens with the expected comparisons for the beauty of the beloved (flowers, gems, sweet winds, natural beauty); but he also focuses all experience on the beloved's virtue, which becomes an emblem of all natural harmony and good,

Make you a world of Harmony,
Tis not for these I serve, or sue,
Nor is it them I doate upon, but you.

The ideas of the poem are unoriginal: what is perhaps more interesting is the way in which Fanshawe subdues another, more profane convention of amatory poetry to the cool Platonism which dominates the poem.

There is a tradition of poems which list the graces of the beloved's body, but which do not necessarily include that cool chastity which dominates Fanshawe's poem. Two representatives of that tradition which appear to bear some relation to Fanshawe's work are Lord Herbert of Cherbury's 'A Description' and Herrick's 'The Descripcion: Of a Woman', both of which remained in manuscript until long after Fanshawe had composed the poem in question, so any speculation about influence must remain in doubt. In Herbert of Cherbury's poem, however, there occur certain lines which appear to be echoed in ll. 17–18 and ll. 37–8 of Fanshawe's:

> Her Hair, Sun-beams, whose every part
> Lightens, enflames, each Lover's heart...
> Her Front, the White and Azure Sky,
> In Light and Glory raised hy...

(Edward, Lord Herbert of Cherbury, *The Poems English and Latin*, ed. G. C. Moore-Smith, Oxford, Clarendon Press, 1923, pp. 2–5). The echoes in Herrick are even stronger,

> Each cheeke resembling still a damaske rose...
> Over the which a meet sweet skin is drawne
> Which makes them shewe like roses under lawne...
> Thus every part in contrariety
> Meets in the whole and makes a harmony...

(Robert Herrick, *Poems*, ed. L. C. Martin, London, Oxford Univ. Press, 1968, pp. 359–61) bearing resemblance to ll. 31–2 and ll. 21–2 of Fanshawe.

An Oade on the sight of a Gentlewoman at Church (pp. 41–2)

This 'Oade' is very much concerned with distant and spiritual love: so that the lines (34–6) which describe red lips and the wounds of Cupid seem curiously at variance with the rest of the poem. There are a number of seventeenth-century poems which make use of images of perfume, spice islands, and scented wind over sea. Notable amongst these are Edmund Waller's 'The Night-Piece, or a Picture drawn in the Dark' (*Poems written upon Several Occasions*, London, 1668, pp. 233–4) and Herrick's 'The Dirge of Jephthah's Daughter' (Herrick, pp. 359–61); but the use which Fanshawe makes of the image to express a distanced attraction remains individual.

The image of pilgrimage which concludes the poem (one which seems to derive from Spenser's *Daphnaida*, ll. 372–4, p. 532) establishes both the reverence and distance which characterize the whole poem.

Of two most beautifull Sisters... (p. 43)

The two poems to Lord Aston's daughters were written in the autumn of 1636. The second poem, 'Of two most beautifull Sisters...', was thoroughly revised by Fanshawe between its composition, the copy in Constantia Aston's own commonplace collection (MS C), and the copy in H. The reason for the revision is clear: the first, spontaneous version contained obvious borrowings from Spenser, which Fanshawe reduced in his revision. In the first version, Fanshawe is indebted to Spenser not only for the swans of the *Prothalamion* which survive into the final version, but also for all the details of the opening lines. The revised version still bears a strong resemblance to Spenser in:

> Two stately swans sayle downe the Trent I saw
> (Like spotlesse Ermynes charg'd on silver feild)

To which the Doves which Venus chariot drawe,
And Venus selfe, must Beautyes Scepter yeild.
Jove was not halfe so white when he was one,
And courted Laeda . . .

lines which come almost directly from ll. 37–44 and 60–2 of the *Prothalamion* (p. 601):

With that I saw two Swannes of goodly hewe,
Come softly swimming downe along the Lee . . .
Nor *Jove* himselfe when he a Swan would be
For love of *Leda*, whiter did appeare . . .
. . . or to be that same payre
Which through the skie draw Venus' silver Teame . . .

Fanshawe's first version of the opening lines is uncomfortably close to Spenser:

I saw two swans come proudly downe the streame
of Trent, as I his silver curles beheld.
To which the doves that drawe fayre Venus' Teame,
And Venus selfe must beautie's scepter yeild.

The revision does not remove Spenser altogether, but it makes a gesture of independence in the introduction of the image, heraldic and cold, of the ermine, to provide a stronger contrast with the erotic, 'Gongorist', ll. 9–12 (cf. Petrarch, *Trionfo della Morte*, ll. 19–21, *I Trionfi di Messer Francesco Petrarca*, ed. C. Giannini, Ferrara, Bresciani, 1874, p. 38).

This poem, indeed, stands at a point of transition in the development of Fanshawe's style: the early influence of Spenser is still very strong, but the second half of the poem, with its play on 'impossibilities' of fire and water, as well as with its newly sensual movement, shows that the influence of Gongora and his followers is beginning.

For the circumstances of the composition of these two poems to the daughters of Lord Aston, reference may be made to a letter from Constantia Aston to her brother Herbert Aston, which enclosed the now lost copies of the poems which are printed in *Tixall* (p. 215):

[Colton, 1636 (Autumn)]

DEAR BROTHER

That you may see how Mr Fanshawe has spent his time here, I have sent you these verses, which are of his making, sense his coming hither, and has presented them to my sister and mee. The first was made upon this occasion: Wee wer all walking in the owld halle, and looking upon Trent, and I was speaking how you used to course your boy Dick about that meadow, and talking of many such things. But the next morning he came out with these verses which I doe not think but you will like very well, for methinks they are very prity ones, if they had bin made of better subjectes. Wee made him beleeve that you should fight with him when he came into Spaine againe, for abusing your sisters so, in flattering of them so infinightly as he has don in these verses. But how to come to speak of these other verses of his, which are made in particular to my sister Gatt. The occasion of making of them was this: We had bin one evening at bowles, and when we caime in, my sister was opening her hayre with her fingers, and bid him tell you that she would not curle her hayer no otherwaies than it curled itselfe till she saw you againe. Uppon which theame he made these other verses, which are much admired by all here, and by the Thimelbyes. I have sent you a little picture which you did love much when you were here, and then I could not get one for you, but sence having got one for you, I was most willing to send it to you. Once more, my dear brother, adieu.

Gertrude and Constantia were the daughters of Walter Aston, 1st Lord Aston of Forfar (1584–1639) who was Ambassador to Madrid (1635–8) when Fanshawe was in his Embassy. His aunt by marriage was Susannah Fanshawe, daughter of Henry Fanshawe (*c.*1506–68), Fanshawe's great-great uncle. This letter is addressed to Lord Aston's second son, who was also in the Madrid Embassy. Herbert Aston's commonplace book is in the Beinecke Library at Yale (Osborn B4 1634).

The manuscripts from the Aston's houses at Tixall and Colton are dispersed. All that remains with reference to Fanshawe are the fragments of eight letters from Constantia Aston to Herbert Aston which the editor of *Tixall* chose to preserve (pp. 383–4),

Wee hear Mr Fanshawe is in London, and porposes to com downe, which I rejoyce at mightyly (Colton, the 11th of August 1636).

Mr Fanshawe has made us beleeve a great while he would come downe, but it seemes his bisnes is such it will not permit him, for he has just this day sent us letters of yours from him, which he has kept all this time, thinking to bring them himselfe. I will send your letters safe to Mrs Thimelby.

You writ me word in your letter by Mr Fanshawe, that heretofore you sent me verses which began (Whilest here Eclipesed) this letter did I never receave, nor verses which I am most truly afflicted att, and if you doe truely love me doe not denye me, but send them me againe; for you know not how much I suffer that they are lost; therefore, prethee, dere brother, send them me agane and I hope they will have better lucke. Ah when shall I see you.

Mr Fanshawe sent us word he went within two dayes, and soe I was fayne to send won up secretly to his post with a box which I hope he will safely bring you; for I was soe desirus you might have it by him, because I know not when I should get it so safely convey'd to you.

To a freind fearing his relapse into an old Love (pp. 44–5)

A free translation of 'Estas libre Damon? Pues no blasones' by Bartolome L. de Argensola. B. L. and L. de Argensola, *Rimas*, ed. Blueca (Zaragoza, 1951), ii. 238.

ll. 5–8 The fine image of the falcon is Fanshawe's invention. The original has the conventional images, 'No se juzga por libre de prisiones, / El can por mas que rompa la cadena.'

The Sonnets Translated from the Spanish (pp. 45–9)

The element which entered Fanshawe's work after his first residence in Spain in the 1630s comes unexpectedly: he suddenly reveals a capacity for rendering the most developed productions of the Spanish Baroque in an English style no less luxuriant than the originals. This English Baroque of Fanshawe's is not like the Mannerist wit of Crashaw, but relates rather to some of Lord Herbert of Cherbury's imitations from the Spanish: 'Entre tantoque L'Avril', 'Sonnet to Black Itself', 'La Gralletta Gallante' (Herbert of Cherbury, pp. 8–9, 39, 69–70).

Fanshawe kept this 'Hispanic' style running concurrently with a plainer English style throughout his poetic career: poems in both voices appear in *1648* with *Il Pastor Fido*, but *1652* is altogether in the English manner deriving from Jonson and May. *Querer por solo Querer* (translated in 1654) is wholly in the Spanish manner of its original, although some English rustic speech intrudes amongst the pastoral characters, to bizarre effect.

The versions from Gongora are, in general, faithful translations of the Spanish; but a curious phenomenon may be observed in Fanshawe's translations from the lesser poets, the Argensolas. In these diffuse and thin originals there is a lack of argument and imagery, a conventional conceit often being thinly stretched over the fourteen lines of the sonnet. When he comes to the translation of these pieces, Fanshawe does not hesitate to invent his own images and expansions in the manner of the Gongorist Baroque. These interpolations are extraordinarily convincing: Fanshawe has so thoroughly absorbed the manner and idiom of Spanish literature that the inventions only betray themselves when comparison is made with the original.

Sonnets translated out of Spanish

I (p. 45) Numbered 1 in MS F. From Gongora, 'No enfrene tu gallardo pensamiento', *Obras Poeticas* (New York, Hispanic Society of America, 1921), i. 57.

II (pp. 45–6) Numbered 2 in MS F. From Gongora, 'La dulce boca que a gustar convida' (i. 56.)

III (p. 46) Numbered 4 in MS F. From Gongora, '*En la muerte de Giomar de sa Muger de Juan Fernandez de Espinossa*', 'Pallida restiuye a su elemento' (i. 532.) Both this poem and ll. 5–8 of Fanshawe's 'The Spring' (ii. 121) bear certain resemblances to an unpublished poem in the commonplace book of Herbert Aston, Fanshawe's friend and colleague in Madrid, which derives from the same Spanish sources as Fanshawe's poems, and may owe something to Fanshawe's advice or collaboration. The poem is not recorded in Margaret Crum's *First Line Index of English Poetry 1500–1800 in Manuscripts of the Bodleian Library Oxford* (Oxford, Clarendon Press, 1969):

Upon the funerall of Mrs. Pawley's daughter.

Say not because no more you see
I'th' fayre armes of her mother tree
This infant bloome; the winde or time
Hath nipt the flowre before the prime
  Or what ev'r Authume promis'd to make good
  In early fruite is wither'd in the budd.

But as when roses breath away
Their sweet consenting soules, none say
The still deflowres those virgin leaves
But them extracts, exalts, receaves
  Ev'n so hath Heaven's Almightyes Chymick here
  Drawne this pure Spirrit to its propper spheare.

Sadd Parents then recall your greefes
Your little one now truely lives;
Your pretty messenger of Love,
Your new intelligence above,
  Since God created such immortall flowres
  To grow in his owne Paradice not ours.

(Beinecke Library, Yale Univ., MS Osborn B4 1634, ff. 50v–51r.)

IV (pp. 46–7) Numbered 11 in MS F. From Lupercio de Argensola, 'Amor, tu que las almas ves desnudas' (i. 67.)

l. 14. Fanshawe is playing on the idea of crystals of red cinnabar, which were used in the seventeenth century to make rouge.

V (p. 47) Numbered 13 in MS F. Source unidentified.

VI (pp. 47–8) Numbered 14 in MS F. From Bartholome L. de Argensola, 'Ya el oro natural crespes o estiendas' (ii. 46).

l. 1 *trence*. Possibly from the Spanish *trenzar*, to braid or plait.

VII (p. 48) Numbered 16 in MS F. From Bartholome L. de Argensola, 'Con tyranicas leyes nos aprieta' (ii. 61).

l. 6. *minyon-flower*. Could be generally any tender flower or specifically the blossom of the minion-peach (cf. John Evelyn, *Kalendarium Hortense*, ed. Rosemary Verey, London, Stourton Press, 1983, p. 58).

VIII (pp. 48–9) Numbered 17 in MS F. From Gongora, 'Aunque a rocas de fe ligada vea' (i. 70).

l. 6. *graines*. 'Grane'; a snare.

IX *The Praise of the Winde* (p. 49) Numbered 18 in MS F. Source unidentified.

Effigei Inscriptum (pp. 49–50)

Translation:

An epigram inscribed upon a likeness of James, Duke of York, a distinguished youth, son of His Serene Majesty King Charles the First of Great Britain, the second son of a second son, aged about thirteen, virginal in his countenance as in his life, an exile by fate, he is represented as one in peril on a stormy sea, the captain thrown overboard, the ship broken up, thrust upon a rock, but clinging to an anchor, the trident of the ruler of the sea. To this office he was even then marked out first by his father of illustrious memory, and afterwards by his very august brother.

Prophetic Epigram
AD 1648

Younger than his only brother, James stands out in the British World as a secondary glory and hope of the widowed throne. Younger than his only brother, he is depicted in this tablet as destined to reign with despotic sway over his brother's seas. Lo! a Venus in armour, a child of the sea, like the Cyprian, still a boy, hardly yet worthy of this curving marble. Yet sink down ye waves, lest he should clothe himself in fury like yours, he in whom rough valour lies hidden under a gentle appearance.

Fanshawe's 'Effigei Inscriptum' was composed (presumably in Paris in 1648) for a sculpture, portrait, or engraving of James, Duke of York. An engraving seems more likely, in view of the propagandist text, although no copy appears to have survived.

It seems likely, however, that the inscription, together with the image which it describes, identify the kind of visual image which seems to have given Andrew Marvell the central idea for his enigmatic poem 'The Unfortunate Lover'. Marvell was travelling in France at the time when Fanshawe's inscription was composed and it is not impossible that he saw a copy of it. 'The Unfortunate Lover' is an elusive poem, even by Marvell's own standards of obliquity, but there are elements in it which bear a striking resemblance to Fanshawe's inscription. The bulk of the poem presents an emblem of the 'unfortunate lover' of the title, portrayed almost exactly as the Duke of York is portrayed in Fanshawe's inscription:

See how he nak'd and fierce does stand,
Cuffing the Thunder with one hand;
While with the other he does lock,
And grapple, with the stubborn Rock:
From which he with each Wave rebounds.

(Andrew Marvell, *The Poems and Letters*, ed. H. M. Margoliouth, 3rd edn. rev. by P. Legouis and E. E. Duncan-Jones, Oxford, Clarendon Press, 1971, i. 29–31).

This is not to suggest that Marvell's poem is exclusively 'about' royal children, although there are indications in it that an image of overthrown and exiled royalty is one element in the complex emblematic figure of the 'Unfortunate Lover': in l. 16 there is the barely concealed pun on '*Cesarian Section*', and ll. 25–6, with their 'masque of quarrelling Elements', constitute a parody of the kind of festivity which might be expected to attend the birth of a royal child. The use of 'Malignant Starrs' in l. 59 invokes the contemporary, political use of 'Malignant'. A full account of the specifically political use of this imagery of the rock in the stormy sea may be found in Martin Warnke, *Political Landscape: The Art History of Nature* (London, Reaktion Books, 1994), pp. 123–4.

Poems Published with *Il Pastor Fido*, 1648

General Note

In Fanshawe's collection of poems published with *Il Pastor Fido* in *1648* there is a double vision which unites a troubled England with an imaginary Arcadia: Fanshawe turns to the appropriation of Classical and Continental texts to reflect on the disasters which surround him, and to express his oblique hopes for their resolution. The Prince of Wales is the political focus of the collection: it is to him that Fanshawe looks, in actuality and in metaphor, for the renovation of a ruined England.

After his return from Spain in 1638 and after a period with Strafford in Ireland, Fanshawe followed the Court to Oxford, being appointed Secretary for War to the Prince of Wales in 1644 and following his Royal Master thereafter through the West Country and the Channel Islands to France (cf. Chronology, pp. xii–xiii).

Throughout the *Pastor Fido* poems the Prince is addressed on a level which is at once personal and public. However personal the origin of some pieces in *1648* may be, Fanshawe could not but be aware that the dedication made his book a public document and a statement of political affinity with the Prince.

The collection succeeds in both its private and its public voices: the future King is placed in parallel with the virtuous Aeneas and with the fortunate shepherd-kings of Guarini's pastoral. As a whole, the collection allows Fanshawe to offer the Prince versions of poems which will educate him in governance and morality.

The thematic unity of the book is simple and compelling: the Prince is urged to prepare himself for the just government of his people at the same time as he is presented in the role of potential healer of his people's disorders. The introduction to the 1647 volume is explicit in this regard, as is the very presentation of Guarini's play accompanied by two poems which specifically present Charles in his role of the restorer of unity and peace.

The Epistle to the *Il Pastor Fido* (1647) makes this application of Guarini's play to contemporary circumstances clear:

Just so our Authour (exposing to *ordinary view* an Enterlude of Shepherds, their loves, and other little concernments, with the stroke of a lighter pencill) presents through the *perspective* of the *Chorus*, another and more suitable object to his *Royall Spectators*. He shews to *them* the image of a *gasping State* (once the most flourishing in the world): *A wild Boar* (the *sword*) depopulating the *Country*: *the Pestilence* unpeopling the *Towns*: their gods themselves in mercilesse *humane Sacrifices* exacting bloody contributions from *both*: and the *Priests* (a third Estate of misery) bearing the burthen of *all* in the *Chorus*, where they deplore their *owne* and the *common* Calamitie. Yet in the *Catastrophe, the Boar slain; the Pestilence* (but this was before upon that miserable composition with their Gods) *ceased*; the *Priests* above all others *exulting* with pious joy: and all this miraculous change occasioned by the presaged Nuptials of two of Divine (that is Royall) extraction; meaning those at that time of the *Duke of Savoy* with the *Infanta of Spain*, from which fortunate Conjunction hee Prophecies a finall period to the troubles that had formerly distracted that State: *So much depends upon the Marriages of Princes*... Yet because it seems to me (beholding it *at the best light*) a *Lantskip* of these Kingdoms, (your *Royall Patrimony*) as well in the former flourishing, as in the present distractions thereof, I thought it not improper for your Princely notice at this time, thereby to occasion your Highness, even in your recreations, to reflect upon the sad *Originall*, not without hope to see it yet speedily made a perfect *parallell* throughout; and also your self a great Instrument of it. Whether by some happy Royall Marriage (as in this *Pastorall*, and the case of *Savoy*, to which it alludes) therby uniting a miserably divided people in a publick joy: or by such other wayes and meanes as it may have pleased *the Divine Providence* to ordain for an *end of our woe*; I leave to that Providence to determine. (Sir Richard Fanshawe, *Il Pastor Fido* (London, 1647), sig. A4r and v.)

Fanshawe's preface to the full collection, *1648*, places even more emphasis on the importance of the Prince, who is addressed as 'The HOPE AND LUSTRE: Of Three Kingdomes', and the purpose of the 'Additionall Poems' is made explicit:

and, to take up and minister such *Discourses* in your *Presence*, as (for the *Subject-matter* therof, though in no other respect) may bee in some sort fit for a *Prince* of Your high *Birth* and *Hopes* to entertaine vacant Houres with; at least, that may not with any *Scurrility* offend at once both Your *Dignity* and your *Vertue*.

Fanshawe's translation of Guarini hints at a miraculous settlement which avoids the question of the living and reigning King altogether. In the same way, the parallel which he makes between the Prince of Wales and the exiled Aeneas altogether avoids the living and present problem of the King. At the conclusion of the prose 'Discourse' which ends the volume of *1648*, Prince Charles is explicitly placed in parallel with the Emperor Augustus, the monarch who rules justly when the Civil Wars (and the murder of Caesar) are over. Fanshawe is loyally vague about his aspirations: he seems to be looking forward to some time of future prosperity when the rule of the future Charles II will restore a divided England.

When the poems in the collection are considered in this light, as works intended to 'take up and minister... *Discourses*' to the Young Prince, a striking thematic unity becomes apparent. The two poems addressed to the Prince which conclude the 1647 volume offer direct exhortation to Roman virtue and express hopes for a pacification of the country.

The 'Ode Upon occasion of his Majesties Proclamation...' offers a vindication of Royal wisdom and a recollection of an Arcadian England. 'The Escuriall' is a celebration of a King who rebuilt that which war had destroyed in a form more glorious than the original. The poem 'On His Majesties Great Shippe' reminds the Prince that the achievements of his ancestors, and of the earliest English kings, were founded on the unity of the people under a wise monarch, not too proud to take an active hand in their concerns. 'Dominae Navigaturae' is a love song charged with political aspirations: Fanshawe implicitly makes it to the absent Henrietta Maria, gone over the sea to raise support for the King. 'A Canto of the Progresse of Learning' is a poem which clearly stems from Fanshawe's personal concerns at an earlier period, yet in the position which it now occupies it is possible to see it as a vindication of an idealistic loyalty against the 'craft' of the legalistic mind, and as an encouragement to those who would put truth above expediency.

The translated sonnets offer general reflections on hope and fugacity, but also the specific adaptation to present circumstances of Gongora's sonnet on the fall of the Spanish court favourite, Don Rodrigo Calderon, becomes, in the context of *1648*, a stern warning not to repeat the weakness which sacrificed Fanshawe's old commander, the Earl of Strafford, to the Parliament. The translation of the Fourth Book of the *Aeneid* provides a point of focus for the collection: while this was the section of Virgil's poem which obviously held the greatest appeal for seventeenth-century readers, as the numerous versions of it testify, it has also a great weight of specific reference to the circumstances of Fanshawe and his Prince. It offers both consolation and a warning: consolation, in that it sets forth the idea that no kingdom can be destroyed beyond the hope of continuance, if the Prince is only prepared to avoid all compromise and distraction, holding the good of his people as his only aim. The poem on the Earl of Strafford succeeds less well in making the point by direct methods which has already been set forth powerfully by the translation of Gongora. The first of the two *Odes* from Horace has strong thematic connections with the earlier poems: the Prince is urged to strength and virtue, to the strength which can only come of virtue. The second offers a remote and beautiful vision of a land removed from civil war, a kingdom refounded and restored. In the 'Discourse' which concludes the volume there is no great attempt to parallel every event in the Roman civil war with recent events in England; but the parallel of Prince Charles with the young Augustus, ruling his pacified country with wisdom and strength, could hardly be clearer.

An Ode Upon occasion of his Majesties Proclamation (pp. 55–9)

General note. The idea which dominates the first part of the poem—that of Britain as an enchanted and enclosed paradise—derives from a line in the first Eclogue of Virgil, 'et penitus toto divisos orbe Britannos' (Virgil, *Eclogues*, ed. A. G. Lee, Liverpool, Francis Cairns, 1980, p. 10), a line which had been extended into something of a commonplace of compliment to the peaceful foreign policy of James I and Charles I (cf. Ben Jonson, *Love Freed from Ignorance and Folly, Works*, vii. 368; Aurelian Townshend, *Albion's Triumph*, ll. 410–16, London, 1631, p. 20; Thomas Carew, 'In answer of an Elegiacall Letter upon the death of the King of *Sweden*', *Poems*, ed. R. Dunlap, Oxford, Clarendon Press, 1949, pp. 75–7). The use which Fanshawe makes of it, however, owes less to the example of his literary predecessors than to the intensity of his own feelings about the halcyon England of the 1630s. The catalogue of European disasters with which the poem opens is oddly unreal: the wars and rebellions are distant in space and are further distanced by Fanshawe's diction. But his contrasting evocation of the felicity of the England of the 1630s finds a powerful echo in Clarendon's *The History of the Rebellion*, i. 162 (Clarendon, *The History of the Rebellion*, ed. W. D. Macray, Oxford, Clarendon Press, 1888, pp. 94–5) and indeed in a whole nexus of Royalist evocations of a spoiled garden, a lost golden age.

The praise of the country life in the second half of the poem is part of a flourishing tradition in the poetry of the earlier seventeenth century, one which ultimately derives from the second *Epode* of Horace. There are elements in common with James I's own poem on his Proclamation of 1622, which is, however, generally more satirical in tone than Fanshawe's 'Ode' (*The Poems of James VI of Scotland*, ed. Craigie, Edinburgh, Scottish Text Society, 1958, ii. 179). Comparison might also be made with Thomas Randolph's 'An Ode to Mr.

Anthony Stafford to hasten him into the Country' (Thomas Randolph, *Poems*, ed. G. Thorn-Drury, London, Etchells and Macdonald, 1929, pp. 79–82).

Title. Fanshawe refers to a proclamation issued by Charles I on 9 September 1630, which repeated a proclamation issued by James I on 29 May 1603. Charles repeated the proclamation on 20 June 1632.

ll. 1–20. The Thirty Years War was at its height: war against the Spaniards had restarted in 1621 in the Netherlands with the end of the treaty of The Hague. On 11 November 1630 Marie de Medici had failed to overthrow Richelieu. Gustavus Adolphus began his campaign in Germany on 4 July 1630. The opposing Imperial General, Tilly, had taken Bohemia after the defeat of the Elector Fredrick at the Battle of White Hill, in November 1620 [B.] ([B.] marks a note substantially in agreement with *Bawcutt*.)

ll. 39–40. Cf. Psalm 91: 4.

l. 77. Cf. Virgil, *Eclogue* I, in which Tityrus is the contented shepherd. A compliment to the King is contained in the reference: Meliboeus, the other shepherd in Virgil's poem, bewails the bad effects which Augustus' wars have had on husbandry, whereas English countrymen may sow their seed secure in the knowledge that they will enjoy the crop.

l. 85. Cf. Horace, *Odes* III, 29, ll. 11–12.

ll. 86–90. Cf. Horace, *Epode* 2, ll. 1–4 and 43–4.

ll. 94–6. Cf. *Epitaph on Thomas Whitbread*, in Great Baddow Church, Essex: 'The fat'ning Dew which on the Branches fell, / Chear'd and supply'd the wants of all below.'

ll. 127–8. Cf. Horace, *Epode* 2, ll. 7–8.

The Escuriall (pp. 60–9)

It is as a poem describing a rebuilding after the disasters of war that *The Escuriall* finds a place in the collection of *1648*: a reminder to the Prince that a time will come when it will be his duty to rebuild those things which the war has destroyed. The style of the poem owes a certain debt to Spanish models, especially in the very Gongorist descriptions of the paintings in the palace and in the long implied parallel between the aspects of kingship and the diverse functions of the Escorial.

l. 12. The siege of St Quentin in Belgium was on 10 August 1537. Philip II was at war with France; and the French under Gaspard de Coligny were defeated by Philbert Emmanuel of Savoy aided by English troops.

l. 43. *Geryon*. A mythical three-bodied King of Spain, killed by Hercules.

l. 43. Bawcutt (*Bawcutt*, pp. 90–1) correctly contradicts Bullough's contention (G. Bullough, 'The Early Poems of Sir Richard Fanshawe', *Anglo-Americana* [*Wiener Beiträge zur englischen Philologie*, 57] 1955, pp. 27–36) that Fanshawe is making use of Jose de Siguenza's *Historia de la Orden de San Jeronimo* (Madrid, 1605). A more convincing although untraceable source is mentioned by Lady Fanshawe: 'It [the

Escorial] is in every particular exactly described in a book writ by the fryers and sold in that place, and you [Fanshawe's son Richard] have it amongst your father's books' (*Memoirs*, pp. 168–9).

ll. 85–6. Cf. Virgil, *Aeneid* i, ll. 403–4.

ll. 115–24. King Roderick 'Roderigo el Gozo', the last Visigothic King of Spain, ravished the daughter of his General, the Count Julian, who, in revenge, opened the gates to the Moors. Cf. Melveena McKendrick, *A Concise History of Spain* (London, Cassell, 1972), p. 25. There is some difficulty in these lines: the paintings in the *Sala de Batallas* now represent the defeat of the Moors at Higuernela on 1 July 1431.

ll. 149–50. Cf. Donne, 'The Extacie', ll. 13–14 (*The Elegies and The Songs and Sonnets*, ed. Dame Helen Gardner, Oxford, Clarendon Press, 1965, p. 59). Cf. also Donne's sources: Tibullus, *Elegies* ii. 5, ll. 45–6; Ovid, *Metamorphoses* viii, ll. 11–13.

l. 158. In honour of St Laurence, the ground-plan of the Escorial is in the shape of the gridiron on which the Saint was martyred.

l. 181. *Gen'rall Blacks.* The mourning of the people, 'lachrymis populi' in the Latin.

On His Majesties Great Shippe (pp. 70–7)

General note. This poem continues that education in governance which runs through all the poems of *1648*; but what is less expected in an official poem on an official occasion is the sheer freshness and delight which Fanshawe feels in the contemplation of the Great Ship, both as an object of beauty and as an emblem of a well-governed state.

Fanshawe's was, naturally, not the only poem written in or after 1637 to celebrate what was then England's supreme achievement in naval architecture. *Heywood* contains verse by Heywood himself and by a 'T.C.', most probably Thomas Cary of Tower Hill. Henry King's 'A salutation of his Majestie's Ship the Soveraign' (Henry King, *The Poems*, pp. 92–3) dates from the same years and, like Fanshawe's poem, draws heavily on *Heywood*.

King's and Fanshawe's poems converge in predictable areas: the invocation of the Baroque sea-gods, the consideration of the dual functions of such a ship in peace and war, the expression of hopes for the future of the ship and the kingdom. Fanshawe is individual in his use of the common source in his insistence on the symbolic significance of the ship as the emblem of a harmonious country governed by a wise monarch. Throughout this poem he has drawn very heavily on Thomas Heywood's pamphlet *A True Description of His Majesties Royall Ship, Built this year 1637 at* Wooll-*witch in* KENT (London, 1637).

ll. 7–8. Cf. *Heywood*, p. 25.

ll. 10–12. Ibid., p. 39.

ll. 15–16. Ibid., p. 1.

ll. 17–19. Ibid., p. 26.

ll. 33–56. A complex series of echoes of *Heywood*, pp. 29–34.

ll. 57–66. Cf. *Heywood*, preliminary pages sig. A1 V.

ll. 79–80. Ibid., p. 28.

l. 81. Ibid., p. 27.

ll. 95–100. Cf. Catullus, *Carmen* 4, ll. 25–7.

ll. 100–4. Cf. *Heywood*, pp. 27–8.

Maius Lucanizans (pp. 77–9)

Translation: May's imitation of Lucan

O Lucan, you live! your dark shade is called back from your funerary urn, and I mark your greater image. Your veins, emptied by the crime of Caesar [Nero] fill again, while a better Caesar in the Capitol, dying, spattered his own Jove with blood (and was avenged by your verse). You have done this O May; heir to his divine bosom [i.e. his genius], powerful in tongues; [1] whether you render in the song of your native land what was the wandering Muse sang to her Romans; or you dare to continue further after the leader was carried off, and carrying the victorious signs of the English Muse which the Roman Muse left lying, [2] or [3] you are a translator of your own work, in which wars were sung which only a few ears heard before, which you now return to Rome in a Roman dress. Your famous tongue describes hesitating Cato who died with the whole world watching as in a theatre.

You outstripped your author and were able to scale both peaks of Parnassus, and were read by both the learned and the vulgar, when you sang of savage triumphs at the river Thames in varied voices, and the trumpet echoed from both banks; from one side, the Roman language resounds, and from the other, the British replies: the English boast of Lucan, and the Romans of May!

O bring back many things for us! How many battles remain to be immortalized by you? What love poems does your Muse hold buried within her? Alas! do you not undergo so many deaths to live for ever? Death does not prove merit: [against] the irascible people, the end of wretched Brutus, [see] the honour of his wife—alas, alas! for her, linked with such a man, and emulous of her father [Cato]! He [Cato] ordered, as you recount, that same outlawed senate and Cicero himself by dire law to hear the supreme complaint of Liberty (already oppressed by three tyrants). First the Muse spoke to you of Cleopatra, and asked you at once to reach the heights of song, even though everything shines, and strives for more light in the middle part, deprived of death, the Queen fears the snakes her servants, unless you hurry to her aid with your high-sounding verse and smooth her spirits with your words. Paint the form of a victorious leader; it is no time for the conquered: paint a Duke conquered, with his fierce neck in a soft shackle: the battle-line of Actium, where the shining glories of the Tyrians came to an end. Often the conscious virtue of men, of old makers, draws back, and the inborn Desire of Mars [war], but in a naval battle more can be tested, the watery Venus. Fleeing whom he was able to conquer, he followed the victorious fugitive: and withdrawing from his part of the empire, handed the slack reins to Augustus.

Raise the trumpets here. Here, Maro [Virgil] and Flaccus [Horace], with Naso [Ovid], and the sweet chorus [of the Muses] acknowledge your work. The splendid conqueror, with the world made peaceful by a song, hears you, and they yield the whole olive [the crown of poets] to the ivies [the crown of Bacchus]. The veteran poet goes to his rest under that grace.

Fanshawe's marginal notes:

[1] A translation of Lucan into the English tongue.
[2] A supplement to Lucan in the English tongue.
[3] A translation of the supplement into the Latin tongue.

Written for Thomas May's *Supplementum Lucani*, Leiden, 1640, a continuation in Latin verse of Lucan's *Pharsalia*. This poem must have been written for Fanshawe's friend and literary mentor shortly before the political quarrel mentioned by Aubrey (*Brief Lives*, ii. 55). It is characteristic of Fanshawe to reprint the poem in *1648* and *1658* when the Civil War had ended the friendship which inspired it.

Methodus Amandi (pp. 79–82)

'Mr T. C.' is not Thomas Cary of Tower Hill, but the Thomas Cary who was a Gentleman of the Bedchamber to Charles I (Cf. Malone, f. 24v).

Dominae Navigaturae (p. 83)

The English original was a popular poem in the 1630s and 1640s. 'T.C.' is a weak candidate for its authorship. The poem seems to be the work of the Scot William Fowler. For discussion of its date and authorship cf. *Scottish Poetry from Barbour to James VI*, ed. M. M. Gray (London, Dent, 1935), pp. xxi–xxii.

A Canto of the Progresse of Learning (pp. 84–95)

The first version of this lengthy Spenserian poem, in MS A, dates from Fanshawe's years in the Inner Temple, and may be seen as a more extended treatment of the questions which received attention in the 'Oade, Splendidis longum valedico nugis' (pp. 36–8).

In the literary circle of Thomas May, of which Fanshawe appears to have been a peripheral member, there is no doubt that Spenser was held in esteem as a poet who had expanded the literary potential of the English language. Sir Kenelm Digby's short treatise 'Concerning Spenser that I wrote att Mr. May his desire' confirms that May's circle esteemed Spenser's achievement highly and thought that he had, together with Jonson, formed a workable 'literary' English style for long future use (*Spenser, the Critical Heritage*, ed. R. M. Cummings, London, Routledge and Kegan Paul, 1971, pp. 148–9).

In this atmosphere, and inspired by that personal admiration for Spenser which the frequent echoes in the earlier poems suggest, it was not surprising that Fanshawe should attempt an allegorical poem in Spenser's style. The first version found in MS A was abandoned; and Fanshawe's second attempt at the subject, the poem which is found again in MS A, in *1648*, and in MS F, is more leisurely and more intricate than the first version. It appears that an external influence intervened to shape the final version of the poem: the text and illustrations of George Sandys's version of the *Metamorphoses* of Ovid (George Sandys, *Ovid's Metamorphosis, Englished, Mythologised and represented in figures*, Oxford,

1632). The opening lines of Fanshawe's allegory derive from the account of creation which begins the *Metamorphoses*. He may have taken the idea for the final apotheosis of 'Wit' from the soaring, eagle-mounted figure which flies above the created world in the engraving which faces the beginning of the first book of Sandys's translation.

The externalization of an interior conflict in the form of a trial owes a debt to Spenser's *Mutability Cantos*; and particular use is made of the seventh and eighth *Cantos of Mutabilitie* (Cf. Spenser, pp. 400–6).

There are other, lesser Spenserian echoes, particularly of the *Four Hymnes*: Fanshawe's account of creation owes some of its vocabulary to the *Hymne in Honour of Love* (cf. Spenser, p. 587, ll. 57–77) and Wit's inspiriting of man has its source in the *Hymne in Honour of Beautie* (Spenser, p. 590, ll. 50–63). It is the *Hymne in Honour of Love*, however, which supplies much of the vocabulary for the apotheosis with which 'A Canto of the Progresse of Learning' concludes (Spenser, pp. 587–8, ll. 183–9).

It might be noted that Fanshawe's friend Sir John Denham published a poem which was also entitled 'The Progress of Learning', but it is a historical account of the spread of knowledge cast in epigrammatic couplets, and bears no relation to Fanshawe's work (Sir John Denham, *The Poetical Works*, ed. T. H. Banks, New Haven and London, Yale Univ. Press and Oxford Univ. Press, 1928, p. 112).

ll. 5–6. Cf. Donne, 'The First Anniversary', ll. 112–16 (*The Epithalamions, Anniversaries and Epicedes*, ed. W. Milgate, Oxford, Clarendon Press, 1978, p. 55). Also ll. 135–6, p. 59.

l. 10. Cf. Ovid, *Metamorphoses* i, ll. 8–9.

ll. 15–16. Cf. Boethius, *De Consolatione Philosophiae*, Metrum III, ii, ll. 13–14.

ll. 20–1. The image here suggests that Chaos is monophonic and therefore incapable of harmony, whereas the ordered world is polyphonic and therefore potentially harmonious.

ll. 28–32. Cf. Claudian, *De Raptu Proserpinae*, iii, ll. 35–45.

l. 40. The image is that of a silver *tabula rasa*, to be chased with a diamond-headed burin.

ll. 55–61. Cf. [Ferrar], *Conversations at Little Gidding*, ed. A. M. Williams (Cambridge, CUP, 1970), p. 208.

ll. 64–6. Cf. Horace, *Odes* I, 3, ll. 27–33.

ll. 83–90. Cf. Sidney, *A Defence of Poesie*, in *Miscellaneous Prose*, ed. K. Duncan-Jones and J. Van Dorsten (Oxford, Clarendon Press, 1973), p. 121. Cf. also *Conversations at Little Gidding*, p. 205.

l. 105. Cf. the False Florimell in Spenser's *The Faerie Queene*, III, viii, 5, p. 183.

l. 109. Cf. *The Faerie Queene*, I, i, 35, l. 5, p. 7.

ll. 112–17. Cf. *The Faerie Queene*, II, vii, 16–18, p. 101.

l. 126. The legal term '*in Capite*' is used with precision: Craft is presented as the chief feudal tenant, holding all land directly from his sovereign and which he may let out in turn.

l. 153. Play is made with the use of gall in making ink. Cf. Sir Hugh Plat, *The Jewell House of Art and Nature* (London, 1635), p. 40.

ll. 154–9. Fanshawe is drawing on his legal knowledge: Craft claims dominion over the world on a Plea of Merit (i.e. that his claim is just) and he does not invoke the Law of Possession, which puts the onus on the pretender to prove the justice of his claim.

l. 217. Cf. Fanshawe's 'Soare high, my Love, check not thy gallant flight', ll. 9–11 (p. 45).

ll. 235–9. Cf. Sir Kenelm Digby, letter to an unnamed correspondent *c.*1625 (E. W. Bligh, *Sir Kenelm Digby and his Venetia*, London, Sampson Low, Marston and Co. Ltd., 1932, p. 17, transcribed from British Museum, Add. MS 41,846, f. 63r and v).

ll. 253–4. The first line is an adaptation of Ovid, *Metamorphoses* ii. 56. The second line appears to derive from the *Dicta Catonis*, II, 2: 'Ad di sint caelumque regnant, ne quare doceri / Cum sis mortalis, quae sunt mortalia, cura.' *Dicta Catonis quae vulgo inscribitur Catonis Disticha de Moribus*, ed. Geysa Nemethy (Budapest, 1895), p. 24.

The Ruby (p. 96)

Cf. Pliny, *Historia Naturalis* xxxvii, ch. 25, and Ovid, *Metamorphoses* iii, ll. 183–5.

A friends Wedding (pp. 96–7)

ll. 3–5. Cf. Propertius, *Elegies* ii. 15, ll. 27–8.

ll. 11–12. Cf. Propertius, *Elegies* iii. 3, l. 5.

l. 25. Cf. Fanshawe's translation of Boethius, *De Consolatione Philosophiae*, Metrum III. 12, ll. 45–7 (p. 20).

Sonnets translated out of Spanish

General Note

Only some of this collection of translations from the Spanish form part of the thematic unity of *1648*: 'A Picture' and 'A Rose' both offer reflections on the unstable nature of experience and the transience of earthly things, and 'Hope' offers a stoical consolation in misfortune. The translation which Fanshawe has entitled 'The Fall' has been altered in the process of imitation so as to have a direct English relevance. The original is Gongora's sonnet on the fall of a court favourite 'En la muerte de Don Rodrigo Calderon',

Sella el tronco sangriento, no le oprime,
De aquel dichosamente desdichado,
Que de las inconstancias de su hado
Esta picarra apenas le redime;
Urna que el escarmiento le ha negado,
Padron le erige en bronce imaginado,
Que en vano el tiempo las memorias lime.
Risueno con el, tanto como falso,
El tiempo, quatro lustras en la risa,
El cuchillo quica embainava agudo.
Del sitial despues al cadahalso
Precipitado, o quanto nos avisa!
O quanta trompa es su exemplo mudo!

(Gongora, *Obras Poeticas,* New York, Hispanic Society of America, 1921, ii. 348.)

A considerable adaptation has been made to fit the circumstances of the fall of Fanshawe's friend and commander, the Earl of Strafford: the Spanish describes the time of Don Rodrigo's prosperity as 'quatro lustros' which may be interpreted as four Roman 'lustra', that is, four terms of 5 years. Fanshawe's substitution of 'Ten yeares' is appropriate to the career of the Earl of Strafford if one dates his high career from his appointment as Deputy in Ireland in January 1631/2 to his downfall in 1641.

A Rich Foole (p. 98)

From Gongora, 'Lugar te da sublime el vulgo ciego' (iii. 2).

Hope (pp. 98–9)

From Bartolome L. de Argensola, 'Fabio, las esperanzas no son malas' (ii. 248).

Constancie (p. 99)

From Gongora, 'Peniava al sol Beliza sus cabellos' (ii. 319).

The Fall (pp. 99–100)

From Gongora, 'En la muerte de D. Rodrigo Calderon', 'Sella el tronco sangriento no le oprime' (ii. 348).

A Rose (p. 100)

From Gongora, 'Vana Rosa', 'Aier naciste, i moriras mañana' (iii. 27).

A Picture (p. 101)

From Bartolome L. de Argensola, 'A una dama que estaba mirando un retrato de Mario', 'Mario es aquel que del Minturno lago' (ii. 229.)

A River (pp. 101–2)

From Gongora, 'O claro honor del liquido elemento' (i. 25).

A Nightingale (p. 102)

From Gongora, 'Con differencia tal, con gracia tanta' (i. 55).

A Cupid of diamonds presented (p. 102–3)

The source remains unidentified. H. Thomas, in 'Three Translators of Gongora', *Revue Hispanique*, 48 (1920), 230–43, compares Gongora's 'En el cristal de tu divina mano' (i. 300). The resemblance is slight. Cf. Sir Robert Ayton, 'Upon a Diamond cutt in forme of an hart sett with a Crowne above and a bloody dart peirceing it sent in a New Yeares gift' (Ayton, *The English and Latin Poems*, ed. C. B. Gullans, Edinburgh, Scottish Text Society, 1963), p. 181; see also Gullans's note on the poem, p. 295.

The Spring (p. 103)

From Gongora, 'Los blancos lilios que de ciento en ciento' (i. 300).

The Fourth Booke of Virgill's Æneis, On the Loves of Dido and Æneas

General Note

Fanshawe's translation of Book IV of the *Aeneid* stands alone, bearing no relation to that mainstream of seventeenth-century Virgilian translation which is discussed in Proudfoot's *Dryden's Aeneid and its Seventeenth Century Predecessors* (Manchester, Manchester Univ. Press, 1960). The chief translators in this tradition are 'One who has No Name' (?1622); Robert Stapleton (1634); Edmund Waller and Sidney Godolphin (1658); John Ogilby (1650 and 1668); and John Vicars (1652). The first two of these translate Book IV only.

Fanshawe's translation is set apart by his choice of the Spenserian stanza in preference to the iambic couplet. But this form is appropriate to Fanshawe's Spenserian interpretation of Book IV: it emphasizes the supernatural and romance elements of his original. This translation of Virgil has a central place in the thematic unity of *1648*, both as a depiction of a Prince in exile and adversity and also as a lesson in the governance of the self and the nation.

Fanshawe does not focus on Aeneas to the exclusion of Dido: the last section of the Book is both tender and frightening. Fanshawe's appropriation of Spenserian enchantment works to convey the confusion of desolation, magic, and bewilderment in which Dido dies.

It is, however, in the treatment of the supernatural messages to Aeneas that Fanshawe has the greatest success: the poetical world out of which he took the style for this translation (Spenser and, to a certain extent, the Jacobean drama) provides him with an existing style to make the numinous passages tell and thereby to redress the ambiguity which appears, in most translations, to surround Aeneas' behaviour. This success may be seen when Fanshawe is compared with Denham, a comparison which also points up the chief weakness of Fanshawe's version: its lack of narrative impetus. After Mercury has given Aeneas the divine command to leave Carthage, Virgil has:

> tali Cyllenius ore locutus
> mortalis visus medio sermone reliquit
> et procul in tenuem ex oculis evanuit auram.
> At vero Aeneas aspectu obmutit amens,
> arrectaeque horrore comae et vox faucibus haesit.
> ardet abire fuga dulcisque relinquere terras,
> attonitus tanto monitu imperioque deorum.

(*P. Vergili Maronis, Aeneidos Liber Quartus*, ed. R. G. Austin, Oxford, Clarendon Press, 1963, p. 10)

which Denham translates (p. 181):

> Having at large declar'd *Jove's* Ambassy,
> *Cyllenius* from *Aeneas* straight doth flye;
> He loth to disobey the God's command,
> Nor willing to forsake this pleasant land

and Fanshawe (ll. 317–23) renders:

> This having said *Cyllenius* vanisht quite
> From mortall eyes, and back to Heaven flew.
> *Æneas* at the vision shakes with fright,
> His tongue cleaves to his jawes, his hair stands bolt-upright.
> Hee is on fire to goe, and flye that Land
> Of sweet inchantments, being skar'd away
> By no lesse warning than the Gods command.

Denham's narration is rapid and compelling, but all the terror and poetry have vanished. Fanshawe, on the other hand, may fall short of the dignity of the original and it is immediately clear that a sustained narrative in this manner is not going to flow easily; but the terror and the poetry are still there and the matter of the original is alive. The reality and horror of the supernatural visitation must be credible if Aeneas is to retain his heroic stature; and the reaction of Aeneas, theatrically preserved by Fanshawe, serves to keep the balance of the narration. Fanshawe's rendering of 'dulcis relinquere terras' has caught the resonance which Denham's indifferent 'willing' misses completely; Fanshawe's Aeneas is like a Spenserian knight breaking out of an enchantment, disenchanted by stronger magic, resolved but perplexed.

This is a fair representation of the general achievement and failure of Fanshawe's translation. He succeeds in making his Aeneas credible as a lonely and pitiable man, troubled by visions and aware that he has higher responsibilities than he might desire. He understands Book IV as a moral and spiritual poem as much as a narrative of unhappy love. He succeeds particularly in the supernatural passages; but the defects of Fanshawe's translation are bound up with the style and stanza which he has chosen: if the poetry of individual lines comes across entire, the narrative does not, and in this the work of Denham and Dryden succeeds and establishes the style for future translators. Their works are continuous, as is the *Aeneid* itself, whereas Fanshawe offers illuminations line by line, but never attains a rhythm for the work as a whole.

ll. 1–50. In *1648* these lines are italicized for no apparent reason. Given the degree to which they vary in F, it may be conjectured that the final version of these lines came to the printer later than the copy for the rest of the book.

l. 18. The extended last line of the stanza is used with great success to represent the faltering of Dido's speech.

l. 154. Cf. Nicholas Cox, *The Gentleman's Recreation* (London, 1677), p. 52.

l. 250. *Beaver* translates 'semiviru'. In the seventeenth century, beavers were believed to castrate themselves at the approach of danger. Cf. Sir Thomas Browne, *Pseudodoxica Epidemica* (*Works*, ed. Sir Geoffrey Keynes, London, Faber and Faber, 1964), ii. 167 ff.

l. 322. *sweet inchantments* for 'dulcisque relinquere terras' suggests that Fanshawe is thinking of Aeneas as an enchanted, Spenserian knight. Cf. *The Faerie Queene*, II. i. 23 (p. 72).

ll. 448–50. Cf. Webster, *The White Devil*, V. vi. 140–2 (ed. F. L. Lucas, London, Chatto and Windus, 1958, p. 129).

l. 663. This represents perhaps the extreme of Fanshawe's baroque mode in adapting 'adnixi torquent spumas et caerula vertunt'.

ll. 704–12. Something of a *locus classicus* of the 1640s, in view of the widespread story that Charles I lighted upon this ominous passage while consulting the *sortes Virgilianae* during the years which the Court spent at Oxford. The written source for the anecdote appears to be a passage of Aubrey not included in Clark's edition of the *Brief Lives* (John Aubrey, *Remaines of gentilisme and judaisme*, ed. James Britten, London, 1881, pp. 90–2; from British Library, MS Lansdowne 231, ff. 155, 157, 158). The first text of Cowley's translation of the passage, supposedly made extempore on this occasion, is found in *Miscellany Poems by Buckingham, Milton, Prior and others* (1692), p. 26.

A Happy Life out of Martiall (p. 129)

From Martial, *Epigrams* X, 47. Cf. Thomas Randolph's version (*The Poems of Thomas Randolph*, ed. G. Thorn-Drury, London, Etchells and MacDonald, 1929, p. 88).

On the Earle of Straffords Tryall (pp. 129–30)

Fanshawe had been Secretary to the Council of War in Ireland under Strafford from 1639 until 1641, and was a friend of Strafford's son, from whom he rented Tankersley Park in Yorkshire in the 1650s. The Earl was brought to trial on 22 March 1641 and executed on 12 May in the same year. Cf. Clarendon, *The History of the Rebellion*, iii. 200, ed. W. D. Macray (Oxford, Clarendon Press, 1888), p. 339.

l. 31. Marcus Salvius Otho (AD 32–69) was the husband of Poppea and was honourably exiled on her marriage to the Emperor Nero. Because he was chosen Emperor by the Legions of the Danube and the Euphrates his suicide in AD 69 technically prevented a civil war.

Presented to His Highnesse . . . At his going into the West (p. 143)

Cf. *Memoirs*, p. 114.

Presented to His Highnesse . . . In the West (pp. 143–6)

Taken from the *Genethliacon Jacobi Sexti Regis Scotorum* by George Buchanan, *Poemata* (Edinburgh, 1615), sig. D7r and v. The first nine lines of the original are given for comparison.

Cresce puer patriae auspiciis felicibus orte
Ex pectate puer, qui vatum oracula priorum
Aurea compositis promittunt secula bellis,
Tuque peregrinis toties pulsata procellis
Exere laeta caput, cohibe pacalis olivae
Pene tuo toties excisa Britannia ferro,
Fronde comam, repara flammis foedata, ruinis
Confulsa, et pulso cole squalida tecta colono.
Pone metum, aeternam spondent tibi sidera pacem.

l. 76. Expansion of the original via Psalm 28: 5.

SELECTED PARTS OF HORACE

The Place of 1652 *in the Seventeenth-Century Tradition of Horatian Poetry: General Note*

When Sir John Denham praised Fanshawe as a translator in the commendatory poem which was published with the 1647 edition of *Il Pastor Fido* (Denham, pp. 143–4) he attributed to Fanshawe virtues which he hardly possessed. The 'free and bolder stroke', the 'foording his current', and the 'new names, new dressings and the modern cast' may express Denham's own attitude to the translation of foreign or classical poetry, but hardly apply to Fanshawe's practice as a translator. Fanshawe's *Selected Parts of Horace, 1652*, represents the utmost which can be achieved by a translator without forsaking strict translation for the 'imitation' which Denham's poem appears to identify and praise.

There is little point in entering into complicated comparisons to fix the place of *1652* in the tradition of seventeenth-century Horatian poetry, because *1652* is a collection of uneven style and quality which was compiled over a number of years. Such extended analysis is also fruitless in that the position of the best poems of *1652* is comparatively simply defined: they exist at the point of maximum freedom and invention which may be achieved without departing from the twin policies of faithful translation of sense and line-for-line translation of verse. As a whole the collection breaks no new ground.

Fanshawe's work places itself essentially within a continuing tradition of reading Horace as moralist first and poet second. The other strain of influence on his trans- lation comes from those versions from Horace which were made by Ben Jonson, who appropriated Horace to form his image of himself as a poet within society.

The exponents of the 'moral' tradition were numerous, but can be represented by the work of Sir Thomas Hawkins, who first published his *Odes of Horace* in 1623. Fanshawe's first Horatian translations, in MS A, which date from a few years later, are not dissimilar in adopting in some poems a very literal style of translation emphasizing the didactic content of the original. Hawkins occasionally varies his metres and there is a perfunctory attempt to match them with the metres and stanza-forms of the original, although this goes no farther than using an eight- rather than ten-syllable line for the more lyrical Latin forms, such as the Sapphic. Fanshawe from the beginning attempts the matching of Latin and English stanzas which may be seen in his final version.

Apart from the work of the 'moral' translators, the chief influence on Fanshawe's first Horatian versions is that of Ben Jonson, whose versions of *Odes* III, 9 (viii. 293) and of *Epode* 23 (p. 290) provide examples of his vigorous, limited freedom with his original. The comparison of a few lines from *Ode* III, 9 points up both the extent of the influence and the degree to which Jonson's translation has an ease which Fanshawe's version lacks:

> Whilst, *Lydia*, I was lov'd of thee,
> And ('bout thy Ivory neck,) no youth did fling
> His armes more acceptable free,
> I thought me richer than the Persian King.

Fanshawe's version (p. 184) clearly derives from Jonson, but is more circumspect:

> Whilst I possest thy love, free from alarms,
> Nor any *Youth* more acceptable Arms
> About thy Alablaster Neck did fling:
> I liv'd more happy then the *Persian King*.

In his version of the second *Epode*, Fanshawe comes nearer to Jonson's achievement, but he also translates very much in Jonson's shadow, imitating verse-form and even diction.

The translations from the Latin poet which were made in the second half of the seventeenth century moved into an area of experiment altogether independent of the kind of faithful version which Fanshawe made. It is possible, however, to claim for Fanshawe a certain place in the development of Horatian imitation, in that the versions of the *Satires* and *Epistles* which are contained in *1652* have a certain colloquial freedom and rapidity of versification which look to the future. Fanshawe, however, never presents his Roman original in modern English dress. Such modernization is represented in *1652* only by a glancing and unconvinced attempt to give the 'ides' and 'calends' mentioned in the last lines of *Epode* 2 a modern guise as the financial quarter-days (p. 209). This experiment brought down upon Fanshawe the satire of Samuel Butler, who assumes negatively (as Denham assumed positively) that Fanshawe's translations consistently take inspired liberties with the matter of the original:

Besides their nonsense in translating
For want of *Accidence* and *Latin*,
Like *Idus* and *Calendae* Englisht
The *Quarter-days*, by Skilful Linguist.

(Samuel Butler, *Hudibras*, Part II, Canto II, ll. 15–19, ed. J. Wilders (Oxford, Clarendon Press, 1967), p. 178.)

It is perhaps incorrect to talk of the 'making' of a collection such as *1652*, which in its final form still displays considerable unevenness of style and poetic quality, with poems which had been translated as much as 20 years earlier remaining in their original form. Some are revised in verbal details, but are not subjected to any extensive revision to bring them into line with the greater sophistication of the poems which were added to the collection in the years between the compilation of F and the printing of *1652*. It is, however, possible to trace a certain development in Fanshawe's reading of Horace through the additions which he made to his earliest stock of Horatian translation in A, first in F and finally in *1652*.

The contents of A suggest that Fanshawe's initial intentions regarding the translation of Horace were chiefly moral and didactic. MS F is a graver collection: the single 'libertine' *Ode* found in MS A (III, 20) is omitted. MS F adds translations of *Epodes* 1 and 14 as well as four translations from the *Odes*. As yet there are no translations of the *Satires* or *Epistles*. Such verbal revisions as are made to the text as it stands in A are not extensive. Overall the tone of the Horatian collection in F is unified in its seriousness: there are no poems of compliment, but the presence of a revised version of *Epode* 16 is not without significance: it appears that Fanshawe was coming to an awareness of the relevance which Horace might have to the condition of a divided England. *Epode* 16 was published in *1648* as well as *1652* (for the text see pp. 211–13).

Clearly at some point in the mid-1640s Fanshawe must have decided to form the work which he had completed into two collections, *1648* and *1652*, rather than publish a single volume (along the lines of the manuscript F) of miscellaneous poems and translations. It is significant that two Horatian translations are published in *1648* and are obviously intended to form part of the commentary upon contemporary events which that volume makes. One point in *1648* also deserves notice: Horace is mentioned in the 'Discourse' which concludes that volume, in the context of a larger discussion of Roman Civil War, in such a way as to suggest that Fanshawe retained a degree of identification with the Latin poet (pp. 139–40):

this same despairing *Horace* did live to see, and particularly to enjoy, other very different *times*, when the Common-wealth, after the defeat of *Mark Anthony* at the Battell of *Actium, being now quite tired out with civill Warres, submitted her selfe to the just and peacefull Scepter of the most Noble Augustus.*

This feeling of identification is also present in certain poems of the completed collection of *1652*, particularly in the revised version of *Ode* IV, 4 and in *Ode* IV, 9. Between the compilation of F and the printing of *1652* Fanshawe added the fluent and vigorous translations of the *Satires* and *Epistles* which represent the most advanced element in the collection.

[I, 4] (pp. 155–6) l. 19. Perhaps a recollection of the extraordinary scene (III, 5) in Fletcher's *The Lover's Progress*, set in a haunted inn, in which the 'Dead Host's Song' includes elements of this *Ode* and of *Ode* I, 9 (Beaumont and Fletcher, *Fifty Comedies and Tragedies*, London, 1679, p. 501).

[I, 8] (p. 157) l. 5. *twits.* Controls by the mouth.

[I, 13] (pp. 158–9) l. 2. *henge.* Hinge; 'neck'.

[I, 37] (pp. 163–4) l. 20. The preposition is in accord with seventeenth-century custom. Cf. Nicholas Cox, *The Gentleman's Recreation* (London, 1677), pp. 87–9.

[II, 1] (pp. 164–5) l. 19. *shog.* Start; shake.

[II, 3] (pp. 166–7) ll. 5–6. Cf. Song in Fletcher's *The Nice Valour*, III. i (*Comedies and Tragedies*, London, 1647), p. 157.

[II, 8] (pp. 168–9) l. 22. *gripple.* Niggardly; tenacious.

[II, 13] (pp. 170–1) l. 1. The fifth word of this line is marked by empty brackets in *1652* (both states) and in Brome's *Horace* (1661, 1671, 1680). All available copies have been consulted and the annotation recorded is the earliest discovered. The reading is obviously offered with hesitation. Possibly the original word was an impropriety: seventeenth-century senses of 'prick' would admit of a triple play on insult, horticultural tool, and *membrum virile*. Cf. Eric Partridge, *A Dictionary of Slang and Unconventional English* (rev. edn., London, Routledge and Kegan Paul, 1961).

[III, 4] (pp. 179–81) ll. 15–16. Cf. Fanshawe's Inscription to the engraving of Camões, l. 16 (*The Lusiad*, London, 1655, frontispiece).

[III, 11] (pp. 185–6) l. 12. *backing.* Breaking to the saddle.

[III, 24] (pp. 188–90) First printed in *1648*, pp. 299–301.

[III, 27] (pp. 190–2) ll. 11–12. Fanshawe has substituted a contemporary superstition for the original 'corvum . . . ab ortu'. Cf. Sir Thomas Browne, *Pseudodoxia Epidemica*, iii, ch. 10 (ii. 86 ff.).

[III, 30] (pp. 194–5) l. 10. Cf. Spenser, *Ruines of Rome, by Bellay*, ll. 37–8 (p. 509).

[IV, 2] (pp. 195–7) ll. 17–20. These lines have been tentatively restored because (unlike a couplet which seems to have been removed from *Ode* IV, 7 to unify the tone of the poem) they fit both mood and argument. With these two exceptions, although he translates on occasion freely, Fanshawe preserves every line of his original in some form.

IV, 4 and Andrew Marvell's 'An Horatian Ode upon Cromwel's Return from Ireland'

General Note

The most interesting point which arises from Fanshawe's *1652* collection is the part which Fanshawe's translation of *Ode* IV, 4 may have played in the making of Marvell's 'Horatian Ode'. A degree of relation between the two poems cannot be doubted: Marvell echoes stanza-form, diction, and imagery. Fanshawe's poem is Horatian in that it translates an *Ode* from Horace, hinting at a contemporary application, but without significant modification of the original. Marvell's poem (*The Poems and Letters*, ed. H. M. Margoliouth, 3rd edn., rev. by P. Legouis and E. E. Duncan-Jones, Oxford, Clarendon Press, 1971, i. 91–4) is Horatian in that it approaches a difficult topic in a way which resembles the rapid and allusive progress of a poem by Horace, imitating his technique of indirect exposition. This clearly suits Marvell's preservation of his ambiguous stance in the 'Horatian Ode': the Horatian procedures allow him to reserve personal judgement at the same time as he advances diverse possibilities to the reader.

At this point it is necessary to give a brief account of the resemblances between the two poems: both employ the same stanza, a stanza of a four-stress iambic couplet followed by a three-stress iambic couplet. Both poems begin with the image of a gentle youth led out of retirement into active life, and contain images of an avenging hero as a bird of prey: Asdrubal in Fanshawe and Cromwell in Marvell both run through the air like fire and storm. Hannibal in Fanshawe is a wolf attacking the sheep, Cromwell in Marvell is a hunter of Picts. Asdrubal's 'red ghost' appears in Fanshawe; Marvell's Cromwell is surrounded eventually by the spirits of the dead. There are also verbal resemblances: in ll. 11–12 of Marvell, 'But through adventrous War / Urged his active Star' there is a resemblance to ll. 75–6 of Fanshawe, 'And their own prudent care / Clews through the Maze of War'. There is another, more direct echo in ll. 55–6 of Marvell, 'While round the armed Bands / Did clap their bloody hands' of ll. 23–4 of Fanshawe's version, 'Their long Victorious Bands / Subdu'd by a Boy's hands'.

Fanshawe's poem gives every appearance of predating Marvell's by a number of years. No definite conclusion can be drawn as to the first possible date for Marvell's poem in some form, as no version of it survives from the 1650s; but there is no reason to suppose that it is any earlier in its origins than its title indicates. Fanshawe's poem, on the other hand, clearly existed, at least in a first version, as early as the mid-1630s on the unequivocal evidence of its appearance in manuscript A. It might be conjectured that Marvell is most likely to have seen Fanshawe's translation in a lost manuscript version of the late 1640s, containing the text in an intermediate state between F and *1652*.

Fanshawe's choice of stanza-form appears to be dictated by his consistent practice in the translation of Latin poetry of matching the stanza-form of the original with an English stanza of similar shape. It appears to have suggested possibilities to Marvell, being a stanza which encourages concise statement in the four-stress couplet and equally concise development in the three-stress couplet which follows. In Marvell's hands the enforced rhythmic pauses become a mimesis of the difficulties and ambiguities raised by the poem's subject.

Fanshawe, however, offered Marvell more than a stanza-form and appropriate cadences. In a simple way, he makes his poem apply to the political events of contemporary England. Although this translation of *Ode* IV, 4 offers no overt parallel (Drusus and Charles II; Hannibal and Cromwell), his choice of vocabulary is very close to that which he used in *1648* to give voice to his aspirations for the young Prince. There is evidence that such a parallel was present in Fanshawe's mind as he made the final version of his translation: in ll. 45–8 (lines which are echoed by Marvell) the movement of the verse is designed to place emphasis on the word 'restored'. In ll. 53–6 there is some reference to another parallel which was implied in *1648*: that between the Prince of Wales and the fugitive Aeneas. The firmest use of the parallel vision of the poem may be traced in the revisions which Fanshawe made to the text of this *Ode* between the compilation of F and the printing of *1652*: while the final version remains in most respects a faithful translation of the Latin, the revisions suggest that Fanshawe developed his reading of the poem and increasingly came to think of Drusus as an analogue for Charles II. In ll. 2–5 the sex of the royal eagle is changed from female to male, and revisions are made with similar intentions in ll. 9–10. In ll. 23–4 (lines which are again echoed by Marvell) 'land' is revised to 'Bands' so as to make a possible reference to the Civil War; the general phrase 'a young hand' becomes the specific 'a Boy's hands'. Line 34 has the most precise revision whereby 'vertuous' becomes 'Princely'. In the same way, in l. 45 'thy *Youth*' (echoed in Marvell) replaces the earlier 'our State', a phrase which could not apply to a monarchy in exile. It might, in conclusion, be noted that ll. 57–60 stand unaltered in Fanshawe's revised version as their original, by coincidence, could hardly offer a more convenient sentiment to a Royalist translator.

[IV, 7] (pp. 202–3) The couplet which follows l. 18 in MSS F and A appears to have been left out of *1652* because it introduces a satirical disturbance of the melancholy unity of the poem.

[IV, 9] The supposition that this translation was important to Fanshawe and his circle is supported by the record left by his wife: in her *Memoirs*, when she describes her husband's death, she quotes the second half of this translation as a summary of the virtues and qualities which she has valued in him. This poem of firmness and endurance in adversity (which is also a poem about the perdurability of poetry and of the irrelevance of worldly fortune) may have furnished Fanshawe's family with some consolation in their misfortunes in the years 1650–2, and the use which is made of it in *Memoirs* suggests that it held some private meaning for them. The mood and cadence of the poem is very similar to that of another Royalist poem of endurance in adversity, Lovelace's 'The Grasshopper' (Richard Lovelace, *The Poems*, ed. C. H. Wilkinson, 2nd edn., Oxford, Clarendon Press, 1930, pp. 39–40).

[IV, 9] (pp. 205–6) l. 39. *Tenters.* Hooked boards for stretching cloth.

[Epode 2] (pp. 208–9) Seventeenth-century versions are numerous. Cf. especially Randolph's in *The Poems*, ed. G. Thorn-Drury (London, Etchells and Macdonald, 1929), pp. 47–9.

[Epode 16] (pp. 211–13) First printed *1648*, pp. 301–3. There is no substantive textual variance.

[Satire I, 6] (pp. 214–18) l. 24. *Naule.* Meaning obscure; there is a cognate contraction of *noli prosequi* recorded in *OED*, which might give the required sense that Horace votes but makes no speeches in public matters.

l. 31. *List.* Border; edging.

l. 36. *Small.* The calf of the leg (translating 'sura').

[Satire II, 6] (pp. 221–4) l. 40. Fanshawe was himself appointed Master of the Requests in 1660. Cf. *Memoirs*, p. 141.

ll. 49–51. In roman in *1652*: italicized as obviously representing reported speech.

[Epistle I, 2] (pp. 228–30) l. 52. *Culter.* Plough-share.

Ausonius His Roses (p. 233–4)

The status of Ausonius (*c.*310–94) was surprisingly high in the sixteenth and seventeenth centuries. His graceful and epigrammatic verse appealed powerfully to the Italian humanists of the fourteenth century. Petrarch, Boccaccio, and Coluccio Salutati were three of the most important scholars to own anthologies of Ausonius' poetry, while at least twenty other manuscript collections of Ausonius were copied in Italy between the fourteenth and fifteenth centuries. Further, odd works, particularly short poems such as *de rosis nascentibus*, appear in poetic miscellanies, not always ascribed to their author. The printing history of Ausonius' poetry attests to continued interest in his work. The *editio princeps* was printed in Venice in 1472 by Bartholomaeus Girardinus, and eleven others appeared before 1600, mostly published in Italy or France. All this is an indication that Ausonius, though now little read, was very much part of the Classical tradition as it was perceived by humanists, and his works were readily accessible to an early-modern writer. *De rosis* is echoed by the influential and widely imitated humanist Latin poet Giovanni Giovano Pontano (1426–1503), in his poem *Ad Fanniam* ('puella molli delicatior rosa').

l. 48. Cf. Sir Henry Wotton, 'A Description of the Countrey's Recreations', ll. 43–5, *Reliquiae Wottonianae* (London, 1651), pp. '232–333', i.e. 532–3.

La Fida Pastora

General Note

The 'Tragie-comedie' of *The Faithfull Shepherdess* by John Fletcher (1579–1625) was written and first performed in 1608–9, and its undated first quarto was printed in 1609–10. The play was not well received at its first performance, but was successfully revived both at Court and in the theatre in the early 1630s, where it enjoyed a considerable success. This was perhaps due to a more favourable climate created by the Caroline court vogue for pastoral drama, a fashion influenced, if not entirely instigated, by Henrietta Maria.

The play is very much in the manner of Court, Continental drama, being clearly indebted to Guarini's *Il Pastor Fido*, which in itself may well have influenced Fanshawe to attempt his translation. While this stylistic affinity found the play an appreciative élite reception in the 1630s, it did not ensure its success at its first Jacobean public performance. In his indignant epistle 'To the Reader', which precedes the first quarto of 1609/10, Fletcher justifies his stylistic intentions as a dramatist and expresses his disappointment with and contempt for the first audience of the play, showing pre-emptive exasperation with, if not despair at, the play's initial reception.

If you be not reasonable assurde of your knowledge in this kinde of Poeme, lay downe the booke or read this, which I would wish had been the prologue. It is a pastorall Tragie-comedie, which the people seeing when it was plaid, having ever had a singuler guift in defining, concluded to be a play of country hired Shepheards, in gray cloakes, with curtaild dogs in strings, sometimes laughing together, and sometimes killing one another: And missing whitsun ales, creame, wassel and morris-dances, began to be angry... But you are ever to remember Shepherds to be such, as all the ancient Poets and moderne of understanding have receaved them: that is, the owners of flockes and not hyrelings. A tragie-comedie is not so called in respect of mirth and killing, but in respect it wants deaths, which is inough to make it no tragedie, yet brings some neere it, which is inough to make it no comedie; which must be a representation of familiar people, with such kinde of trouble as no life be questioned, so that a God is as lawfull in this as in a tragedie, and meane people as in a comedie. Thus much I hope will serve to justifie my Poeme, and make you understand it, to teach you more for nothing, I do not know that I am in conscience bound. (*The Dramatic Works in the Beaumont and Fletcher Canon*, gen. ed. Fredson Bowers, play ed. Cyrus Hoy, Cambridge Univ. Press, 1976, iii. 497.)

The prefatory verses to the first quarto edition of the play display the indignant solidarity of Fletcher's professional peer-group in their consolatory (as well as traditional commendatory) tone. They demonstrate the author's genuine gratitude to his patrons, including Sir Walter Aston (Lord Aston of Forfar), the ambassador in whose embassy Fanshawe would serve in Spain. Fletcher's patron was also the father of Fanshawe's friends Herbert and Gertrude Aston and of

Constantia Aston, to whom Fanshawe seems to have been emotionally attached in the 1630s. The association with the Aston family would provide a strong motivation for Fanshawe's translation of the piece, looking back, as he did consistently in his Interregnum translations, to his happier *milieu* in the 1630s. Fletcher's verse epistle to Sir Walter Aston emphasizes the élite intention of the text (Hoy, pp. 493–4):

To that noble and true lover of learning,
Sir Walter Aston knight *of the Bath.*

Sir I must aske your patience, and be trew.
This play was never liked, unlesse by few
That brought their judgements with um, for of late
First the infection, then the common prate
Of common people, have such customes got
Either to silence plaies, or like them not.
Under the last of which this interlude,
Had falne for ever prest downe by the rude
That like a torrent which the moist south feedes,
Drowne's both before him the ripe corn and weedes:
Had not the saving sence of better men
Redeem'd it from corruption: (deere Sir then)
Among the better soules, be you the best
In whome, as in a Center I take rest,
And proper being: from whose equall eye
And judgement, nothing growes but puritie:
(Nor do I flatter) for by all those dead,
Great in the muses, by *Apolloes* head,
He that ads any thing to you; tis done
Like his that lights a candle to the sunne:
Then be as you were ever, your selfe still
Moved by your judgement, not by love, or will,
And when I sing againe as who can tell
My next devotion to that holy well,
Your goodnesse to the muses shall be all,
Able to make a worke Heroyicall.

Given to your service
John Fletcher.

It is likely that the success of the play in the 1630s also influenced Fanshawe's decision to make a Latin translation. Fletcher has clearly taken a tone and an aesthetic from Guarini: it is not impossible that he had attended or seen a text relating either to a reputed English-language performance of 1601 or to a Latin performance at King's College, Cambridge in *c.*1605. His play would have fitted naturally into the cultural policy of the Caroline Court, with its reticence, diffused Platonism, and echoes of Continental courtly drama. Indeed, the 1633 performance can be seen to fit aesthetically into a sequence of pastoral dramas patronized by Henrietta Maria. De Racan's *Artenice* was performed on 21 February 1626, with the Queen and her Court as performers; Walter Montagu's *The Shepherd's Paradise* was given on 9 January 1633, and 2 February 1633; *Florimene*, a French-language play performed by French actors, was given on 21 December 1635. It is clear that the Court performance of *The Faithful Shepherdess* was by the professional company of 'His Majesties Servants' (The King's Men), but fits exactly the tone and atmosphere of the series defined above.

In *The King's Arcadia* the authors suggest that Jones may have provided scenery for this Court performance (*The King's Arcadia: Inigo Jones and the Stuart Court*, John Harris, Stephen Orgel, and Roy Strong, 1973, p. 10). If so there are no clearly identifiable surviving designs. Orgel and Strong (*Inigo Jones and the Theatre of the Stuart Court*, Sotheby and Univ. of California Press, London and Berkeley, 1973, ii. 505–36) give designs for Montagu's *The Shepherd's Paradise* which could obviously be used also for Fletcher's play performed in the same year. They also (ii. 802–3) give an unassigned forest scene and (ii. 465) a forest scene with cottage, either of which might relate to Fletcher's play.

What is really important about the Court connection is that it might well have brought to Fanshawe's mind (even though he was in Spain in 1633, and could not have seen the performance) that *The Faithful Shepherdess* had by the 1630s found a context for itself as a Court piece and a piece specifically associable with the Continental aesthetic of the Court. This influence, together with the relationship to Guarini of which Fanshawe writes in his Epistle to *1658*, and the connection with the Aston family, come together to provide a credible set of reasons for Fanshawe's decision to undertake the translation.

Although initially unpopular on the stage, *The Faithfull Shepheardesse* was clearly in demand amongst readers in the earlier seventeenth century. The first quarto is datable to 1609/10; a second quarto appeared in 1629; a third, containing material specifically relating to the Court performance, appeared in 1634. (There was a further quarto edition in 1665, perhaps relating to a successful revival in 1663, which was attended by Pepys, who commended the excellence of the scenery.)

It is not easy to state with confidence which edition Fanshawe translated. He gives page numbers in the margins of the text of *1658*, but these would work for any of the first three quartos, which reproduce page layout and page division from one to the other. *1658* appears to relate typographically more to Q2 and Q3 than to Q1, particularly in the layout of the songs. Possibly Q3 would have been the most readily available to him in the 1650s, though it is always possible that he had obtained a copy of Q2 earlier.

The details of Q3 are:

THE / FAITHFVLL / SHEPHERDESSE. / ACTED AT SOMERSET / House before the KING and / QUEENE on Twelfe night / last, 1633. / And divers times since with great ap-/ plause at the Private House in Blacke-/ Friers, by his Majesties Servants // *Written by* IOHN FLETCHER. // The third Edition, with Addition. // [fleuron ornament] // LONDON / Printed by *A.M.* for *Richard Meighen*, next / to the Middle Temple in Fleet-/ Street. 1634.

and its Stationer's Register entry is:

S.R. 1634 . . . Acted at Somerset House before the King and Queene on Twelfe night last, 1633. And divers times since with great applause at the Private House in Blacke-Friers, by His Majesties Servants. (E. K. Chambers, *The Elizabethan Stage*, Oxford, Clarendon Press, 1923, iii. 221–2.)

The modern reader may refer to the text of Fletcher's play in vol. iii of *The Dramatic Works in the Beaumont and Fletcher Canon*, ed. Cyrus Hoy (Cambridge, Cambridge Univ. Press, 1976, gen. ed. Fredson Bowers), pp. 483–602.

Author ad opusculum (p. 240)

Translation:

The author to his work: go forth, little book, let the dangers be what they may, shipwrecked from your house, to swim on this tablet, and to obtain some little bit of patronage and suffrage, mostly among foreigners (for why should I deny it?). Behold here the very beginning of THE FAITHFULL SHEPHERDESS, a hateful title and ambiguous as well, though it has evoked an opportunity for the highest imitation. O Icarus, where are you flying? For now, it is not so that you may perpetuate your name by perishing, but that you may perish in taking over some alien work. It is evidently a shield. The hasty author named you, not I, from which I ought not to retract in any way. But accident itself may make a way, it does not agree [joke, grammar] no more than that which is said in English and which I made into Latin hurried me away from the diction of the ancients. This is the problem, indeed, how much I admire GUARINI and how much as I respect him, *Pastor Fido* itself stands witness, which has always been most esteemed amongst those Italians who seek the pure well-spring of their tongue: thus now, even among our people, even though twice-cooked and translated by me, it will be numbered among delights. If the ports of the English graciously receive the foreign wares of that same GUARINI and foreign ports take them in from day to day (I speak now of writings and languages), at the very least, who would forbid writings which can be called their freemen (for indeed the Latin tongue is the tongue of the world) to be opened together with English wares? Certainly if many more divine Poems are contained (trapped) in the narrowness of this Northern Island on account of the peculiarity of its language, they ought to be written from the beginning in one which is of greater familiarity; or if to some extent their souls may transfer themselves, with a happy theft, in a Pythagorean transmigration, they should be thus sent forth. I see nothing to despise in the Muses of England (particularly in her dramatic Muses), whether by France or by Spain, or (and nothing greater can be said) by ancient or modern Italy. How I am carried away, full of my native land! I return to you: go forth little book.

Prose Works

A Proclamation (pp. 318–19)

Cf. *Memoirs*, pp. 115–17.

A Message from his Highnesse the Prince of Wales (pp. 320–6)

Cf. *Memoirs*, pp. 122–3. The date of the *Message* contradicts Loftis's chronology (*Memoirs*, pp. 94–9) and casts considerable doubt on the dating of events in Lady Fanshawe's work.

Letters

Letter 1 (pp. 329–30)

John Heath (later knighted), poet and Royalist, was the son of the Lord Chief Justice of the Common Pleas, Sir Robert Heath. He appears to have been a close friend of Fanshawe's from the 1620s onwards. MS Eg. is composed mostly of his papers and papers of his family and circle.

The 'Master' of the letter is Thomas Wentworth, First Earl of Strafford, under whom Fanshawe was serving in Ireland. The Earl was brought to trial in March 1641.

It may be conjectured that the 'Mistress' is Constantia Aston. The details of the letter are too allusive to confirm this conjecture, but they do nothing to dismiss it: 'She is preferd if the other fall' might possibly refer to Strafford's policy in Ireland and to the fact that the Astons were Catholics; 'climbd too high' might refer to the difference in social status between Fanshawe and the Astons.

The second paragraph contains the interesting suggestion that Fanshawe and John Heath not only exchanged copies of verses informally (which is the suggestion of the presence of Fanshawe's work in Eg.) but that they may have belonged to some literary circle or society, the details of which seem unfortunately to be lost. The contents of Fanshawe's 'torne blotted Papers' can only be conjectured: it is likely that by 1640 the canon of his work would have included all the poems in A, with the addition of those works directly and indirectly inspired by his Spanish travels of the 1630s.

Letter 2 (p. 330–1)

Sir Richard Browne, Bt. (1605–83), John Evelyn's father-in-law, was the King's Resident at Paris and was related by marriage to Lady Fanshawe (Cf. *Memoirs*, p. 133). For this letter Cf. *Memoirs*, pp. 119–20. The text of *Memoirs* is highly ambiguous at this point concerning the passage of time. Loftis in his Chronology (*Memoirs*, pp. 94–9) appears to date the visit to Caen in the August of 1646. This interpretation of a thoroughly confusing passage does not square with p. 120 of *Memoirs* which, taking Fanshawe's nervousness about an unagreed composition with the Government (which can hardly have lasted for over a year) together with the firmer evidence of Lady Fanshawe's pregnancies, implies that these events (the visit to Caen and separate return to London) *must* be placed in the August of 1647, the 'that year' of p. 120, l. 8. This interpretation agrees with the date of *Letter 2* here, which cannot be in error as to *year* since *Il Pastor Fido* is mentioned as being already in print. We must assume, in the end, that the date of the letter is correct and that ambiguity and confused recollection in the *Memoirs* have misled all of their editors. Indeed the date '1646' (*Memoirs*, p. 119, l. 5) from which the following paragraphs are dated is an interpolation in the manuscript (cf. Textual note, *Memoirs*, p. 224). If this redating is accepted the chronology of these years in the *Memoirs* must be viewed with great caution.

Letter 3 (p. 331)

It will be observed that new-style dating is used in the text of this letter, while old-style is used to date it. For the reasons given in the note to *Letter 2* the date 1647 is offered soon after Fanshawe's return from Caen to London. A new lodging in London is implied in the text of the letter (cf. *Memoirs*, p. 119, l. 37–p. 120, l. 2).

Letter 4 (p. 332)

Cf. *Memoirs*, p. 122: the date of the letter accords with the date of the death mentioned in the first sentence. There is no doubt that *Memoirs*, p. 122, ll. 24–9 describe the same incident, in which case the *Memoirs* are confused as to the year, which was that of the Prince's death but not the 1648 of the visit to Paris. The account of the voyage should rather be applied to the journey described on p. 132 of the *Memoirs*. William Beale (d. 1651), a former master of Jesus College, Cambridge, and a Royalist, died in exile.

Letter 5 (p. 333–4)

Cf. *Memoirs*, p. 136:

> In this winter my husband went to waite on his good friend the Earle of Straford in Yorkshire, and there my Lord offered him a house of his in Tankersly Parke, which he took and payd 120lb a year for...
>
> In March we with our 3 children, Ann, Richard and Betty, went into Yorkshire, where we livd an innocent country life, minding only the country sports and the country affairs. Here my husband translated Luis de Camões...

John Evelyn's 'essay upon the first Booke of Lucretius' was published in 1656.

Letter 6 (p. 335)

Cf. *Memoirs*, p. 180: Lady Fanshawe notes the receipt of the letter two days later in Madrid.

Letter 7 (pp. 335–6), *Letter 8* (p. 336)

Cf. *Memoirs*, p. 181: Lady Fanshawe records the arrival of three posts from her husband in quick succession. This letter could have arrived on either 2 or 5 March. Sir Robert Southwell (1635–1702) was a diplomat. The Duke of Medina Sidonia was praising Fanshawe's son.

INDEX OF FIRST LINES